VOLS

Three Decades of Big Orange Football
1964-1993

Russ Bebb

Sagamore Publishing
Champaign, IL

Production supervision and interior design: Brian J. Moore
Dustjacket design: Michelle R. Dressen
Photo insert design: Amy L. Todd
Editor: Susan M. McKinney
Proofreader: Phyllis L. Bannon
Dustjacket photo: Tom Raymond

Library of Congress Catalog Card Number: 94-67275
ISBN: 0-915611-99-6

To La Wanda, my wife and best friend of 40 years, who is, and always has been, everything to me.

To my children, Kim, Rusty, and Chris.

To my grandchildren, Nicolas, Alex, and Meghan, and those who might follow.

To Steve, the world's greatest brother.

And to the memory of my wonderful parents, Alice and Andy Bebb.

Contents

Acknowledgments

It is with pleasure that I acknowledge the assistance that made this book possible.

I was fortunate to have the support of Bud Ford and Tom Mattingly of the University of Tennessee Sports Information staff, who helped tremendously in rounding up pictures. Tom also helped with the editing and seemed to be constantly ransacking his remarkable memory for first one thing and then another.

I would like to thank Haywood Harris, with whom I have shared a long and enduring friendship, for his help in editing the contents and for sharing his extensive knowledge of Tennessee football.

I benefited from discussions and interviews with University of Tennessee coaches and players, past and present. To them I am indebted.

And I must not forget those Vols, particularly those included within these pages, whose on-the-field contributions made Tennessee football something to write about.

Finally, I shall forever be indebted to my wife, La Wanda, who persuaded me to write this book in the first place, who nursed me through a heart operation just as the book was getting underway, and then continued to encourage me during those times when I didn't think I could write another word. It was a most fortunate day for me when I married her 40 years ago.

My sincere thanks to them all.

All photographs in this book, including the dust jacket photo, were supplied by the University of Tennessee Sports Information Department. Credits should go to the following photographers who are known to have shot pictures obtained from UT:

Laughead Photographers
Michael Patrick, *Knoxville News-Sentinel*
Action Sports
Phillip Schmidt
Action Sports of America
Charles Pugh
John D. Smith
Hugh Lunsford, *The Knoxville Journal*
Jim Garner
DiAnne Milam
Bill Shipley
Glenn Thackston

Foreword

Russ Bebb knows the inside and outside of Tennessee football as well as anyone.

OUTSIDE . . . for more than 38 years, first as a reporter, then as executive sports editor of *The Knoxville Journal*; he was an objective journalist, reporting and editorializing on the events and people who have made University of Tennessee athletics the biggest single activity in the state. His ongoing communication with coaches and players gives him a perspective from the outside that is totally unique.

INSIDE . . . for three decades as statistician for Vol Radio Network football broadcasts, no person alive has chronicled each Volunteer football game in such detail. The intense concentration required to chart every single yard gained, every single tackle made, gives Russ Bebb a perspective from the inside that is also totally unique.

Above all, he has been a close friend, who understands that the foundation of Tennessee football . . . yesterday, today, and tomorrow . . . is the Big Orange fan.

Just like Russ, that fan is totally unique.

John Ward
Voice of the Vols

Preface

Russ Bebb's latest book on University of Tennessee football fills in some big gaps for me as far as my own knowledge of that subject is concerned.

And it is a subject that is very dear to my heart. As a UT student, 1937-41, I was privileged to be backstage in one of the greatest eras in Vol football history, the unbeaten and untied seasons of 1938-39-40. I worked as an English tutor for the players, helped out as an assistant to the publicity director, and in general did what General Robert R. Neyland told me to do. (Come to think of it, everybody did what Neyland told them to do in those days.)

Then after World War II, I returned to Knoxville to start my career as a sportscaster. With Neyland's blessings, I started the Vol Radio Network, and once again was privileged to witness a prosperous era for the Vols, the great seasons of the early '50s which peaked with the national championship team of 1951.

After that, my work took me elsewhere, and although I tried to keep up with the Vols as best I could, I just did not have the opportunity to follow them closely. But now, Russ's new book is here to fill me in on some of the years that I missed.

Football books are always fun, I think, and it is fun for me to read about the coaches who came after Neyland and the great players who helped keep the Tennessee tradition alive. I know of no one better qualified to write a book on Tennessee football than Russ Bebb, who covered it for so many years for *The Knoxville Journal.* He saw it all from a front row seat.

Lindsey Nelson
Hall of Fame sportscaster

Introduction

Geographically speaking, its epicenter, Neyland Stadium, is at 35 degrees, 58 minutes north latitude and 83 degrees, 35 minutes west longitude.

It is called Big Orange Country, and therein live two types of people: those who worship Tennessee football and those who are simply too young to comprehend its importance.

This is where the season never ends, where lives a fervent group that ties its fortunes to the welfare of Heath Shuler and Friends on autumn Saturdays. It is a matchless time of year. Fans cast aside their personal cares and worries and become emotionally involved instead with the lot, good or bad, of a football team.

The setting is intoxicating. It quickens the pulse and invigorates the senses. The air at Neyland Stadium on Game Day is like wine. You don't breathe it; you drink it.

No matter what the time of year, a Vol fan can let his mind wander to The House That Neyland Built, its 91,902 seats filled with fans awash in orange and white and comprising at that moment the state's "fifth largest city." He can picture the Pride of the Southland band marching onto the field, then swinging into "Rocky Top." Memory's eye can see the team run through the giant T formed by the band. The cacophony of sound at that moment is like very few other places in sports.

This is where time seems to stand still after a loss, where the fans have trouble dealing with the fact that life and the football season must go on. Even those certain members of the crowd who never let the outcome of the game affect the celebration that takes place afterward eventually awake to the awful realization that Tennessee has lost a football game.

The Big Orange is steeped in tradition. Tennessee is the 10th winningest team in the nation and ranks fourth in both all-time bowl appearances and bowl victories. Tennessee has the winningest overall athletics program in the Southeastern Conference with 99 SEC team titles and has won 11 SEC football championships, three since 1985. Tennessee teams have been to 34 bowls and have been on television 118 times. Ten Vols have been first-round NFL draft choices in the past seven years. The Vols have had three Heisman Trophy runners-up—Johnny Majors (1956), Hank Lauricella (1951) and Heath Shuler (1993).

Football is legend at Tennessee. Enough so that you could easily be brainwashed into believing that Andrew Jackson was once head coach and Davy Crockett a star halfback.

When it comes to supporting their football team, UT boosters rank second to none. Other schools make similar claims, of course, and admittedly it's impossible to measure the depth of affection that stirs in the heart of a fan.

But when 73,801 turn out for a spring scrimmage, that's an impressive gauge of loyalty. After all, nobody ever mistook UT's Orange and White game for the Super Bowl.

In 1986, the game closed out spring practice on April 26 and it afforded Vol fans their first chance to salute their 1985 SEC champions since the rousing Sugar Bowl victory over Miami four months earlier. Even the Guinness Book of Records, which keeps tabs on such things, took note that the turnstile-authenticated count made it the largest crowd ever to see a spring game in U.S. college football history.

Tennessee football is more than just a game. To some it is a passion; to others it is an obsession. To be sure, it exerts a mystical grip on citizens of the Volunteer State. In the early 1980s, *The Knoxville Journal* had a nationally recognized newspaper research company survey its readership. The results of that months-long study revealed that in more than 60 previous surveys of major metropolitan daily newspapers, researchers had never before encountered a phenomenon like the one they found in the Knoxville area.

"Never have we come upon a situation where an entire community is so in love with an athletic team," a survey spokesman said.

And the coffers of the University of Tennessee athletic department reflect just how much of a love affair exists between Tennessee football and its followers. No matter who the opponent, no matter what the opponent's record, and usually no matter what the weather, the tradition and grandeur draw capacity-plus crowds in the 95,000 range through the portals every time the gates open at Neyland Stadium. A Vol football game is an event of monumental proportions. The third largest crowd in stadium history, 97,372, turned out to see the 1985 Vols play a Vanderbilt team that had won only three of 10 games. The average attendance for the 1993 season, 95,326, was more than three times what it was in 1963, the year before Doug Dickey became head coach. The total attendance for seven home games in 1993 was an all-time UT record, 667,280.

Yes, Tennessee football occupies a special place in the hearts and minds of UT fans, young and old alike, no matter when and where they saw their first Tennessee game. It is a year-round subject of discussion in barber shops, on church steps, at alumni gatherings or any place Vol fans get together.

When you're a Vol fan, you're already halfway to heaven. You are expected to dress louder, yell louder, spend more, suffer more, exult more and care more. You usually go everywhere the team goes. You mix and mingle with friend and foe alike. You revel in victory and die in defeat. But either way, you always come back for more.

No, the season never ends. A year is divided into four parts: the football season, recruiting season, spring practice and preseason practice.

When it was decided that this book would be about Tennessee football of the modern era, it was all too obvious that that era would have to begin with the 1964 season — a sort of natural dividing line between two distinct periods of Vol football.

This, then, is the story of the 30 Big Orange seasons of that era — 1964 through 1993. The story does not end with the 1993 season; it really has no ending, because the tradition is still living, still growing. For as surely as past memories fade, Tennessee's greatest moments lie ahead.

CHAPTER 1

A CALL FROM KNOXVILLE

It is August 1963, and longtime assistant athletic director George Cole is throwing his customary fish fry for Arkansas staff members. It has become an annual ritual that serves to unofficially kick off the football season at Fayetteville.

Among the guests is Bob Woodruff, acting athletic director at Tennessee, who has come to Fayetteville ostensibly to study the Razorback football program and to meet with his old friend and coaching associate, coach Frank Broyles. There is little doubt that Broyles knows Woodruff has come to look at more than facilities and the inner workings of a highly successful football program. The wily Vol AD is more interested in 31-year-old Douglas Adair Dickey, an assistant on Broyles' staff and a quarterback for Woodruff at Florida a decade earlier. In the intervening years, Dickey may have been out of sight, but not out of mind as far as Woodruff was concerned. On this occasion, Woodruff and Dickey exchange the usual pleasantries, but their encounter is nothing out of the ordinary.

Woodruff had seen in the quarterback of his 1953 team unmistakable traits that would serve him well as a head coach.

"Doug was one of the brainiest quarterbacks I ever saw," Woodruff said. "He could see things as a game rolled along that showed me he had the makings of a smart coach. I knew him as a man of unusual intelligence, and you can't overestimate the value of brains.

"Doug took over at Florida when Haywood Sullivan left school to accept a baseball bonus. Doug led our team into the Gator Bowl in 1952. He was a self-made athlete who made himself into a football quarterback, basketball player and baseball pitcher."

Broyles, who shares Woodruff's admiration for Dickey, knows that it is just a matter of time before the call from Knoxville comes. "I knew a long time ago that I was going to lose Dickey to Tennessee. Every time I saw Woodruff, he would ask about Doug's progress," he said. "I knew that he regarded Doug as potentially a fine head coach."

Woodruff heads back to Knoxville, where Jim McDonald is about to embark on his first season as Tennessee's head coach. And his last, as it would turn out. He had been named as successor to Bowden Wyatt, who just six years earlier had stood tall in the coaching saddle. But Wyatt's program had declined steadily, resulting in his ouster in the spring following a 4-6 season.

Woodruff and McDonald have been touring the state, trying to sell Tennessee football to the disillusioned orange-clad masses. Even though both Woodruff and McDonald were hired on a one-year basis, everywhere they go Woodruff is introducing McDonald as "Tennessee's head coach for 1963 and many years to come."

But McDonald is doomed from the start. Having been named head coach in mid-June, it is obvious even to the lay observer that three months is not nearly enough time for a new coach to get things in order before the start of the season. He even has to accept Wyatt's assistant coaches, some of whom he doesn't particularly want. And although McDonald manages to instill a new spirit in Tennessee football, fan disenchantment born of a downward spiral in the program takes its toll; average home attendance (30,141 in a 52,227-seat stadium) is the lowest in five years.

As McDonald and his team struggle toward a 5-5 season, it becomes increasingly clear that Big Jim's days are numbered, even though just about everybody would agree that a break-even season would be a creditable achievement under very trying circumstances. By midseason, some prominent names have already surfaced as a possible successor — Georgia Tech's Bobby Dodd, Murray Warmath of Minnesota, and LSU's Paul Dietzel, among others.

After the Ole Miss game, a 20-0 loss for UT, Woodruff is sent to Minnesota to see if Warmath, a Vol guard of the early 1930s, can be enticed to take the Tennessee job. The lure is $28,000 annually, a princely salary at the time, and a 10-year contract as coach and athletic director. Woodruff realizes that he is, in effect, offering Warmath his own job. Warmath is at first interested but not overly eager, a circumstance that, for obvious reasons, suits Woodruff just fine.

Woodruff is in touch with Dickey, who expresses a genuine interest in the job. Broyles is willing to release him. But he has some advice for his young assistant.

"Some good job offers are going to come your way," he said, "but that Tennessee job is a tough one. You will just have to make up your mind." Broyles said nothing to encourage him to take the Tennessee job should it be offered. In fact, he told Dickey that the Georgia job, which was about to come open, would be a more attractive situation.

Woodruff again calls, telling Dickey that he is prepared to offer him the Tennessee job. But first, he says, there is someone he wants him to meet with. And that someone turns out to be Tom Elam, who has the assignment of sizing up the Arkansas assistant. So, on November 23, as the nation mourns the assassination of President John F. Kennedy the day before, Dickey climbs aboard his Arkansas National Guard L-19 liaison plane, stops in Little Rock to refuel, then heads toward Union City in northwest Tennessee and a very important meeting with Elam.

"I landed in some little field out there and Tom and his wife, Kathleen met me. They drove up and I got in the car and we rode around. I guess Tom just wanted to look me over."

Elam remembers the meeting well, even recalls that he balked at the assignment at first.

"It made me mad to begin with because I had never heard of Dickey," Elam said. "I asked Woodruff who he was. He said this guy is another Darrell Royal or Frank Broyles, who were two of the leading coaches at the time. I said I didn't care if he was another Knute Rockne. 'We're playing at Kentucky that day and I haven't missed a Kentucky game.' He said go see him anyway."

So Elam and his wife meet Dickey and drive around for perhaps two hours. Elam is interested in two things: How Dickey plans to recruit in Tennessee and how he will make the transition from the traditional Tennessee single wing to the T formation, even offering his opinion that the time had come to junk the single wing.

"That's right; I wouldn't do it any other way," Dickey says. And in a classic example of oversimplification, he adds, "It's not very complicated. The schemes aren't that different. You just take that blocking back out of the game and put a guy in there to play quarterback and get on about your business."

Tennessee was the last bastion of the single wing offense, but even the traditionalists realized the time had come for it to go the way of the flying wedge. The star high school quarterback, exposed to the glamor of professional football on television, was already playing T formation and wanted to play the T in college to prepare himself for the National Football League. Two cases in point were Steve Sloan of Bradley Central High School in Cleveland and Steve Spurrier of Johnson City Science Hill. Both spurned Tennessee, Sloan choosing Alabama and Spurrier winding up at Florida, where he won the Heisman Trophy in 1966.

As for in-state recruiting, Dickey again was to the point: "If you can't recruit your own home state football players, you're in trouble. That would be a major objective with me."

Chalk up another score for Dickey.

"Dickey impressed me as an intelligent, competent young man," Elam said. "I liked the answers he gave on those two major questions. He made an impression on me and I was sold. Once I've got a firm position, I stay with it."

On the wall of his Union City office, attorney Elam displays evidence that he did indeed stay with it for the young man who was to become Tennessee's 17th head coach — a picture of Dickey with the inscription: "Thanks for having faith in a young coach."

A week after the meeting with Elam, Dickey receives another call from Woodruff. "It's a done deal," Woodruff tells him. But there is a bit of trickery involved, made necessary, Woodruff believes, by the incessant digging of the press.

"We'd like you to come to Knoxville, but I want you to take the train from Memphis that gets in here about 6 in the morning. If you get on the train at night and arrive very early in the morning, nobody will know you're here and we can announce your hiring at a press conference. Dr. Holt wants to have breakfast with you; he has to leave town but he wants to meet with you before he goes."

Dickey is flown from Fayetteville to Memphis by a National Guard buddy, who lets him off at Mud Island. Dickey rides a boat across the Mississippi River, takes a cab to the railway station and prepares for a 425-mile train ride.

It is 10 o'clock at night on Dec. 1, a Sunday. Dickey is on the Night Train to Knoxville. No doubt he and Woodruff feel rather clever for having outsmarted the press. But he hadn't been on the train more than five minutes, he recalls, before a reporter appears from nowhere and begins asking questions. A newsman's telephone call earlier in the day to the Dickey home in Fayetteville had produced a startling bit of information: Dickey was on his way to Knoxville. By train. So much for cloak-and-dagger.

After arriving in Knoxville at 6 a.m., Dickey goes straight to Dr. Holt's West Knoxville home, where Dr. Holt, perhaps the most popular president UT ever had, is about to leave on a fund-raising trip. After they meet one another, Dickey notices a battered old suitcase by the front door. "You don't want to look too sharp when you go raising money," Dr. Holt explains. "You want them to feel sorry for you."

"I found out that Dr. Holt just basically had confidence in Coach Woodruff," Dickey said as he thought back to those developments of three decades ago. "He and Tom Elam didn't know me, but Bob Woodruff did, and I think he had confidence that I could do the right thing for UT."

On the night of the season's final game, a 14-0 victory over Vanderbilt, UT president Andy Holt meets with Woodruff and members of the Athletics Board. They are bitterly divided. Debate goes on for hours. There is a serious push for Warmath, led by UT Athletics Board members Herman "Breezy" Wynn, Knoxville industrialist and a former Warmath teammate, and Jerome Taylor.

The Warmath proposal is rejected. Wynn, feeling he has been double crossed, walks out of the meeting and later resigns from the board. There is heated debate about McDonald. Some members want to give him another year. They maintain that by removing the word "interim" from his title when he was named coach, the university had obligated itself to give him a second year in order to assemble his own staff and succeed or fail on his own. But there are powerful forces dissatisfied with the decline of UT football since the late 1950s, people who are convinced that the only answer is an infusion of new blood. It is finally agreed that the affable McDonald will not be shown the door. He will become assistant athletic director.

Woodruff, by this time named permanent AD and backed by Dr. Holt and powerful board member Tom Elam, is given the green light to hire a new coach. And he already has his man—Doug Dickey. The next afternoon, McDonald is informed that he is being replaced as coach. The news is delivered to the media at a Sunday night press conference, along with the announcement that McDonald will remain as assistant athletic director.

The following morning, the front page of *The Knoxville Journal* informs Tennessee fans that an Arkansas assistant unknown to them will become their new coach. The appointment is made official later that day, and Dickey meets the press for the first time as a head coach.

In an unusual twist of irony, Dickey's move to Tennessee creates a vacancy at Arkansas, and Broyles hires a promising assistant coach off the Mississippi State staff, 28-year-old Johnny Majors. Even more ironic, Arkansas would go from a 5-5 record in Dickey's final year on the staff to an 11-0 record and the national championship in Majors' first year at Fayetteville.

Dickey got busy trying to put a staff together.

"Coach Woodruff said, 'Here's who is here. These are the people I think you probably ought to keep and here are the guys who are already gone to other jobs.' It got down to where there were two or three coaches I had to make some decisions about and that was probably the most uncomfortable thing I've ever had to do in my life.

"There was Johnny Mauer, for instance. I ended up offering him the freshmen coaching job, but he decided to go with the pros. He was a wonderful person and he had been my football and basketball coach for two years in college."

Dickey was desperately trying to find Vince Dooley to offer him a job. But so was Georgia athletic director Joel Eaves. Needless to say, Eaves won out and Dooley went on to serve as Georgia's head coach for 25 years, 1964-88.

McDonald occupies a unique position in the world of college football. He is the only man who was involved in both games that were voted the two best of all time in an Associated Press poll several years ago. As a player at Ohio State in 1935, McDonald took part in the Buckeyes' 18-13 loss to Notre Dame, the No. 1 game on the list. As an assistant coach at Tennessee, he was on the sidelines when the Vols beat Georgia Tech 6-0 in the 1956 classic at Atlanta, the No. 2 selection among history's greatest games.

PUTTING THE PIECES TOGETHER

It didn't take Dickey long to figure out what he would have to do to compete with Bear Bryant, Shug Jordan, and Johnny Vaught, all of them already legends in the coaching profession.

"What we would have to do would be to outhustle them," he said. "There weren't any rules in those days about how many times you could go someplace on recruiting visits. So we simply attempted to get busy with our recruiting with the idea that we were going to outwork people. We were young, all of us, so we thought we could do that."

It didn't take his coaching associates long to find it out. Within an hour after the Athletic Board named him Tennessee's 17th head coach on December 2, 1963, Dickey huddled with his assistants in the Athletic Department conference room. Dispensing with non-essential matters, he immediately brought up the subject of recruiting, an area in which Tennessee had failed to keep pace in recent seasons. Less than 24 hours later, he and McDonald hit the recruiting road. McDonald was only too eager to show him the recruiting ropes and they embarked on an in-state trip on which Dickey would strike it rich, landing one of the finest players he ever coached on his very first recruiting stop.

McDonald told him, "Come on, get in the car with me and I'll take you to see some people that we think are key prospects. You don't know where to go or who those people are. "

The first stop was at Cleveland, 75 miles south of Knoxville, where Bob Johnson of Bradley Central High School was considered a blue chip prospect. Then they headed toward Pikeville, 50 miles to the northwest. There they visited with John Boynton, a strapping tackle for Bledsoe County High. Johnson and Boynton were destined to become three-year starters in Tennessee's offensive line.

"These guys were great-looking prospects," Dickey recalls. "I hadn't seen any football players in six years at Arkansas who looked like either one of them. We had a bunch of little runts compared to Johnson and Boynton. And I thought to myself 'This has got to be the greatest job in America if the first two guys I see look like that.' "

Johnson had been heavily recruited by McDonald and was all set to sign with Tennessee. He was keenly disappointed when McDonald was not given a second year as coach.

Johnson was summoned from class when Dickey and McDonald came calling at Bradley Central, the same school that had sent Steve Sloan not to Tennessee, but to Alabama two years before. And he took an immediate liking to Tennessee's new head man.

"I made up my mind after that first meeting with him that I was going to go ahead and sign with Tennessee. I was very impressed. Coach Dickey was hired one day and he was at my school the next day. He came across as a very earnest coach and I thought he was terrific. So I signed on the first signing day."

Johnson signed with UT along with 52 other freshmen, recruited by both McDonald and Dickey. And it turned out to be a fine recruiting class, given the uncertainty of the coaching transition.

That first recruiting class produced some of the players who would pave the way when the Dickey Era shifted into second gear a year later. In addition to Johnson and Boynton, there were names like Charlie Fulton, Bubba Wyche, Walter Chadwick, Derrick Weatherford, Albert Dorsey, Elliott Gammage. As seniors, the freshmen of 1964 would form the backbone of Tennessee's outstanding 1967 team that finished No. 2 in the nation behind Southern Cal.

And there were some talented holdovers from the 1963 season, the most notable among them middle guard Steve DeLong. A year earlier, he had become Tennessee's first All-American in six years and was about to embark on another All-America season in which he would also win the Outland Trophy as the nation's best interior lineman.

Johnson went on to All-America honors as a center at Tennessee and finished No. 6 in the Heisman Trophy balloting in 1967 — a rare achievement for an offensive lineman. He was the second player taken in the 1968 National Football League draft and was the first player the legendary Paul Brown drafted when he formed the Cincinnati Bengals. Johnson went on to spend 12 years (1968-79) in the NFL. Johnson, president of his own company in Cincinnati today, was inducted into the National Football Foundation College Hall of Fame in 1989. Two of his brothers, Tom and Paul, followed in his footsteps as centers at Tennessee.

Johnson starred in the classroom as well. An engineering major, he was an Academic All-American and was named a National Football Foundation Scholar-Athlete in 1967.

Nearly three decades later, Dickey looked back on a 25-year coaching career and unhesitatingly called Johnson his favorite player.

"If you went to the blackboard and drew up a football player, you might come up with Bob Johnson," he said. "Physically, he was able to play his position in as commmanding a way as anybody you might imagine. Secondly, he was a guy who assumed the leadership role with as much dignity and with as much respect as you could ever ask from any athlete. Thirdly, he was a quality student, so highly respected by everybody on campus. His lifestyle, his academics, his leadership in the athletic program and the way he played his position just made him an ideal player. You could hardly draw up anybody on the board who would have been a higher level performer in intercollegiate athletics, then or now, than Bob Johnson."

But before that 1964 season got underway, it was obvious to Dickey that there would have to be some kind of offseason conditioning program.

"The players here had never had anything like that at all," Dickey says. "We had started a program about two years before at Arkansas but it was really sort of new in college football at the time. There wasn't much weight training to it; it was more agility and conditioning work. Weight training was still three or four years down the road and workouts consisted mainly of isometrics and some strength training."

Although taking shape, Stokely Athletics Center was still two years away, so those winter workouts were held beneath Section X, a 1500-seat section in the northwest corner of Neyland Stadium. The conditioning program took on the appearances of a Marine boot camp as Dickey and his staff attempted to toughen up the Vols.

"All those guys on the '64 and '65 teams still remember old Section X," Dickey said. "Underneath it was the worst old storage room you ever saw. It looked like something out of the Civil War. We put in some mats, hung a rope and we wrestled and climbed rope and did agility drills in there. It was just a stinking mess, that room. Guys would get sick and throw up and it would smell just terrible.

"The players paid a price, but in the end they loved it, because it restored some pride. They worked through it and every one of those guys will never forget Section X. It made a real impact on them. When the going gets tough for them now, they can remember that they made it through the Section X program."

Not all the players remember it with fondness. About 15 or 20 of them quit, unable to endure the oppressive winter workouts.

Dewey Warren, star quarterback of the early Dickey years, remembers it quite well. "It was like a Marine boot camp," he said. "No, it was probably worse than a Marine boot camp. It was like a cellar in a prison, dark and wet and smelly. It was without a doubt the worst place I've ever been in. After we worked out in there we had to go out and run the stadium steps. Toughest thing I've ever been through. It was unbelievable.

"Everybody just despised it. But I'm not sure that the workouts at the ag farm barn weren't almost as bad. It was nasty. There was bull and cow manure everywhere and we got in there and were rolling around in it. That didn't last very long; it was just too nasty."

"I think Coach Dickey was going to separate the men from the boys," Bob Johnson claims. "It was tough. We wrestled and we did agility drills. It was some strange stuff. They would start one guy on one side of a mat and another guy on the other, like he was playing defense. You could do anything you wanted to but you had to get to the other side of the mat. The other guy's job was to keep you from getting to the other side. It was unbelievable.

"We had one drill that coach P.W. Underwood used. One-on-one and it was whoever was on top at the end of a minute or so. But it was the most frenzied minute you've ever been involved with. A whole bunch of people were trying to figure out ways to get out of that. They'd say, 'Well, I've got a bad back or a bad this or a bad that.' P.W. decided that was a bunch of junk; he was very irritated by somebody who wasn't participating. He'd lay them down on a concrete floor and and stand over them. He'd make them lift a big medicine ball up to him and then he would drop the ball down on their stomach. It wasn't as sadistic as it sounds, except he did it for probably a minute. I think it was as much embarrassing as it was physically tough.

"But through it all, you really wanted to be on that team. It was very unpleasant, and it was meant to be. And we ran the stadium steps. It was really something.

"I thought that practices under Coach Dickey, not so much in the spring but in the fall and winter workouts, were the most physically demanding I've ever done, including my 12 years with the Bengals."

The workouts at the ag farm arena resulted from Dickey's search for a facility where his Vols could get in some offseason running. So he sent them to the rodeo arena in a building at the UT agriculture farm. Since the arena was frequented by cattle, it didn't take long to realize that it was less than ideal for running. Trainer Mickey O'Brien was worried that the players would end up with some type of body sores. The scene shifted to a tobacco barn on Knoxville's east side, where track coach Chuck Rohe's runners had been holding workouts.

Through it all, Dickey says, came an esprit de corps like he had never seen. "I think those guys could sense we were going to do something worthwhile, and it was going to be exciting. So they put their hearts into it. I think we sold them on the Tennessee tradition, in which you are expected to do well, to play hard and do it with a lot of excitement."

Following spring practice, Dickey figured that his maiden team had a chance to be competitive. And that was because he suspected that his defense would be something special. "You build your defense first," he said, "and then you build your offense around whatever your talent base is. And we got busy trying to build our defense around Steve DeLong and actually played pretty well defensively the first year. We had some other pretty doggone good defensive players—Frank Emanuel and Paul Naumoff and Tom Fisher could play the game awfully well. As a result, we weren't bad at all on defense; we just couldn't make anything happen on offense.

"We had Art Galiffa and David Leake, who was a walk on, at quarterback. Leake had worked in the dining hall and came out for the team. And he was a good-sized guy who ran pretty well and had good intelligence. He had two or three great games for us and he beat Georgia Tech in Atlanta that year."

Junior Hal Wantland became Tennessee's very first official T formation quarterback but he lacked the quickness needed for that position and was moved to wingback.

Johnson remembers the square-jawed Wantland as a study in toughness. "Hal was just one of those guys you couldn't tire out. He was a rather average athlete; he wasn't particularly big and not a bit fast. He wasn't really very skilled. But he was as mentally tough as can be. He was, to my way of thinking, the epitome of that 1965 team. He really played tough."

The recruiting emphasis was on quarterbacks.

"Recruiting had been struggling because of the single wing," Dickey said. "By switching to the T, we could sign five to seven quarterbacks a year and some of them ended up playing all over the place, including defense. Steve Kiner, who became an All-America linebacker, had been a high school quarterback. So we had a lot of former quarterbacks and fullbacks doing a variety of things. And we immediately picked up some speed and we got to where we could throw the ball with some effectiveness."

Recruiting areas were reevaluated. Tennessee had not been working the state of Georgia, which had been a happy hunting ground for college recruiters. Vince Gibson, who had come from Florida State to head up the defense, was convinced there were a number of prospects in the Atlanta area that the Vols could and should become involved with. And UT recruiters continued to work Ohio, Pennsylvania and New Jersey.

Although most areas of North Carolina were closer to Knoxville than many points in Tennessee, UT scouts went recruiting in North Carolina hardly at all because the interstate through the mountains hadn't been completed. So they concentrated all the more in Tennessee. Dickey set a lofty goal for in-state recruiting: 100 percent of the prospects in East Tennessee, 75 to 80 percent in Middle Tennessee and 50 percent in West Tennessee. "If we do that, we'll be doing well," he said. And that's just about the percentage the recruiters returned home with.

Tennessee fans approached the 1964 season just like their new coach did—hoping for many victories but expecting very few.

Dickey could thank the schedule maker that the first opponent was Chattanooga, Tennessee's favorite patsy over the years. The Moccasins were held to a mere 38 yards rushing and 42 passing, but managed to give Dickey cause for concern before bowing 10-6. The Vols themselves weren't exactly awesome; only six first downs and 148 total yards.

The defense, credited with the victory over Chattanooga, stood tall the following week against Auburn, which had gone 9-1 and played in the Orange Bowl the year before. Don Lewis kicked a 42-yard field goal in the fourth quarter to end the Vols' upset bid. For Tennessee, it was the fourth straight loss to Auburn by four points or less, 24-21, 22-21, 23-19 and this one by 3-0. Oddly, Tennessee had blown leads of at least two touchdowns in each of the previous three losses. But that had been in another world, another time, as far as UT fans were concerned.

Tennessee fans in general, and Dickey in particular, saw a silver lining in the way the defense performed that day at Birmingham's Legion Field. On the other hand, after scoring but 10 points in two games, it was obvious that the I-formation offense was a bit impotent, to put it mildly.

Kicking specialist Fred Martin was the hero of the next two games, his toe providing the difference in a 14-13 victory over Mississippi State at Memphis and a 16-14 win over Boston College at Knoxville. After four games, the Vols had won by 4, 1 and 2 points and lost by 3, but the record was a surprising 3-1.

Dickey's first meeting with Bear Bryant had enough mistakes to last a season. Tennessee lost three fumbles, two interceptions and had two punts blocked. Alabama fumbled away the ball twice, was intercepted three times and had one punt blocked. But the Tide prevailed, and Dickey was left to wonder just what kind of grip Bear Bryant could exert on a game.

"I remember Ron Widby hit a bad punt early in the game and I said, 'By golly, I think Coach Bryant is really controlling this game a little bit' because Widby almost NEVER hit a bad punt. Coach Bryant and I went on to have a wonderful relationship. He was a very inspirational person."

The game was closer than the scoreboard indicated, a 19-8 Tide victory, and Tennessee fans exited Neyland Stadium that day with renewed hopes. And developments of the next several weeks demonstrated just how good this Alabama team was, because it went on to a 10-0 season and the national championship. If ever a loss can be encouraging, this was one.

"This was the kind of defeat that can do us a lot of good in the long run," Dickey said after the game. "We played hard. We were in the game in the fourth quarter. I was pleasantly surprised we played that well."

In their first pregame meeting, Alabama's Paul Bryant had told Dickey: "Doug, I wish you all the bad luck in the world," a remark that didn't sit too well with Dickey.

"I thought, 'Well, that's a heck of a thing for a guy to say to me,' " Dickey said. " 'But if that's the way he wants to play, let's get on with it.' He had all the players, then wanted me to have all the bad luck, too."

In five more meetings with Bryant, Dickey would win three, lose one and tie one.

The doubters began to have second thoughts a week later. The Vols were called on to face LSU in an afternoon TV game at Baton Rouge, one of the most demanding assignments in college football. Few teams lived to tell the tale after visiting Tiger Stadium, known by various nicknames like the "Snake Pit" and the "World's Largest Outdoor Insane Asylum."

LSU was undefeated and had allowed just 16 points to its four victims, Texas A&M, Rice, North Carolina and Kentucky. And the Tigers had one of the best field goal kickers in the nation in Doug Moreau. If the Vols were intimidated, they didn't let it show. It was 3-3 at the half after Moreau and Martin traded field goals.

The drama was saved for the second half. LSU recovered a fumble at the Tennessee 15 and began pounding its way toward the UT goal. DeLong led the defense that stopped Rusty Schwab at the one-foot line in one of the most famous goal line stands in UT history, and Moreau missed three field goals from inside the 30 in the second-half. Vol punter Ron Widby's second half punts of 50, 54, 50, 47 and 59 yards played a big role as the Vols got out of Baton Rouge with a 3-3 tie.

A tie may be like kissing your sister to some people, but this one was like kissing Miss America as far as the players and coaches and even the fans were concerned.

Dickey felt that the standoff at Baton Rouge was a giant step for the young program. "It was on television and it was the first time that we really established ourselves as a real competitor. That defensive team of 1964 was a very good outfit. They just didn't have any help to speak of on the other side of the ball."

Next up for Tennessee was a trip to Atlanta and a meeting with old rival Georgia Tech, undefeated and favored by 9 points. The Jackets mounted a 14-9 lead but the aroused Vols rallied for a 22-14 victory — their highest point total of the season.

Tennessee headed for the Mississippi-Kentucky-Vanderbilt homestretch with a surprising 4-2-1 record. Big Orange supporters found out in a hurry that elation can change to despair in no time flat; the Vols could manage only seven points in losses to Ole Miss (30-0), UK (12-7) and Vandy (7-0).

While Dickey's maiden season might not have been an artistic success—4-5-1—it was a victory at the box office. A record average attendance of 38,000 turned out at Neyland Stadium for five home games. In 1965, the figure would rise to 43,000. Then in 1966, even that record would be surpassed, the 45,419 average placing Tennessee among national leaders in attendance.

With the 1964 season behind them, the coaches plunged headlong into recruiting. No longer did Doug Dickey want to see most of the talent on the opposing team.

Enter Chuck Rohe.

CHAPTER 2

IN SEARCH
OF SPEED

Chuck Rohe was his name and recruiting was to be his game. A veritable reservoir of energy and boundless enthusiasm, he was seemingly always on the go. He arrived on the scene as head track coach a couple of years ahead of Dickey and his track program's success had been nothing short of sensational. UT officials decided that the indefatigable Rohe could carry out additional responsibilities, so he was added to Dickey's staff. Officially, he was an assistant football coach whose duties would include coaching the freshmen. But since he did absolutely no on-field coaching, recruiting coordinator would have been a more appropriate title. Under his guidance, Tennessee recruiters ranged far and wide and with unusual success. Rohe's recruiting operation undoubtedly landed more All-American football play-ers and track performers than any other in the nation. He proved to be as good a recruiter as he was a track coach.

And track coach that he was, Rohe convinced Dickey that there is something to the adage that luck may be important, but it certainly ranks somewhere behind speed when it comes to football. So Dickey decided to build his team around speed, and that, as they say in the locker room, was right down Chuck Rohe's alley. Speed may kill, but speed also wins.

Dickey already knew the importance of being fleet of foot. "I had been associated with speed at Arkansas, so I had a lot of faith in it. We tried to recruit as much speed as we could. Chuck had the track-football player relationship—sprinters, hurdlers and even some high jumpers who could do some things in football. We packaged that thinking into our recruiting."

Dickey established a policy that enabled an athlete to participate in both track and football. In his first year, a track-football athlete would be required to attend spring practice, but not engage in much heavy contact work. After his freshman season, he would not have to participate in spring football at all. That applied to people like Flowers, high jumper Karl Kremser, shot putter Chip Kell and sprinters Chick McGeehan, Andy Bennett and Stan Trott, among others.

Rohe put together an offseason conditioning program that stressed running and speed as much as strength training. By learning how to get off to a quick start, players improved their 40-yard dash times by two- and three-tenths of a second; not impressive on paper perhaps, but significant when wideouts were going one-on-one in the secondary.

The speed training became so successful, in fact, that the UT coaches produced a training movie, "The Winning Edge," and marketed it nationwide. Tennessee became the first school to employ the track-football concept. Coaches from around the country dropped by to check out the UT program, because a school that had never been known for speed had suddenly developed a reputation for speed. Within a few years, Tennessee became known as "Wide Receiver U."

One of the first football players who arrived at Tennessee via the track route, and by far the most celebrated, was Richmond Flowers Jr. He was the most sought-after athlete in the country that year and became the object of a major recruiting tug of war between Alabama and Tennessee. Flowers, from Sidney Lanier High in Montgomery, Alabama, was such a recruiting jewel, that Alabama coach Paul "Bear" Bryant, conceding that the Tide didn't have much of a track program, told Flowers he would build a new track at Tuscaloosa and went so far as to hire Billy Hardin, an Olympic hurdles medalist, to coach Alabama's hurdlers.

Because of the spirited battle for Flowers, Rohe and Dickey crossed paths often with the man who was well on his way to becoming one of the most famous football coaches of all time. "We ran into him a number of times and in a number of places," Rohe recalls. "At Richmond's home, for instance. And we were both at Richmond's athletic banquet."

With no restrictions at that time on the number of visits coaches could make with prospects, Dickey partook of many an evening meal in the Flowers home. Richmond Flowers Sr., attorney general of the state of Alabama, was much in the public eye and preferred to be the entertainer rather than the entertainee when recruiters came calling.

"Mr. Flowers was such a public figure that he preferred to be at home," Dickey said. "He didn't want to get Richmond out publicly in a situation where everyone would be stopping by the table to see him. And being the state attorney general, he had too much notoriety and didn't care for that. He also had a daughter and just wanted to be at home with his family. So I got to know the family extremely well. Mr. Flowers must have cooked me at least half a dozen steaks at his house.

"You know, they made a television movie about Richmond's career a few years back and I thought the actors who played the mother and father did a tremendous job of portraying them as they were.

"In the end, we just stayed with recruiting Richmond week after week after week. Some of the other national teams got in there a bit, but it was basically an Alabama-Tennessee thing. I made a lot of trips to Montgomery and went to a lot of track meets. We just simply tried to keep waving our flag and it paid off."

As Flowers improved in track as a senior, the more he leaned toward Tennessee and one of the premier track programs in the nation. But Bryant and Alabama hung tough and the recruiting battle for the handsome young speedster became just as intense as the celebrated Alabama-Tennessee football series. Even so, there is little doubt that Flowers felt deep down that Bryant's real interest in him was as a football player rather than a track man.

Seemingly, the more Flowers improved, the more he began to lean toward Tennessee, picturing himself as a world-class hurdler in a world-class track program. But the Southeastern Conference football signing date, in early December in those days, came and went, and Flowers remained unsigned. Most prospects signed before Christmas, but the recruiting struggle for Flowers carried well into the spring.

"Richmond just couldn't make up his mind for sure and he wanted to wait and see how well he did in track that spring," Rohe said. "And I think that Coach Dickey's attitude about an athlete combining track and football careers was an important factor. But it was a long, long process. We actively recruited him for eight or nine months."

That spring, at the National AAU Youth Championships in San Diego, Flowers ran his first race over college-height hurdles— and beat the silver medalist of the 1964 Olympic Games.

Rohe, recruiter extraordinaire, landed some of the nation's top track athletes; his 20 SEC championships in eight years are proof of that. But he also was responsible for getting many of Tennessee's top players during the Dickey era and he unhesitatingly called Flowers the No. 1 catch of his seven years as Tennessee's recruiting coordinator. That same year, Rohe signed Larry Kelly, who had broken the national record in the 880, giving Tennessee two national record holders in one recruiting year.

Flowers was blessed with unusual speed, but Rohe had at least three sprinters on the track team who could beat him at 100 yards — Carroll Thrift, Gary Wagner and another footballer, Chick McGeehan. But it was in the hurdles, and eventually football, that Flowers excelled.

He was without question one of the world's top young hurdlers. His hurdling form, close to perfect, was as good as any Tennessee hurdler, before or since. Richmond Flowers going over a hurdle was poetry in motion.

But, great track star that he was, he went on to exceed all expectations as a footballer.Generally speaking, track performers aren't tough enough to be football players; Flowers was. His first success in football was as a wide receiver. Later in his career he became an outstanding running back. And, of course, every team feared his tremendous speed.

Quarterback Dewey Warren, the inimitable "Swamp Rat" of 1965-67, was one of Flowers' biggest fans.

"Richmond didn't have the best hands, but he worked at it and got better," he remembers. "He could absolutely fly; I'm telling you, he could smoke it. I could throw it as far as I could and he could run under it. It was ungodly how he could run.

"I always tell this story about Richmond. The first time he ever got in a huddle he had his head tilted real funny, with one ear pointing toward me and I couldn't figure out what he was doing. I finally found out he was deaf in one ear. So I always tried to put him to the side where he could hear the checkoffs. There were a lot of times when he didn't hear the checkoffs, because if his bad ear was toward me he just couldn't hear."

But he heard well enough and often enough to make All-SEC and All-American his senior season.

"Richmond was a lot tougher than he appeared," Warren says. "He had a small waist and broad shoulders and real big thighs. He could take a lick and he could deliver a lick. That was obvious because he went on to the pros as a safety (with Dallas and the New York Giants)."

The lore of Flowers' astonishing speed was not confined to America's tracks and football fields. In the summer of 1967, Warren and Flowers were serving as counselors at a camp at Coker Creek, near Tellico Plains, about 50 miles southeast of Knoxville. Seldom did a day go by that Warren wasn't playing throw and catch with Flowers. The idea, of course, was to improve Flowers' pass-catching ability.

Ted Hamilton, an entrepreneur of sorts in Tellico Plains, saw a chance to put Richmond's celebrity to good use. Hamilton owned a large horse arena. Flowers would race against the fastest quarter horse in the area.

"So they built this thing up for about a month," Warren recalls. "They put posters up everywhere saying that Richmond Flowers, the great UT receiver, was going to run against the fastest quarter horse in the area. Well, they had more people for the race than they had ever had there for a rodeo or anything. There were people there from Madisonville and Tellico Plains and Sweetwater and all around. They were 20 deep around the outside. I was Richmond's business manager; I carried his bag for him.

"They brought that quarter horse in and they smoothed the arena surface. Richmond was going to get a headstart, about five or 10 yards as I recall. There was a lot of betting going on; you could hear it everywhere. Well, Richmond beat the horse at 40 yards, not by much, but he did beat him."

Following the 1964 season, the Vol staff came up with a plan to improve recruiting, to stay a jump ahead of rival schools on the one hand, and NCAA rules on the other.

"We were just trying to find some way to do things a little bit better and get a winning edge," Rohe says. "We would come up with some kind of recruiting system that was successful, one that was beating the heck out of other people and then the NCAA would pass a law, so we would have to do something different. We'd take prospects to Gatlinburg and then they ruled that you couldn't recruit more than 25 miles from campus. We started taking them on the Tennessee River on boat trips and they said you couldn't recruit in the summertime anymore."

Rohe hit on the idea of feminine persuasion. He formed the Vol Hostesses, a group of Knoxville high school girls, who would date prospects visiting the UT campus.

"We solicited applicants and interviewed them. I guess we selected about 35 girls each year as Vol Hostesses. Every Saturday morning they would come to Gibbs Hall and help check the guys in. They would go to lunch with them, sit with them at the ballgame and go to a party we always had for them that night. Sometimes we would also do it on Friday night and make it a two-night weekend. The girls would write them a nice letter afterward, saying they hoped they would come back to Tennessee. The Vol Hostesses were very successful. They were a big help in our recruiting for eight or nine years."

CHAPTER 3

A SEASON OF
UPS AND DOWNS

    Chuck Rohe had been on a recruiting trip to Atlanta, calling on a quarterback/hurdler, the day after Tennessee had earned a dramatic 7-7 tie with heavily favored Alabama in Game 4. As he drove back to Knoxville that Sunday night, the rest of the staff was meeting to map plans for the following Saturday's game against Houston. It was the last time the staff would ever be together.

    At 6:53 the next morning, at a railway crossing in West Knoxville, a Southern Railway passenger train slammed into a Volkswagen carrying three young assistant coaches to work. Bill Majors of the famous football family and Vol tailback of 1958-59-60, and Bob Jones, who had been on the staff just two months, died instantly. The driver, offensive line coach Charlie Rash, never regained consciousness and lingered for five days. It was he who, following the marvelous showing against Alabama, had left notes to each of his linemen in their dormitory boxes. "Play like that every week," he wrote, "and you will go undefeated."

    "I got back to Knoxville about 1 or 2 in the morning," Rohe said, "then got my kids up and took them to cross country practice at about 6. After they finished running about 7, I went to the training table and the news was that three of our coaches had been involved in a terrible accident."

The players, trying to get ready for Houston, were stunned by the ghastly turn of events. The hurt was deep, the mood gloomy. "It was simply devastating," Bob Johnson said. "Between those three coaches there were, I think, seven children and all of them under the age of six. I just remember seeing those three young widows with all those small children."

Houston offered to cancel the game, but the Vol players voted to play, and UT officials conferred at length before deciding it would be best to go on.

Within three days of the tragedy, one replacement coach had joined the staff, 24-year-old Ray Trail, an All-Southwest Conference guard and captain of the 1962 University of Arkansas team. If being a winner made a difference, Trail was in on the ground floor, for he had never played in a losing game in his three seasons at Arkansas. The Hogs won 25 and tied 5 in his three campaigns. He had just two years of coaching experience when he arrived in Knoxville, one year as line coach of the undefeated Razorback freshman team and one year at an Arkansas high school. Dickey, of course, knew him well from his days at Arkansas.

"Coach Dickey told me 'I'm not offering you the offensive line job; let's just see what kind of job you can do.' "

There is no doubt that he performed to Dickey's satisfaction, for he would spend 12 years on the Tennessee staff and could count a long succession of players who earned All-Southeastern Conference and All-America honors under his tutelage.

The Vols, their hearts not in the game, their helmets adorned with the familiar orange "T" but also black crosses, turned in a bizarre but winning performance against Houston. The offensive line, for instance, was totally out of sync, the result of an unusual Houston defense, not to mention the emotional strain of the week. So it was decided that on plays designed to go between the tackles, they would simply wedge block. The scheme worked wonderfully, and a grim Tennessee team won 17-8. If ever a victory had little meaning to players, coaches and fans, it was this one.

Trail's introduction to big-time coaching was awkward, to say the least. "The week of the Houston game, which was my first week, was tough. It was an unusual situation because I was trying to coach kids who had been coached by Coach Rash. I didn't want to come in and say 'Just forget what you've been taught by Coach Rash.' Coach Dickey helped me a lot in those times."

It had been a helter-skelter week, but Dickey never stood taller. He spent long hours keeping a vigil at Rash's bedside, comforting the families, dealing with the media, helping with memorial services for coaches Majors and Jones. His assistants carried on at practice as best they could.

"I think that if ever Doug showed his merits and strength, it was during that week," Rohe said. "Pulling the staff together and the players together and just bringing everybody closer."

"Coach Dickey felt deeply about those guys," Johnson said. "He could be inspirational, but for him to be personally emotional, to shed a tear in front of the team, was not his style. He absolutely cried talking about those coaches. There was a warmth between players and Coach Dickey that I don't think would come easily. That accident did help emotionally tie players and coach."

Col. Tom Elam, chairman of the Athletics Committee Board of Trustees at the time, also recalls the way Dickey handled the tragedy. "He was marvelous. He didn't panic. He didn't moan or shout. He was a gentleman about it. He did what he could. Dickey produced a textbook display of how a man should react to a terrible situation like that. The team carried right on after it happened."

If ever a team faced a season of ups and downs, it was that Tennessee squad of 1965. The team was stocked with Dickey's first signees—sophomores who made an immediate impact and were destined to play prominent roles in Tennessee's return to the ranks of college football's elite. Their maiden campaign turned out to be one of the most extraordinary a Vol team ever encountered, albeit a bittersweet one. Certainly no Tennessee team ever faced a run of such triumph and tragedy, exhilaration and heartbreak.

It began with a 21-0 victory over Paul Dietzel's Army team, and ended exactly three months later with a one-sided triumph over Tulsa in the Bluebonnet Bowl. In between came the sensational tie with Alabama and a never-to-be forgotten duel with UCLA in the so-called Rosebonnet Bowl. But the deaths of the three assistant coaches thrust the team into mourning and cast a pall over what turned out to be a banner season.

Dewey Warren was one of those sophomores who would gain fame as the "Swamp Rat," who spent more than half the season on the bench watching the heralded Charlie Fulton operate at quarterback. Fulton, from Memphis, was the run-pass quarterback Dickey knew he needed. He was a skillful passer and, in Dickey's words, a "knuckleball runner," the type a tackler would have a most difficult time drawing a bead on.

Fulton was signed by Harvey Robinson, who had succeeded Gen. Robert R. Neyland as Tennessee's head coach when Neyland retired in 1953. Robinson, one of the most knowledgeable coaches the Vols ever had, told Dickey that Fulton was the best player Tennessee would sign that year, and he was probably right. Dickey called him the "most dynamic" player UT had. Fulton was certainly that. "He was the quickest guy I had seen in a long time," Dickey said. "I hadn't been around anybody with that kind of quickness who could accelerate like Charlie could; he was as quick as anybody out there today for sheer quickness and acceleration and the ability to stop, start, dart, that sort of thing. He was a dandy."

The free-wheeling Fulton guided the Vols to a 4-0-2 record, then went down with an injury in the seventh game, against Ole Miss at Memphis's brand-new Memorial Stadium. It was Warren to the rescue — almost. Though Tennessee fell by a single point, 14-13, Warren and the Vols would return to Memphis three weeks later, there to take on UCLA in the Rosebonnet Bowl — to this day one of the most memorable games in Tennessee history. And the Swamp Rat would lead the Vols to victory over their last four opponents — Kentucky, Vanderbilt, UCLA and Tulsa in the Bluebonnet Bowl game at Houston.

Ron Widby, one of the most versatile athletes in Tennessee history, achieved All-America status in 1965 as a forward in basketball and a punter in football. Naturally, his extraordinary talent made him much in demand, but the basketball and football teams were in December action simultaneously, the cagers in the Gulf South Classic at Shreveport, Louisiana, the football squad in the Bluebonnet Bowl at Houston.

Widby played Friday night at Shreveport, was hustled to the airport where he flew on a UT plane to Houston and then participated in the bowl game that afternoon, which the Vols won with ease, 27-6 over Tulsa. He was then flown back to Shreveport in time for Saturday night's tournament finals.

Lowly scout squad members were routinely told by coach George Cafego: "When you get your chance to play, don't ever let the guy have his job back." And Warren never forgot that sage piece of advice. After Fulton went down, the Swamp Rat was Tennessee's quarterback for the remainder of his college career. Fulton first shifted to wingback, then went to tailback a third of the way through his junior season and became one of the Southeastern Conference's premier running backs. But he had to share playing time with Walter Chadwick, among the most underrated Vols of all time. Chadwick was a talented running back, but his passing statistics were remarkable, to say the least.

He attempted two passes his senior season, and both went for touchdowns. Naturally, he often told quarterback Warren to call the halfback pass and he would show him how to throw the ball. And he became a crowd favorite for his habit of hurling the ball into the stands following a score, which he did 11 times his senior season.

Warren and Chadwick, who became best of friends, once collaborated on a play that caught Dickey off guard.

"We called an off-tackle fake and ran tight end Austin Denney across the middle," Warren said. "I faked to Walter and he went down about 15 yards, turned around and was wide open. He came back to the huddle and said, 'Run the same play. I was wide open; nobody has seen me yet.' So I called the same play and hit him over the middle and he runs for about 20 yards for a first down. When that series was over Coach Dickey wanted to know where we got that play. I told him, 'Well, that's just one we stuck in.' We had guys who would do things like that. We would cut up but we stayed together, we ran together, we played together and we had fun."

Warren, excitement in a football uniform, was a favorite of the press corps. He never uttered a few words when a thousand would do. He was a study in confidence. And his cocksure ways permeated the entire team. An assistant coach once gave an idea of how much his teammates believed in the portly Swamp Rat when he commented: "Dewey could walk down the street in front of the athletic dormitory, and half of the football players would fall in behind him even if they didn't have any idea where he was going."

While he was a study in confidence, Warren inwardly didn't feel as though he was the greatest thing ever to pick up a football. "As I look back now, I really didn't look like a quarterback (he was a bit pudgy). I couldn't run. I couldn't do any of that stuff. But we won. We did what I could do and that was throw the football. I knew my limitations, so I had to get some things out of some other players."

Warren had a rather intimate acquaintance with obscurity through more than half the 1965 season, and must have felt he was meant for better things all along. "I always tried to outdo the other team's quarterback; I wanted to outshine him. I put my pants on like the rest of them did but when I walked out on that field, I believed I was in charge. If I could do that and show the rest of the players that I had confidence, then it was bound to help them."

Confident, yes. Presence of mind, not always. In his very first game, when Fulton was injured on the first play against Ole

Miss, Warren went rushing into the huddle, then had to call a timeout because in the excitement of the moment he had not bothered to take his headgear with him.

Warren's cockiness obviously rubbed off on his teammates. The fourth team up was Alabama, which had beaten Tennessee four straight years by an average margin of 24 points.

"Alabama was just another team to us," Warren said in an interview nearly three decades later, a brash statement by most anybody else's standards, but not the Swamp Rat's. "We didn't fear Alabama. We had good coaches. I'll say this: when we walked out on the field we were prepared. Coach Dickey had a good staff. Several of his assistants became head coaches: Vince Gibson, Charley Coffey, Ken Hatfield, P.W. Underwood. Charlie Rash and Bill Majors probably would have been had they lived."

Warren was still riding the planks that third Saturday in October at Birmingham's Legion Field. Alabama, the defending national champ, was heavily favored, and not without reason. Steve Sloan, a product of Bradley Central High in Cleveland, Tennessee, was one of the Tide quarterbacks. The other was sophomore Kenny "Snake" Stabler, later to gain fame with the NFL's Oakland Raiders as one of the most accurate passers and most poised quarterbacks who ever played the game.

The Vols didn't seem to be impressed by Alabama's reputation, almost as though Warren had told them not to be impressed. The game was knotted at 7-7 in the fourth quarter when Sloan engineered a 61-yard drive to the Vol 5, then was replaced by Stabler. Two plays lost yardage, but Stabler eluded tacklers on third down and made it to the 3. Then came the play that became as big as any in the storied Alabama-Tennessee series.

As kicker David Ray got ready to rush onto the field to kick the game-winning field goal, Stabler took the snap from center, stood up and deliberately threw the ball out of bounds, stopping the clock with seconds to play. The concept was impeccable. Unfortunately, it was based on Stabler's notion that he made a first down.

It wound up 7-7. Bryant and his players were numb. Dickey and the Vols were exuberant. As far as Alabama was concerned, it was a loss. For Tennessee, it was like a victory. Both Bryant and Dickey let it slip out in impulsive postgame comments. "I take responsibility for the loss," Bryant said. "Our punter had a lot to do with the win," Dickey said. As things turned out, the tie wasn't as damaging to Alabama as one might have imagined at the time, for the Tide went on to win the '65 national championship.

Dickey was pleased and thankful. "We were lucky to get the tie," he said, surely without fear of contradiction. Bryant was apologetic, as he usually was after a loss. "I lost the game, pure and simple because a coach is supposed to be more organized than I was today," he told his players. "You would have won without me."

Without prompting, the Bear went on to salute his old rival. "Tennessee is getting better. They are going to be tough in the future." How right he was. Alabama would beat Tennessee only once over the next five seasons.

The tie was a tremendous psychological boost for the Vols, a needed tonic for their fans. The Tennessee program turned the football corner on that October afternoon. There was little doubt that Dickey had the UT program back among the upper crust. Tennessee was playing even-up with a program that had won a national championship the year before and was headed toward another one that season.

The highlight of Warren's career was unquestionably his 1965 performance against UCLA. And that landmark win, coming over a team fresh from victory over Southern Cal and bound for the Rose Bowl, served notice that Tennessee football was indeed back. Even now, three decades later, Vol fans love to relive the details of the thriller at Memphis because, for sheer drama, few games in UT history can match it. Vol wideout Johnny Mills caught 10 passes before suffering a broken arm on that memorable afternoon, a school record that lasted exactly one game, and it was the acrobatic Mills who broke it in the season opener against Auburn nine and a half months later.

The lead swapped hands six times, first the Bruins forging ahead, then Tennessee charging back to assume a tenuous lead. By halftime, Warren had two pulled groin muscles. They were retaped in the dressing room and Fulton started the second half, but Warren reentered the game.

"We were down 34-29 when we got the ball the last time," Warren said. "I came to the sideline to Coach Dickey but he didn't say too much. I remember going back into the huddle and saying, 'This is it. We have one last shot. You guys block and I'll throw and let's go down the field and go win the game.' I felt like we could do it."

Warren hit Austin Denney for a crucial first down. Three plays later, it was fourth-and-goal from the 1. The play was supposed to be a pass to Hal Wantland.

"The play was a rollout pass to Hal, a play we had been using all day. They don't come any tougher than Hal, but they just clobbered him, knocked him off his feet. Mills was out with the broken arm. David Leake got in the back of the end zone, but he was just getting out of the way; the play was designed for Wantland all the way."

With no receivers in sight, the Swamp Rat tucked the ball and began to circle left end. And he didn't finish circling left end until what seemed like an eternity to UT fans, but he made it to the end zone. Warren then passed to Denney for two points.

"I rolled left and I've got two pulled groin muscles. As Austin Denney has always said, it took me about two days to get to the end zone on that play. I was surrounded by a lot of good football players, and Austin was one of them. He was a big, tough tight end. I threw to him a lot and he caught seven touchdown passes the year before to set a school record. I don't understand why a lot of teams today don't throw more to the tight end; a good tight end will open up the middle."

The game didn't end with Warren's touchdown. Bob Petrella intercepted star quarterback Gary Beban at the Vol 6 in the final minute and, in a classic example of discretion not being the better part of valor, Petrella set sail down the sideline. Bruin fullback Paul Horgan came off the bench and cut him down with a savage forearm, closing the game on an ugly note.

Shortly after game's end, UCLA coach Tommy Prothro exploded in the postgame interview. He minced no words in telling the press that his team had been beaten not by Tennessee but by the officials, claiming among other things that Warren had not made it to the end zone on the final TD.

"For the first time in my life, I am ashamed to be a Southerner," proclaimed Prothro, a native of Memphis. That remark, uttered several times, did nothing to help the tense civil rights feelings of the time, not to mention relations with the University of Tennessee. Prothro, obviously unable to handle the loss that his proud Rose Bowl hosts had suffered at the hands of an underdog team headed to the relatively obscure Bluebonnet Bowl, continued to rant and rave after the Bruins returned home to Los Angeles.

As a result, Tennessee threatened to cancel the other two games of the contract, at Los Angeles in 1967 and Knoxville in 1968, unless an apology was made. Prothro and athletic director J.D. Morgan later issued a formal apology and those games went on as scheduled, as did six more in the series.

Dickey remembers the Rosebonnet ending as a "bad situation," Horgan flattening Petrella after the issue had been decided. "It was just an unfortunate thing that that guy stepped off the bench and did that to Petrella," Dickey said. "We had a great football game and we won, and Horgan lost his cool. Of course, Bobby made a mistake in running with the ball; he should have got on the ground, because the worst thing you could do in that situation would be to fumble the ball while running with it. He should have just run out of bounds. He invited trouble. But UCLA was just not prepared for us to be in the football game with them and we were."

The excitement of the game and Prothro's rude behavior combined to make UCLA vs. Tennessee an instant rivalry, and Tennessee now leads the series 4-3-2.

Dickey's second campaign ended 8-1-2, a far cry from preseason forecasts that tabbed the Vols as the ninth-best team in the Southeastern Conference. The lone setback was the 14-13 loss to Ole Miss — the Vols' seventh straight to Johnny Vaught's Rebels.

Thus, in only two seasons, Dickey had brought about a football revival in Knoxville, a recovery that was stunning in its swiftness. And Dickey and Tennessee football appeared to be the perfect marriage. In 1965, he and his wife, JoAnne built a new home in West Knoxville—and they painted its front door Tennessee orange. "It was a brick house with white trim so we thought the front door should be orange," Dickey explained matter-of-factly.

It wasn't the only novel idea Dickey introduced. He had Tennessee's white headgear fitted on each side with an orange "T," which has since become one of college football's most familiar emblems. And he came up with the idea of UT's Pride of the Southland band forming a giant "T" on the field for the players to run through as they take the field just before kickoff, a sight that still gives Vols fans goosebumps. For the team to be able to run through the "T," it was necessary for Tennessee to break with tradition and give up its bench on the east side of the field and move to the west sidelines. But there was method to his madness.

"In those days, I felt like the west side was an advantage," Dickey said. "We didn't play much night football then, so we figured we'd be better off on the west side by letting the opponent look into the sun. But as we began to play night football, and with the weather turning cold in November, I'm not sure that was a great decision. I think now that you're as well off on one side of the field as the other, because having to look into the sun is offset by the cold on the other side."

A Southeastern Conference directive in 1993 made it all a moot point anyway. The SEC ruled that visiting teams must not be seated in front of the home team's student cheering section, which they had been doing at Neyland Stadium for nearly three decades. So the Vols moved back to the east sidelines.

Dickey's colleagues around the SEC voted him 1965 Coach of the Year, and only two coaches finished ahead of him in the balloting for National Coach of the Year honors.

Dickey's performance had not gone unnoticed. Oklahoma was looking for a new coach, and its president, who had stood with Dickey's father when Doug was born in South Dakota 35 years before, was the first to call.

"Dr. Cross phoned and said they had a coaching position open and asked if I was interested. So we thought about it for a little bit. We had pondered it and we were at the table with our four sons. Each of them had been born in a different state — one in Arkansas, one in Colorado, one in Florida, and one in Georgia. We told the boys that we had an offer and we were considering it and one of them said, 'Well, Daddy, you can't go to Oklahoma because we don't have a Tennessee baby.' " (The Dickeys welcomed the Tennessee baby, daughter Jaren Anne, several months later.)

Dickey finally decided that the position at Oklahoma would not be any better than the one he had at Tennessee, so he called Dr. Cross the next day to say he wasn't interested. Jim McKenzie got the job and lasted one year.

Michigan contacted Dickey a year or so later, asking him to come to Ann Arbor for an interview. Again, he decided that would be a parallel move. The Wolverines eventually hired Bo Schembechler. Georgia Tech also came calling, and was told the same thing.

"If you get to be a popular coach, obviously there are some people who will want to talk to you," Dickey said. "But I never let it go past the point of saying 'Thank you, but I'm not interested in anything else. I have an excellent job.'" After spurning Oklahoma, he said "If such an offer came from my alma mater, (Florida) I might be interested. Otherwise, I'm staying at Tennessee."

A few years down the road, of course, such an offer did come and he was indeed interested.

Ill fortune continued to plague the 1965 team in later years.

Three of its members, linemen John Crumbacher and Gerald Woods and linebacker Tom Fisher, met with tragedy in the spring of 1966. As they were returning from spring break to Knoxville for spring practice, their car and a truck collided near Benton, Tennessee. Fisher, perhaps as fine a linebacker as Tennessee has ever had, and Crumbacher were killed. Woods was critically hurt; he recovered but never played again. Though he played nearly three decades ago, Fisher still holds the UT records for primary tackles (21) and total hits (28) in a single game.

"This tragedy took away two people at a very young age and left a tremendous emotional scar on a lot of people," Dickey said. "The parents, the roommates, the teammates, people that they were with just yesterday. The death of young people is always especially tragic. It's not so much a setback for the program, because you replace people. But it's the tragedy of it that grabs you so. When you hear about a traffic accident in Seattle that killed four people you don't think anything about it. But when it is your people at your office or your school or your team then it's a different thing because you are personally involved.

"Tom Fisher would have gone on and been an outstanding professional football player. He was just a great player for us."

EUPHORIA TURNS TO ANGUISH

The shock of losing 6-3 to Georgia Tech in Atlanta, coming on the heels of smashing victories over Auburn and Rice, failed to dampen fan spirit a week later. It was the third Saturday in October 1966, and Alabama was in Knoxville. Despite intermittent rain, a record turnout of 56,368 was at Neyland Stadium. Most Vol partisans were willing to forgive and forget; just beat Alabama, they pleaded. And that refrain has been heard more often than not in the intervening years.

Tennessee cashed in early on an Alabama mistake and went on to seize a 10-0 lead before the game was 15 minutes old. Euphoria had taken hold in Big Orange Country.

Kenny "Snake" Stabler, the goat of the bizarre 7-7 tie the year before, directed his team to a touchdown on the second play of the fourth quarter, and the Tide converted a crucial two-pointer to make it 10-8. Steve Davis hit a 17-yard field goal for an 11-10 lead midway through the quarter.

Tennessee had a dandy field goal kicker, Gary Wright, who just happened to be from Heflin, Alabama. And it was his lot to have the game come down to one swing of his right leg. All the Vols had to do was get the ball in position for Wright to do his thing. And they did, although it was not exactly a bull's-eye.

With 3:23 remaining, Tennessee drove from its 30 to the Alabama 3, primarily on some beautifully executed passes from Warren and Fulton. But it was then that the comeback fizzled out.

The coaching staff later received much criticism for what some fans perceived as an obsession of achieving victory with a touchdown instead of a field goal. With the ball well within Wright's range, prudence called for moving the ball toward the center of the field, from where Wright could probably chalk up three points blindfolded. But fullback Bob Mauriello slammed into the line without success as the clock ticked ever closer to the end. The ball wound up at the 3, but on the right hashmark; a decidedly tough angle made even more difficult by the rain. The clock said 16 seconds. Wright had made this kick a million times in his mind, the winning boot against his homestate university. This one slid to the right, missing by only inches. At least referee Charles W. Brown said it did, and his was the only opinion that mattered. Many Vol players, and surely most every Vol fan in attendance, were sure the kick was inside the uprights. Bear Bryant, they insisted, did not deserve to walk on water that day. And to this day, many Tennessee fans consider the loss perhaps the most disappointing a Vol team ever suffered.

"I still think the field goal was good," said Bob Johnson, who snapped the ball on the play. "Did you see the picture in the student newspaper the next day? You can see the ball nestling into the stands and it sure looks good in that picture."

Warren, the holder, had an excellent view and he, too, begs to differ with the officials. "I had a super view of the kick. I have always believed, and will always believe, that the kick was good. Gary thought he had made it. And to think we had them beat."

Wright kept his head down during the kick, as he had been coached, then was horrified when he looked up. "When I looked up from the kicking tee, the ball was soaring over an upright, drifting badly to the right. I looked at the official and when he called it no good, I wanted to hide."

Later that night, Wright went to a concert, trying to erase the abortive kick from his mind. And some teammates went looking for him, thinking perhaps he might have headed for the Gay Street Bridge.

Bear Bryant, among others, voted the kick wide. "Call it fate, good fortune or just plain luck; we're grateful for the win," he said. "But I don't think their kicker should feel so bad. If he had kicked it straight, we would have blocked it."

In all likelihood, the direction of Mauriello's run cost the Vols a victory. Had his route been east, south or north, the outcome probably would have been different. The play called for him to run straight ahead, but he bounced off a would-be tackler and to the outside. West, toward the right hashmark. Had he arrived at his intended destination, either in the middle of the field or in the end zone, the Bear and his players almost surely would have departed for Tuscaloosa with their only loss of the season. As it turned out, however, Alabama wound up 11-0, better than either of its national championship squads of 1964 (10-1-0) and 1965 (9-1-1). But Bama ranked No. 3 in the nation behind Notre Dame (9-0-1) and Michigan State (9-0-1), both of which finished 9-0-1 after battling to the famous 10-10 tie in their final regular season game. Neither went bowling. The Tide's impressive 34-7 victory over Nebraska in the Orange Bowl went for naught as far as rankings were concerned, because in those days, the final polls were taken before the bowl games.

Johnson still thinks the call giving Mauriello the ball was the correct one. "We should have gotten the touchdown on that play. There was a gaping hole and I think Mauriello just decided he could jump over the pile. But he took one step to the right. Had he gone where the call was, and I'm not blaming him, he probably would have scored. I think the run was absolutely the correct call."

Denney almost broke loose for a touchdown on the pass play that set up the ill-fated field goal. "I wish I had scored," he said. "It would have saved Gary Wright a lot of disappointment." Not to mention that of a lot of Tennessee fans.

By missing, Wright became a footnote in Big Orange history. Had he made the field goal, his name probably would have slipped from memory of most UT fans.

Wright was an unfortunate victim of a 20-yard what-might-have-been. His middle initial was "W" and he became known as "Wide Wright," a sobriquet that he did not deserve. He had, after all, kicked a 40-yarder through the rain earlier in the game. He remained upbeat. Years later, he said of the 1966 squad: "We had the best 8-3 team in the nation." And he was probably right. The Vols finished 8-3, beat a Syracuse team led by future NFL stars Larry Csonka and Floyd Little in the Gator Bowl, and wound up No. 14 in the nation. With 14 more points at strategic junctures, Tennessee would have had an undefeated season, as the three losses were by a total of 11 points: Alabama (1), Georgia Tech (3) and Ole Miss (7).

So on that dark, dreary October 15, 1966, at Neyland Stadium, Dickey knew how Bryant had felt a year earlier, following that wacky 7-7 tie in Birmingham. And he told him so when they met at midfield.

"We really made a great drive to get back in the game,"Dickey recalled. "We hit some big passes, one to Bill Baker where he made a great reception, sliding under the ball at midfield. We had it first-and-goal and not much time but we decided to give it to

Mauriello off tackle with the idea that we are going to run it in there and see if we can score, and if we don't we'll kick the field goal.

"Mauriello hits the hole and bounces outside and runs around right end. Now that puts the ball way over on the right hashmark instead of in the middle of the field. It's not the place you want to kick a field goal from at anytime. The angle is a bit sharper. You're better off in the middle of the field but we ended up on the hashmark. We'd have been better off if we'd left the damn thing in the middle of the field and kicked it from there.

"There's not much you can say. But it told us that it's 7-7 one year and 11-10 the next and we're in the hunt with Alabama for sure. I was awfully disappointed for Gary Wright and for the whole team, but there's nothing you can do; we did everything we could do on that given day. I think we felt we were in the hunt now for the championship, when we could play Alabama to basically a standstill two years in a row."

Little did he know it at the time, but Alabama, which had not lost to Tennessee since 1960, would not beat the Vols again until 1971. The loss of '66 set the stage for what was to come over the next four years.

The 18-12 Gator Bowl triumph was a case of the Vols giving the Orangemen a sound beating in the first half, then having to hold on. Tennessee mounted an 18-0 halftime lead and then Little ran wild in the second half.

Dickey saw the bowl win as a milestone of sorts. "The bowl victory over Syracuse was a great win for us against a very talented team. Again our offense and defense worked very well together and that was another step in the direction we needed to be going with the program. The only thing left was to win the conference championship."

And that's exactly what awaited the Vols a year down the line, an SEC championship, their first since 1956.

The national media began to take notice of Tennessee. Four members of that '66 squad made one All-America team or another: Johnson, linebacker Paul Naumoff, tight end Denney and punter Ron Widby, who also starred on the Tennessee basketball team.

Johnny Mills, the lanky receiver from Elizabethton, earned his reputation as the clown prince of the squad. After breaking his arm late in the 1965 UCLA game, he had to wear a cast during the winter months as doctors tried to get him ready for spring practice. It seemed that almost every week he would show up with his cast broken, and it would have to be replaced.

Coaches discovered that Mills was catching an early morning train to Etowah as it passed behind the football stadium. "The train would come through and Mills would grab the train ladder with his cast," assistant coach Ray Trail recalls. "He would ride to Etowah and eat breakfast and then catch another train back to Knoxville. This was about sunrise. He told us, 'It's beautiful when that sun comes up over the mountains. Nothing else is that pretty.' "

Mills was called "the Duck," a nickname he gave himself in the days when the Vols had no first-rate passer, the days before Dewey Warren. So he called himself a decoy, as in a decoy duck, and as he left the huddle he would go "Quack! Quack!"

As things turned out, though, Mills became much more than a decoy; he became one of Tennessee's greatest receivers ever. He enjoyed a banner senior season in 1966, hauling in 48 passes for 725 yards, both school records. He caught 10 passes against UCLA in 1965 to tie the school record for catches in a game, then broke it one game later, with 11 receptions in the '66 season opener against Auburn. More than a quarter of a century later he still holds the record for single-game yardage, 225 against Kentucky in 1966.

It is noteworthy that a 24-year-old assistant coach, who already had served under Bud Wilkinson at Oklahoma and Paul Dietzel at West Point, joined the UT staff for the 1966 season as receivers coach. He replaced Bob Jones, one of the three assistants who died in the car-train accident the previous season. No one could imagine at the time that the handsome, young Alabamian, Bill Battle would be head coach of the Vols less than four years down the line. He made an early impression; the '66 receivers established five individual school records under Battle's tutelage.

But for a twist of fate, Battle might never have been on the Tennessee staff to begin with. Jerry Elliott, a childhood chum of Battle's in Birmingham, was Dickey's first choice as the replacement for Jones. But Elliott, then an assistant coach at Auburn, turned the job down and it went to Battle. Elliott, eight years older than Battle, had played at Auburn and later tried unsuccessfully to recruit his old pal for the Tigers. They would be reunited later when Elliott joined Battle's Tennessee staff as a replacement for Larry Jones.

It was about this time that Tennessee coaches began to take notice of a number of prospects at Franklin County High School in Winchester, Tennessee, 135 miles southwest of Knoxville. Among them were a couple who would someday make their marks in Tennessee football: Bobby Majors and Phillip Fulmer.

Majors, of course, was more or less destined by birth to be a Vol, being from the first family of Tennessee football. Two of his brothers, Johnny and Bill, had already starred as Vol tailbacks. Another brother, Joe, had played quarterback at Florida State. Their father, Shirley Majors, was head coach of the University of the South and one of the most respected coaches around.

So it was Fulmer, 6-1, 215, who received the most recruiting attention. UT coaches saw him as perhaps a linebacker, possibly a tight end, probably an offensive lineman. But never in their wildest dreams did they imagine him as head coach of the University of Tennessee a quarter of a century later. Nor did Fulmer himself. A doctor or dentist, perhaps—a coach, no way.

His decision to sign with the Vols two years later, in the winter of 1968, was a momentous occasion, both for him and the University of Tennessee. He just as easily could have signed with Alabama, and thereby changed the course of Tennessee football history 24 years later.

CHAPTER 4

A RECRUIT
NAMED FULMER

There was no mistaking Ray Trail. He came smoking a cigar and wearing cowboy boots and a cowboy hat and speaking in his Arkansas brogue.

Most college recruiters had their calling cards. But none of them had one like Tennesee's offensive line coach—a Pontiac GTO convertible, with orange body, white top and white leather upholstery. Whenever a high school player saw that car in the school parking lot, he knew Coach Ray was on the recruiting trail. There was no denying that Ray Trail was a "character."

For five or six years, Trail drove those special order orange and white cars, on loan from a Pontiac dealer in Cleveland, Tennessee. "The one thing about that car was that when I drove up to watch practice at a high school, they all knew that Coach Trail was there. For youngsters that age, cars are a big part of their life, especially one like a GTO. It was a hot car, had the big engine. It got me in a lot of doors."

And one of the biggest doors it opened was in Winchester, Tennessee, where Trail and his signature automobile were frequent visitors at Franklin County High School, a particularly happy hunting ground for college recruiters. There were football prospects to be had—Bobby Majors, Phillip Fulmer, Jimmy

Moss, Bill Rudder, Greg, Robert and Johnny O'Neal, Robert
Fraley and Greg Mantooth.

Winchester sits near the Alabama-Tennessee border, and
there was quite an Alabama following in that little pocket in
southeast Tennessee. So into Franklin County Bear Bryant
dispatched two of his aides who were characters in their own
right—trainer Jim Goostree and assistant coach Ken Donahue.
Donahue, a Vol tackle in the post-World War II era, was from the
Gary Cooper school of conversation, even bore a resemblence to
the legendary movie hero, and went on to a distinguished career
as builder of great Crimson Tide defenses. Goostree, a one-time
assistant trainer at Tennessee, was an expert pool shooter, and
he was all but unbeatable in 25-cent games with the players
around Winchester.

"There was this little place where we all went to shoot pool,"
Fulmer remembers. "Coach Goostree, of course, tried to convince
me to go to Alabama. He even wanted to shoot me a game where
if he won I would sign with Alabama. But I didn't buy into that,
not after I saw what he could do with a cuestick.

"Coach Donahue was always calling and coming around
like Coach Trail and I was a little embarrassed because in
Winchester there was only one place to go and have any kind of
meal at all and I ended up going to the same place with different
coaches two or three times a day. It was good in a way because
at the time I was trying to get bigger, so I might have an early
dinner with one recruiter and a later dinner with another."

While Winchester can't boast of being the dining capital of
Tennessee, Fulmer had nothing to be embarrassed about, inasmuch as neither Donahue nor Trail hailed from what might be
called a metropolis. Donahue hails from Corryton, Tennessee, a
rural community just north of Knoxville and Trail from Forrest
City, Arkansas.

While young Phil was out with the Alabama recruiters, Trail
was gaining ground in the Fulmer home. "Coach Trail did it
probably the way it should be done," Fulmer said. "He got real
close to my parents. And I believe in the long run that was the
difference. Tennessee was on top at the time and everybody was
trying to convince me that Coach Bryant was about ready to
retire. But 12 years later I was still going against him.

"Another thing is, when it came down to choosing between
Alabama and Tennessee, Coach Trail did a great job of selling me
on the state loyalty business, that Tennessee needed the best
players to stay in state. And he also said I could continue the
string of great Tennessee linebackers." (The Vols had had two
recent All-America linebackers, Frank Emanuel in 1965 and

Paul Naumoff in 1966, and two others were on the verge of greatness, Steve Kiner and Jack Reynolds.)

Since it was more or less a foregone conclusion that Majors would follow two of his four brothers to Tennessee, Trail was able to spend more time with the other Franklin County players, particularly with Fulmer. Even though Fulmer was the No. 1 prospect among the group and a "blue chip" recruit, Tennessee didn't regard him as a sure-fire star of the future. He wasn't sought by a single Big Ten school, mainly because his size (6-1, 210) wasn't up to Big Ten standards of the day.

"I believed Phillip was the kind of player you took with the idea that he was going to be a good football player, a good solid player. He was the kind of player you would want on your team, because he's a good citizen, he's going to work hard and he'll be at practice every day. He could play. What I'm saying is that he wasn't one of those players you go after with the idea that he is destined for greatness immediately. He wasn't that at all. And, as it turned out, he was never what you would call a great player at Tennessee. But he was solid. He was the kind of player who did his job well and would never hurt the team.

"Phillip was not easy to recruit. He was a quiet sort of guy until you got to know him. I guess that, being a typical small town kind of guy, there was so much swirling around him at the time. Alabama and Auburn were after him, and really every other SEC school too, I guess.

"I got to know his parents and his sisters real well. In recruiting, I always tried to get acquainted with the parent because, in most families, I thought it was going to come down to the mother having the final say; not the daddy, the mama. I spent a lot of time with her. Phillip was from a good family, a good home. So sometime in that recruitment he was going to sit down with his family and ask 'What do you all think I should do?'

"It got close to time for him to make a decision and I took him back into a little room right off the coaches' office at his school. I sat him down and said, 'Phillip, you are a Tennessee boy. If anything good is going to happen to you, it's going to happen at Tennessee. It's not going to happen at Alabama. If anything good is going to happen at Alabama, it's going to happen to a boy from Alabama.' And I think Phillip finally realized that he was a Tennessee guy."

Once at Tennessee, Fulmer did perform well, to be sure. His college linebacking career lasted but a few practice sessions. "I looked at the freshmen and we had Jackie Walker and Ray Nettles, and there was a bunch of guys like Steve Kiner and Jack Reynolds and James Woody on the varsity. There were a lot of guys who were really good players, and I began to look for a place where I could play and help the team. Having been a tight end in high school, that's where I hoped to play."

But he eventually moved to offensive guard and became what Ray Trail had envisioned him being, not a star, but a solid performer. As a senior in 1971, he was elected alternate captain, which to this day he considers one of the biggest honors of his life. "I wasn't a great player, but I hoped that the people recognized that I was a team guy."

Had Fulmer's mother not objected, young Phillip might have wound up at the University of Hawaii as a player and, who knows, perhaps the Rainbows' coach. He was invited to visit, but she considered the 50th state to be a bit too far from home. And Georgia and Vanderbilt were at least on Fulmer's list. He seriously considered Georgia for a while. And, being a Middle Tennessean, he looked at Vandy, because new coach Bill Pace had instilled some enthusiasm in Nashville.

Another reason that Fulmer picked Tennessee was in hopes of becoming a two-sport athlete. His Franklin County team had won the state baseball championship, and baseball might have been his best sport. But his budding diamond career was short-lived once he arrived in Big Orange Country. "I found out real quick that I couldn't spend the time with both sports and be effective in either one of them. With me, baseball was just about equal with football. I enjoyed the success we had in high school and at that time I considered myself a good defensive catcher and a good hitter. But I didn't have a great arm so anything in baseball after college probably wasn't there and I realized that."

Like so many college freshmen, Fulmer enrolled without the slightest idea of what he wanted to do in life, and he wrestled with a major for quite some time. He considered dentistry and even fancied himself as a doctor. Chemistry courses put an early end to those notions. He then took some courses that would be required if he decided on a law career. He also took courses in real estate. He thought about a career as a school principal. But a coach—never. He ended up majoring in history and graduated on time.

Tennessee also landed Majors, Moss and Rudder off that Franklin County team. Fraley and Mantooth went to Alabama, and the O'Neals to Vanderbilt.

A couple of years earlier, UT officials decided the time was right to begin recruiting black athletes. The university itself was integrated; all the high schools were integrated; UT coaches had wanted to sign blacks long before. So they began to look around for that "special" black athlete who would fit into the program and, at the same time, be certain to become an oustanding player. That person was Albert Davis, a running back of extraordinary ability from nearby Alcoa High School.

"Albert came along at the time that we needed to make our integration happen," Doug Dickey said. "He was the right person; no doubt about it. Everybody was in accord that it was obviously the thing to do."

"It was a tough issue and we had been debating it," said Bill Battle, an assistant coach at the time. "Taking the first black, yes, it was a big issue. But really, all we wanted was the best athletes, no matter what color.

"We brought Albert Davis in and took him to a basketball game and introduced him to the crowd during halftime. He got a standing ovation, and the crowd started chanting 'We want Albert.' There are bigots and problem people everywhere. But I think Tennessee was ready for the change."

Obviously, it would have been impractical to bring just one black athlete into a predominantly white environment, so Dickey and his staff began to look for a second one.

Davis signed with the Vols; it was decided to also sign Lester McClain, a lanky Nashville running back/receiver who had been highly recommended by Bill Garrett, a UT booster who often helped UT recruit players in the Nashville and midstate area. McClain signed with the Vols and was going to be Davis' roommate. But Davis was never admitted because of problems with a qualifying test, and he ended up at Tennessee State. So McClain was left to go it alone.

"Everything fell apart," McClain said in a newspaper interview several years later. "All the great planning fell through . . . and I had to have a white roommate. And when my dad and brother left me at Gibbs Hall, I was all alone. That was a helluva feeling."

Suddenly, McClain was thrust into the role as Tennessee's and the SEC's first black scholarship football player. And it was a perfect fit.

"Lester was the youngest child from a very nice family; his father was a preacher," Dickey said. "I guess you had to be part of the 1960s to comprehend Lester's position. He handled it with a lot of class. He turned out to be just a wonderful person. And so did Albert Davis."

McClain was readily accepted by his white teammates. Having a black teammate didn't become an issue. Dickey says he cannot recall a single problem of any significance. "I might have gotten a little bit of mail, but I don't remember anything of a negative stature."

McClain, who graduated in 1971 with a degree in business administration and went on to become a successful insurance executive, was a three-year starter at wingback. In his junior season, 1969, he hooked up with quarterback Bobby Scott for an 82-yard touchdown pass against Memphis State—a school record that stood for 10 years.

"Lester was just a teammate, and that was it," said Scott, who arrived with McClain in the freshman class of '67. "He did what was asked of him as everyone else did. It might have been a big deal to a lot of people, but it wasn't to us. We just looked to each other to do our jobs, prepare for the games and win."

Tim Priest, another classmate and captain of the 1970 squad, remembers all the publicity that accompanied McClain's arrival. "Maybe I'm looking back at it through rose-colored glasses, but Lester was good friends with everyone, and everyone liked Lester. He was an exceptional athlete, and that helped. Lester was also very bright and had an engaging personality that made it easy for him to deal with people and with whatever situation he was in."

CHAPTER 5

9-1: "A PRETTY GOOD YEAR"

There was a Hollywood setting for the start of the 1967 season. The Vols, arriving in Los Angeles to face touted UCLA and star quarterback Gary Beban, walked off their chartered airplane to be met by 30 UCLA girls who greeted them with kisses. They visited Disneyland, saw the sights, got caught up in the whole California scene.

Tennessee was expected to be among college football's elite in '67, even though three of the first four opponents ended 1966 ranked among the top 10 teams in the nation. But the Vols were coming off an 8-3 season and a bowl victory. UT football was on solid ground. Not only the football program, but the entire athletic plant had become the talk of the South. A Los Angeles writer once referred to it as the Taj Mahal of college athletics. Athletic director Bob Woodruff's budget was almost $2 million. Almost 6,000 new seats had just been added to Neyland Stadium, boosting its capacity to 58,122. Season ticket sales were up to an astounding 25,000. UT also boasted an outstanding track program. The basketball program was prospering. Visitors came from across the country to see the Tartan Turf basketball floor, the Tartan track (both indoor and out), the sparkling swimming pools, the dormitory for athletes.

Coach Doug Dickey, with a three-year record of 20-9-3, had seen his salary increase from $16,000 to $20,000. And he was making another $20,000 or so through his television program.

The road to the Orange Bowl and the SEC championship was a difficult one, to say the least. The Vols went down to defeat before most other college teams had even left the starting gate, losing to the Bruins 20-16 in a night game on September 16, and thus dropping out of serious top 10 consideration for a while. It was a defeat that annoys members of that team even today. Johnson calls it the most disappointing loss of his UT career, and there were but six defeats during that three-year span.

Beban, the losing QB in the classic confrontation at Memphis two years earlier, applied the coup de grace this time. Tennessee, thanks to seven UCLA fumbles and two interceptions, held the lead until only 10 minutes remained. That was the point at which Beban, on a fourth-and-two situation at the UT 26, picked his way through the Vol defense, not only for a first down but the game-winning touchdown as well. And he was off and running toward the Heisman Trophy that would be his at season's end. Warren, the nation's most efficient passer in 1966, wound up No. 8 in the 1967 Heisman balloting, his chances hampered by a knee injury suffered against Auburn. He would not reclaim his starting job until three games later.

The UT offense fell far short of expectations against UCLA but the loss revealed a glaring chink in the Vols' defensive armor. Wholesale changes were to follow. The four-point difference was not at all indicative of UCLA's superiority. The Bruins piled up 26 first downs and 412 yards, almost double Tennessee's 14 first downs and 211 yards. Only five UCLA turnovers made it seem close. Even so, the Vols had a shot at winning, but Warren missed tight end Ken DeLong, open in the end zone.

"We were floating around," All-America center Bob Johnson says. "We were a bunch of people who had never been to California. I look back on it and I played terrible. Of course, we had read during the whole offseason about how good we were going to be. Gary Beban had a couple of great big individual plays. But we should have beaten them. We were a better team."

The Vols limped back to Knoxville, welcoming an open date, but realizing that Auburn was the next opponent. Practices were demanding; offensive players learned to block better; defensive players learned to tackle better. Substantial changes were made on defense.

The team would go on to win the next nine games but was hounded by crippling injuries to key players, one or more popping up in almost every game, to such an extent that Big

Orange followers felt that the team would be hard put to match the 7-3 record chalked up by the 1966 team.

The way the Vols were able to overcome these adversities and win their last nine games in succession to finish No. 2 in both national rankings stands as one of the most inspiring chapters in the history of Tennessee football, a history replete with teams, players, and coaches who have become legends.

Big things had been predicted for the 1967 Vols, and not without reason. They looked to have the best offensive line in the Southeastern Conference, anchored by Bob Johnson at center. Seniors Elliott Gammage and John Boynton were two-year starters at tackle and junior guard Charley Rosenfelder had started as a sophomore. Senior Joe Graham, shifted to offense by a bad knee, held down the other guard spot. The defense might have been suspect in the beginning, but improved in a hurry. Steve Kiner and Jack Reynolds blossomed into as fine a pair of linebackers as Tennessee ever had, both making All-American before finishing their careers.

Boynton was probably the unsung hero of the group. Line coach Ray Trail says a tougher player never wore the orange and white. "One day in practice, Coach Dickey was giving a pep talk and asked, 'Who is the toughest guy out here?' You'd think everybody would say 'I am' but everybody said, 'Boynton is.' John never said a word, but you sure didn't cross him.

"I think a lot of players on that '67 team played better than they were. Coach Bryant always told me that your great players have to play great and your average players have to play real good. He said that was the secret to being a great coach."

Following the loss to UCLA, the Vols spent the off-week shoring up the defense. The practice sessions were demanding, even reminiscent of two-a-days. Dickey told his players, "We are going to learn to tackle; we aren't going to miss tackles anymore like we did against UCLA."

The defense improved—immediately. It was seldom better than it was the next time out, against visiting Auburn. The Tigers made just one first down rushing, and the Tennessee offense, with the Gammage-Rosenfelder-Johnson-Graham-Boynton blocking front leading the way, was impressive. The only negative was a knee injury to Warren in the third period. No problem; Fulton stepped in admirably, directing the Vols as they expanded a 14-13 lead into a 27-13 triumph.

Fulton's stay at QB was short-lived. The gifted Memphian himself was the victim a week later, suffering broken ribs against unbeaten Georgia Tech. With Warren and Fulton both sidelined, that left the quarterbacking up to third stringer Bubba Wyche, a smiling young man from Atlanta whom many Vol fans had not known existed. And his pinch-hit work over the next couple of weeks would have put Cinderella to shame. Against Tech, he performed like a veteran, throwing two touchdown passes to Flowers as the Vols prevailed 24-13.

Next up on the Vols' dance card was Alabama, the SEC defending champion, winner of 25 games in a row, the longest streak in college football. The Vols had lost 11-10 the year before, and tied the Tide 7-7 in 1965. Fans of both sides drooled at thoughts of the rematch. Did the Vols finally have Alabama's number? That was the question. It loomed as the biggest game of Dickey's young career, the game that would show whether he could at last cut it with the big daddy of college football, Bear Bryant. And he had to do it with a third-team quarterback, Wyche.

The UT coaches hoped to at least slow the great Kenny Stabler-to-Dennis Homan passing combination, considered the best battery in college football and the real heart of the Alabama offense. So they devised a combination man-to-man and zone pass defense scheme in which Jim Weatherford would play man-to-man on Homan about half the game and the other side of the secondary would play zone. The strategy confused Stabler, who, seeing zone coverage at one glance and man-to-man at another, overthrew receivers and wound up being intercepted five times as Tennessee won by a 24-13 score for the second straight week.

Senior Albert Dorsey, a relatively obscure defensive back heading into the season, picked off three of Stabler's passes on consecutive series in the fourth quarter. He ran one back for the clinching touchdown and made All-American in one afternoon; actually in one quarter. Only a few months before, Dorsey's chances of making the Vol squad, much less All-American, were less than certain. He had dropped out of school for academic shortcomings, missed spring practice and had to attend summer school to regain his eligibility.

And this particular Third Saturday in October came on October 21—his 22nd birthday. "It's my birthday! It's my birthday!" he exclaimed. "Boy, what a birthday present. We beat Alabama and I score my first touchdown."

Dickey was equally thrilled. "This is the greatest victory of my life, for certain, beating Alabama in Birmingham."

It was a storybook setting, so much so that *Sports Illustrated* sent a team to Birmingham and wound up giving it cover treatment in its October 30, 1967 issue. The cover photograph shows Vol Mike Jones clobbering star receiver Dennis Homan on a pass play. Across the top, on an orange background, was the headline: "Tennessee Overwhelms Alabama." And there on Page 13, alongside a marvelous color photograph of orange and crimson jerseys engaged in savage football warfare, was the main headline: "One Way To Dam The Tide."

Perhaps the most remarkable story from that game was the play of Wyche, the third-stringer, the "who's-he?" of the UT squad. Wrote John Underwood, an associate editor for *Sports Illustrated*:

"All right, you long sufferers. You have been looking for the way to beat Alabama. Here is how you do it. Very simple. First thing you get two top quarterbacks, one who passes like a professional and runs like he would rather not (call him Swamp Rat Warren, just for fun) and one who is a terrific natural athlete (call him Charlie Fulton) who also doubles as a tailback and frightens people no matter what he plays. Are you getting this down? Then you make a raid into Alabama and grab a prospect from under the nose of Bear Bryant. That's the hard part. Better do that at night. Call this prospect Richmond Flowers Jr. of the Montgomery Flowers. Flowers can catch, and he can run with what he has caught. Then you go down to Tampa, Florida, and get a couple more quarterbacks and shove them onto the defensive team. They will love it.

"Now pay attention, because this is where it gets tricky. You allow both Warren and Fulton to get hurt before the game. Knock them right out of the action, see? And you bring up a quarterback with a name nobody can pronounce. Bubba Wyche. Does it rhyme with tyke, rich, psyche, rice or swish? His father says with 'I-ch.' Bubba is a fellow who has been hanging around for four years, serving time as a red shirt on the meatball squad and aching to get a chance to earn his laundry money.

"Bubba gets a lot of unattention, and richly deserves it. Even the week before, when he makes his debut on national television because Warren and Fulton are hurt and he beats Georgia Tech, nobody thinks about him. Who's Georgia Tech? Beat Alabama, that's the thing.

"So, on a lovely clear day in late October you put the baby-faced, blue-eyed, turned-up-nose and nice-as-can-be Bubba Wyche on the painted turf of Legion Field in Birmingham before the largest crowd (72,000) ever to see an Alabama-Tennessee football game. Then you add expatriate Flowers, who once got a wire from Alabama that said, 'The Bear will make you regret your unfortunate decision,' and those two former quarterbacks from Tampa, defensive halfback Albert Dorsey and linebacker Steve Kiner. You tell Wyche to throw passes, Flowers to catch them, Dorsey to intercept when Ken (The Snake) Stabler throws and Kiner to intercept Alabama's runners. And there you have, in a capsule, how Tennessee beat Alabama last weekend by a score of 24-13.

"With its victory, up went Tennessee to the top of the Southeastern Conference, which is called The Really Big Ten, with justification. Down went Alabama's 25-game undefeated streak. Up went Coach Douglas Adair Dickey's first victory over Coach Paul (Bear) Bryant. This story will serve to explain how an aspiring young coach just four years into the race and with a name like Douglas Adair can beat a famous older coach named Bear."

That afternoon, following the game, a wag back in Knoxville called a newspaper and inquired, "Does Coach Dickey intend to come back to Knoxville on the plane with the team or will he just walk up the river?"

Years later, Dickey credited Dorsey and his defensive mates for the monumental win. "We beat Alabama in Birmingham really with defense. We had enough offense to win the game, but we really did it with defense. It was a milestone; that really was the victory that got us the SEC championship. We had to go back home and win it and we managed to do that."

Looking back at the triumph a quarter of a century later, Dickey called it his favorite game as Vol coach. "It was the key turning point in this program." There is no disputing the fact that it remains one of the brightest jewels in Tennessee's football crown.

Of his six squads at Tennessee, Dickey felt a special closeness to that 1967 team. "We were not a collection of outstanding football players. We had some good ones, of course. You have to have good ones to win. But our strength lay in being a TEAM. The players had unity. They had purpose. They thought of themselves as a team."

While Dickey praised the defense, '67 captain Bob Johnson, who went on to greatness in the NFL, saluted his mates in the offensive line. "That was really one of the highlights of my life," said the man who went on to a standout 12-year career with the Cincinnati Bengals. "You know, John Boynton was a great player. Joe Graham had bad knees but they ran plays that he could still physically handle and he was terrific. Charlie Rosenfelder was a wonderful player. Of the five of us, Elliott Gammage was probably the very best athlete. I'm probably looking back too fondly, but I just can't believe there were very many offensive lines that were any better than that bunch."

Following the tumultuous victory at Birmingham, the Vols clicked off six more wins in a row, the most notable being a 20-7 triumph over Ole Miss; notable for the fact that it ended the longest losing streak in the school's modern history. Eight straight losses to the Rebels had begun to stick in Tennessee's craw.

The Vols' ninth consecutive victory, a 41-14 romp over Vanderbilt, wrapped up Tennessee's first SEC championship since 1956, the No. 2 national ranking and an Orange Bowl berth opposite Oklahoma. The '67 Vandy game was the last played on grass at Neyland Stadium for 26 years; the Vols switched to artificial turf in 1968. The turf came up following the 1993 season, replaced by grass for 1994.

The Vols were razor-sharp for much of the season, but the Orange Bowl battle with Oklahoma was another matter. The Sooners had compiled a 9-1 record mainly on the brute inside running of Ron Shotts and Steve Owens, but fooled the UT staff by passing and going outside with option plays. Oklahoma cruised to a 19-0 halftime lead and then withstood Tennessee's gallant second-half comeback. The Vols actually had a chance to win after Oklahoma gambled and lost on fourth-and-1 at their own 43. Warren worked the ball to the 27 from where Karl Kremser, UT's first soccer-style kicker, was wide on a 44-yarder at the gun.

The Vols lost their opener under the lights at Los Angeles and their finale under the lights at Miami. In between, there were nine victories, one SEC championship and a thousand thrills.

Before the bowl game, Dickey summed it up with the understatement of the year: "When you go 9-1 and beat Alabama, LSU, Ole Miss and Auburn, you have had a pretty good year."

Dickey was named SEC Coach of the Year and Kiner was selected the conference Sophomore of the Year. Johnson, Dorsey, Rosenfelder and Boynton made the All-SEC first team. Johnson, Dorsey and Flowers were named All-American, Johnson making 10 different A-A selections. Johnson also was named the SEC's Most Outstanding Lineman and won the Jacobs Blocking Trophy as the SEC's best blocker, an honor bestowed on Hal Wantland two years earlier.

CHAPTER 6

BUBBLES AND A BAD DAY IN BIG D

Bubbles Cash was her name and stripping was her game. As fate would have it, she hailed from Tennessee. Soddy-Daisy, just outside Chattanooga, a hundred miles or so from the very center of Big Orange Country. So if one could assume she was a Vol fan, one could also assume that she came by it quite honestly.

The curvaceous Bubbles was the featured stripper at a nightclub in Dallas. She was also a football fan; at least that's what she told other observers at Tennessee's Cotton Bowl practice sessions. More than once she showed up at practice, wrapped in a mink coat and little else, temperatures in the teens.

The Vols had been turned loose their first night in Big D and a dozen or so of them just happened to drop in at the club where Bubbles performed. It was one of several "private" clubs where you could bring in your own liquor, not that the UT players brought any. Bubbles was an eyeful and was not "silicone-enhanced," as one Vol who asked to remain nameless put it. "It was all her. What you saw was definitely Bubbles.

"We were Tennessee boys and right away she became enamored of Bubba Wyche. She would come to practice. In fact, the day before the game, it was cold; I mean really cold. It was in the teens and the wind was howling and we went to the Cotton

Bowl to practice. And she showed up in the stands. As we were leaving the field after a light workout, we headed up the tunnel and she's standing in there. She's waiting to say hello to Bubba.

"A bunch of us decided to stay an extra day after the game. Most of the team had already gone back to Knoxville, including Bubba. A teammate and I were trying to find a way back. We didn't have a car or anything. I knocked on his door to tell him that we had to get to the lobby and find somebody heading to Knoxville. And guess what? Bubbles answered the door. She really got around."

It was an interesting end to a stimulating season, one for which Doug Dickey had feared the worst as he headed into his fifth season as UT's head man. Gone were his first signees, the freshmen of 1964 who had spearheaded the championship season of 1967 as seniors, along with the group of '64 redshirts like Dewey Warren, Joe Graham and Derrick Weatherford. Except for Charlie Rosenfelder, the great offensive line of 1967 had marched off down the graduation aisle. Furthermore, speedster Richmond Flowers, the brilliant pass receiver, had taken a leave of absence to prepare for the Olympic Games at Mexico City.

But 1968 might have been Doug Dickey's finest coaching job. The Vols turned in an 8-2-1 record and finished No. 7 in the UPI poll and No. 13 in AP.

Earlier that year, Flowers was the No. 1 hurdler in the world. He beat his chief rival, Willie Davenport, in the last meet of the indoor season and again two or three times outdoors. But in early June, he pulled a muscle working out at Tom Black Track and wasn't able to run in the National AAU and some other big meets. He recovered sufficiently to run in the Olympic Trials, but was far from at his best. He finished fourth, and Davenport won the Trials and also the Olympic gold medal.

Flowers had already told Coach Dickey he would forgo the 1968 season for the Olympics and then return for his senior football season in '69. He had no doubt that he would make the Olympic team.

"I have always believed that Richmond would have won the gold medal at Mexico City if he hadn't gotten hurt early that summer," Chuck Rohe said. "I remember after Richmond lost in the Trials, Doug had asked me to call him because he was anxious for Richmond to come back and play football if he didn't make it to Mexico City. I found a phone and called Doug. He said, 'Get Richmond on the phone.' Richmond was all teary-eyed and dejected and I told him Coach Dickey wanted to speak to him.

"Get your fanny back here," Dickey told him. "I have a spot at tailback waiting for you." Flowers replied, "OK, I'll come." He packed his bag, went home and went to football practice after a day or two. He did not arrive back in Knoxville in time for the season opener against Georgia, but the Vols had an open date following Georgia and Flowers went on to play first-team tailback the entire season. The coaches had talked with him about moving to tailback, but he really hadn't anticipated doing it because he had his heart set on being in the Olympics.

Flowers had an athletic, but almost skinny build, slim at the waist but with broad shoulders and well-developed thighs. To be sure, he did not look the part of a college running back. But he impressed his coaches—and the opposition as well. He gained 417 yards, second on the team behind Richard Pickens, and caught 25 passes. He wound up with 101 career catches, a school record that stood until Larry Seivers broke it with 117 eight years later.

Assistant coach Ray Trail was one of his biggest admirers. "Richmond was a good football player, tough as nails. I don't know how he took the punishment that he did. But I never heard him complain. Never heard him gripe one time about getting hit, about anything. He had a great attitude. He might have looked skinny, but gosh he was tough. I thought he did as much with his ability as anybody who's been at Tennessee."

Ironically, Flowers later received his law degree from the University of Alabama, the school that had tried so hard to wrest him away from Tennessee in the beginning. And it was Bear Bryant who helped get him into Alabama's law school after Flowers had been unable to get into Tennessee's.

With Flowers and sophomore end Lester McClain, the Southeastern Conference's first black scholarship player, Tennessee had speed like few other teams. And the Vols still had quarterback Bubba Wyche, hero of the win over Alabama the year before.

The opener against Georgia was significant for a number of reasons, not the least of which was that the game was played on Tennessee's new artificial field. Which brings up an interesting story.

Some time earlier, Vol athletic director Bob Woodruff had received a phone call from the 3-M Corporation in St. Paul, Minnesota, the company that had installed Tennessee's Tartan track and basketball surfaces years before. The company had been developing a new synthetic turf for football. Then in the spring of 1968, 3-M notified Woodruff that the turf was available. Woodruff and Dickey visited the company in St. Paul and liked what they saw. UT officials ordered the new turf at a cost of $230,000. Tennessee would become the first big-time football school to have an artificial playing surface. Installation of the turf began in the spring and in no time at all everybody was calling it "Doug's Rug."

When he was notified by telegram in mid-June that Tennessee was in the process of installing the turf, Georgia athletic director Joel Eaves was livid. "It's a radical move that should have been considered by the conference," Eaves said. "Why didn't Tennessee bring this up when all of us met at Biloxi in May? No one from Tennessee mentioned the possibility of installing such a field. No one knows anything about this field, what it's like when it's wet, or anything else. We're thinking about voiding the contract. Maybe Tennessee can just put on an intrasquad game for the TV audience September 14."

The week before the game, Bulldog coach Vince Dooley and six of his assistant coaches hopped aboard a private jet to Minnesota in order to conduct some firsthand research on this mysterious new surface. They carried with them five different types of shoes.

"We all came back and reported that the ball bounced a little higher when it hit the surface and that it would roll a little bit farther," Dooley says. "But we finally adopted the attitude that it doesn't matter whether you play in a cow pasture or on artificial turf or whatever. The game is still football and you've just got to go out and play the game."

Woodruff attempted to calm the issue by offering the Georgia team special shoes. He even invited Dooley to bring his team in early to try out the new field. Georgia declined but showed up in Knoxville and the game went on as scheduled, before a packed house of 62,000 and a national television audience.

It was an unforgettable game. A storybook finish by Tennessee put the emphasis back where it belonged — on the game itself. After an 80-yard touchdown run by Georgia's Bruce Kemp, the Vols found themselves trailing 17-9 in the dying moments of the game. The scenario would be repeated, even down to the score, 25 years later when Tennessee faced defending champion Alabama at Birmingham. The Vols made their way downfield and were at the Georgia 20 as the second hand of the clock on the hillside scoreboard started its final sweep.

On fourth down, facing a do-or-die situation, Wyche took the snap from center just before the final buzzer and delivered a strike to split end Gary Kreis in the end zone. Like the thousands of Vol fans around him, Kreis felt it appropriate to celebrate. He kicked the ball high into the stands. That reduced the margin to 17-15. Then Wyche faded back under a hard rush and found tight end Ken DeLong open for the two-point conversion that gave the Vols an almost unbelievable 17-17 tie. Tennessee had gained an improbable tie, but lost a second football, DeLong tossing the ball into the stands, as was his custom. "A lot of our sophomores grew up out there today," Dickey said.

The Vols might never have pulled it off had not Wyche bothered to take a cup of dirt to the game. Wyche was used to rubbing his fingers with dirt before taking the field and, with there being no dirt on the synthetic field, he had to furnish his own.

For Georgia, it was hardly the end of the football world. The Bulldogs went on to finish undefeated but twice tied (the other a 10-10 standoff with Houston) and lost to Arkansas in the Sugar Bowl 16-2.

Not many players liked the new surface, including Vol fullback Richard Pickens. He went diving over the line on one play and came down on his head. He was out cold for a few minutes.

Flowers, back in an orange uniform for the first time after his abortive Olympics hurdling bid, played well in his debut at tailback as the Vols got past Memphis State 24-17. Then they mauled Rice 52-0 at Houston. McClain speared two touchdown passes a week later in a 24-7 romp over old rival Georgia Tech and the Vols' record was up to 3-0-1 as Alabama headed for Neyland Stadium.

Where Albert Dorsey had been the hero of the 24-13 victory over Alabama the year before, this time it fell to another defensive back, Jim Weatherford, to steal the show. He blocked an Alabama field goal attempt with five seconds remaining to preserve Tennessee's 10-9 victory. "I just kept thinking about that 11-10 game here two years ago," he would say after the game, alluding to Gary Wright's missed field goal in the rain.

In an amusing sidelight, Bama quarterback Scott Hunter had a run-in with Smokey, the Vol mascot, and a lecture by Coach Bryant that day. "We were warming up before the game and one of their cheerleaders kept letting their mascot dog come over close to us and bark," Hunter said. "I got tired of it and took a kick at that old hound. When we were walking to the dressing room before kickoff, Coach Bryant came to me and said, 'Scott, we've got enough trouble up here without you trying to kick their dog.'"

An easier-than-expected 42-18 win over UCLA set the stage for a showdown with Auburn at Birmingham. The Vols were almost out of it before you could say "Mike Currier." The Tiger back caught three touchdown passes in the first half as Tennessee fell behind 21-0. Auburn, withstanding a Tennessee rally in the second half, went on to win 28-14 and eliminate the Vols from the SEC title chase.

Tennessee bounced back to blitz Ole Miss 31-0, intercepting Archie Manning seven times. The one-sided victory might have doomed the Vols a year later, for the Rebels would remember that crushing defeat in the 1969 "Jackson Massacre."

With an 8-1-1 record, Tennessee earned a Cotton Bowl bid to meet Texas, the Vols' first trip to the Big D since 1953. Tennessee was a good team, better than expected, but probably had no business playing Texas. The Longhorns, showing off their new-fangled wishbone T offense, destroyed Tennessee 36-13 and rolled up 513 yards in the process.

Tim Priest, then a sophomore defensive back, thinks that Cotton Bowl loss was the only game in his three years in which the Vols were simply outclassed.

"Texas had tied Houston in their first game that year and lost to Texas Tech in the second and then they went to the wishbone. They were the first team to run it. They were bigger than us and stronger than us. They had Cotton Spreyer at end, had Ted Koy and Chris Gilbert at halfbacks, Steve Worster at fullback and James Street at quarterback.

"They wore those burnt orange jerseys that were the same color as the football and you couldn't find the ball in that triple option. They'd run a play and, hell, I didn't know where the ball was. I don't think anybody else on our team did either. I believe our coaches tried; they told us before the game, 'We've got it figured out. We're the first team that really knows how to defend this triple option.' But we didn't know how. Or at least we weren't capable of carrying out the game plan.

"I remember playing monsterman part of that game. I remember standing up there on the line of scrimmage and they didn't even block me. And I didn't know where the ball was; I couldn't find the ball. It was a very difficult situation.

"And poor Jimmy Weatherford. He was the toughest guy I ever played with. But he was sick all week long, had a temperature of 103 before the game and they played him anyway. He just basically had Cotton Spreyer man-to-man all over the field. Anybody else would have been in the hospital, but not Jimmy. We really didn't have anybody else who could run like he could. Spreyer scored a couple of long touchdowns against Weatherford.

"I remember that Alabama ran three straight bombs against him; three straight times they came out and threw the home run and he knocked down all three of them."

Dickey may have had an inkling of what was to come. In the locker room before the game, he told the squad "Whatever happens today, you guys have had a great season," or words to that effect.

"I didn't take it that way at the time," Priest said. "But later I realized that he probably knew we were in over our heads. He knew that we were a team of over-achievers. I think Coach Dickey would tell you this today, that he never expected that team to be in a New Year's Day bowl game. He had to totally rebuild his team from that great '67 outfit."

Dickey remembers it as a most miserable week, beginning with the weather. "The temperature must have been down around 15 to 18 degrees the whole week and we couldn't even practice because of the cold. And trying to practice and coach against the wishbone was all but impossible; we couldn't get our own team to get out of the huddle, much less run the wishbone. We were just too far behind defensively to where we needed to be to play that game.

"I don't know that we were outmatched so much. But nobody understood the wishbone; we'd never seen it. We didn't know what to do. The B team didn't know what to do. The coaches didn't know how to run the thing and I didn't know much about it."

All-America linebacker Steve Kiner missed curfew one night and Dickey gave him the choice of going home or running at 6 a.m. every morning during winter quarter. He ran, as everyone who learned about it knew he would.

Dickey almost lost assistant coach Bill Battle to Alabama that season, a move that would have drastically changed the course of Tennessee football, and perhaps Alabama's as well.

"Coach Bryant called and asked if I would be interested in becoming receivers coach for him. I just told him I wouldn't be interested in going from receivers coach here to receivers coach there. But I did go down to Tuscaloosa to talk to him. I really liked Tennessee and liked the staff. I was comfortable with where we were with the program.

"Coach Bryant said he needed some help and wanted me to come back. I asked him who was going to be offensive coordinator. He said he wasn't going to have coordinators, said that when you name one it hurts everybody else in getting a head coaching job because other teams think they ought to go after the coordinator. I told him I didn't care about the title but I wanted to know who was going to call the plays. He just hemmed and hawed around.

"I found out on that visit about the competitiveness of the press. It was all over the papers. I never would have gone down there if I thought it was going to get all the press that it got. I was serious in going down there because I loved Alabama and I loved Coach Bryant. There's no doubt that he influenced my life more than anybody except my parents.

"The thing is I really liked it at Tennessee. I liked Doug and he let me coach. We had a good young staff and I was able to have a lot of input. I thought the program was doing well and that we were going to have another good team. And we had good teams for quite a while."

Battle stayed on and fulfilled a date with destiny. In just one year, he would be Tennessee's head coach.

The 1968 season not only marked the unveiling of Doug's Rug, but also the debut of the announcing team of John Ward and his sidekick, analyst Bill Anderson. Ward, the "Voice of the Vols," and Anderson, Vol co-captain and wingback of the mid-1950s who later played with the Washington Redskins and world champion Green Bay Packers, have been side-by-side through a period of phenomenal growth of the Vol Network. As Tennessee's home attendance soared during the 1970s and '80s, so did the size and coverage of the far-flung Vol Network. When Ward and Anderson did their first broadcast, the '68 Vol-Georgia game, the network had fewer than 50 stations. During the 1970s, the network mushroomed to about 150 stations and could be heard in 10 Southeastern states. It was second in size only to the Notre Dame network, whose games were carried on an existing national network, Mutual.

Surveys at that time indicated that more than 1,750,000 listeners in Tennessee alone tuned in to the Vol Network each time the Vols took the field, home or away. And thousands more listened in neighboring states. Although the network has shrunk to fewer than 100 stations, it is still the largest in the Southeastern Conference and one of the top five in the country. A number of factors, primarily the plethora of games on television, combined to reduce the number of stations on the network, but broadcasts can still be heard in all parts of Tennessee and in surrounding states. And the network still has the same geographic reach it had in earlier years.

The airing of a Tennessee game has become not merely a broadcast; it has become a happening in Big Orange Country. It is not just a three-hour account of a football game; it is six hours, high-tech hours, of Tennessee football from every angle.

CHAPTER 7

WALKER, KINER, REYNOLDS, ETC.

Lon Herzbrun joined the Tennessee staff as linebackers coach in 1969 with this admonition from Doug Dickey: "We've got some good linebackers; don't screw them up."

Perhaps Dickey spoke in jest, perhaps not. In any event, he did not exaggerate. There was some outstanding linebacking talent wearing orange: seniors Steve Kiner and Jack Reynolds, sophomores Jackie Walker and Ray Nettles, and freshman Jamie Rotella. Kiner had made All-American in 1968. He would repeat in '69 and be joined by Reynolds. Walker would garner A-A honors in '70 and '71 and Rotella in '72. Nettles was All-SEC in '71.

Herzbrun had coached Walker at Knoxville's Fulton High, where Jackie had earned quite a reputation as a linebacker. A Knoxville sportswriter, questioning the accuracy of the Fulton statistician who regularly reported Walker making two dozen or so tackles a game, decided to attend a Fulton game to check it out. By the sportswriter's own count, Walker made 31 tackles that night.

Walker was a defensive back in linebacker's clothing, a big-play specialist of the first order, perhaps the biggest big-play linebacker ever to perform for the Vols. He still holds the NCAA record for interceptions returned for touchdown in a career (five). Nobody else has ever returned more than three. He called the shot on one of them. The '69 Alabama-Tennessee game at Birmingham was played on October 18, which happened to be the birthday of Herzbrun's wife, Wilma. On the eve of the game, Walker told her, "I'm going to score a touchdown for your birthday." True to his word, he took an interception back 27 yards for Tennessee's third first quarter touchdown and the Vols went on to dismantle the Tide 41-14.

Walker was an unlikely looking all-star. His weight was listed at 182 to 200 during his four years, but he never weighed more than 175 or 180. But because of his quickness and explosion he could hit like a Mack truck.

Kiner, however, was the most acclaimed of Tennessee's linebackers. He was already a first-team Associated Press All-American, an honor bestowed in large measure for his play against Ole Miss the previous season when he shed a cast that had encased a cracked wrist bone and proceeded to record 12 tackles and two interceptions.

For another, Kiner played his position without regard for physical well-being, his or anybody else's. He had a reputation for being a bit on the belligerent side.

"I think that's because Steve came from a tough neighborhood in Tampa," Herzbrun says. "Now the times I've seen him in a fight he never started it. But he always finished it. And he had many fights, with teammates in particular.

"One fight I'll never forget. It was with Roger McKinney, who happened to be from the same high school as Kiner (Hillsborough High School). We were having a drill at the stadium and Kiner said something to him, what I don't know. McKinney went into the halftime room and grabbed two scalpels they use to remove tape and came out at Kiner. Steve said, 'Put it down or I'm going to break your neck.' And McKinney kept coming at him, with two of them. He wouldn't put them down and Kiner held him at arm's length and finally—Boom! Kiner decked him.

"When Steve Kiner said something, he meant it. He didn't talk just to hear himself talk. That's one thing that probably got him into a lot of fights. When he said something to someone and they came back to make a fist or have some words with Steve, there weren't any more words spoken. You might call some people a name. You call Kiner a name and you're in a fight."

Teammates also remember Kiner for a fight with a Vol basketball player who was 6-11, weighed 250 and was considered to be unusually strong. The fight, if it can be called that, wasn't even close. At one point the young giant who had incurred

Kiner's displeasure left the room backward at high speed without observing the formality of opening the door.

For assistant coach Ray Trail, whose offensive linemen had more than a few words with the pugnacious linebacker, Kiner was his kind of football player. "He was a unique sort of guy," Trail says. "He was a real competitor. He was mean as hell, mean, and he had an ego as big as a house. He couldn't accept defeat in any way. He is the sort of guy you're always looking for to play."

In spring practice of 1969, sophomore Tim Priest got to work with the No. 1 secondary. On returning to the huddle after getting beat on a deep pass, Kiner was waiting. "All right, rookie," he said, his tone like that of a Marine drill instructor, "we allow that one time, but don't ever let that happen again."

Kiner's mouth often got him in trouble, but he never minced words. In the 1969 victory over Alabama, a 41-14 runaway, Kiner and his first team defensive mates were being removed after the Vols had mounted a 34-0 lead.

Before he went to the bench, he turned and screamed at the Alabama players. He pointed at coach Bear Bryant on the other sideline and shouted, "Look over there at that poor old man. He looks pitiful. Can you see him? You sorry sons-of-bitches have let him down. You should be ashamed of yourselves."

At game's end, Bryant put an arm around Kiner and walked him part of the way to the Tennessee dressing room, chatting along the way. Back in the dressing room, Kiner told a writer how happy he was to have beaten Alabama for the third straight year. "But, I swear, I'm a little sad, too. I can remember when there was some pride associated with wearing those red jerseys."

That remark hit hard at Bear Bryant, but he realized that maybe it was true. The next day, on his weekly statewide television show, he agreed with Kiner. He told his audience, "I guess we'll lose the faint-hearted now. Well, we can do without you. All of you letter-writers, to hell with you. I don't even have time to sort through them, much less read them. I know I'm old and fat but I'm not ready to give up. I hope our players aren't."

Eleven years later, reflecting on that miserable season in which Alabama went 6-5 and suffered one of its infrequent losses to Vanderbilt, Bryant recalled the loss to Tennessee.

"I'll never forget as long as I live how Tennessee humiliated us in Birmingham in 1969. They beat us 41-to-something, could have been nothing, had us down 34-zip, crushed us, embarrassed us, dog-whipped us—you name it.

"That one got me to thinking I'd lost my touch, that it was time to move over, give somebody else a chance. We were outclassed so badly I didn't want to do my TV show the next day. It was all orange. It was sickening. I wanted to puke."

Three sophomore stars emerged in Tennessee's smashing triumph that day—linebacker Walker, fullback Curt Watson and tailback Bobby Majors, last of the five football-playing brothers of the famous football family. All played key roles in the smashing victory, Walker with his interception return for a touchdown, Watson with 116 yards rushing and Majors with a 71-yard punt return for a TD.

Before that '69 season, Dickey decided to change his offense. He and his staff visited the University of Houston to study the Cougars' famed veer offense. But they didn't stop there; they incorporated a passing attack into it to take advantage of quarterback Bobby Scott's passing ability.

"We had a little turnover in personnel from 1968," Dickey said, "but we had a great group with people like Bobby Scott and Curt Watson. Don McLeary was a good junior halfback for us. We had some linemen who had seasoned a little bit and Chip Kell came into that mix. We began to have an excellent offensive team. We came back from Houston and decided we could do more with the veer than Houston was doing. So we put in a mix of the dropback pass with the Houston veer. And I thought we had a great combination in '69.

"We got ahead of the learning curve on the defenses by doing that. They couldn't blitz us because if they did we'd run the veer and Curt Watson would go sailing through there. We got a lot done offensively with that team."

Besides the annihilation of Alabama, another highlight had been an exhilarating 45-19 victory over Auburn, making it one of the few times that Tennessee had beaten Alabama and Auburn in the same year. Tiger sophomore quarterback Pat Sullivan was intercepted five times that day. "It was like a bad dream," he said years later. "I tried to block it out of my mind later, but I kept seeing the ball sailing over receivers' heads into somebody's arms. But it soothed things some that we came back, and midway through the fourth quarter we had a chance to win."

But the Tennessee defense, which came up with nine turnovers for the day, slammed the door shut rather emphatically. In a span of less than two minutes, the Vols turned two fumble recoveries and an interception into 21 points.

Five games into the season, Tennessee held decisive victories over Auburn and Alabama but the Vols faced a trip to Athens, Georgia, one of the more demanding assignments in college football. The Orange defense was magnificent that rainy afternoon, but the day belonged to Watson, the powerful fullback from Crossville, Tennessee. All he did in the 17-3 triumph was ramble for 197 yards on 19 carries to wipe out Tom Tracy's single game rushing record of 192 yards set 15 years earlier against North Carolina.

Watson, not given to vainglorious reminiscence even though his accomplishments would certainly allow him to do so, went on to a splendid career at Tennessee. Three times he made All-SEC. He became the busiest back in Tennessee history, carrying the ball 529 times in three years. He is No. 2 all-time behind Johnnie Jones (1981-84) in rushing yardage, 2,852 yards to 2,364.

Watson consistently carried the ball 20 to 30 times a game and his statistics undoubtedly would have been more impressive had he not been hobbled by injuries at various stages in his career. In 1971, regular tailback Haskel Stanback was hurt against Alabama, so Watson was moved to tailback, with Steve Chancey and Bill Rudder then sharing fullback duties. Watson suffered a broken rib in the season finale against Vanderbilt, which caused him to miss the Penn State game and the first half of the Liberty Bowl against Arkansas. How he managed to play in the second half is a story in itself.

By the time of the bowl, the final game for senior Watson, the rib injury was still causing him pain. Trainer Mickey O'Brien hauled out some old rib pads that he had last used in 1938.

"Mickey fixed me up with those pads and the pain went away," Watson says. "When I had that thing on I was comfortable. When I took it off, if I laughed or sneezed it hurt. At the Liberty Bowl I kept asking Coach Battle to let me play since it was my last game. He was hesitant to use me because he thought three weeks wasn't enough recovery time.

"We hadn't been very productive on offense and I kept bugging him. Finally, about midway through the third quarter he turned to me and asked if I was sure I could play. I told him I felt great, just let me in there. It was as though he put me in just to get me out of his ear."

Arkansas dominated the second half and Tennessee was all but given up for dead as the Hogs appeared to be putting the finishing touches on a 13-7 victory. But the Vols recovered a fumble at the Arkansas 36. Tennessee scored in two plays, Watson rambling 17 yards for the winning touchdown in a dramatic finish to a brilliant college career. George Hunt kicked the deciding point.

The Crossville Comet tried his hand at pro football, first with the New Orleans Saints and a year later with Green Bay. That didn't work. He went on to a distinguished Navy flying career, serving for four years in the Navy's famous Blue Angels squadron.

He almost didn't get into flight school because his weight, about 210 at the time, exceeded the Navy's weight standards. The Navy wanted pilots who would fit into the cramped cockpits of jet fighters, not king-sized former football players.

"The last thing you did before flight school was to have an interview with the flight surgeon," Watson said. "I said, 'Doc, there's one thing I have a question about and that's that I don't fit your weight standards. I never have and never will. I'm as skinny as I've ever been.' There was even a height-weight chart right there on his desk.

"The flight surgeon looked at my height, which was six feet, looked at my weight and said, 'You don't fit. But I'll tell you what let's do; let's just make you two inches taller.' So that's what he did. He filled it in as 6-2 on the physical form."

Watson flew Navy jets for 11 1/2 years, putting in a fourth year with the Blue Angels when he was asked to serve an extra year because of a pilot fatality. He has flown for Federal Express since his retirement from the Navy.

"The best job I ever had was with the Blue Angels," he said. "It was fun. A lot of people say it's a glamorous job and I guess it was. But for some reason I just never could imagine a hillbilly from Crossville, Tennessee, being very glamorous."

Kiner was the central figure in the celebrated "Jackson Massacre" of 1969. When the SEC Skywriters made their pre-season stop in Knoxville, Kiner told them he thought Alabama and Georgia would be Tennessee's toughest opponents.

"How about Ole Miss?" one writer asked. "They look like they have the horses this year."

What Kiner said then is open to conjecture. One paper quoted him as saying "They played more like mules up here last year," no doubt recalling Tennessee's easy 31-0 win in 1968.

Watson remembers Kiner being insulted by the writer. "Kiner said, 'You asked me my opinion and I gave you my opinion. Now you're questioning my opinion.' That really angered Steve. He said, 'Some people go down to the farm and don't know the difference between a horse and a mule.' I really don't think he was talking about the Ole Miss team. But that's the way it got written up. It got written up that Kiner had called Ole Miss a bunch of mules."

Kiner's remarks from early September had major repercussions in mid-November. Tennessee headed for Jackson with a 7-0 record, the No. 3 national ranking and a bid to the Orange Bowl all but in their pocket. There were reports that the Vols would go to Miami even if they lost, provided that they at least played well. But early in the week of the game, Ole Miss coaches hauled out

Kiner's reference to mules. A mule named "Mr. Kiner" was paraded all about the campus. At mid-week, an airplane flew over the Ole Miss campus and dumped three types of leaflets. One said "Archie Who?—Archie Mud, that's who. At least that's what his name will be Saturday." The largest pep rally in Ole Miss history followed.

When the Vols arrived at the stadium, two hours before kickoff, there were thousands and thousands of Ole Miss fans there to greet them. The players had to walk the gauntlet between two lines of Rebel boosters. One Vol said the fans were spitting on players, cursing them. "We weren't necessarily intimidated by that, but it just showed how fired up those people were," he said.

Obviously, the Rebels had a huge psychological advantage that had been won on the bulletin board. To make matters worse for Tennessee, seven Vol starters were injured. They included Kiner, who had a broken arm. But being the competitor he was, he gave it the old college try.

"Kiner couldn't really play," Dickey says. "He had a broken arm and tried to play but couldn't. But Steve Kiner was going to play—broken arm, broken leg, a concussion, whatever. Because of the situation, he'd have been out there no matter what. But we just had a bad day as well as having a very banged-up football team."

Neither the Tennessee coaches nor players had any indication of what lay ahead. The earliest indication that the Vols were in for a miserable afternoon came when the Rebels marched 90 yards to a touchdown the first time they had the ball. By the end of the quarter, it was 21-0 and it was obvious to all that the Rebels were sky-high.

"The Ole Miss players were four feet off the ground when they came out," one Vol said. "They were foaming at the mouth and their eyes looked like silver dollars. They were crazed."

Over on the Tennessee sideline, Watson was out of action, nursing a badly bruised leg. "Their field goal kicker, who was one of the most inconsistent in the conference, tried a mid-range field goal. When it came off the tee it looked like a pitcher throwing a knuckleball. It hit the crossbar and slipped through. I remember turning to whoever was beside me and saying, 'This is going to be a long day.' And Archie told me later that at the same instant he turned to somebody and said, 'Boy, we've got 'em now.' "

It wound up 38-0, one of the costliest and most disappointing defeats in Tennessee history. The loss knocked the Vols out of not only the Orange Bowl but the Top 10 as well. They became just another football team.

Kiner's teammates were quick to come to his defense, none of them blaming him for the defeat. "We all understood what happened," Watson said. "Nobody would ever blame Steve. We were a team; we won together and we lost together. You couldn't blame Steve Kiner for one game after the contribution he made over a three-year period."

Coach Trail felt the same way. "Football is 22 people. No one guy gets you beat. Ole Miss was about as high as any team I've ever seen. Still, we were a good enough football team that we should go out there and squelch that. If we had won that game we had a chance at the national championship. That was one of the saddest days I ever went through as a coach."

Dickey gave the Rebels their just due. "They made a lot out of that pregame stuff and I give them credit for maximizing their performance. But we were not the same football team we were two weeks before that or two weeks after that. We had to come home and beat Kentucky to be able to win the confernce championship and we did that."

The major bowls turned their backs on Tennessee. Two days later, when bowl games still seemed meaningless to players and coaches, and yes, even the fans, UT accepted a consolation trip to Jacksonville, to face Florida's Gators in the Gator Bowl. The matchup didn't seem like any big deal at the time, even though rumors had begun to circulate that Dickey would leave Tennessee to become head coach at Florida, his alma mater. In light of subsequent developments, it would become an unusually big deal in the days to follow.

He might have had occasional attacks of foot-in-mouth disease; but whatever else he was, Kiner was a competitor and an outstanding college football player. He was the SEC's Sophomore Player of the Year, a two-time All-American and the unanimous choice as SEC Defensive Player of the Year as a senior. He was drafted in the third round of the 1970 NFL draft by the Dallas Cowboys, played in the 1971 Super Bowl and later played with the New England Patriots, Washington Redskins and Houston Oilers. He became a pretty good linebacker for a player who, by NFL standards, was undersized and not quite fast enough.

The Jackson Massacre left the Vols with a hangover. They escaped another ambush the following week at Lexington, struggling against Kentucky. The Wildcats subjected Tennessee to a brutal air assault, connecting on 28 passes for a whopping 440 yards, but came up short 31-26. The Vols got the clinching score when punter Herman Weaver dropped a kick dead on the UK 1 and Jack Reynolds recovered a fumble in the end zone on the next play.

It was more of the same a week later against Vanderbilt. The offense was back in gear but the defense was out to lunch for the third straight week and the Vols won 40-27. All that remained was the bowl date with Florida. And an incredible development that left some Tennesseans numb, some bewildered, some enraged.

DEPARTING THE GARDEN OF EDEN

Tennessee fans were ecstatic with the status of their football program. As Southeastern Conference champions, for the second time in three years, the Vols were booked for the Gator Bowl in December, and the outlook could hardly have been brighter. The school's ambitious young coach was building a dynasty that would have Tennessee awash in championships for the next couple of decades. One prominent newspaper columnist had gone so far as to proclaim the end of the Bear Bryant era in the SEC, the implication being that the old man had been rooted out by the hard-charging upstart from Tennessee.

And while the RIP sign turned out to be premature as far as Bryant was concerned, there was no reason to believe anything but prosperity lay ahead for the Tennessee Vols. Shades of Bowden Wyatt's early years as the returning hero of UT football. Shades even of General Robert Neyland's reign as undisputed king of the Southern football coaching landscape.

Maybe things were going too smoothly. As Doug Dickey himself once said, college football is a series of peaks and valleys. Perched on the peak, UT partisans weren't prepared for the valley that lay ahead. If at the end of the 1969 season, Tennessee faithful could envision nothing but clear skies ahead, they were ignoring a rumble in the air that would alter the course of Vol football drastically in the years ahead.

Members of Tennessee's advance party, who had arrived in Jacksonville two days before the team's arrival in order to nail down transportation and hotel arrangements, were jolted by the rumors that came down from Knoxville. The *Knoxville News-Sentinel* had published the unthinkable: Doug Dickey would pull up stakes after the Gator Bowl game and switch his coaching allegiance to his alma mater, the University of Florida. The man who was positioned to guide Tennessee to an era of Neyland-style prosperity was calling it quits. The irony and clumsiness of Dickey coaching his present employer against his future employer was lost in the shock of the news. The awkwardness of the situation was nothing compared to the magnitude of the deed's central theme.

Vol fans were understandably aghast. Pride would not let them accept the notion that somebody would consider another coaching job superior to the opportunity at Tennessee. Kentucky's fabled basketball coach, Adolph Rupp, said it best when he was informed of the news. "What?" asked the Baron of the Bluegrass in his patented drawl. "You mean he's leaving the Garden of Eden?"

To this day when longtime Tennessee fans rehash "the good old days" of football, the subject of Dickey's abrupt departure in 1969 invariably arises. Not so much in terms of the historic effects it produced, but more from the psychological standpoint: Why indeed would he leave the Garden of Eden? What mental machinations would cause a man to forsake the Big Orange head coaching position, in some ways the best job in all of college football, for the uncertainties of a rebuilding project at a different school, even if it happened to be his alma mater?

Let the only man who knows for sure answer those questions. Here is what Doug Dickey says: "Both my mother and Jo Anne's father were alive at the time. It was my home school. I felt that I had done about all at Tennessee that I probably could get done. I had accomplished what I came to accomplish.

"We had been in all the major bowls and we had won championships. We had not won a national championship but we had been very close. And the national championship at that time was not the kind of issue it is today. It has become a different deal, in the polls and all. To be honest, I wasn't aware much of the national championship in 1967-68. I was working my tail off to beat Bear Bryant and Shug Jordan and Johnny Vaught. That was about all I needed to take on; I didn't need anything else in my world at Tennessee."

Unquestionably the lure of alma mater and family play a role in the lives of men. And so it did for young Doug Dickey. But there were members of his staff who still express puzzlement at the strange sequence of events that deprived UT of a winning coach and sent him packing off to Florida where his welcome would be far from overwhelming.

Chuck Rohe, Tennessee's combination track coach/football recruiter, was mystified. "I really didn't think he would do it. Had Coach Dickey stayed at Tennessee, you would probably be talking about him now in the same terms you use for Bear Bryant. We had beaten Alabama three straight. We were the team to beat in the SEC. We had the best program. A dynasty was being built."

A former Tennessee coach summed it up this way: "I personally don't know that there was anything more to it than what Doug says. There was a sense of going home because his mother was there and Jo Anne kind of wanted to go there. When you say he had accomplished all he could, I don't know. He hadn't won a national championship, and he could have had a dynasty for the next 20 years or so. He could still be coaching today. He might be approaching Bear Bryant's won-lost record right now. I never quite understood the move. I knew he was discussing it, but I never did think he would do it."

The scenario that took place was less intriguing than the thought patterns that produced it. Stripped to its bare essentials, it went like this: The University of Florida president, Stephen O'Connell, approached Dickey in the summer of 1969 and asked if he would consider becoming the Gators' head coach after the 1969 season. Ray Graves had agreed to step down as coach at the end of the year and to continue as athletic director only. Dickey declined to commit himself, but said that he would be interested in pursuing the matter after the season ended.

O'Connell called Dickey in December and told him that Florida was definitely going to make a coaching change.

"I told him I couldn't do anything about it right then, that we had this bowl game and would have to wait. I said, 'If you're willing to wait I'll be willing to talk to you. But that's your call, not mine.' And he said he would wait."

Dickey said he met with O'Connell one more time before the bowl game and told him he would have to wait until after the game to make any commitment. Dickey says he had made up his mind that if he were offered the job, he would go to Florida.

Back to Dickey: "If you get to be a popular coach, obviously there are some people representing other schools who will talk to you one way or the other. One time Oklahoma called and said they had a coaching position open and was I interested. I just felt that the University of Oklahoma job was about the same job I had at Tennessee. I never went out there. I called them the next day and told them, thank you, but I'm not interested. I also had an offer from the University of Michigan at the time Bo Schembechler went there. They wanted to know if I would come up and talk to them, but I turned that down too. Georgia Tech got a little involved also, but I really felt I had the same job here as at any of those places.

"Florida had never won the SEC championship. It had been a growing, improving program. Coach Graves had taken it to a new level. And I felt like I might be able to go another step. And at the same time, it was my alma mater. And there were a lot of ties, a lot of personal ties, in the state of Florida that I felt very warmly about. I felt my children would probably end up going to school there, graduating and living in Florida because they had great growth potential in the state of Florida. That obviously has been true."

Dickey made another interesting point, this one concerning his financial arrangements. "I went for the same amount of money I was making here. In fact, I made less money the second year than I had been making here because the television show turned out to be a bummer. It took about four years to rebuild the television show to where I really made any money, more than I had been making at Tennessee.

"So it was never a financial bonanza of any kind. It was strictly a personal decision that I wanted to try to do something at the University of Florida that I felt I was capable of doing. I was not unhappy here at all. I just felt that I had done all I could do, and it was a personal decision that had personal ramifications in it."

As soon as Dickey stepped on the Florida campus in January, 1970, he sensed that something was wrong. Florida had experienced a 1969 season that far surpassed expectations. Some wanted Graves to remain as coach in view of the success that had been attained in his final year—Graves included. There were those resigned to the departure of Graves, but wanting his replacement to be veteran Florida assistant Gene Ellenson, not Dickey. Include the Florida players in that number. They made their sentiments known by carrying both Graves and Ellenson off the field following the Gators' 14-13 triumph over the Vols.

"When I went to Florida, I found that two things had occurred," Dickey says. "One, there was a lot of dissension among the Florida people about how all this had transpired. The press and supporters had been split apart between Ray Graves and Steve O'Connell. It was not a happy scene and I was a victim. I was not aware of that at the time. I was a victim of some significant power plays that Ray Graves and some of them had tried to make.

"And there was a different cultural atmosphere in Florida from what there was in Tennessee at the time. It was a turbulent time and Florida was five years ahead of what was going to happen from the Vietnam war in other places—the cultural change, the long hair and all of that. Probably the most disconcerting time to be on a college campus was in the early 1970s. And I got thrown into the middle of that."

Dickey has called the situation at Florida "the most disheveled mess I've ever been in in all my years as head coach, athletic director or assistant coach."

Florida under Dickey never reached the heights he had anticipated when he heeded his alma mater's call. But that's a story for another book.

Another jolting development that Dickey came face to face with in Gainesville was integration, which he had experienced at Tennessee in 1967 without major incident.

"We brought in black players at Florida in 1970 and there was a much more significant redneck backlash than we ever experienced at Tennessee. I was extremely surprised by it. It came from a lot of the West Florida rural element and it continued to be a rather nasty level of irritation.

"I didn't have too many real problems with it, but one day we did have the threat of a boycott by several of our black players. I'll never forget that Vince Kendrick came in and I said, 'Vince, what kind of problem do we have here?' And he said, 'You ain't going to have a problem, Coach. I'm going to take care of it for you.' Vince was a kid from a very poor black family in Miami. Some people were trying to set up a boycott over various issues, trying to bring a divisiveness to the squad, but Vince wasn't going to have any of that. He and his brother Preston did a great job of managing that thing. So we had a variety of things going on over a three- or four-year period that were kind of messy."

The one thing that is indisputable is that Dickey, as he left for Florida, had taught the Vols how to win. He hadn't left many stones unturned in Big Orange Country. But his alma mater was calling.

As for Tennessee, the Vols were forced to begin a search of their own for a new head coach.

CHAPTER 8

ENTER
BILL BATTLE

When he was a senior at the University of Alabama, Bill Battle's goal in life was to make $10,000 a year. Shortly after he turned 40, after he got out of the coaching rat race, he was a millionaire.

In 1962, Battle was president of the A Club, Alabama's lettermen's organization. He was in coach Bear Bryant's office one day talking A Club business and got a lesson in finance from the Bear himself. They began to talk about coaching.

Bryant told him that two of his former players, Bobby Drake Keith and Gene Stallings, were doing very well in the coaching profession. "They're making $10,000 a year," Bryant told him, "and there aren't many people in our profession making $10,000 a year."

That little tidbit, coming as it did from the man who would have such a powerful influence on his life, made a tremendous impression on young Battle.

"I believed what Coach Bryant said. I doubt that my dad, who was athletic director at Birmingham Southern and had been there for 20 years or so, was making that much money. So that was my goal in life, to make $10,000 a year. If I could ever do that I thought I would have it made."

And for a time, it probably seemed to him that he would never make it. In his first job out of college, as an assistant to Bud Wilkinson at Oklahoma in 1963-64, he was working toward a master's degree. He was making $103 a month. And that had to support a wife and new baby and pay for his tuition, books and fees.

"That was a lean year," Battle remembers. "With that new baby, we had to buy all the baby formula the first of the month so we would be sure we had some for the last week because the last week got hairy around our place.

"You got 12 cents a mile if you went recruiting, so every time they asked who wanted to go where, I asked to go the farthest because I had a new car and I could get 12 cents a mile and that helped. And I was out hustling at night, refereeing rec league basketball for $5 a game. That was an interesting year."

Barely five years later, after brief coaching stints at Oklahoma and West Point, Battle had already surpassed his $10,000-a-year goal. He was making the princely sum of $14,000 as an assistant to Doug Dickey, who had hired him in 1966 to replace Bob Jones, one of three assistants killed in a car-train accident in 1965. Little did Battle know that his salary was about to be doubled. The Bear would be pleased.

Like a bolt out of the blue, Dickey resigned unexpectedly following the 1969 Gator Bowl and Battle was shocked to learn that he was one of three candidates for the head coaching job, along with fellow assistant coaches Jimmy Dunn and Doug Knotts. He had no advance warning that he was about to become a head coach at the ripe old age of 28.

"We didn't find out that Doug was talking to Florida until we were well into bowl preparations. We all lived down in Crestwood Hills and we were driving home from work when Jimmy Dunn told me about it and that was kind of a shock. When we got down to the Gator Bowl things were a little tense. One day Coach Woodruff came out on the field and said he'd like to have lunch with me. Now that was kind of unusual because the athletic director never invited me to lunch.

"We went out to Ponte Vedra Beach for lunch. Coach Woodruff told me he thought Doug was going to go to Florida. Rumors were pretty rampant at the time but I just couldn't believe he was going to go. And Doug still hadn't talked to us; at least he hadn't talked to me about it. Or the team."

"I think we have a good staff," Woodruff told him. "There are three guys on the staff capable of being a head coach, Jimmy Dunn, Doug Knotts and you."

Woodruff asked Battle where he would be after the Gator Bowl game. Battle said he was going to his hometown of Birmingham for a few days. Woodruff asked for a telephone number in Birmingham where he could be reached. "If it happens, we may need to call you," he said.

"Even then I didn't think Doug was going to go," Battle said. "At that time I felt like I was ready to be a head coach. But I didn't think I would get it. Both Dunn and Knotts had told me that if they got the job they wanted me to be offensive coordinator. But I felt like I could go to Florida with Doug because I thought Dunn was going to get the job."

Back in Knoxville, university officials gave Woodruff a free hand in picking Dickey's successor. They could veto his selection, of course, but they remembered that it was Woodruff who had hand-picked Dickey six years earlier. Woodruff wanted to choose a successor from within and released a statement saying Battle, Dunn and Knotts would be considered for the job. Dunn, 33, was considered the frontrunner. Knotts, 36, had been defensive coordinator and was also in the picture. Battle, only 28, was the sleeper. There were also factions that wanted to bring Johnny Majors, the All-America tailback of 1956, back home. He had just finished his second straight 3-7 season at Iowa State. That move would be delayed for another six years.

Woodruff, obviously trying to keep as many coaches as possible, called the three candidates together. He told them that whichever one got the job, the other two would get significant salary raises, and specified the amount. Battle recalls that it was something in the $22,000 to $24,000 range, significantly more than any of them were making. Dunn and Knotts, the coordinators, were making $16,000 each; Battle was making $14,000. All were paid a bowl bonus of $2,000.

Battle, the receivers coach, was sort of the golden boy of the Dickey staff: boyish, handsome, intelligent, quiet, studious, level-headed, very popular among fellow coaches and players.

Woodruff arranged to meet with the three of them individually the next morning. It was then that Battle first realized he had a real shot at the job.

"Coach Woodruff didn't tell me but it was the first real clue that I had a good chance. Things moved pretty quickly after that and it was in the next day or two that it all happened."

The real tipoff came when Battle and Woodruff went to the West Knoxville home of university president Dr. Andy Holt. Once there, Dr. Holt called Battle into a room to talk privately. He dropped a pretty big hint when he told Battle, "You know, Bob Woodruff's a smart guy and we never thought about this but when he told us what he wanted to do, we wondered why we didn't think of that; it's the logical thing to do."

Dr. Holt, no doubt remembering the troubles that led to Vol coach Bowden Wyatt's downfall 15 years before, asked Battle if he drank. Only socially and even then not very often was the answer. Dr. Holt was very much against drinking and it was his way of emphasizing to the young coach that one could get caught up in all the festivities that go on in a big-time college football program.

"Dr. Holt didn't tell me to not do it. It was just some fatherly advice. We didn't talk about football; we talked about church and a few other things. And finally he said, 'Let's go meet some other people.' And he had the athletic committee there. I met with them and the press conference announcing my appointment was later that day."

Just as he had done in hiring Dickey in 1963, Woodruff surprised everyone by plucking a young assistant coach to lead Tennessee back toward the top. Young but knowledgeable. He had soaked up a lot of football from four of the game's top teachers — Alabama's Bryant, Oklahoma's Bud Wilkinson, Army's Paul Dietzel and Dickey. Battle's appointment was announced on Saturday, January 3, 1970, just 26 days after his 28th birthday. Just eight years after he had earned a national championship ring at Alabama. And because it was the same scenario as Dickey's hiring, it was met with wide acclaim. The one-time Alabama end would be paid $28,000—twice what he had been making. And nearly three times the amount that really grabbed his attention in a meeting with Bear Bryant eight years earlier.

"It took guts on the part of Coach Woodruff to give me the job," Battle said. "But I've always wanted to be a head coach. I always felt I'd be a head coach some day. I've learned a lot of football from Coach Bryant, Coach Wilkinson, Coach Dietzel and Coach Dickey. I've learned, too, that you've got to be yourself. I can't be any of them. I've got to be Bill Battle. And I have to do what I think is correct."

If Battle thought he was facing a stacked deck for being an Alabamian, he never showed it. Even though the specter of Johnny Majors hovered over him almost from the day of his appointment.

"When you get into coaching," he would say later, "you understand that your longevity isn't necessarily good. But I didn't worry about it. I was too dumb, I suppose, to worry about things like that. I didn't worry about contracts. I never tried to negotiate for any more money; I didn't understand how to do it, even if I had wanted to.

"I was very naive, I guess. I didn't understand the newspapers. I wasn't a political kind of guy. I wanted to coach; that's all I wanted to do. I didn't even know who was on the board of trustees. Which wasn't very smart on my part. And I didn't politick; I didn't do anything. I just wanted to be left alone and coach, and if I did it good enough that would be all right, and if I didn't, that would be all right too.

"I thought I had a good background and I knew that I worked hard. I wasn't worried about a job. I felt like one day I was going to be a head coach; I just got there a little sooner than I thought I would. And after I got there I didn't worry too much about them running me off. When we were 31 and 5, Tennessee people were saying 'Oh, don't go back to Alabama, don't go back to Alabama.' And I was saying 'I just hope you don't run me off from here.' And they would say, 'Oh, no, we wouldn't ever do that.'

"But I didn't worry about it. You understand that when you win, you are a hero far beyond what you deserve. And when you lose you are a goat far beyond what you deserve. And you really don't worry about it too much. If you did, you wouldn't have gotten into coaching in the first place."

Battle's appointment met with the approval of the players. He had earned their respect, even though he was only five or six years older than some of them.

"I wish I had another year or two so I could play for him," said senior split end Gary Kreis, who had been tutored by Battle as the receivers coach.

"He has a keen football mind," said junior quarterback Bobby Scott. "I think we'll have a terrific offense next season." And he hit the nail on the head. The '70 Vols, with Scott leading the way, would go 11-1, score 370 points and set school records for total offense.

Battle would become the first Division I head coach ever to win 11 games in his rookie season. He was joined later by John Robinson of Southern Cal (11-1, 1976), Gary Blackney of Bowling Green (11-1, 1991) and Terry Bowden of Auburn (11-0, 1993).

Battle had to rebuild the staff. Dunn, Knotts, George McKinney and Jack Hall accompanied Dickey to Florida. Ray Trail, Lon Herzbrun, Bob Davis, George Cafego and Ken Hatfield decided to stay at UT. Battle went after and got Larry Jones, Dietzel's top assistant at LSU, Army and South Carolina. He talked Buddy Bennett into leaving East Tennessee State, where he had done a masterful job coaching the secondary, a job he would handle with even more success at Tennessee. Jim Wright left Mississippi State to become offensive coordinator. Rex Dockery, Vol guard of 1960-62 and coach of a state championship team at Morristown, became freshman coach, assisted by Dewey Warren, the star quarterback of the mid-1960s. Warren had spent the previous two years in pro football, 1968 and part of 1969 with the Cincinnati Bengals and the remainder of 1969 with the Las Vegas Cowboys.

For Warren, it was the first step in a coaching career that would take him to Brigham Young, where Lavell Edwards had just become head coach. Warren helped to install the Cougars' now-famous passing game. It was nothing for Brigham Young to throw 50 to 60 passes a game.

"We were real surprised that Battle was chosen," says Tim Priest, captain of Battle's first squad. "He was respected. He had run our winter workout program and it was extremely rigorous, a tough, tough program. Everybody considered him a genuinely good fellow and a bright young guy.

"To tell the truth, the staff he put together in 1970 was a marvelous staff. We had more fun that fall than any of the teams had before us with the possible exception of the '67 team, which had so many characters on it, guys always pulling pranks. Larry Jones and Buddy Bennett and Lon Herzbrun ran the defense and they were so laid-back. Those guys would have killed for us. We just had a ball playing that year."

Offensively, the Vols were armed to the teeth as the Battle era began. It was the defense, or supposed lack of same, that caused concern. And unnecessarily, as things turned out.

Tennessee had lost not one, but two, All-America linebackers, Steve Kiner and Jack Reynolds. Ray Nettles, Jackie Walker and Jamie Rotella showed promise. There were two untested and unknown cornerbacks, David Allen and Conrad Graham, joined in the secondary by Priest and Bobby Majors. That group went on to establish a Southeastern Conference record that year with 36 interceptions. The following season, the secondary set an NCAA record for interception return yardage that still stands, 782 yards and also established standards for highest average per interception return (31.3 yards) and most touchdowns by interception returns, 7.

One of Tennessee's closest calls that year was a 20-18 victory over South Carolina at Columbia, the winning margin coming when George Hunt rammed home a 31-yard field goal with 11 seconds to play.

That game got off to a rocky start for Nettles, one of the Vols' toughest players.

"We figured we were going to have a cakewalk, that we were going to kill them," Priest recalls. "They had three big old fat linemen. This was back when nobody weighed more than about 230 or 235, but Carolina had a center and two tackles who must have weighed 280 each. Nettles lined up on the center's nose most of the time.

"They came out of that first huddle and those big fat guys just waddled up to the line. And you could just see the gobs of fat. Nettles looked at this center, Jim Poston, and said, 'You fat son of a bitch, I'm going to knock your ass off.' That guy snapped the ball and he just buried Ray. They proceeded to block us all day long. And they moved the ball on us all day long. Hunt's field goal really saved our season that day."

Nettles' playing weight that year was listed as 211, but it's a wonder he didn't fit the "fat man" category of those Gamecocks. Watson recalls an example of just how much food the junior from Jacksonville could put away.

"The reason I remember this so well is that my dad always thought it was one of the most remarkable things he had ever seen. That spring I invited the whole squad to Crossville for a chicken cookout, with water skiing and a fun afternoon. It was rather chilly that day but we got in some water skiing anyway and then we went out to Catoosa Wildlife Area, where one of my dad's friends had a cabin. Dad had ordered up 260 pounds of chicken and only about a third of the guys showed up, most of them with dates. But they ate every last bit of the 260 pounds.

"The thing that my dad never forgot was that Nettles ate five whole chickens at one sitting. That didn't include the baked beans and cole slaw and potato salad and bread that he ate along with the chicken. Many years later, when my dad was past 80 and I'd come in from the Navy to see him, he would look up at the ceiling and say, 'Five whole chickens!' "

DOUG DICKEY RETURNS

Any Tennessee fan worth his salt would never consider anybody but Alabama the No. 1 enemy on the schedule. And yet it happened.

As fate would have it, one of Tennessee's and Florida's infrequent matchups was scheduled for the fall of 1970, just 10 months after Florida had hired Doug Dickey away from Tennessee. A Hollywood script writer couldn't have come up with a more dramatic setting for Tennessee's sixth game of the season, October 24.

Dickey could be considered a victim of the luck of the draw. The Florida team he inherited from Ray Graves was not a very good one; the Tennessee team Battle inherited from Dickey was. And that's putting it mildly. The Gators had been mauled by Alabama 46-15 and would go on to lose four games. The Vols were fresh from an impressive 24-0 romp over the Tide the previous Saturday, and were anxious to meet up with their old coach. Not to mention the team that had beaten them in the Gator Bowl 10 months before.

Naturally, the game got a tremendous buildup. A fan in Loudon, Tennessee, composed a song titled "Tricky Dickey," which sold several thousand copies and aired on radio stations in Big Orange Country. A Florida B-team player responded with one called "Bad Billy Battle, You Mean and Nasty Boy." The song may have been a hit in Gatorland but the title was hardly appropriate because almost everybody, including his severest critics, would agree that the boyish Battle was about as friendly and easygoing a person as one would ever meet.

Needless to say, a lot of Tennessee fans were in a vengeful and unforgiving mood. UT officials feared the worst as Dickey brought his Gators into Neyland Stadium, where the leather-lunged boo-birds were out in force in the highly partisan crowd of 64,000. Surprisingly, nothing of a nasty nature transpired. That was probably due to the outcome, a rousing 38-7 Tennessee victory. Dickey, in fact, was given a standing ovation by Vol fans as he left the field, their way of saluting him for the quality he had restored to the UT program in his six years in Knoxville.

The triumph, unquestionably the centerpiece of Battle's first season, was highlighted by a brilliant performance by quarterback Bobby Scott. He riddled the Gator secondary for 21 completions, two touchdowns and a school-record 385 yards. His Florida counterpart, John Reaves, one of the Gators' all-time passing greats, had a miserable day, completing but nine of 22 passes for a paltry 91 yards against the aggressive Vol secondary. Two of his passes were intercepted and returned for touchdowns, one of 19 yards by Jackie Walker, another of 36 yards by Conrad Graham.

Dickey says he wasn't expecting anything ugly on his return to Knoxville that day and remembers the ovation at game's end, which he has referred to as one of the most touching moments of his life.

"It was a nice moment and I appreciated the fans. Coming back to face the fans wasn't difficult; the most difficult thing was that I didn't have a very good football team. We had lost all the offensive linemen and all the defensive backs from the team of the

year before, which was a very good football team. So, consequently, we had a poor situation that we put ourselves into.

"Tennessee fans are very good fans, very knowledgeable,
and they are really a class crowd, then and now. They were more
conservative then than they are today and didn't wear as much
orange and all that. They are basically a really conservative
crowd, as East Tennessee people generally are. And not much
rabble rousing. We just needed to play the game and get out of
here. And I appreciated the reception."

At least Dickey fared better than Bear Bryant, who got
headaches instead of ovations in another emotionally charged
encounter the week before. The Tide, down from its remarkable
prosperity of the 1960s, was in the midst of its second consecutive 6-5 season. But to Tennessee fans, Alabama is Alabama, no
matter what.

The media jumped on the Battle vs. Bryant angle. Battle
tried to downplay the confrontation. "When we play Alabama
Saturday, it won't be Bryant vs. Battle, but Alabama vs. Tennessee. Coach Bryant won't make a single tackle out there and
neither will I."

Of the 59 victories Battle recorded in seven seasons at
Tennessee, that 24-0 triumph over Alabama probably ranks as
the most satisfying. For the first time in 115 games, Alabama had
been shut out, the second-longest streak in college history. It was
the fourth straight loss to Tennessee, the first time a Bryant-
coached team had been beaten four years in a row by any team.

The ball-hawking Tennessee defense was never better.
Eight times it picked off Alabama passes, five of them thrown by
Scott Hunter. That prompted Tide receiver David Bailey to
remark, perhaps not altogether in jest: "Scott, this time throw the
ball to them and see if I can intercept it."

The eight thefts, still a school record, was the high-water
mark in a season in which the Vols of 1970 set an NCAA record
for interceptions in a season, 36. Captain Tim Priest, who had
three interceptions in that '70 Alabama game, patrolled the
secondary with David Allen, Conrad Graham and Bobby Majors.
He believes the record was the result of a combination of things.

"We had some pretty good people rushing the passer that
year; not great players but darn good ones. The coaches rotated
four sophomore tackles—Bill Emendorfer, John Wagster, Frank
Howell and Carl Johnson. We had really outstanding linebackers
in Jackie Walker, Ray Nettles and Jamie Rotella.

"Our secondary coach, Buddy Bennett, had a scheme. He
ran some zone coverages that people hadn't seen before. The first
year we went to a four-deep secondary from a three-deep with

monsterman. Most people were still playing a three-deep in those days. We played a lot of teams that had average quarterbacks but thought they had great quarterbacks, so they threw the ball a lot. We probably had more passes thrown against us than any Tennessee team ever had."

Priest was correct. The 11 opponents of 1970 attempted 358 passes, a record at the time. Only two Vol teams since have had to defend against more aerials—1987 (368) and 1989 (402). True, the 1970 team had more opportunities for interceptions than all but two other Tennessee teams, but on an interception-to-pass ratio, it is no contest. The 1970 defenders had a goal of one interception for every 10 passes thrown at them. With 36 interceptions in 358 attempts, they just about hit that goal on the nose. Priest is still the career interceptions leader with 18. The '70 Vols also recovered 18 fumbles, giving them a whopping 54 turnovers in all.

Bennett's Bandits intercepted at least one pass against every opponent but one, Wake Forest in Game 7. Surprisingly, it was one of the Vols' easiest victories, 41-7.

The Bandits worked long and hard in practice. There was little tackling, but much agility work.

"Coach Bennett worked us hard on breaking to the ball," Priest says. "We would go out there and he'd throw the ball to one side of the field and all four guys had to touch it before it hit the ground. The first guy would knock it up in the air and the next guy would tip it, and so forth. He'd have one guy running from hash mark to the other sideline. And the other three would have to keep it in the air. If it hit the ground, you'd do it over again. He almost worked us to death, so the games themselves were a piece of cake. We almost never got tired in a game after what he put us through in practice."

The only blot on that 1970 record came in the second game of the season, an early Southeastern Conference showdown with Auburn. It came a week after the Vols had throttled SMU and its great senior passer, Chuck Hixson, holding him without a touchdown pass since early in his sophomore season and intercepting him twice.

Expectations were high as the Vols headed for Birmingham. But Pat Sullivan, who would win the Heisman Trophy a year later, riddled the Tennessee secondary for 268 yards in the Tigers' 36-23 victory. The loss wasn't due so much to Sullivan passing to Terry Beasley as it was a 5 1/2-minute series of setbacks in the second period in which Tennessee gave up an interception that set up a touchdown, a 40-yard pass play, an interception return for a touchdown, a third interception, a lost fumble and a safety.

"That was one of the finest games we ever played as a team," Sullivan said later. "Tennessee jumped out to a 10-0 lead and we came back. That was what got us going that year."

For the Tigers, it was revenge for the 45-19 blowout at Knoxville the year before, a game in which Sullivan was intercepted five times. For Tennessee, it was the only loss of the season, a defeat that not only ruined a perfect campaign but relegated the Vols (4-1) to a second-place SEC finish behind LSU (5-0).

But in the weeks ahead, the Vols would build an impressive string of 10 victories, including the pair of emotionally charged games against Alabama and Florida on back-to-back Saturdays at Neyland Stadium. They came awfully close to getting a legitimate shot at the national championship, but the luck of the draw did them in. The chance died when Tennessee accepted a Sugar Bowl bid to meet Air Force, rather than waiting for a possible matchup with Nebraska in the Orange.

The Sugar Bowl had beckoned, inviting Tennessee to face Air Force, which was undefeated at the time but would be annihilated 49-19 by Colorado in its final regular season game. Many Vols wanted to take on Nebraska in the Orange Bowl, but the Orange was holding out for a Nebraska-Notre Dame matchup. Tennessee was second choice behind the Irish.

Notre Dame officials said their team would go to the bowl offering the highest-rated opponent. It turned out to be the Cotton Bowl and top-ranked Texas. By opting for a rematch of the previous Cotton Bowl, the Irish also got a chance to avenge a 21-17 defeat.

Tennessee officials, remembering the previous year when a 9-1 LSU team was left out of the bowl picture altogether, were determined that their team would not finish the season all dressed up with no place to go. They allowed the seniors to vote on whether to accept the Sugar Bowl, or to wait for the Orange and hope the call came.

"The Sugar Bowl won by one vote as I recall," Priest said. "Coach Battle came in and gave us a talk first. He explained that if we voted for the Orange Bowl and Notre Dame ended up going we might get left out of the bowl picture. I don't know if he would have gone with our vote if it had turned out the other way.

"I wish the vote had been for the Orange Bowl because as it turned out LSU went to the Orange Bowl with a 9-2 record and played Nebraska a tough game before losing 17-12. If we had gone to Miami, Nebraska might have beaten us, but we might have beaten them."

Nebraska's win over LSU, coupled with Notre Dame's 24-11 triumph over the Longhorns, gave the Cornhuskers the national championship. The Irish wound up second, followed by Texas and Tennessee.

Air Force was no match for the Vols, much like the Tennessee team that was taken apart by Texas in the Cotton Bowl two years before. The Vols rolled to a record 24-0 lead in the first period on a pair of touchdown runs by Don McLeary, a George Hunt field goal and a 10-yard TD pass from MVP Bobby Scott to Gary Theiler. Tennessee won 34-13, and the Vols and their fans were left to ponder what might have been.

"I wish we could have played a better team," linebacker Rotella says. "We were ranked No. 4 in the country, but if Notre Dame or Nebraska or just anyone else had been our opponent, I'm sure we would have beaten them. We were rolling along awfully well."

It is universally agreed that the turnstiles are linked directly to the scoreboard, and that certainly was the case for Tennessee's high-flying athletic program. The Vols had gone into the 1970s with two SEC football championships in three years, they were dominating the conference in track and cross country, they won the 1970 tennis title, were runner-up in swimming and baseball and competitive in basketball and golf. UT was the conference's all-sports champion for the second straight year.

And it was all tied to football, whence cometh just about all the bucks to operate the overall program. It was during this period of phenomenal growth that season tickets became such a treasured commodity. So treasured that it was not at all unusual for their ownership to be contested in divorce settlements.

CHAPTER 9

PLAYING AT FULL SPEED

Art Reynolds' older brother had been an All-America linebacker for the Vols and was in the first year of a standout 15-year career in the National Football League. Art thought he could follow in Jack's footsteps. So he came as a walk-on.

And not a very promising walk-on at that. He weighed 155 pounds, soaking wet. He ran a 5.5 forty. In college football, that's slow, very slow. No way could he play major college football with that kind of size and speed. Not at linebacker. Not anywhere.

He did play, defying the odds. He didn't make All-America like his brother, Jack, four years his senior. The best he could do was second team All-Southeastern Conference his junior year. He wasn't an all-star as a senior. But he became one of the great success stories of all time at Tennessee.

"I think I enjoyed coaching Art Reynolds more than anybody I ever coached," says Lon Herzbrun, who tutored a succession of outstanding linebackers in his eight years on the Vol staff, including four first-team All-Americans. "He didn't have Jack's size, but he had that same ingredient inside—everything he did he did at full speed. I could see him getting better and better.

"Art comes back for his senior year, 1973. He has gotten his speed down from 5.5 to 4.9. He's up to about 210 now. The first day we have a 12-minute run to see what kind of shape the guys are in. You run 12 minutes to see how many laps you can make. We had some speedsters on the team who could do it real well.

"Art takes off full speed, running bow-legged like he always did. The coaches and I are laughing about it. This is funny. Doesn't Art know we're going to run for 12 minutes? He keeps on going and he passes everybody at least once. He lapped some of them twice. Now I'm worried that he's going to die. It went from laughter to worry.

"He comes through and beats everybody on the squad. He doesn't fall down; he comes over to me and he's breathing very, very hard. I grab him and start walking him, forgetting about everybody else at the time because this was incredible to me. I'm walking with him and I said, 'Art, how did you do that?' He said, 'I just put pain out of my mind; I wanted to win.'

"I knew right then that I had me a player. Later, after fall practice started, he's running first string middle linebacker and Coach Battle remarked that we had to come up with a middle linebacker, that we couldn't have a walk-on playing middle linebacker at Tennessee.

"I said, 'Coach, Art isn't going to let anybody beat him out. He'll die first. If we go to war, I want to go with Art Reynolds.'

"We were playing Kentucky in the mud Art's senior year and Kentucky had a center who probably weighed 260. And I had told Art 'You have to whip their center if we're going to win.' About the second or third play this guy drives Art back five yards and I pulled him out of the game and said, 'Art, I told you if you don't whip him we can't win.' And Art says, 'Let me back in there.' And he ripped that guy unmercifully the rest of the day."

Reynolds wound up with a sensational 21 individual tackles and assisted on three others that day in probably his finest day as a Vol. Tennessee won 16-14 after Kentucky's Ron Steele missed a 34-yard field goal with only seconds left.

Art's brother Jack was half the tandem of the late 1960s that became synonomous with great linebacking—Kiner and Reynolds. While Kiner was a unique individual, Reynolds was also a free spirit of the first order. Long before he became a standout with the Los Angeles Rams and San Francisco 49ers, Reynolds made a name for himself not only on the football field, but off it as well. The most famous incident earned him the nickname by which he became famous: "Hacksaw."

Herzbrun tells the story:

"When Jack was at Tennessee, he had an old Jeep. He would take it out in the woods and run over things. He did that all the time. He would run over small trees just to see what the

Jeep would do. He was an outdoors person and he just wanted to get out by himself. He stayed by himself a lot, in fact.

"He was so frustrated after a game in his senior year—I guess it had to be the loss to Ole Miss—that he got a hacksaw and cut his Jeep in two. What did he do with it then? Junked it, I guess. You don't do much with them when they're cut in half. Jack didn't talk about it; in fact, I didn't hear about it until after it happened. He just didn't brag about things, didn't talk about himself. He just got the job done.

"Jack spent a lot of time watching films, watching the guys who would be trying to block him. The defensive coordinator of the 49ers told me one time that Jack would go to the film room and have 30 or 40 pencils and big note pads and he would take down just loads of notes on the next opponent."

Jack was one of the best-fed Vols on game day. Kiner had a nervous stomach and rarely ate much of the pregame meal. Reynolds ate his and Kiner's as well.

Another of Jack's peculiar habits once he got to the NFL was to be taped and in game uniform before ever leaving the team's hotel on game day. When the other players went to the team buses for the trip to the stadium, they were dressed in street clothes; Reynolds was in full battle gear, ready for the kickoff. And when he got to the football field, his rpm's were on redline all the time. Hacksaw was a buzz saw.

Herzbrun, who with columnist Bob Gilbert did a Saturday morning sports show on a Maryville radio station, arranged to interview Reynolds live on Saturday, the day before the 49ers were to meet the Cincinnati Bengals in Super Bowl XXIII.

"When we called him that morning, Jack said, 'I'm not going to do it,' " Herzbrun says. "I asked why, pointing out that he had agreed to do it, and he said, 'I have to look at film.' I said, 'This is your old coach calling and I need to interview you.' Jack said, 'I don't care. I'm not going to do it.' "

Herzbrun never learned why Reynolds decided not to be interviewed.

A teammate of Art's who became a study in achievement was Eddie Brown, the captain of the '73 squad. He made All-American as a defensive back his senior year but might just as easily have been All-American as an offensive player.

"Eddie just never got a chance to show what he had on offense because he was a defensive back from the day he got to Tennessee," said the man who recruited him, line offensive coach Ray Trail. "He played tailback in the single wing. He was a great punt returner. He could have played anywhere because he was a winner.

"I went to Eddie's home his junior year. He weighed 165 pounds. I told him I would give him a scholarship if he got up to 175 by the next fall. And the next fall before we started practice I went by his home and he had moved everything out of the living room. There was no furniture; they had stored it all in the back of the house and made the living room into a weight room for Eddie.

"I went to practice and Eddie grabbed me by the arm and took me over to the scales. He weighed 176. I said,'OK, Eddie, we made a deal; you have a scholarship.' So Eddie wrote to the schools that had sent him correspondence and told them he wasn't interested, that he was going to Tennessee."

Brown became one of Tennessee's finest defensive backs ever and a superb punt returner. His greatest day came against Kansas and its standout quarterback, David Jaynes, in a 1973 thriller at Memphis. Eddie's magnificent performance kept Jaynes from building an impossible lead. First he blocked a field goal try with his face. When he returned to the sideline, he found three of his front teeth embedded in his mouthpiece. Apparently annoyed by the loss of his incisors, Brown became a raging ogre in orange. After Tennessee had fallen behind, he intercepted what would have been a touchdown pass and returned it 74 yards downfield to set up a Vol TD. He also had a 48-yard punt return and a fumble recovery.

After the Vols had come from 21-7 behind to 28-21 ahead, Jaynes had one more arrow in his quiver. He rifled a 17-yard touchdown pass, cutting Tennessee's lead to 28-27. The Jayhawks lined up to go for two and it was Jaynes vs. Brown. This time Jaynes came up one arrow short as Brown led a wave of defenders in stacking up Jaynes short of the goal.

The Jayhawks might have won but for a crucial mistake on the two-point attempt. The play was a flood route, but one receiver failed to enter the game, so Kansas was unable to stretch the Tennessee defense with only 10 men on the field.

Brown had a long and productive career in the National Football League, much of it with the Washington Redskins and Los Angeles Rams under coach George Allen. He also played with the Cleveland Browns, and the Chicago Blitz and Arizona Wranglers of the USFL.

Eddie Brown maintained a close relationship with his old coach. When George Allen died on the day that Tennessee defeated Virginia in the 1991 Sugar Bowl, Brown walked into a radio studio where Condredge Holloway was doing a show.

"I couldn't believe how sad Eddie looked," Holloway says. I asked him what was wrong. "George Allen just died," he said.

A teammate of Brown and the Reynolds brothers, Phillip Fulmer, never has been regarded as a hell-raiser, but one incident from his freshman year at UT, out of character though it may have been, tells us that the future head coach of the Vols didn't leave all the mischief to others.

In 1968, he and Carl Johnson, a fellow freshman from Palatka, Florida, faked an altercation on the third floor of the athletic dorm, Gibbs Hall, all for the benefit of a janitor and a couple of maids.

"It was just one of those crazy things that 18-year-old guys will do when there's nothing else to do," says Curt Watson, another member of that freshman class and a witness to the caper. "Phil and Carl staged this fight, with the janitor and maids looking on. Carl had a knife and Phil had a .22 rifle with a blank shell in it. After they struggled awhile, Carl pulled the knife and said, 'I'm going to cut you from ear to ear.' Phil pulled the rifle and said, 'Well, see if you can cut this bullet.'

"Carl took off running and Phil let him get quite a way down the hall before he fired; you know, blank bullets have some wadding in them. Phil drew a bead on Carl's back, just like in a western movie. He pulled the trigger and BOOM! It made a tremendous noise in that hallway.

"As soon as the gun fired, Carl put on the greatest act you could imagine. It was worthy of an Academy Award. He threw his arms up and let out this yell. He fell and slid face-down on that tile floor.

"By this time, the janitor had locked himself in the closet. The maids were beating on the door trying to get in there with him. One of the maids finally went over to Carl and asked if he was all right. He couldn't hold his laughter any longer. By then, she was about ready to kill him herself. I don't know if those people ever forgave us for that. They took care of us and cleaned up after us; they were like a part of our family.

"Phil Fulmer was a rather serious young man. Not that he didn't have fun but he wasn't usually an instigator. He left that sort of thing to Johnson and Anthony Edwards and some of the other guys."

At a practice session at Neyland Stadium the following spring, offensive guard Fulmer and defensive end Tom Bennett were going against each other in a one-on-one drill. Like the other sophomores-to-be, they were competing for playing time come fall.

"When Tommy got up I sort of hit him when I shouldn't have," Fulmer says. "We started this awful fight that eventually involved just about the whole football team. The funny thing is

Tommy and I stood over on the sideline and watched the whole thing. Coach Trail got knocked down before it was over. They got it all on film and it was really funny to watch."

Somebody came up with an idea that made Tennessee's oft-hated film sessions at least tolerable, if not downright enjoyable at times.

The game films contained a number of "nudies," a few frames of shapely young women spliced in at various points. They were intended, of course, to keep a young man's attention on the screen at Sunday afternoon sessions of reviewing movies of the previous day's game.

Where there had been football on the screen, there suddenly would appear two or three frames of a young woman decked out in little more than a Tennessee helmet. "It would wake them up," assistant coach Ray Trail says. "They didn't go to sleep; it would keep them loose for the whole film session."

The nudies were routinely removed from the film following the Sunday film session. But at least once it wasn't. Assistant coach Lon Herzbrun was scheduled for a Thursday night Big Orange meeting in Chattanooga. It had been an unusually busy week and Herzbrun was running late. He grabbed the film as he headed for his car.

It wasn't until he was showing the film that night to the 100 or so people at the meeting that he realized that he had forgotten to edit out the nudies. One of the nude shots popped up on the screen just for an instant. Herzbrun, flustered by the turn of events, hit the reverse switch and she appeared again.

A MAGICIAN IN SHOULDER PADS

For one who aspired to a career in baseball, Condredge Holloway had quite a fling with football. He began playing the game at age 7 in his hometown of Huntsville, Alabama, and didn't stop playing until he was 33, in Vancouver, British Columbia.

Had his mother not so steadfastly insisted that he play football at the University of Tennessee, Holloway's football career would have ended there in Huntsville, when he was 16. When he graduated from Lee High School, he would have signed a baseball scholarship with Arizona State, not a football scholarship with Tennessee. Big Orange fans would never have heard of him, except perhaps as a major league baseball player. Instead, he is remembered as one of the most popular athletes in Tennessee history.

Holloway was picked No. 4 in the major league draft and actually signed a contract with the Montreal Expos when he was 16, but his mother refused to also sign it. The contract was not binding without her signature. And still the Expos tried desperately to sign him. They offered him $80,000, a handsome sum of money in the early 1970s. They even offered him an opportunity to fight his mother in court. "How are you going to win that one?" he asked. "If you win, you lose; if you lose, you lose."

Holloway was an extraordinary baseball infielder. That year the Topps All-America had 10 players because there were two shortstops named to the team: Condredge Holloway and Robin Yount.

Looking back today, Holloway has no regrets about the millions that might have been. "It might not have worked out in baseball. A lot of people don't make it. You just never know."

Recruiting Condredge Holloway had gotten to be an all-consuming endeavor. For nearly two years, Ray Trail had been courting the highly touted quarterback in Huntsville. He finally got Holloway's signature on the Southeastern Conference grant-in-aid in February 1971 and on a national letter-of-intent a few weeks later.

Then the Expos jumped into the picture in a big-time way. Trail had to more or less set up camp in Huntsville that summer.

"I was probably in Huntsville more than I was at home," he says. "I finally told him, 'Look, Condredge, I'm spending three or four days a week in Huntsville. I've got to take a vacation with my family. I'll be gone two weeks. Can we trust each other for two weeks?' "

"Sure," Holloway replied. "I'll not do anything until you get back. I'll guarantee that."

They shook hands.

The Trails headed for the Ozark Mountains of Arkansas, to a chalet owned by Mrs. Trail's father. It was an out-of-the-way retreat and had no telephone. Nobody but Holloway knew where they would be.

About three days after they arrived, a man drove up in a Jeep and said he was looking for Ray Trail. "That's me," Trail said. He was told there was a telephone call for him at the lodge. His first thought was that it was Holloway. Had something happened? He gritted his teeth and headed for the lodge.

The caller was head coach Bill Battle back in Knoxville. "Ray," he said, "you have to get home. Condredge is about to sign with the baseball folks."

"Coach, Condredge gave me his word that he wouldn't do anything for two weeks. They offered him $80,000 a few nights ago. That was a lot of money and there it was all in one big bundle. There's no use to come home unless Condredge calls me and tells me he needs me."

More phone calls from Battle followed, the head coach continuing to worry that Tennessee might lose the gifted Holloway.

Trail told him, "Coach, he gave me his word and if a man's not good for his word, then me coming home isn't going to help any. I'm not coming home. I've given my family two weeks out of this year. I have spent a whole year recruiting Condredge and I've got to give my family a little time."

In two weeks, the Trails returned home. Holloway called, saying he was ready to make a move. There was a meeting set up with Montreal scout Mel Didier. Holloway asked Trail to be at the meeting. Trail balked at first, thinking Didier would hardly welcome him with open arms.

"I figured if he didn't want Coach Trail there, then he must have something to hide," Holloway says. "But Mel's a professional guy, so why would he have anything to hide?"

"We met at a little restaurant in Huntsville and I could tell that Didier wasn't very happy to see me there," Trail said. "Just as I wouldn't have been happy if our roles were reversed. We talked about several Montreal players and how they went back to school. Didier had his money in a briefcase and finally he looked at me and put it on the table in front of Condredge and opened it up to show the money."

Holloway remembers Didier saying, "I can give you this money legitimately. Tennessee can't do that. It's illegal for them to do anything like that."

The insinuation was clear: Montreal could give Holloway money on top of the table; any money that Tennessee gave him would have to be under the table.

"I understood what he was saying," Holloway says. "At that point, I saw a different side of Mel Didier. Here was a guy who regularly used money as a tool, as opposed to a guy who has to use books, tuition, an education and opportunity as a tool.

"Professional sports isn't a buddy system; it isn't a scholarship system. It's 'What can you do for me today? And if you don't do it I'll cut you and get somebody else. I don't care about your family.' No, professional sports is strictly a business.

"That was my first encounter with that sort of thing and I guess it kind of showed me that I wasn't ready for that. Because it did bother me when he said what he did."

As they left the restaurant, Holloway looked at Trail and said, "Coach, I'm ready to go to Tennessee."

At first Holloway was devastated that baseball, for all intents and purposes, was out for him. But it wasn't; he would go on to become an All-America shortstop for the Vols. And once he got into fall football practice shortly afterward, he put baseball out of his mind.

Looking back, Holloway says there is no doubt that, given the choice, he would have pursued a baseball career. "I was a better baseball player than football," he says. A lot of Tennessee football fans would argue the point, whether they had seen him on the diamond or not.

No matter what the sport, Holloway could play it. At the ripe old age of three he made his first goal in basketball. It was during halftime of a basketball game at Alabama A&M College in Huntsville, where his father was a teacher and coach. The halftime show consisted of the local kids going onto the floor and having a shootaround. It was all young Condredge could do to launch the ball up to the standard-height rim. In high school, although he was only 5-9, he became quite a cager and played in the Alabama high school all-star game, a fact that did not go unnoticed. John Wooden, UCLA's legendary coach, contacted him.

"I guess that was the highlight of all my recruiting contacts," Holloway says. "Coach Wooden said he thought I could play point guard. I never did get very serious about it because I didn't want to pursue a basketball career."

He did quite well at ping pong, among other sports. Shortly after he arrived in Big Orange Country, he was playing in the game room at Stokely Center and he found that his reputation as a ping pong expert had preceded him. "I understand you are a pretty good player," said Coach Battle, himself a ping pong player of some renown. "Well, I play pretty good, I guess," Holloway answered. "Then how about playing me?" the coach said.

They played a couple of games and Battle won both. As they started out of the room, another football player said, "Holloway, I thought you were supposed to be a pretty tough player." Holloway replied, "Hey, man, you don't beat the head coach."

Overhearing the remark, Battle said, "What'd you say? You don't want to beat the head coach? Get your fanny back over to the table."

They played another game. Holloway won 21-5. The head coach didn't insist on another game.

Holloway ended up at Tennessee because Battle promised him a shot at being the Vols' quarterback. Bear Bryant wanted him in the worst way, too, but lost out because of a racial barrier that still existed in Alabama at the time.

"I wanted to play quarterback and I respected Coach Bryant because he was honest about it. He told me I couldn't play quarterback, that they just weren't ready for that at Alabama. He could have told me anything. A lot of coaches did. Coach Bryant was the only one who told me I couldn't.

"Another thing was that Coach Battle told me that once I established myself in football I could play baseball in the spring. Coach Bryant told me the same thing but all the other coaches wouldn't commit to that. "

Holloway was recruited by most all of the Southeastern Conference schools and also Ohio State, Arizona State, Michigan and UCLA. He visited Ohio State, liked what he saw, but lost interest. "It was just too impersonal there," he says.

When he signed with the Vols, Holloway was 5-9 and about 155. But as far as Ray Trail was concerned, his star signee was 5-11 and 171. "Coach Trail must have lied a little bit to get Coach Battle to take me," he says.

Trail and Holloway have maintained a closeness through the years. After he left UT, Holloway gave the Trail family a painting of himself in action as a Vol, with this inscription: "To Ray, Sandy, Kim and Karen, a family that I felt part of simply because they cared for me and my family. Thanks for all the kindness you've given me. I'll always remember you."

Holloway began his Tennessee career with a bang, hurling two touchdown passes in the first period and directing the Vol freshmen to a 51-13 conquest of Vanderbilt. A season-ending game with the touted Notre Dame freshmen lured 31,300 curious fans to Neyland Stadium—an astonishing turnout at a time when freshman games usually attracted 2,000 to 3,000. They were there partly to see a Notre Dame team in the flesh for the first time; they were also there to check out this new quarterback phenom they'd been hearing so much about, Condredge Holloway.

The Notre Dame frosh boasted a massive offensive line, said by *Sports Illustrated* to be bigger than that of the Los Angeles Rams. Holloway and his mates won 30-13 over the Irish, led by quarterback Tom Clements, later a Notre Dame All-American.

Already, in just five freshman games, Holloway had established himself as one of the most exciting players ever at Tennessee. He was a master of the escape, leaving the fans breathless and on the edge of their seats. It was no wonder he became known as "The Artful Dodger" and "Houdini." Later on, Bill Battle would describe Holloway as "indescribable," probably as good a description as anyone could have come up with.

Many years later, long after he had left the coaching ranks, Battle said this of his nimble quarterback of 1972-73-74: "When he was healthy, not only could you not tackle him; you couldn't even touch that little sucker. He was incredible. He'd play hurt and you could see the pain on his face and yet he'd stay in the game. He'd hang in there and, gosh darn it, you'd die for somebody like that. And to think that some people back then started talking about a black quarterback, saying you couldn't win with a black quarterback."

Ten months after the victory over the Notre Dame frosh, it was Opening Day 1972, Tennessee vs. Georgia Tech, at Grant Field in Atlanta, heart of the deep South. Holloway was about to become the first black quarterback in the Southeastern Conference. A reporter had asked, "How does it feel to be the first black quarterback in the SEC?" Holloway's answer: "I don't know; I've never been a white one."

The game was on national television, and the Yellow Jackets also had a black QB, senior Eddie McAshan. The media did its best to bring up the angle of two black quarterbacks going against one another.

"We had a football game to play and these guys were concerned about me and McAshan," Holloway says. "You can't go out on the football field worried about being Martin Luther King. That's not going to work. He was for non-violence; but it's violent out there on that field.

"I said, 'Wait a minute, guys. I'm worried about a guy named Rock Perdoni (Tech's defensive star) on the other team because he can hurt people, and you're talking about me vs. Eddie McAshan?'

"Me going against McAshan was the furthest thing from my mind. Here I was in my first game, going against a senior quarterback, on national TV, in the other team's hometown. I had more things to worry about than being black. I just said, 'Hey, guys, I've been black all my life.' I think the media realized then that I didn't want to talk about it.

"I wanted to talk about football. But I wasn't going to get into any political statement because I didn't have one. I just wanted to play football."

Faced with the pressure of debuting before the national TV cameras, he responded with the aplomb of a battle-hardened veteran as he guided the offense on early marches that were a refreshing combination of passing and running. It was a rousing 34-3 victory.

A star was born. But he was not a star to many fans. Because he was black. He got mail, plenty of mail. Hate mail.

"You wouldn't believe what I went through my first two years at Tennessee," he says. "They would screen my mail; they had to. Everybody talked about how bad it was going other places but it was bad here at Tennessee. We didn't have many blacks here at the time. I don't know if the others had a problem; at least they didn't discuss it with me. And I didn't discuss mine with them. I just tried to ignore it all. After the first two years it wasn't too bad.

"Just being on the team is one thing, but being the quarterback is different. The position brings a lot of publicity, a lot of responsibility. And a lot of blame. And a lot of undue praise, too."

The experience wasn't exactly new to Holloway. He had been through a similar situation once back at Lee High School in Huntsville, when a group of blacks decided to boycott. Holloway didn't join in. "I told them I wasn't going to miss an opportunity to get a scholarship. I told them that I would be out of there and they'd still be there pumping gas. I figure that before you have a cause that you want to jump on, you'd better know what you're doing. And a lot of those kids didn't know. They were followers. They let somebody else tell them what to do.

"These same kids had been my classmates at St. Joseph's Catholic School, where the only prerequisite was if you could pay the tuition you could go to school. There wasn't any black-white stuff. Then to see those kids go to school and have to take sides. That's crazy.

"I didn't worry about it because I had a place to go every day at 3 o'clock. I was practicing football or basketball or baseball. By the time I finished I went home. I was hungry and ready to go to bed and go back to school the next day. I didn't have time to sit around and worry about how to get back at somebody. I had competition on that practice field every day. That's where I could get all my anger out."

With all the racism that swirled around him at UT, Holloway never had any problems with his teammates. There was a great equalizer on the football field. "Everybody out there on that field gets hit in the mouth by a helmet the same way," he says. "It's when you don't play that all of a sudden you become an expert on things you know nothing about."

Holloway wanted only to play football. And play he did. As the starting quarterback for three years, he led Tennessee to a 25-9-2 record and three bowl games. His sophomore season, 1972, the Vols went 10-2 and he was Sophomore of the Year in the SEC. Holloway wasn't the only starring act on the squad. Haskel Stanback blossomed as a runner a year behind schedule after going into the 1971 season billed as the "super soph." Bothered by a rash of injuries as a sophomore, Stanback came back to cap his junior season by rushing for 890 yards, thereby surpassing Hank Lauricella's school record for rushing yardage in a season. Lauricella's mark of 881 yards, set with the 1951 national championship team, fell when Stanback gained 143 yards in the season-ending game with Vanderbilt.

CHAPTER 10

BLUE MAX TO THE RESCUE

———————

The 1971 season could be called 1971 BC — Before Condredge. It wasn't the Year of the Quarterback — it was the Year of the Quarterbacks. Plural.

While the coaching staff and fans anxiously awaited the day when freshman Holloway would become eligible for varsity play, Tennessee went through a procession of quarterbacks. At the midway point of the season, the Vols were still searching for a QB who could muster some offensive clout to go with a defense that was ranked among the nation's best.

Dennis Chadwick, Chip Howard and Phil Pierce all tried their hand in the season opener, a 48-6 romp over an outclassed California-Santa Barbara team that couldn't have won even if coach Bill Battle's mother had lined up at quarterback for Tennessee. Battle wasn't impressed. Chadwick was shifted to wingback and Howard opened against Auburn the following week. The Tigers, playing nine men on the line for most of the game, won a defensive struggle 10-9. Howard moved to wide receiver.

Pierce, a senior from Athens, was the third starting quarterback in as many weeks as the Vols faced Florida at Gainesville. Pierce's career had been beset by misfortune the two previous seasons. He had suffered a broken leg against Army in 1970. In the spring of '71, he had been a defensive back.

The teams were deadlocked at 13-13 when the Gators downed a punt at the Tennessee 1. Pierce faced a forbidding test as he trotted onto the field, his team 99 yards from the end zone. After the play of the Vol offense up to that point in the season, it could just as well have been 99 miles.

But Pierce brilliantly directed the Vols on the winning touchdown march, accounting for all but 25 of the yards on the drive with some nifty runs and accurate passes. His 20-yard TD pass to Stan Trott was the clincher.

An interesting sidelight is that the 20-13 victory marked the first time a Tennessee team had ever won a game while wearing white jerseys.

After pulling out a 10-6 triumph over Georgia Tech in an old-fashioned defensive duel, it was the Third Saturday in October, Chapter 51. An Alabama team that Bear Bryant had armed with the ground-gobbling wishbone offense waited in Birmingham. Tennessee headed south armed with not much more than the old maxim: "The best offense is a good defense."

It simply wasn't Tennessee's day. A questionable ruling by an official as the Vols went for it on fourth down at their own 29 with three minutes to go opened the gates for the Tide's final 10 points. It was shades of the previous year, when the Tide lost a fumble and eight interceptions in a 24-0 loss to the Vols. This time, however, Tennessee lost four fumbles and four interceptions and, quite naturally, the game.

Bama fell behind early, but went ahead 22-7 in the third quarter to seemingly put the game out of reach. But the Vols cut the lead to 22-15 on Curt Watson's 9-yard run and a 2-point conversion by Chadwick. Following the abortive fourth-down try, the Tide kicked a field goal, the Vols lost a fumble at their own 5, and Bama added a touchdown, but it was much closer than the 32-15 final indicated.

"It just kills me that Alabama got all those points in the last minute," says Watson. "The score makes it look like they drilled us. I swear we got rooked out of the ball on the fourth-down play. Our defense really hung in there, particularly after we had a lot of turnovers early in the game, when it would have been easy for us to get run out of the stadium."

Injury befell Pierce again at midseason. Enter Jim Maxwell. He wasn't overly talented, especially as a runner. The 1971 UT media guide devoted all of three lines to him, noting that "Jim doesn't quite meet the requirements needed as a runner in the

Southeastern Conference, but he is an excellent passer, perhaps the best of the lot."

Somehow the Vols rallied behind this fifth-year senior from Nashville, an erstwhile B-teamer who had been little more than practice field fodder for the varsity. Under his direction, the Vols would not lose again that season. Few stories in Tennessee history have had more of a Cinderella touch.

Up to that point in his career, Maxwell's only claim to fame had been as holder for place kicker George Hunt for three years. The year before, 1970, Tennessee attempted 318 passes; quarterback Bobby Scott threw 252 of them, quartrback Chadwick 64 and quarterback Maxwell two. He had played a mop-up role in an easy win over Vanderbilt and made a token appearance in the Sugar Bowl victory over Air Force.

So here he was, well on the downhill side of his career, five years after signing on with Tennessee in 1967.

"I sort of figured that after being on the team for five years, and I'm five or six games into my last season, the odds were pretty much against me playing at all," Maxwell says. "You just look on it as one of those dreams that didn't come true. By then you have to believe that your career isn't going anywhere."

Actually, it was the beginning of a rags-to-riches story that seems too improbable to be true.

Five games into the season, without an effective quarterback, Tennessee had become type-cast: a run-oriented team with no passing game to speak of. Three different quarterbacks had completed only 23 of 68 passes for a paltry 373 yards — little more than a good afternoon's work for an Andy Kelly or a Heath Shuler two decades later.

The coaching staff, perhaps at wit's end over the lack of an effective offense, continued to search for a quarterback—and found one right under its nose. Probably out of sheer desperation, the coaches turned to Maxwell in practice the week of the Mississippi State game at Memphis. Offensive coordinator Jim Wright devised a pass play off a fake option, a throw down the middle to the wingback. Maxwell was to be the passer.

Blue Max, as he came to be known, entered the game in the second quarter and stayed at the controls for the remaining six games. Maxwell remembers his reaction when Battle dispatched him into the game. "Out of nowhere your name gets called and you ask yourself, 'What's going on here?' I was scared to death. I remember trotting onto the field and wondering, 'What am I going to do now?' "

His first play was the specially-designed play to wingback George Silvey. He rifled the ball right on target but the State defender made a perfect break on the ball and stripped it away from Silvey. Tennessee prevailed 10-7, getting its points on Hunt's 51-yard field goal and a 42-yard interception return by linebacker Jackie Walker. The Vols had won a game and uncovered a quarterback.

The following week, Maxwell got his first start, against Tulsa at Neyland Stadium, and the 62,000 who turned out for Band Day had a new hero—the Blue Max. Tennessee won 38-3 and, even though the oft-beaten Golden Hurricane was the victim, Vol fans were thrilled to see their team light up the scoreboard for the first time since the opening-day rout of Cal-Santa Barbara.

Maxwell went 5-for-10 passing and even scored the first touchdown on a 5-yard run, really an oddity because he wasn't much of a runner, even by his own admission.

"I always thought I could throw the ball," he says, "but running just never was my game. As far as the stop watch goes, I wasn't much of a runner. Now, I'm not saying I *couldn't* run. Because when the defense was breathing down my neck, I could run better than you might think."

Maxwell endured the ultimate embarrassment for a quarterback somewhere in that seven-game string of victories—leaving the huddle and lining up behind a guard instead of center Tom Johnson. And he believes the guard was a teammate of some renown, Phillip Fulmer. "I just vaguely remember it and in the back of my mind it seems that it was Coach Fulmer."

"The thing about Max," says fullback Watson, "is that he just hung in there. He had talent but he didn't have talent like, say, Bobby Scott. Once he came in to play, we never lost another game from that point on. We started being more productive offensively. We had been sputtering, to say the least.

"Why, the highlight film that year was called 'The Year of the Offensive Defense.' We weren't very productive at all that year but we didn't need to be, with the defense we had. I'm just glad I didn't have to play against that defense. They ate people alive. They just killed Penn State."

Maxwell, the Vol who finally played in the twilight of his career, signed on as a free agent with the Philadelphia Eagles of the NFL. His professional career never got off the ground. He suffered an elbow injury in an exhibition game and was placed on injured reserve. The elbow was still bothering him when he reported to training camp the next year. He underwent surgery and spent another year on injured reserve. After being cut by the Eagles, he tried out with San Diego but gave up on an NFL career after a couple of weeks.

Without a doubt, the biggest play of the 1971 season occurred against Kentucky on a cold and windy day at Lexington. With five minutes to play, Tennessee was leading 14-7 and trying to hold on as the Wildcats drove goalward. With the ball at the UT 9, defensive end Carl Johnson picked off a Bernie Scruggs pitchout and rambled 87 yards for an insurance TD and it wound up a 21-7 victory. Struggled might be a better word than rambled, because several Vols caught up with Johnson as he strained goalward. Watson had a banner day with 156 yards and scored on a 26-yard run. The other Vol TD was also scored on a run, a 4-yarder by none other than the Blue Max, Jim Maxwell.

Bobby Majors, last of the five football-playing brothers, came up with an electrifying performance in closing out his home career against fifth-ranked and previously undefeated Penn State. The Nittany Lions, riding a 15-game winning streak, had averaged more than 44 points a game in compiling their 10-0 record. Twice they had scored in the 60s. A Cotton Bowl date with Texas waited. Foremost among their stars were running backs Lydell Mitchell and Franco Harris and linebacker Jack Ham.

After the Majors family had been honored in pregame ceremonies, the All-America safety put on a show for 59,000 at the stadium and millions more on national TV. He returned two punts for 82 yards and a touchdown and hauled two kickoffs back 113 yards to spearhead the Vols' surprisingly easy 31-11 triumph. Conrad Graham, a secondary mate of Majors, grabbed a mid-air fumble by the Lions' John Hufnagel and darted 76 yards for an early touchdown, setting the stage for a brilliant day by the Vol defense.

A dramatic turnaround near game's end enabled Tennessee to beat Arkansas 14-13 in the Liberty Bowl. The Razorbacks, with a 13-7 lead and the momentum, were apparently home free. But an Arkansas receiver fumbled after a catch and, in a hotly disputed decision, the officials ruled that the Vols recovered.

The game film showed clearly that an Arkansas player fell on the ball but the Vols on the field and most of those on the sideline—almost as one—pointed toward the Hogs' end of the field in an "our ball" gesture. The officials agreed, perhaps influenced by all those orange-clad arms, perhaps not. In any event, Carl Witherspoon came up with the ball. Granted a reprieve at the Arkansas 36 with time running out, the Vols scored in two plays, Watson carrying the final 17 yards to cap his outstanding career. Hunt, with Maxwell holding, kicked the winning extra point, and Battle's second season ended 10-2.

After routing Georgia Tech 34-3 in Holloway's varsity debut, the Vols did another number on Penn State in the second game of the 1972 season. Lights had been installed at Neyland Stadium in the 9 1/2 months since Penn State's first visit to Knoxville. Tennessee again prevailed over the pride of the East, holding on for a 28-21 victory after holding a seemingly comfortable 21-0 lead at the half. Stanback got the clinching touchdown, his third of the game.

The season got off to a roaring start but sagged in the middle with two losses. The losses were particularly painful because they came at the hands of the same two teams that beat them the year before, Auburn and Alabama. And in both games, Tennessee was just a play or two away from victory.

The Alabama game was especially traumatic. For 58 minutes, the Vols played a near-perfect game. After Alabama drew first blood with a field goal on the last play of the first half, Tennessee came back with a touchdown by Holloway and Townsend kicked a 36-yard field goal early in the fourth quarter for a 10-3 lead. With the clock showing 2:39, the nation's No. 3 team was all but given up for dead and a record crowd was all set to erupt in one of the happiest celebrations ever at Neyland Stadium. But suddenly, in the span of just 36 seconds measured in scoreboard time, there was nothing for Vol boosters to cheer about.

The Tide used just three plays to make it 10-9. The crowd of 72,049 was stunned when Bear Bryant shunned a two-point try, sending kicker Bill Davis out to try an extra point kick that would tie the game. Bama fans were astonished that their coach would go for a tie. Tennessee fans booed.

Bryant got the last laugh.

Davis kicked the PAT. On Tennessee's next possession, Holloway was running a draw play on third-and-12 when he was hit by linebacker Mike Dubose. The ball squirted free and was recovered by end John Mitchell at the UT 22.

On the first play, wishbone quarterback Terry Davis faked a handoff, feinted toward a trailing halfback, then tucked the ball and scampered 22 yards to score. It ended 17-10, unquestionably one of the most disappointing losses in Tennessee history.

"We outplayed them the whole way," Holloway remembers. "We had them beat for 58 minutes. We made just one defensive mistake and it cost us."

Actually, Tennessee made two defensive mistakes, one on each touchdown. Each one involved a stunting linebacker getting tied up inside and not being able to commit to either the quarterback or fullback.

It is indisputable that the Tennessee defense did a masterful job otherwise, holding the Alabama wishbone to a mere 113 yards rushing — up to the moment of Davis' 22-yard game-winner.

Nobody took the loss harder than Bill Battle. Many years later, he confided that he would still wake up in a cold sweat in the middle of the night thinking about that defeat. He says he was as shocked as anybody when Bryant decided against a two-point conversion.

"I couldn't believe they went for the tie," he says. "I knew Coach Bryant wasn't going to go for a tie in Knoxville. That had been instilled in me. That was the Alabama way. I told our players to watch for a fake."

Many observers have always felt that Bryant played for the tie because the Tide played one more SEC game than anyone else and a tie wouldn't ruin its chances for the conference championship.

Bryant made the decision to go for one at the urging of none other than Pat Dye, an Alabama assistant coach that day and later head coach at Auburn.

Ken Donahue, the Tide's longtime defensive coordinator, says Dye went to Bryant on the sidelines. "He told Coach Bryant he just had a feeling that we could hold them, get the ball back and win with a field goal. Coach Bryant already had a two-point play called."

For the second straight year, Tennessee was 10-2, capped by a 24-17 Astro Bluebonnet Bowl victory over LSU and star quarterback Bert Jones. The Vols scored all their points in the first half in registering their third consecutive bowl win. Holloway ran for two touchdowns and passed to Jimmy Young for the third.

The 1972 season marked the end of an era for UT. Trainer Mickey O'Brien, who had worked under eight Tennessee coaches, decided to call it a career after being on the job since 1938.

The 10-win season enabled Tennessee to boast about its record of having won at least eight games for eight consecutive years, the only school in the nation to turn that trick over that time span. But it didn't go unnoticed that there had been two straight years of losing to both Auburn and Alabama. And little did anyone realize that it would be 15 years before Tennessee would again win 10 games in a season.

CHAPTER 11

MORGAN THE MAGNIFICENT

At an early fall practice in 1973, when the fleet-footed Stanley Morgan was a freshman, he was exhibiting his outrageous skills on the practice field, not in a showy manner, but by doing what came naturally to this gifted athlete. Condredge Holloway and some other upperclassmen decided to show the freshman phenom a thing or two.

"This was the first time I realized just what kind of athlete we had in Stanley Morgan," Holloway says. "He was out there on Hudson Field catching passes everywhere. He was just beating everybody, catching little hitches and he was gone. Nobody could catch him in practice. Boom! He was gone; he would just run off and leave everybody.

"So some of us got together and said, 'Well, we'll just grab his young ass and tie him up to the goalpost.' Of course, we were just kidding around. We were going to tie him up after practice and leave him out there on the practice field. I remember Haskel Stanback and Eddie Brown were in on it and there were a couple more but I don't recall who they were. But I'm pretty sure there were five of us.

"Well, there were three fields laid out side by side and we chased him all over all three of them and couldn't catch him. He would dodge us and run. We tried to get him in a corner and he would just juke us and take off. We never did catch him. We finally decided that we weren't going to chase him any more. He was just amazing."

Not many people ever caught Stanley Morgan. Not on the practice field, not on the playing fields of the South, not in the stadiums of the National Football League, where he enjoyed a sparkling 14-year career as one of the NFL's all-time great receivers.

Freshman quarterback Pat Ryan also had a memorable first meeting with Morgan.

"They dressed all the scholarship players alike, but at our first practice I see this black kid wearing orange tennis shoes with black laces. And I figured he must be a walk on. The coaches line up the quarterbacks to throw fade patterns and this and that. So this kid lines up and takes off down the sidelines and he was just gone. I threw the ball pretty hard, but about 15 yards short of him. It just shocked me how he could run. It was very apparent that this kid was a phenomenal talent. And that's the last we freshmen saw of him. That afternoon he went to the varsity."

Early in fall workouts of 1973, linebacker coach Lon Herzbrun and offensive coordinator Jim Wright were timing players in 40-yard dashes in Stokely Athletics Center. They put their stop watches on Morgan. As he blazed past, Herzbrun shouted to Wright, "What'd you get?"

"Four-three," Wright answered. "What'd you get?"

"I got four-three, too."

Later, in the athletes' cafeteria, Herzbrun and Wright were eating together.

"Lon, when we were timing Morgan, why were you so quick to ask what I got on my watch?"

"Because I really got four-one-five."

"Hell, I got four-one-five, too."

"Why didn't you just say so at the time?"

"Because I know that nobody runs a four-one-five and I didn't want to look like an idiot."

Before Morgan came up with the first of his many starring roles, Holloway made another of his. It came against an underdog Duke team in the season opener, a night game at Neyland Stadium. The Vols scored off their first possession, then proceeded to leave five fumbles lying on the Tartan Turf. By halftime, Duke held a 17-7 lead and the Blue Devils maintained that advantage through most of the third quarter. Tennessee needed a miracle.

The miracle appeared in the form of Holloway, who broke free from a bearhug tackle to dart 49 yards to a touchdown. On an aborted pass attempt, he set sail into heavy traffic, disappeared for an instant in the embrace of three Duke players, suddenly appeared again and set sail down the west sidelines. Tennessee fans hadn't seen a run like that in a long while.

"The one thing I remember about that run is that I ran into somebody I didn't even see," Holloway says. "I cut back into a group of people, just trying to protect the ball. And I think I got hit so hard in there that I got knocked out into the open. I remember ducking under somebody's arm and the next thing I knew I was out there by myself."

With three minutes to go, it was 17-14 Duke, and Tennessee was clearly on the brink of defeat. The 70,000 fans didn't know it, but this was to be a two-part miracle. Linebacker Eddie Wilson caused a fumble at the Duke 24 and tackle Robert Pulliam came up with the ball. With the clock winding down, the Vols faced fourth-and-4 at the Duke 6. The Vol coaches decided there would be no field goal, no tie, not this night. They called on Holloway for one last Herculean feat. About to be tackled by the ankles at the 5, he dived to the 1. First down. Stanback for the touchdown.

There was a feeling of nostalgia attached to Tennessee's visit to the United States Military Academy the following week. It was there that Bob Neyland learned most of the basics of the football philosophy that he later used to build a dynasty at Tennessee. Furthermore, both Bob Woodruff and Bill Battle had served as Army assistant coaches.

It had been exactly 50 years since a Tennessee team had visited the United States Military Academy at West Point, and not many of the 3,000 traveling Vol fans cared to remember that the 1923 Vols had come off rather ingloriously, losing 41-0.

The Vols survived the most devastating passing attack ever unleashed by an Army team, but won handily 37-18. Newspaper headlines went to Army quarterback Kingsley Fink, who completed 24 of 36 passes for 347 yards, and his favorite target, Barry Armstrong. But Tennessee came up with an exciting aerial battery of its own, Holloway to Morgan. The exciting speedster from Easley, S.C., hauled in scoring passes of 52 and 29 yards.

Then it was "Beat Auburn Week" in Knoxville and the expectancy was accompanied by a measure of fear because the Tigers had beaten Tennessee three years running. This time the Tigers had to visit Neyland Stadium. Developments of the previous Saturday had ensured that they would go against one another undefeated and untied. For that reason, the city had been at fever pitch all week.

Saturday dawned dismal and damp. Rain was in the forecast. Ricky Townsend, Tennessee's barefooted All-America placekicker, kicked two first half field goals and Holloway fired a seven-yard TD pass to Emmon Love making it 13-0 at halftime. Then the heavens unloaded and the second half was played in a driving rainstorm. As a result, Battle opted for caveman football, having punter Neil Clabo kick on first down a number of times, and his kicking with a soggy football kept the Tigers bottled up. One of those first-down punts, a booming 71-yarder, sailed over the safetyman's head and was downed at the Auburn 5. Tennessee fans ate it up.

Linebacker Hank Walter applied the coup de grace, scoring the only points of the second half when he rambled 38 yards with an interception in the fourth period that made the final 21-0. Walter, credited with 12 tackles, eight assists and a fumble recovery, was named the AP's national lineman of the week, duplicating Holloway's feat of the Duke game two weeks earlier.

A rain-drenched Bill Battle, savoring his first victory ever over Auburn, came up with the crack of the year. "Rain, what rain?" he asked. "I didn't see anything but sunshine out there."

Two games later, after the 28-27 thriller over Kansas at Memphis, Holloway put on another show, this time against Georgia Tech in Knoxville. For the fourth time in five games, the Vols showed that they liked to do it the hard way, falling behind at the beginning. In the normal swing of things, that's not the way a 4-0, nationally ranked team prefers to do it. But that's the way Holloway did it.

No wonder they called him "The Artful Dodger."

"How would you describe Holloway's play?" Battle was asked following Tennessee's 20-14 triumph. His answer: "Indescribable."

The two Holloway plays that decided the outcome were crammed into a one-minute span of the second quarter. On the first, he somehow managed to elude the grasp of five Tech players and fired a tying pass to Bill Rudder in the end zone. After an Eddie Brown interception on Tech's next possession, Holloway pulled off another of his patented escape acts, breaking away from no fewer than six Jacket defenders on a 20-yard jaunt for a TD that left everybody in the stadium wondering if they had indeed seen what had just unfolded before their eyes. Interestingly, the last Tech player with a shot at him was Randy Rhino, but it wasn't Rhino's final shot at the Houdini from Huntsville. They would play against each other in Canada over the next 10 years.

So much for dramatics. So much for warmups. So much for quasi-exhibition games. It was the Third Saturday in October again; Alabama vs. Tennessee.

They met in Birmingham at the exact midway point of the season, and for the first time in 27 years, both teams came in with perfect records. It was a perfect football day; Legion Field was jammed with 72,226 fans, and ABC-TV was there to record the action for a regional telecast that was being beamed to most of the nation.

There was no preliminary grappling, no jousting. Any fan who was firing up a cigarette after the opening kickoff probably missed the game's first score. On the first offensive play, quarterback Gary Rutledge passed to split end Wayne Wheeler, all alone behind the Vol secondary, and it was an 80-yard touchdown. So much for anticipating the usual wishbone fullback dive on the game's first play. The Tide, buoyed by the success of that play, pressed its advantage, scoring again for a 14-0 lead. The Vols, however, weren't ready to die.

Holloway began to find soft spots in the Alabama defense, hitting John Yarbrough with a 42-yard touchdown pass. The Vols again fell behind by two touchdowns but answered with a six-yard scramble for a TD by Holloway. What had started out as an apparent blowout had turned into a dogfight by halftime, with Alabama leading, 21-14.

The Tennessee faithful had reason to whoop and holler when Holloway hooked up with tight end Mitchell Gravitt for a 64-yard touchdown at the outset of the second half. The Vols appeared to have the upper hand but the wild offensive pyrotechnics gave way to some old-fashioned trench warfare and it was still 21-21 as they headed into the fourth quarter. That's where Battle figured his Vols would prevail.

"We felt we could win the fourth quarter. We talked about it today, we've talked about it all week, we've talked about it since August. We weren't afraid of Alabama; we weren't awed."

But Alabama owned the fourth quarter, as the Tide was wont to do in those days. A relatively obscure player named Robin Cary, known more for being a second baseman on the Tide baseball team, was sent in to receive a Clabo punt. He fielded it at the Alabama 36, broke one tackle, fell in behind a wall of crimson-jerseyed blockers and ran 64 yards to the end zone. And that was that; the floodgates opened and in rolled the Crimson Tide. A few minutes later, Wilbur Jackson got outside and raced 80 yards for a TD. Then Cary got into the act again, recovering a kickoff, setting up an easy score from the 3, and with stunning swiftness, the Vols' football world had fallen apart.

One thing that made it a particularly difficult pill to swallow was the fact that Cary was a backup; he had been inserted to field the ball, not necessarily to run it back for a touchdown. And he was unusually slow for a kick returner. "That little guy couldn't outrun his sister," said teammate Robert Fraley. "It took Robin two days to get to the end zone," said another teammate, Mike Dubose.

The final score, 42-21, in no way told the story of the game. The old saying certainly fit in this case: the game was much closer than the score indicated.

Bear Bryant paid Holloway his due, saying, "Holloway has more moves and is harder to get a hold on than any back I ever saw."

For the third straight year, Bill Battle walked across the field to congratulate his old coach, Bear Bryant. There also seemed to be something symbolic about it. Bill Battle was walking not just across a footfall field, but walking the plank as well.

There was griping back in the Volunteer State. To many Vol fans, distressed by a third straight loss to Alabama, Battle was no longer the fair-haired boy of Tennessee football. One can never foresee the odd twists and turns that lie ahead for a football team. Or a football coach. Just how true that was became obvious two weeks later.

Following a 39-7 blowout of outmanned TCU for win No. 6, Tennessee faced Georgia, which was fresh from back-to-back losses to Kentucky and Vanderbilt. It was homecoming on The Hill and the old grads in the crowd of 71,000 no doubt already had this one chalked up in the "W" column for Tennessee. Especially after the Vols drove 76 yards to score on their first possession. It turned into a shootout after that, then Tennessee carved out a 31-21 lead with a 17-point third quarter. The Dogs clawed back to within three, 31-28, with a 79-yard drive midway through the final period.

With his team having fourth-and-2 at its own 28 with 2:27 to play, Battle faced probably the biggest quandary of his coaching life: Kick it away and hope to hold Georgia? Or try to keep the ball away from the Dogs with a fake punt, make a couple of first downs and win the game? Battle was a conservative person and coach by nature. The last thing he wanted to call was the fake punt. But because Georgia had run almost at will against the Vol defense up to that point, he felt that was Tennessee's only chance to win. Even if the Vols had punted, a Georgia drive of 70 or 80 yards was hardly out of the question.

The ball was snapped to upback Steve Chancey, who was tackled immediately. The Bulldogs took over and scored the winning touchdown with a minute to play, quarterback Andy

Johnson turning a busted play into a TD and a dramatic 35-31 win.

Ron McCartney, a sophomore linebacker on that team, remembers the scene:

"When Mike Overton snapped that ball, Chancey was stopped almost in his tracks. The momentum of the whole game changed right there. On a third-down play Andy Johnson misses the handoff. Our whole defense swarms the running back who was supposed to have taken the handoff and Johnson pulls the ball down and runs nine yards around end for the winning touchdown."

With typical courage, Battle took full responsibility for the defeat. In the locker room he told his players: "It was a dumb call. And I want to apologize to you guys for losing the game for you after you fought so hard."

Holloway, among others, would have none of that. "Coach Battle didn't try to put the blame on anybody else. In the dressing room he told us he had made a stupid call, that he had made a mistake. I think it was Ronnie Wheeler who first got up and said something and I said something too. Basically what we both said was, 'Hey, Coach, we're in this thing together. We will win and lose together.' "

It was without question the low point of Battle's career. Years later, he admitted the Georgia loss was the beginning of the end of his tenure.

"I don't know any one thing that led to my resignation in 1976, but the fake punt would definitely be high on the list. I felt at that time that was the only way we could win the game. It was odd how we got in that situation. It had been third-and-7 and we throw a flare pass to Stanback and we've got our best running back one-on-one against a defensive back. If he makes first down, we stay alive, and probably win the game. But that guy makes a great tackle and we've got it fourth-and-2. Gosh dang, that guy made a great tackle.

"We couldn't stop Georgia all day and I didn't think we could stop them there if we punted. I felt like the only way we could win was if we maintained possession; I sure didn't want to give it back to them. But I told our guy, 'Fake punt, run right, but don't do it unless it's a gimme. The play we had called in that situation was that if Georgia lined up a certain way, our guy was supposed to say 'Kick the ball' and we'd go on and kick it. Georgia puts eight men on the line, four on each side.

"I see that and I'm over on the sideline hollering 'Kick the ball! Kick the ball!' And Condredge is there hollering 'Kick the ball!' But, you know, they went on with the fake play and it didn't work. But you don't blame the players. It's the coaches' job to get the player to do what he's supposed to do."

Seven years later, three days before the Georgia-Tennessee season opener, Bulldog coach Vince Dooley was asked in jest if he anticipated another fake punt call by Tennessee like the one in 1973. "I think it's always a possibility. But what a difference it would have made if Tennessee had pulled that one off. Had Tennessee gotten that first down I am confident they would have won that game."

Despite the wave of criticism that followed the loss to Georgia, Battle felt no immediate backlash from Vol fans. "Even after that game, the fans were great. It was incredible the number of letters and messages that came in that were positive. But that play was one you'd like to call back. Those kind make you look so stupid."

Not always. In a rather bizarre twist 19 years later, in another Georgia-Tennessee game, the football gods were smiling on interim coach Phillip Fulmer as he filled in for the recuperating Johnny Majors in the second game of the 1992 season. He fared much better on fourth down than Battle had, converting a pair of them en route to a victory by almost the identical score, 34-31. Battle talked with Fulmer after that game and told him, "Phillip, you got a lot of credit for those two fourth down calls, but they can go the other way on you. And I'm living proof!" In a further bit of irony, guess who was a member of Battle's coaching staff in that 1973 season. None other than Phillip Fulmer.

Ole Miss, taking note of the ease with which Georgia had rushed for 356 yards, went the Bulldogs four yards better and Bill Battle suffered back-to-back defeats for the first time in his four-year administration. But unlike the loss to Georgia, which went down to the wire, the Vols were never in contention in the 28-18 loss.

The embattled Tennessee defense surrendered 323 yards to Kentucky, but gobbled up five Wildcat fumbles and prevailed 16-14. Vandy also came close, scoring 17 points in the fourth quarter but bowing 20-17, thanks to punter Barry Burton's decision to run rather than punt on fourth down at his own 24. Townsend, the Vols' barefoot wonder, booted the game-winner from 37 yards out.

Holloway engineered the field goal drive after making a remarkable recovery from an ankle injury that put him out of action in the first half. He retired to the sideline, where the Vol training staff erected a makeshift "tent" around him and made some classified repairs on the ankle. Most fans in attendance guessed that the repairs were in the form of an injection, which seemed as likely an explanation as any. Asked years later just what went on inside the tarp, Holloway smiled and said, "Just a good tape job."

Tennessee continued its brinksmanship ways to the bitter end, losing 28-19 to Texas Tech in the Gator Bowl. The Vols fell behind 14-0 but battled back and had a chance to go ahead with a 32-yard field goal try by Townsend in the final period. The kick missed, Tech added a meaningless touchdown late in the game and a season of peaks and valleys was at an end. There had been too-close-for-comfort victories over Duke, Kansas, Georgia Tech, Kentucky and Vanderbilt, disheartening losses to Alabama, Georgia, Ole Miss and Texas Tech. It added up to 8-4—not bad by anyone's standards, but a comedown from Battle's 11-1, 10-2, 10-2 start.

CHAPTER 12

DOWN BUT
NOT OUT

Although there were relatively minor grumblings—relative, that is, to the uproar that would occur a couple of years later, the Bill Battle regime was still on rather solid ground heading into 1974. Even though he had lost four games in 1973, his four-year record was a sparkling 39-9. The outlook was good, perhaps even great, because of the presence of senior quarterback Condredge Holloway, probably the most electrifying player ever to wear the Orange and White. He had been a second-team All-American as a junior and his return was the key to Tennessee's dreams of continued football success. His spectacular gridiron deeds had even inspired a song, "Go, Holloway."

Tennessee had not had a legitimate Heisman Trophy candidate in 18 years, since tailback Johnny Majors finished runner-up in 1956. Holloway changed that. The great little quarterback went into the season as one of the leading contenders for college football's most prestigious award. All that had to happen was for him to stay healthy and Tennessee to have an outstanding season. Neither came about. Holloway had a date with injury, one that would plague him and his team throughout the season.

Holloway and his understudy, Randy Wallace, were forced to give up summer baseball early in order to get back to Knoxville in time for fall practice. They were playing for the Liberal (Kansas) Beejays, who had reached the finals of the NBC national tournament. The Beejays went on to win the tournament after the two Vols traded in their gloves for shoulder pads.

The season opener against UCLA was the resumption of an intersectional rivalry that began with the memorable Rosebonnet Bowl game at Memphis in 1965, and had since earned a reputation as college football at its best. ABC-TV had picked the game to kick off its 1974 national television schedule. And the bigwigs at ABC couldn't have foreseen the drama that was to unfold at Neyland Stadium.

Early in the game, Holloway ran an option left. He turned upfield, where he and inside linebacker Frank Manumaleuna were on a collision course "Manumaleuna's eyes rolled back in his head and we both went down," Holloway says. "I got up before he did, but I knew I was hurt."

Trainers examined Holloway on the sidelines and feared he had a shoulder separation. He was loaded into a van and taken to University Hospital three miles away. X-rays showed only a slight separation. "Nothing that I couldn't play with" is how Holloway describes it today.

Before Tennessee's first possession, backup quarterback Pat Ryan had slapped Holloway on the back with these words, "Have a good game, Condredge. Just don't leave me stranded out there."

But now Ryan was stranded out there. He had been enjoying the anonymity and comfort of the bench. And now fate had dealt him another hand, a place in the spotlight, a role on national television. He was 18 years old, a sophomore. He had never taken a varsity snap.

"I wasn't even supposed to be the backup," Ryan says. "Randy Wallace was second team and he was sick, had some kind of elbow infection that lasted about a month. So all of a sudden I was the backup. Hell, I had never played any. I had never seen guys like those from UCLA. They had a couple of big Samoan linebackers, with hair down to their shoulders, unusual looking guys. It was scary. I don't mind telling you that I was scared to death. But once I got in, things were OK."

When the second half commenced and Holloway was still missing, Vol fans were concerned, even though the Vols led 10-3. Near the end of the third period, after the Tennessee defense had made a great goal-line stand, the Vols were backed up to their one-yard line. Ryan carried on a quarterback sneak, trying to wedge the ball out to give punter Neil Clabo some kicking room.

He got "stood up" and the ball popped loose. UCLA's Rick Kukulica recovered for a touchdown to make it 10-10.

By early in the fourth quarter, with the Bruins having gone ahead 17-10 and still no Holloway, concern had turned to panic. Suddenly, a huge roar went up from the stands. Holloway had emerged from the chute leading from the Vol dressing room on the east side and was trotting around the north end headed for the Vol bench on the west sideline. The conqueror riding in on his white stallion. ABC's Keith Jackson noted, "Condredge Holloway is coming back into the stadium. He has been to the hospital and there is obviously nothing broken."

Holloway himself was unaware that the cheers were for him. "I thought something good had happened out on the field," he says.

Battle didn't realize it either. "I heard all that cheering and I didn't know what it was for because nothing was going on out on the field," Battle recalled 18 years later. "But Condredge was coming back into the stadium and I didn't realize it. I thought they had announced that Alabama was getting beat or something like that.

"We thought he had been hurt pretty bad in the first half and they told me he was probably through for the season. I didn't even know he had gone to the hospital. When they say he's out for the season, you forget about him for the time being and go to the next guy, who happened to be Pat Ryan."

Incredibly, Battle had been so engrossed in the game that he thought Holloway had been on the bench the whole time.

"Condredge came up and grabbed me and said, 'I'm OK, Coach. Put me in.' I thought he did that because he was just tired of seeing us wallowing around out there. I told him to get the doctor to tell me that, and the doctor did. I turned back to Condredge and said, 'Well, get your butt out there.'"

With only four minutes to go, Holloway drove Tennessee 80 yards to the tying touchdown. He capped it off as only Condredge Holloway could do it. From the 12-yard line, he set sail. Met near the goal by two Bruin defenders, he dived the final two yards, landing on his head as he turned a flip into the end zone.

"He goes in and takes us to a touchdown," Battle says. "They hit him as he flips head over heels into the end zone, and when they do, they tear the cartilage in his knee. So after that he can't run very fast and he has lost all his quickness. And that plagued him for the rest of the year."

John Ward, the Voice of the Vols, says it couldn't have happened any other way. "There are not many stars," he says, "but Condredge Holloway was a star. And so he was the player that people expected to come back, even if his leg was broken. He was a star and he came back and, not really deliberately but just naturally, he played it to the hilt. When he came back on the field and came over to the west sideline, everything he did was done to build the moment."

So the '74 season got off, if not on a winning note, then certainly not on a losing one, thanks to Holloway. It wasn't a victory, but it was the next best thing to one, as former Kentucky and Cleveland Browns coach Blanton Collier was fond of saying. But Tennessee had to pay a price. Because of those injuries to his shoulder and knee, Holloway was just never again the dazzling, dashing quarterback who had terrorized defenses for two years. Consequently, Heisman Trophy talk at Tennessee faded, and would not be heard again for 20 years, until another prodigiously gifted quarterback arrived on the scene in the person of Heath Shuler.

A Holloway operating at less than 100 percent still displayed moments of brilliance, but not nearly often enough to keep Tennessee on the straight and narrow. The Vols were mauled by Auburn 21-0, barely beat Tulsa, then dropped back-to-back decisions to LSU and Alabama. It was mid-October, the season already was in a shambles, 2-3-1, and everybody— coaches, players and fans—was wearing a frown.

There was no joy in Big Orange Country. There was, in fact, sickness in Big Orange Country. On the Monday afternoon following the 28-6 loss to Alabama, a moving van pulled up in front of Battle's home in the fashionable Fox Den neighborhood in west Knoxville. Of course, Battle wasn't at home at the time; but his wife Eugenia was. And she was eight months pregnant, which only added to the classless act. Tennessee fans were horrified.

Mrs. Battle took it in stride. When the coach learned about the moving van at work, he telephoned his wife.

"How are you doing, honey?"

"Fine."

"Has anything unusual happened today?"

"No, everything is fine."

"Tell me, did somebody send a moving van out there?"

"Yes, but I told them to leave, that it was a bad mistake."

The players downplayed the moving van incident. "It just didn't affect us a great deal," Seivers says. "We weren't in tune with that stuff very much, certainly not as much as we should have been. Because we kept thinking, 'Well, next year's going to be great; everything will be OK in '76.'"

Said quarterback Ryan: "Everybody thought the moving van thing was pretty crummy. Everybody liked Bill Battle. He was a good guy. His main fault, I think, was that he was too nice; he surrounded himself with inferior coaches."

Clearly, there was growing discontent with the Battle regime. If the moving van incident didn't offer enough evidence, then the "For Sale" sign that popped up later in Battle's yard and the arrival of an exterminator at his office surely did.

It was at this time that Battle, troubled by his team's failures and distressed by the beating that his senior quarterback was taking, offered Holloway an out so he could remain relatively healthy for a baseball career.

He called Holloway into his office and told him: "You've done enough; you're hurt. If you have any aspirations to play pro baseball you've got to remember that you have a banged-up shoulder and your legs can't run fast any more. I think you have done your all for Tennessee. If you want to call it quits, I'll understand; I'll go to bat for you."

Holloway at first thought Battle was putting him on. He finally told him thanks, but no thanks.

So it was on with the season — the New Season, as they called it. From their 2-3-1 start, and fresh from a 28-6 loss to Alabama, the Vols won four in a row, beginning with a stirring 29-28 triumph over Clemson. And it was another of the Holloway miracles that pulled it off.

Trailing 28-27 and in desperate need of a two-point conversion, Tennessee sent Holloway optioning to the right side. The problem was that Clemson had anticipated the play, which had gone for a TD earlier, and was there to meet him at the corner. Holloway, looking like the Artful Dodger of old, reversed his field and retreated back to the 22. He spotted split end Larry Seivers in the end zone and, just as a Tiger defender lowered the boom, lofted the ball to Seivers, who made the catch over his shoulder.

Just another routine scramble, Holloway says. "We practiced scramble plays some because we didn't have a great offensive line. They were young and learning, so we were forced into scramble plays quite a bit."

Seivers remembers getting instructions from Holloway before the play unfolded.

"Condredge had told me to get to the end zone. He said if he ran and didn't make it to the end zone that he would fumble on purpose and for me to be ready to recover it in the end zone. When he was back there doing all that scrambling, I was on the other side. He screamed "Larry, go the other way," or words to that effect. I got over just in time for him to throw it to me."

Seivers, who would make one seemingly impossible catch after another for three seasons, calls the one against Clemson probably the most memorable of his career.

"That one stands out in my mind for two reasons. One, it was a remarkable play by Condredge. And two, it was the first time I felt like I had done something at Tennessee."

One thing it did do was launch the Vols on an October-November stretch run during which they would go unbeaten. And after a dismal 2-3-1 beginning, that was almost enough to set off dancing in the streets.

In the next game, a 34-6 romp over Memphis State, Holloway overtook Bobby Scott as Tennessee's all-time total offense leader. He went on to finish with 4,068 yards, a record broken five years later by Jimmy Streater.

Over the last six games, the only blot on the UT record was a 21-21 tie with Vanderbilt, a tie that by all rights should have been a loss. It wasn't, because for the second straight year, a miscue by Vandy punter Barry Burton gave the Vols a chance. Back to punt on fourth down and his team leading 21-13, Burton bobbled the snap from center at the Commodore 12. Stanley Morgan got the TD with seven seconds left, but the Vols had to have a two-point conversion. The call? Why, Holloway to Seivers, of course. Seivers went up for the ball at the very back of the end zone. The 21-21 tie earned the Vols their tenth straight bowl trip, but it ended Tennessee's claim of having won at least eight games every year since 1965.

Burton's muff had been damaging enough to the Vandy cause, but no more so than one by the officials on the two-point play.

There are many who were there, including no less an authority than Seivers himself, who say he did not catch the ball. Because the officials were so intent on the landing point of Seivers' feet at the back of the end zone, they didn't pay much attention to whether he caught the ball. Perhaps they had come to believe, like most everyone else, that whatever Seivers touched, Seivers caught.

"The ball hit me right in the hands," Seivers says. "It was raining and freezing cold; I couldn't even feel my hands. And that ball just rolled right down my body so nice that it probably looked like I was tucking it in. But I didn't catch it. After the play, I was over on the sidelines with my head down. I saw the controversy out on the field and I said to myself, 'Well, I didn't catch it and they caught me.' The Vanderbilt people were really fussing about it. Meantime, Tommy West has started a fight out there and there's a lot of commotion. I just figured they were conferring about the catch but the referee said it was good, so I guess all's well that ends well."

Tennessee met Maryland in the Liberty Bowl and managed a 7-3 win, thanks to another of Seivers' scintillating catches. Randy Wallace, subbing for the injured Holloway, was on the throwing end from 11 yards out with 2:44 to go.

Maryland's Randy White, later a standout with the Dallas Cowboys, almost single-handedly kept the Vol offense at bay. First he sent Holloway to sleepy town with a vicious hit, and whipped tight end Tommy West unmercifully.

"Tommy West was so fired up for that game it was unbeliev-able," remembers Seivers. "On the very first play of the game, which was going away from Tommy, he sort of clipped Randy White, just trying to cut him off. When Tommy got back to the bench, he said, 'Oh, man, I hit that guy as hard as I could and bounced off him! He just kept going. This is going to be a long day.'"

And that it was. Before the game, sportscaster Jim Lampley offered to bet West $100 that he would not be able to knock White off his feet. Later on, he said he would make it easier for West, that he would give him the $100 if he put White on the ground just one time. Lampley never had to pay off.

"Not once did Randy White go down," Holloway says. "He was all over us all night. We couldn't block him. One time he was standing next to a pileup and came up to Tommy West and hit him with everything he had. And he went after Tommy at the end of the game.

"Jim Richardson went into the game after Tommy got thrown out and when he came back off the field, he asked Tommy, 'What the hell did you do to Randy White? He's not even trying to get to the play; he's going after me on every play and he's been kicking my ass.'"

The Vols even tried running away from White, but he would catch option plays from the back side.

Holloway's recollections are not first-hand. He woke up in the dressing room, not knowing who had won the game. He assumed that Tennessee had lost because there was no celebra-tion. But the gloom of the locker room was due to the death of Battle's father in the stands during the game. It was an especially difficult time for Battle, who had lost his mother a short time before.

CHAPTER 13

THE TIDE TURNS
THE TIDE

———————————

There were no rent-a-win opponents on the first half of Tennessee's 1975 schedule.

When the Vols reported for fall practice, they were issued T-shirts with a message on the front: "MUALA."

It wasn't the name of some hot-shot player at the University of Hawaii, the team the Vols would face in their 12th game of the season. It was the acronym for the the first five opponents of the season: Maryland, UCLA, Auburn, LSU and Alabama—a meatgrinder stretch of games that figured to make or break the Vols. Shockingly, however, it was the second half of the schedule that did them in.

A bad omen came early. In the final scrimmage before the season opener against Maryland, starting quarterback Pat Ryan was slammed to the ground by linebacker Carl Velander. Ryan's collarbone was broken and he was lost for the season. That left the quarterbacking job to redshirt sophomore Gary Roach and junior Randy Wallace. They split playing time early but Roach fell out of favor with the coaches after making a bad pitch in a game and played little from there on.

Tennessee got through the MUALA stretch with a 3-2 record, beating Maryland, Auburn and LSU and losing to UCLA and Alabama. Whew! There were no heavyweights left; in fact, there were some real creampuffs, like North Texas State, Colorado State, and Utah. Even Ole Miss, usually a tough nut for the Vols to crack, was in a down year, with losses to Baylor, Texas A&M, Tulane, Alabama and South Carolina. UT fans felt smug in the belief that their team would wade through the remaining seven games for a 10-2 record and an eleventh consecutive postseason bowl game.

What they didn't realize was that the 30-7 loss to Alabama at midseason had been a ruinous defeat, and would foster further disaster. The Tide had almost toyed with the Vols in winning on the Third Saturday in October for the fifth straight year. The one-sided beating simply drained the Vols' spirits. They began to be booed by their own fans, which didn't help matters; frustration set in.

Tennessee had gone into the Alabama game with injuries to several of its best players—Wallace, Larry Seivers, Stanley Morgan and Andy Spiva among others. Battle could have used that as an excuse. He didn't.

One thing he did do, for the only time in his coaching career, was to plan ahead for an opponent, in this case Alabama. The week before facing the Tide in Birmingham, the Vols were at home against a struggling LSU team that had beaten only Rice in its first four outings. Battle decided to more or less look past LSU, to concentrate on Alabama and its devastating wishbone offense.

"I called all our people together," he said, "and told them that I'd heard rumors that LSU might be going to the wishbone as a last resort. I said maybe we ought to work against the wishbone in preparation for them. But the truth was that I was getting a jump on preparations for Alabama.

"We were ready for Alabama, at least mentally. But physically we were crippled. And Alabama just beat the heck out of us." The guy who did most of the beating was defensive end Leroy Cook, who had four of the Tide's 10 sacks. The Alabama defense turned in a classic performance, holding Tennessee to a mere 117 yards, including a paltry 12 yards on 39 rushing attempts. The Tide wishbone, directed by Richard Todd, gained almost 400 yards.

With the MUALA stretch thankfully out of the way, it was time to launch a brand-new winning season against a lineup of sitting ducks.

The first pushover, North Texas State, turned out not to be a pushover at all. The Mean Green had served warning by hammering Houston 28-0 just two weeks earlier. Tennessee trailed much of the way but punched across a tying touchdown in the fourth period. Then came the backbreaker on the ensuing kickoff, a 98-yard return by Sears Woods with five minutes to play. The most unthinkable thing that UT fans could think of had happened. The fact that Tennessee rolled up nearly 500 yards in offense was of no consolation, not to the the players, not to the coaches and certainly not to the fans. Even today, most Vol boosters consider the 21-14 loss one of the most humiliating defeats in Tennessee history.

Had the Vols had one more play, they might have won. Seivers hauled in a long pass from Wallace at the North Texas 10, and as he went down the defensive back had a firm hold on his face mask. It went undetected by the officials and the clock ran out before Wallace could stop the clock with an out-of-bounds throw. A penalty would have given Tennessee at least one more play from the 5.

There followed losses to Ole Miss (23-6) and Vanderbilt (17-14). Tight end/punter Barry Burton, a goat in the two previous meetings with Tennessee, played the role of hero this time and was presented the game ball. And he managed to add insult to injury, some Vol players claimed, by spitting on the giant "T" at midfield at Neyland Stadium.

On the eve of the Vols' 17-13 win over Kentucky at Lexington, the *Nashville Banner* reported that if Battle didn't beat both Kentucky and Vanderbilt he was a goner. It wasn't true, of course. "I never saw Coach Woodruff so mad as he was that night," Battle says.

For the first time since 1964, there was no bowl game for Tennessee, but there was a trip to Honolulu where the Vols played Hawaii and Vol fans by the thousands took over Waikiki Beach for almost a week. Stanley Morgan hogged the spotlight in a 28-6 triumph, gaining 201 yards on 11 carries to eclipse Curt Watson's six-year-old school record for rushing yardage in a game, 197.

Seivers was one of the few bright spots in an otherwise drab year, being named a consensus All-American. He led the Southeastern Conference with 42 pass receptions, but the numbers alone failed to capture the impact of many of his catches, some of them bordering on the unbelievable. To be sure, Seivers had the gift of grab.

In 12 seasons as a quarterback with the New York Jets, Pat Ryan saw some of football's greatest receivers. And he insists that Seivers could have played with any of them.

"One of the biggest atrocities that ever happened was Larry Seivers not getting to play professional football. He didn't have great speed but he had ample speed. If anyone had just given him the chance to show what he could do. He had the best hands I've ever seen, college or pro. Of these guys who play every Sunday, not one of them out there can catch it like Seivers could. He could run well enough to play. And he could get open. It's just that pro football is so enamored with burning speed. They will give a guy who can't catch the ball two or three years to develop if he can run a 4.3 or 4.4 forty."

Ryan compares Seivers to Steve Largent, the Seattle Seahawks' great receiver, with whom he played at Putnam City High in Oklahoma City. "Larry was a Steve Largent, just not quite as quick, but he was bigger and probably had better hands. I played with both of them so I believe I can talk about it with some authority."

Seivers was drafted in the fourth round by Seattle but suffered a slight shoulder separation and was idle for a couple of weeks. His pro career was effectively ended at that point.

Seivers had later chances with Tampa Bay, Philadelphia and Green Bay, but none panned out, even though he had sparkling credentials. In 1978, he went to the Packers as a free agent. When he arrived there he sat down with coach Bart Starr and said, " 'Look, no matter what happens, I'll come here if you will throw the ball to me in a preseason game. Once you do that, it's over.' I told him that if he would just put the ball in the air to me in any situation, he would see."

He never made it to a preseason game. Frustrated, he went to visit a buddy in Iowa. He didn't even tell his parents where he was going. "I just called them and told them I was all right, that I would be home in a month or two."

As a member of the 1975 *Look* magazine All-America team, Seivers had to fly from Honolulu following the Hawaii game to New York to be on Bob Hope's television show. The country boy from Clinton, Tennessee, might not have made it had it not been for John Ward. The Voice of the Vols himself was en route to New York after the Hawaii game to broadcast the Tennessee-St. John's basketball game.

"Thank goodness, he took me under his wing," Seivers says. "The only flying I had ever done was on team charters; I had never been on a commercial airliner in my life. United Airlines was on strike at the time so that didn't help matters. When we got to Los Angeles, John knew I didn't have a clue about how to get from there to New York. He saw that my flight number wasn't up on the board. That's because they had me booked on a flight out of San Francisco and I was in Los Angeles.

"John took care of that and when we got to New York he got a cab and took me in the opposite direction from where he was going and made sure I got off at the right place. I would never have made it if it hadn't been for him."

While they were waiting in the LA airport, Ward noticed John Brodie, the former San Francisco 49ers quarterback, sitting in a nearby lounge. Ward had met Brodie once and didn't really know him, but took Seivers over and introduced him. The All-America receiver and the ex-NFL quarterback, who by this time was into television announcing, had a nice chat while they waited for their flights.

The failures of 1975 left Battle terribly disappointed. "This team had a great attitude and we were a good football team in the early going. Then we got beat up some in the LSU game, we lost badly to Alabama and after that we almost turned into a sorry team. After the loss to Alabama, we simply didn't handle adversity very well."

Vol fans would drink to that.

The final 1975 record was 7-5, the most losses since 1964, Doug Dickey's first year as coach. Call it a season of discontent. By now, Battle had been convicted in the court of public opinion. When a team of considerable talent loses to the likes of North Texas State and Vanderbilt, it gets the fans to thinking that perhaps it would be a good idea for the head coach to seek employment elsewhere. There were public outcries for Tennessee to go after Johnny Majors, who was about to embark on a national championship season at Pittsburgh.

Mickey Marvin, the genial giant who made All-SEC three years in a row, 1974-76, says the players felt that, as early as the middle of the 1974 season, the handwriting was on the wall for Battle. "We pretty much knew that it was inevitable that Coach Majors was going to wind up at Tennessee," he says. "We would occasionally talk about it in whispers."

Marvin calls the North Texas State loss "the crusher."

"After that game we would dread coming out on the field. I remember the boos, the things people were saying. I'll never forget playing Ole Miss at Memphis three weeks later (a 23-6 loss for the Vols) and people in the stands shouting things at Coach Battle. They were throwing oranges and liquor bottles."

Marvin took as much as he could, then challenged a fan to come down out of the stands. The heckler, probably noting that Marvin was 6-5 and almost 300 pounds, declined the invitation. It was a most uncharacteristic move by Marvin, described by one of his teammates as a man without a mean bone in his body.

Seivers could also see the end in sight. "Even in 1975 you could tell that Coach Battle's days were numbered, unless we could do great, which we thought we could. The players all thought, 'Well, everything is going to be OK.' But it was inevitable that Majors would get back to Tennessee. If truth be known, Bill Battle was probably too young at 28 to be a head coach. Now the coaching staff he had during my three years, if he had put all the best ones together he would have had a heck of a staff. But he had some loyalty to some coaches and instead of letting them go he would just move them to another coaching position.

"One of the coaches, after he was moved — and I won't name him — had to get one of the players to show him how we got down in a stance. He didn't even know which hand went on the ground."

Battle finally did make some coaching changes. Jerry Elliott had resigned as receivers coach and former Vol wingback Bill Baker, whose position coach had been Bill Battle, joined the staff as Elliott's replacement. He had been defensive coordinator at Wichita State.

Another one-time Vol, Robbie Franklin, left the Georgia Tech staff to coach defensive ends. Jon Conlin came from Southern Mississippi to handle the secondary. Dal Shealy, an assistant at Baylor and one time head coach at Carson-Newman, signed on as offensive coordinator. Tennessee was going to the wishbone, a move that didn't do a great deal to extend Battle's tenure.

Marvin, who went on to play 11 years with the Oakland and Los Angeles Raiders, had a brilliant career at Tennessee, but it seemed beset by one pitfall after another. One he remembers very vividly. Two decades have passed, yet Marvin can take you to the very spot where it happened.

It was a beautiful Sunday afternoon in April 1974, the spring before Marvin's junior season. The giant offensive guard, the first of the really massive linemen to play for Tennessee, had been a first team All-Southeastern Conference guard as a sophomore and the coaching staff had already made plans to move him to tackle in the fall to take advantage of his great size, 6-5 and 280 pounds.

Spring practice had begun the previous week, and this Sunday afternoon was idle time for the Vols. Some of them hit the books and some watched NFL games on television. For others, sitting around the dorm on a beautiful Sunday afternoon wasn't their idea of fun, inasmuch as they would be back on the practice field the next day.

So Marvin and two of his teammates, Joey Bowen and Ed Sears, decided to go horseback riding, as a number of players often did whenever there was a lull in the practice schedule.

They headed for Sherrill Stables, just off I-40 in West Knoxville. "We rented some old nags that looked like they were ready for the glue factory," Marvin recalls. "I think we paid $5 or $10 for maybe an hour. I don't know where we came up with the money, unless we sold some blood like we sometimes did."

Nearing the end of their allotted time, the three Vols headed back toward the stable. "One thing about those horses," Marvin says, "especially if they are carrying 280 pounds, they get kind of frisky when they know they're heading back to the stable. I remember my horse just taking off and I can still see it in my mind's eye now, as though it is happening in slow motion.

"I panicked; I don't know why. I was screaming and hollering. I can see myself sliding off the right side of that horse. I figured I would just put my wrist down to break my fall."

It broke his fall all right, but it also broke his forearm. He was taken to nearby Park West Hospital, where a doctor suggested that surgery might be necessary because he was having trouble setting the fracture.

"I told them to please not operate," Marvin says. "They finally got it set and I ended up wearing a huge cast, one big enough for most people's leg to fit in."

Marvin missed the rest of spring practice and the mishap torpedoed the plans to move Marvin to tackle. Because of the fracture, he wasn't able to work out that summer, and when he reported in the fall he was terribly overweight, about 300 pounds, a circumstance that didn't endear him to certain members of the coaching staff. During preseason workouts, the players were running sixteen 110-yard dashes, one after another with just a short break between. Marvin ran one and missed the next two, ran another and then couldn't finish.

Measured by his other three seasons at Tennessee, his junior campaign was a flop. And so was the team's season, a fact that causes Marvin to blame himself for the 7-5 record.

"When you are young you make mistakes," he says. "Not only was I a disappointment to myself in 1975, I was a disappointment to the University of Tennessee football team. I made All-SEC three years in a row but to be honest I don't think I deserved it in '75. The coaches and all my teammates had looked to me to be a leader of that team, particularly on offense. I let my teammates down, my coaches down, myself down."

He was so downcast after the horseback incident, in fact, that he went home to Hendersonville, North Carolina. Teammates feared he had quit. "I went home because I was upset. I wasn't really thinking about quitting. I was immature. I realized that I had let a lot of people down. Wayne Stiles, the recruiting coordinator, came across the mountain and brought me back.

"The first person I met when I got back to Knoxville was my line coach, Ray Trail. I'll never forget it. Big tears rolled down his cheeks and he said, 'Mickey, I just want you to be as good as you can be.' "

Trail and the other coaches were usually hounding Marvin about his weight. At one practice Marvin was not getting low enough on the blocking cage to please Trail, who growled: "Marvin, I'll bet if I put a biscuit and ham down there you'd get low, wouldn't you?"

Because of his sub-par performance in 1975, Marvin was surprised that he made All-SEC, but not surprised to learn that Battle had not voted for him.

After making All-SEC for the third straight year, as a senior in '76, Marvin went to Battle's office. "I was so tickled about making All-SEC again. Coach Battle had a statue of me that somebody had made and given to him back when I was a freshman. And he gave me that statue that day. He let me know that he had not voted for me All-SEC my junior year, and I had sort of known that. I asked him if he voted me All-SEC this year and he looked at me and said, 'Yes, Mickey, I did because you surely deserved it.' "

CHAPTER 14

BATTLE BOWS OUT

In 1974, after a Tennessee victory, Bill Battle had noted with pride that the backfield that had played most of the game that day was all-sophomore. "Just wait until they're seniors," he said, the implication being that 1976 would be The Year. When 1976 rolled around, the people Battle had referred to — Stanley Morgan, Mike Gayles, Randy Wallace — had reached their senior season. Experts generally agreed that Tennessee had some outstanding football talent.

Without question, this was the make or break season for Battle. His record had slipped in each of the past three years. He hadn't beaten Alabama since 1970 and he was 2-4 against Auburn. He came close against those two old foes, but playing Alabama and Auburn close didn't mean a thing to Tennessee fans.

As the buzzards circled, critics pointed to the steady decline in Battle's record, which looked like this:

1970:	11-1	(.846)
1971:	10-2	(.833)
1972:	10-2	(.833)
1973:	8-4	(.667)
1974:	7-3-2	(.667)
1975:	7-5	(.583)

The players went into 1976 brimming with confidence. "We had a good group of senior players," Larry Seivers says, "and we thought we had a good chance to win the conference championship. But it was strange. The town wasn't pulling together, the team wasn't really together, nothing was going together. The players were looking over their shoulders. Guys made bad plays and were being booed. It wasn't a fun year at all."

The season opener was an omen of things to come. Underdog Duke pulled off a 21-18 shocker. Each team made three touchdowns but the Vols' futility showed in their failure to make a single extra point.

Mickey Marvin was another who expected great things in 1976. "We had as much talent as any Tennessee team in a long time. I think what happened was we got beat by Duke that first game and it was a game we should have won. It was like a funeral march. We should have gone 11-0 that year but we got off on the wrong foot."

It was not a fun season for Bill Battle either. "As early as 1975, the Knoxville press was writing more about what John Majors and Pittsburgh were doing than what we were doing at Tennessee," he says. "And it got worse in 1976."

Fate caught Bill Battle off-guard in 1976. His squad was loaded with senior players and he was not alone in thinking it would be a fine season. "I really thought we were going to be good," he said. "That was when Larry Seivers and Stanley Morgan and Mickey Marvin and Andy Spiva and those guys were seniors. They had come in together as sophomores in 1974 but we had bad schedules in both '74 and '75, just horrible schedules. I thought we had gotten it turned around when those guys were seniors and I thought we had a chance to win the SEC championship. There was so much pressure on those players, probably on all of us if you want to know the truth. But again I don't think the coaches worried about it too much. The wives probably had a hard time with it because they had to deal with it. But the coaches were always working all the time. We never saw anybody. Nobody ever said to us: 'You all are bad coaches.' But they said it to everybody else, I guess.

"You go back and look at that season," he says, "and we lost five games but we lost them in some of the goofiest ways you can imagine. The way we lost the Duke game, I had never seen it before or since. George Cafego was the best kicking coach in America and he worked every day with those guys. And twice during the game the ball slips off the tee and it's like firing blanks because the ball is on the ground and the tee is in the way.

"The year before, we had done a good job of covering kickoffs. Our guys had just flown down there. But in the North Texas State game, we had a single safety, which was a bad mistake, particularly when you put a freshman back there, even though he's a good athlete. Early in that game we had just knocked their jocks off on kickoffs. But on the last kickoff we ran down there and everybody overran the ball and Sears Woods pops out of a pile and there isn't anybody left but him and Billy Arbo, a freshman. And we never had a single safety after that.

"Against Auburn in '76, I never saw anything like it. We can't defend against the long pass. Our guys are falling down and turning around and everything. Auburn didn't have a good passing game but they threw the ball up in the air and our guys would get all twisted and tangled up. And that never happened to us again but it happened in that game."

By the time the Vols faced Auburn at Birmingham, just three games into the season, there was an unrelenting demand for a coaching change. The outcry for his firing was almost deafening. Following that 38-28 loss to Auburn, Battle called a mid-week press conference and most everyone assumed it would be to announce his resignation. They couldn't have been more wrong, for it was a fighting-mad Battle who showed up, and he howled back at the wolves.

"I never reacted much to the garbage dump kind of thinking that has been going around because I felt that it showed class and courage to stand and take it and be quiet," he said. "I am tired of standing and being quiet and taking it. I am tired of the negative people who call themselves supporters of Tennessee. I am tired of the Gay Street quarterbacks who, if they knew as much about their business as they know about mine, would be on Wall Street instead of Gay Street . . . tired of the ten-dollar bettor who bad-mouths whenever you don't make the point spread . . .

"It is tough enough to have to fight the Dukes and Auburns without having to fight your own people."

Battle says he didn't appreciate the lack of Tennessee spirit, which he says was one of the things that attracted him to a job at Tennessee. "We were still fighting to save the season and there were a lot of Tennessee people who had quit on the program. I didn't like prospects coming into my office and saying, 'Coach Battle, I can't come to Tennessee because your fans are pulling for you to lose games, not to win them.' "

The howling subsided somewhat when Tennessee nipped Clemson 21-19. A week later, the detractors were all but silent when the Vols clobbered Georgia Tech 42-7. Stanley Morgan scored three touchdowns out of the wishbone, which frequently employed Morgan and Seivers as double flankers with a full-house backfield.

Then came Alabama, Bill Battle's last round against his alma mater. The Tide was not cut from championship cloth, like the five Alabama teams before it, and had lost two games by the time it arrived in Knoxville. Alabama made it six in a row over Tennessee and to rub salt in the wound, the Tide blocked a Tennessee punt and turned it into a touchdown en route to a 20-13 victory.

"This was another of those goofy games in '76," Battle said in an interview in 1992. "We were playing well, the game was tied in the third quarter and Craig Colquitt was back to punt. Now Craig Colquitt was the fastest punter I ever saw; he punted in the pros for many years. Alabama doesn't rush; they have the return on. They have one guy, Mike Kramer, coming in from the right side. We had our defensive team covering kicks so we had a strong safety back at fullback. Here comes Kramer roaring in and Colquitt is holding the ball a little, which he is supposed to do to let the coverage get down. So the fullback is pointing at Kramer and is fixing to block him and then he just takes off running, doesn't block him. Kramer goes on in and blocks the kick with his head. When our guy gets to the sideline, I asked him, 'Why didn't you block that guy?' He said, 'I wanted to get in the coverage.' And I said, 'Good gosh, you're the safety man; you don't need to get in the coverage.' That was the closest I ever came to wanting to kill somebody on the sideline."

Florida, coached by none other than ex-Vol head man Doug Dickey, pinned a third straight Southeastern Conference loss on the Vols, 20-18, but the Vols got back in victory lane against Memphis State and Ole Miss. Surprisingly, Tennessee was still in the bowl picture despite a 5-4 record. All the Vols had to do was beat Kentucky, which they had done for 11 straight years. But this was one of Kentucky's finest teams, led by brawny quarterback Derrick Ramsey.

"If we beat Kentucky, we go to a bowl," Battle recalled. "It isn't a great year but we go to a bowl game. We really had a good team that year. Kentucky had Ramsey and Art Still and those guys," Battle recalled. "They really had a good team but I thought we were going to beat them because we always beat Kentucky somehow. Ramsey looked like King Kong; he'd go back to pass and our guys would go in there and hit him and just bounce off. He'd dance around and throw the ball anyway."

Ramsey connected on a throwback pass to Greg Woods and he tightroped the sideline for the only score of the game as the

Wildcats won 7-0. Kentucky went on to batter North Carolina in the Peach Bowl 21-0. Tennessee stayed at home. On the same day that the Vols were losing to Kentucky, Majors and his Pittsburgh Panthers, two victories away from a national championship, were accepting an invitation to play Georgia in the Sugar Bowl.

By then, Battle says, it was obvious that his administration was a lost cause.

"At that point, I just decided that there wasn't any need to go on. The Tennessee people really needed to be rallied and it had gotten past the point where I could do it. And I needed to go on and do other things and let Tennessee go on with its football program. And that's when I decided to resign."

On the following Monday, November 22, Battle announced his resignation to a small group of newsmen at a press conference that lasted less than one minute.

Battle says he doesn't remember if he discussed his resignation beforehand with his wife Eugenia. He recalls that former Vol All-American Bill Johnson, a member of the UT Athletics Board, came by the dressing room after the Kentucky game.

"It was gloomy in there and Bill looked at me and said, 'What can I do for you?' And I told him, 'You don't have any choice; you have to go to Pittsburgh.' "

Johnson and Battle had a warm relationship, much like the one enjoyed by Johnson and Johnny Majors until their celebrated split in 1992.

"I think Bill Johnson is a great person," Battle said."If all the trustees and supporters were like Bill Johnson, college football would be a lot better off. When I first came to Tennessee, I had middle Tennessee as a recruiting area, and I would stay at Bill's house whenever I went over there. He and his wife had three pretty little girls and they had a very small house back then. But they would shift around and put two girls together and I'd sleep in one of their beds and my feet would hang off. But it was fun. And Bill would go out and watch high school games with me and talk Tennessee football."

Did he do the right thing in stepping down when he did?

"Yes, yes, yes," he said unhesitatingly. "We couldn't have recruited anybody. When the players you just have to sign—and there are those few that you absolutely have to get if you're going to win—you can't get those guys anymore. They're sitting up in the stands and the fans are booing the players and saying the coaches are going to be gone.

"The best thing an athletic director or president can do is to support the coach, give him enough years on his contract so

everybody won't be saying 'He doesn't have but one or two more years and then he's not going to be here.' You either support him or you get rid of him. When you get into that in-between area—and we got into that area—you have problems."

Battle's final week as coach was like no other week in Tennessee history. He closed practice to the media, even to those reporters who had covered the Vols on a daily basis. The mood was grim as the Vols prepared for the final game, against Vanderbilt.

"I was determined that it wasn't going to be a circus atmosphere," Battle says. "When I decided to resign, I didn't want to talk about it. All I wanted to do was coach one last game, and do it the way I wanted to do it, and go beat the tar out of Vanderbilt. And not worry about it. So it wasn't a bad week at all."

"It was a time when you just wanted to be with the guy," says Mickey Marvin. "He was such a class person. I remember at a team meeting, Larry Seivers made an impassioned plea, saying something like, 'Fellows, we have to send Coach Battle out on top. He has to go out a winner.' We knew we had to do whatever it took to win that game."

Marvin, as mild-mannered a 280-pounder as one could imagine, let the gravity of the occasion get the best of him. In the first quarter, all the frustrations of the season came out at once. Marvin blocked a Vandy player to the ground and began hitting him with both fists. He was ejected and, once on the sidelines, incurred the wrath of Seivers, who screamed at him: "Mickey, you can't do that! We need you!"

Vandy refused to make it easy. Despite three lost fumbles and three interceptions, the Vols gave Battle a going-away present in the form of a 13-10 triumph—perhaps not the biggest victory of his career, but certainly as memorable as any of the other 58 on his record. In a subdued dressing room, Battle thanked his players at his final postgame conference.

"I told our players last Monday that there are a lot of definitions of class. But to me, class is when they run you out of town and make you look like you're leading the parade. And that's what I'd like to do and they helped me do that and I appreciate it."

And so Battle went out leading the parade. As his players gave him a victory ride toward the dressing room, many Tennessee fans who could get close enough reached up to shake his hand, and he obliged most of them. Not only that, but the Knoxville Quarterback Club presented him with a new Oldsmobile only a few days after his resignation.

On his final Sunday television show, Battle told Tennessee fans he hoped he hadn't messed up their program too much. "The years have all been good," he said, "and the good memories far outweigh the bad. I wanted very badly to bring a championship to the University of Tennessee, and wish I could have, for our players and coaches particularly. It wasn't to be. It was a situation where we had some good years, and we have struggled a little bit.

"There was a lot of game-by-game pressure, and in the end that was why I decided to resign. I said earlier that I wouldn't ever leave these players if I thought it was not in their best interest. But it got down to the point where our university people and fans were so divided. I think there needed to be unity and I couldn't unite them.

". . . I know I didn't accomplish what I wanted to accomplish. I have no apologies to make to anyone. I did the best I could."

For Bill and Eugenia Battle, there are no scars. "We have forgotten the bad things now," he says. "We both loved living in Knoxville. And, of course, I loved coaching at Tennessee."

Looking back at his seven-year tenure at a 1992 reunion of the 1972 team in Knoxville, Battle had this to say:

"I don't know how important this is in the great scheme of things, but there has been a lot of negative associated with my tenure at Tennessee. But to me there was so much positive, so many good things. Even after I resigned I was treated pretty well. You get a few people, a small minority of people like the moving van deal, and those few idiots affect how everybody thinks. That isn't how it should be. I don't have any complaints. I was treated fairly and I had an opportunity to do something that I wanted to do. I did the best I could with what I had.

"As it turned out, it wasn't a long-term deal. I had a lot of pride in it and put a lot of myself into it and gave a lot to Tennessee. And Tennessee gave a lot to me. So, I'd like for more positive to come out of it as history looks back at it. Some people say, 'Boy, I hate Tennessee for what they did to you.' But they really shouldn't feel that way. There were a few people who were idiots but they are everywhere. Alabama certainly has them. But there are great people here in Tennessee and that's why Tennessee has done as well as it has."

The Battle Era ended with quite a record: 59 wins, 22 losses and two ties. His winning percentage, .718, is 10th on the list of the SEC's all-time winningest coaches. Ironically, he ranks ahead of such prominent coaches as Vince Dooley of Georgia

(.715), Pat Dye (.711) and Shug Jordan (.675) of Auburn, Tennessee's Majors (.643), Doug Dickey (.641) of Tennessee and Florida and Tennessee's Bowden Wyatt (.622).

But there is no denying that from the dizzying heights of the 11-1 record in 1970 and the back-to-back 10-2 records in '71 and '72, an unmistakable pattern of mediocrity had set in.

Even though he won, Bill Battle was destined to lose because the shadow of Majors hovered over him, particularly during his last three seasons. "It didn't help that the next coach was standing in the wings," he said. "I understand how everyone always screams for the athletic director to fire the coach when things go badly. But there aren't many places where they already have the next coach picked like they did at Tennessee."

The following week, UT athletic director Bob Woodruff called Pitt AD Cas Myslinski to request permission to talk with Majors after the season-ending game with Penn State on Friday night.

On Thursday night, Majors and his wife Mary Lynn left a noisy pep rally on the Pitt campus in the company of two Sugar Bowl representatives. As they rode along, Mary Lynn remarked: "Look, it's starting to snow."

"Honey, that's not snow; it's sugar," said the Sugar Bowl's Charlie Gluck.

The following night, on the eve of the Vandy-Tennessee finale, Pittsburgh wrapped up a perfect regular season by beating Penn State 24-7 on national television. Locked in a 7-7 halftime tie, Pitt sprang a surprise on Joe Paterno and the Nittany Lions at the outset of the third period, simply by moving All-America tailback Tony Dorsett to fullback.

"Let's move Tony up to fullback and run that short trap up the middle," Majors had said. "He's so damn quick they'll never notice him and he'll be gone before they know it."

On Pitt's first play of the second half, the short trap up the middle, Dorsett lined up at fullback. He took the handoff and, sure enough, was gone before Penn State knew it, 40 yards to a touchdown that broke the game open. He went on to rush for 224 yards that night. A few days later, Dorsett won the Heisman Trophy that his coach had barely missed out on 20 years earlier.

In the tumult of the Pitt dressing room, the first question fired at Majors was, "Are you going to Tennessee?" He answered that he had not been contacted by any Tennessee officials, had no announcement to make and had planned no meeting.

In the days leading up to the Penn State game, it had been one rumor after another: Majors would announce his decision following the game; Majors had committed to Tennessee back in

October; Majors had signed with Tennessee two weeks earlier. When Battle had resigned on Monday of that week, the Pitt football office was swamped with telephone calls from reporters.

Because of the media crush, Majors had a recorded message played for callers to his office. It said, "I am not interested in discussing the Tennessee situation or any other situation until our regular season ends."

So with Penn State out of the way, all that remained for Johnny Majors was a date with Georgia in New Orleans and a national championship.

And a move to Knoxville.

CHAPTER 15

A COACH
NO MORE

As Johnny Majors came marching home, Bill Battle went marching off toward the land of milk and honey. Without question, the best thing ever to happen to Battle was to be forced out as Tennessee's head football coach, for he has since become a multi-millionaire. Once shed of the yoke of a job that had become a struggle, he happened into a situation and became prosperous beyond his wildest dreams. Today he is president and owner of an eminently successful collegiate licensing company.

After resigning the Tennessee job, Battle received several coaching offers, a couple of them very lucrative, others not quite so attractive. One came from Miami, at a time when that school had decided to upgrade its program to national prominence. Another came from Purdue, which had gone 31-43-1 under two coaches during the seven seasons that Battle had been 59-22-2 at Tennessee. But because of the trials and tribulations of the previous two or three years, Battle had soured on big-time coaching and its attendant pressures and pains. The yearning to coach was gone, at least for the time being.

"I had a chance to go down to Miami making twice as much as I had made at Tennessee," Battle says. Pete Elliott was the

Miami athletic director at the time and Battle had gotten to know him quite well. They had coached together in the 1974 Hula Bowl and Battle had hired Elliott's son as a graduate assistant coach.

Battle, preferring not to go to Miami and risk getting the press involved, met with the Miami representatives in the Atlanta airport. By that time, Battle had enjoyed about as much of the media as he could stand. He was offered the job and a juicy salary, but declined. The Hurricanes, who had had five head coaches in seven years, hired Lou Saban. He lasted two seasons and was succeeded by Howard Schnellenberger, who in turn was followed by Jimmy Johnson. Who knows but what Bill Battle, instead of Schnellenberger or Johnson, might have been the coach to guide Miami on its national championship ventures in the early 1980s?

Battle then visited Purdue, where Alex Agase had departed following an 18-25-1 record in four years. The job eventually went to Jim Young, who, ironically, would beat Tennessee in the 1979 Bluebonnet Bowl, Johnny Majors' first bowl trip at UT.

"I went up to Purdue," Battle says. "I still didn't know if I wanted to go back into coaching. I wanted to take some time off; I was tired and I was beat down and I wasn't ready to jump back into the fray. But I went up there anyway. I'm not sure if they offered me the job or not, but we talked salary and it was a whole lot more than I had been making at Tennessee.

"But I just really wasn't interested in doing it. I needed to let my head clear. I had worked my butt off ever since I had been out of college, but never really had thought anything about it. We didn't have time to think; at least I didn't. Because we were working 16- and 18-hour days, recruiting or coaching, or watching film or doing something all the time.

"I decided I needed some time. But I went up to Purdue to look at it and I didn't feel that good about the job. I just wasn't interested in going to Purdue; in fact I wasn't interested in going north of the Mason-Dixon line.

"The University of Oregon people came down to see me and I wasn't interested in that either. And then the people at Army tried to get me to come up there for a couple of years. The general at West Point, who had been a colonel when I was an assistant coach there in the mid-'60s, came back as athletic director and he tried to get me for a couple of years.

"I just wasn't ready. I wanted to see how other people lived. So I took nearly a year and looked at a lot of different things. I didn't know if I would be able to stay out of coaching, but I had to find out. I had a lot of friends and associates who had tried to get out and couldn't make the adjustment. But the thing I didn't want to do was bounce around and end up a 55-year-old assistant coach somewhere."

Battle looked toward the business world, checked out, as he says, "some neat things and some fly-by-night things." Finally an old friend, Larry Stripling, talked him into joining him in a business in Selma, Alabama.

"This thing in Selma came up and it looked like a small company about to explode. And, sure enough, it did. As things turned out, it was a great move for me."

The Selma operation was actually two companies, the larger of the two making aluminum windows.

"When I went there the two companies were doing about $10 million a year," Battle says. "Then they made a massive sale with Saudi Arabia. That really put us in another league. And we went to doing about $40 million and started buying other companies. So we ended up with 10 companies under a holding company umbrella doing $60 million. For me, it was a great learning experience in business education. I had been a biology major and a psychology minor and a football coach. You learn whatever you learn in coaching, but it was a great opportunity to get into profits and losses and balance sheets and see how companies are formed and a lot of things. Like what not to do as well as what to do."

"One day we decided to put together a package and take it to the Nicklaus people. This was before Nicklaus hooked up with MacGregor and we got exclusive rights to do Golden Bear gloves and socks and some other things. Larry bought another company while he was down there, Jack Nicklaus Eyewear. So we became licensees for Nicklaus and paid him about six or eight percent on everything we sold with the Golden Bear logo on the template of the glasses frame.

"We brought in another guy who understood licensing and he got the Disney characters to put on children's eyewear. Then he got the rights to Chris Evert Lloyd. So we had a men's line and a ladies' line and a children's line. We paid Nicklaus $60,000 that first year and I thought, 'Man, what a great way to make money!'

"We got invited to the Nicklaus partnership meeting and we went strutting in there thinking we were something big, paying him $60,000. The truth is we weren't even close to anybody else. They were paying hundreds of thousands and even millions."

The company continued to expand. Bear Bryant was an active member of the board and attended every board meeting. At one meeting, Bryant mentioned to Battle that he was about to change agents.

"This was in 1981 when, if he won nine games, he would break Amos Alonzo Stagg's record as football's all-time winningest coach," Battle recalled on a 1992 visit to Knoxville. "And I thought, 'Oh, man, here's Knute Rockne about to change agents.'

"When Coach Bryant said that, I thought, 'Well, we can do for Coach Bryant what our Golden Bear items have done for Nicklaus. Because that Golden Bear logo was generating a fortune for Nicklaus' heirs long after he's gone, I would think. So, that's how we got started doing it. We were successful with Coach Bryant and then people came in and started wanting to use Alabama's logos. Obviously, we didn't have the right to do that so one day in Tuscaloosa I went by the administration and they told me they were going to do something about licensing. They asked me to send them a proposal, which we did. We got Alabama's licensing business, and then we got a few other Southern schools."

Ironically, one of those schools was Tennessee. In 1983, barely six years after he had left Tennessee, Battle's Collegiate Concepts joined with International Collegiate Enterprises, a joint venture known as Collegiate Licensing Co. Together, they had 30 schools. By the fall of 1992, they had 125 colleges and universities, seven bowls and three conferences. By 1994, they had added seven more. There are only a handful of schools not under the Collegiate Licensing banner, choosing instead to do their own licensing.

By the early 1980s, Battle was vice chairman of the board of Circle S Industries, the holding company of the small conglomerate that included Disco Aluminum Window Co., Nelson Brantley Glass Co., American Fine Wire Co., Golden Eagle Enterprises, Otey Crisman Putter Co., and Jack Nicklaus Eyewear. He was also the president of Golden Eagle, the marketing company in the relatively new field of sports management and sports licensing.

By that time, Battle decided the business didn't belong in out-of-the-way Selma, Alabama. So he moved it to Atlanta, where today it is one of the nation's leading sports licensing operations.

Coaching no longer sang a siren song to Bill Battle. Seven years after he left UT, someone asked how much it would take to get him to pick up his whistle again.

"You haven't got that much," he answered.

Battle traveled extensively during the early days of his association with the aluminum window business. The author received a number of postcards, with felicitous messages, from the former coach as he traveled to places far removed from Knoxville, Tennessee, and Selma, Alabama.

From Warsaw, Poland: "Investigated and applied for the University of Poland football job, but was turned down. They said anyone dumb enough to coach at Tennessee for 11 years did not qualify."

From Saudi Arabia: "Applied for the football job at the University of Saudi Arabia. It is now being built and will be magnificent. I withdrew my application, however. If they catch you stealing they cut off your hand. If you commit murder, they cut off your head. Can you imagine what would happen if you went 6 and 5?"

From Athens, Greece, a card with a statue of an ancient Greek athlete on the front: "Finally found the perfect quarterback. Does not require expensive equipment either."

From Tokyo, a card featuring a group of sumo wrestlers: "Am really interested in the University of Tokyo job. I found the darndest prospects for an offensive line. Ray Trail would go crazy with these guys. They don't need much equipment either."

From Switzerland: "Applied for football job here but they have no team. Offered me the uphill skiing team job and recommended that I go back to Poland to recruit."

Tennessee football fans by the thousands may have deserted Bill Battle. His sense of humor had not.

Long after he got out of coaching, a lot of people continued to call Bill Battle "Coach." But their number began to dwindle as time passed. Half a dozen years after he left Tennessee, he said, "People ask me if they should call me 'Bill' or 'Coach' or 'Mr. Battle' or what."

Whereupon Battle, no doubt remembering his later days in Knoxville, always responded: "Call me whatever you want. I've been called a lot of things in my day."

CHAPTER 16

THE ENVELOPE

Somewhere in Henry Lee Parker's home there's a sealed envelope. It has gone unopened since the day in 1976 that University ot Pittsburgh chancellor Wesley Posvar handed it to Johnny Majors.

At the time, Parker was Majors' administrative assistant and, as now, one of his closest personal friends.

"John agonized over the decision about coming back to Tennessee," Parker said in a 1994 interview in his Knoxville home. "I remember when we were young coaches at Mississippi State in the early 1960s, his dream was always to someday be the head coach at Tennessee.

"At Pitt, we had just won the national championship and had the team that he felt could probably win it again the next season. But he wasn't going to let anyone else be the coach here. So I don't really think he ever came real close to not accepting the job."

After the Vanderbilt-Tennessee game on Saturday, November 27, Bob Woodruff and Bill Johnson had flown to Pittsburgh to discuss the UT job with Majors. They talked at length, hammering out details of a contract and a budget for assistant coaches. Majors flew to Knoxville the next day with Woodruff and

Johnson and met with the UT executive committee. He was officially offered the job but told them he would not make a decision until after returning to Pitt to confer with his family and Pitt officials.

"He really wrestled with a decision," Parker says. "We sat there at his home, he and Mary Lynn and my wife Martha Ann and I, until 2 or 3 o'clock in the morning. Finally, he said, 'Henry Lee, pick me up at 7 o'clock.' "

Parker picked him up on schedule. Majors told him to take him to chancellor Posvar's office. "Just go around the block and I'll be ready because I've made up my mind what I'm going to do." He didn't tell Parker what his decision was; Parker didn't ask.

Parker had to go two or three times around the block before Majors emerged from the building, carrying a large envelope, which he placed on the seat between them.

"Well, we're going to Tennessee," Majors announced.

"And what's in the envelope?" Parker asked.

"That's what they offered me to stay here. I don't know what's in that envelope and I don't want to know."

Parker is sure he still has the envelope. "I reckon it's here in my house somewhere. John doesn't have it. Maybe someday I'll find it and open it and I'll tell you what's in it."

Contrary to popular belief, Parker says, Majors took a pay cut to go to Tennessee. "That's one thing that irks me," he says. "A lot of people said John took the Tennessee job only because he would make more money. No way. He made more money at Pitt because he could do endorsements there, which he couldn't do here."

Majors had rescued destitute programs at both Iowa State and Pitt and in 10 years at those schools he had twice been named national coach of the year. He had developed a reputation that was right down Tennessee's alley.

Anyone in Big Orange Country who thought that the new coach would be anybody other than Johnny Majors was a candidate for the funny farm. In fact, to the disappointment of many fans, Majors had been passed over in favor of Bill Battle seven years earlier when Doug Dickey left Tennessee to take the Florida job. And now public demand stipulated that the new coach be no one but Johnny Majors. For UT officials to have even hinted that someone other than Majors would be considered would have invited a fan rebellion.

Because of intense media speculation, the announcement of Majors' appointment came one day earlier than planned. Finally, on Friday, December 3, 1976, as Majors was meeting with his Pitt players to inform them of his leaving, the news was released jointly in Pittsburgh and Knoxville.

As he bade them farewell, Majors was serenaded by some of his Pitt players with "Goodbye, Johnny" to the tune of "Goodnight, Ladies." In Tennessee, the fans were singing a different song: "When Johnny Comes Marching Home."

The following day there was a press conference in Knoxville, at which Majors would be introduced as the new Vol coach. As he began the introduction, UT chancellor Jack Reese set off widespread laughter when he said, "After an extensive nation-wide search . . ."

At that first press conference, Majors wasted no time in telling Vol faithful: "I'm a hard worker, not a miracle worker." He repeated it over and over, hoping to temper the frenzy that had overtaken Big Orange Country, an enthusiasm that knew no bounds. There were T-shirts and bumper stickers proclaiming: "A Majors Change in Tennessee Football."

No conquering hero ever experienced a warmer homecoming than Johnny Majors. Vol fans were clearly expecting him to pack his success in his suitcase and bring it to Knoxville. That sort of thing just doesn't happen, and no one was more aware of that than the new coach himself. Greeted by a standing ovation at a Vol basketball game in January 1977, Majors again told the fans, "I'm a hard worker, not a miracle worker."

He had been a hard worker at Pitt; his rpm's were on red line all the time. Majors has always been mad because they put only 24 hours in a day. Parker recalls early visits to fraternity houses and dormitories in an effort to get students out to the Panthers' games.

"They didn't even have majorettes in the band," Parker says, "so we had to change that.

"John got on his television show one night and he said, 'By the way, we're going to start something new next week. For this home game, we're going to give everybody that comes to the game a little red or green towel. When we've got the ball, that means GO, so the people with the green towels will wave them. When the other team has the ball, we're going to wave the red towels because that means STOP.'

"When I heard him saying that on television I wondered how the hell we were going to get all those little towels. He called me when he got home and said he guessed I had heard about the towels. And I asked him how in the world were we supposed to do that.

"He suggested that the Stop and Go stores in Pittsburgh would probably love to sponsor it. Trouble was the Stop and Go stores had already used all their advertising budget.

"I looked everywhere for red and green cloth. Finally we sent a truck to Altoona and I ended up with cotton cloth, wool cloth, corduroy cloth, every kind of cloth you can imagine. And we cut that stuff up into 12-inch lengths. Everybody who came into the fieldhouse we would make them go down there and cut some cloth. By hand. Anybody who came in—coaches, pro scouts, media, anybody—they had to cut awhile.

"The day of the game it rained like crazy but we passed out the towels. We had hoped the fans would keep them for future games but since they were so wet most of the people just threw them down. They cost us several thousand dollars."

Majors has a policy regarding squad meetings: if the meeting is scheduled for 10 o'clock, the doors are locked at 10 o'clock. You are either present or you are absent; there is no such thing as late. At his first squad meeting at Tennessee, every player was on time. But they learned a couple of Majors' rules right off. He does not allow his players to wear a cap or hat indoors and he does not allow them to dip snuff at squad meetings.

"At that first meeting, all the players were there but Coach Majors didn't say a word. Finally, he looked at me and said, 'Coach Parker, haven't you forgotten something?' And then it hit me just like that: some of the players were wearing caps. Coach Majors doesn't speak to people who wear caps indoors.

"And everybody who has ever worked for John Majors knew just who the head coach was. I always stood by him on the sidelines at games and one night I was giving a talk at Cleveland and somebody in the audience asked 'Does Coach Majors ever ask your opinion?' Well, of course, he asked my opinion about a lot of things. So I just laughed and said, 'Well, sometimes he asks me what we ought to do on fourth-and-one.' I was kidding, of course.

"Somehow John heard about that and he didn't waste any time getting me into his office. He said, 'Henry Lee, you and I are friends and I love you, but I am the damn head coach! And I make the decisions on what we call on fourth-and-one!' "

At a staff meeting early in his tenure at Tennessee, Majors was, as Parker describes it, "really shelling the corn," lighting into assistant coaches on some matter. "I want you to get after them like Grant went through Georgia," he said. "Coach, wait a minute," Parker interceded. "That was Sherman, not Grant." The meeting broke up while everybody had a long laugh.

The first time Majors met with Tennessee players after his appointment, he noticed that they were not nearly as big as the players he had had at Pitt. He was less than impressed with what he saw. "Have you ever seen anything so bad?" he asked Parker.

Majors was criticized by certain members of the media for being too negative about his players. "I'm not down on our players," he said. "They're ours and they're all we've got. I just believe in telling people what I think, how it is, not what they want to hear."

But fans thought what they wanted to think, Majors' grievings notwithstanding. There was a big increase in season ticket sales. The first spring game of the Majors Era drew a record crowd of 26,300. Knoxville area hotels and motels were taking reservations for Saturdays in the fall.

People wondered if Majors had changed.

"I'm still the same guy from Huntland who went to Tennessee to play football almost 25 years ago," he said. "I am a man in a fishbowl. Every move I make will be watched. This one will win the game; that one will win the championship. That's the way I'll be watched. But I'm not going to panic. It's going to take patience, perhaps more patience that I have. But I'm going to do the job my way.

"I'll step on some toes. I hope not, because it's not my nature to offend people. But I am going to do what I think is best for the players and the team. That way, I can go home at night and sleep.

"If we have quick progress, it will be great. If we have slow progress, my friends will still be my friends. I can still visit them in their homes; I can still go bird hunting with them."

Shortly after moving into his new job in Knoxville, Majors found himself at the opposite end of the spectrum from which he had just come. Here he was, the national championship coach and national coach of the year speaking at an athletic awards banquet at Trousdale County High School in Hartsville, Tennessee, population 2500. He later signed two players off that Trousdale County team, tight end Reggie Harper and linebacker Donnie Oldham.

Harper was probably the star signee of Majors' first recruiting class, a blend of those previously pledged to the Battle staff and a dozen or so persuaded to the Tennessee cause by the Majors staff. Harper went on to letter for four years and make All-Southeastern Conference. Oldham lettered in 1977, then fell victim to a knee injury.

While it is indisputable that Tennessee's stock of football talent had sunk to an alarming level, what is abundantly clear is that Majors did inherit some quality athletes. Twelve members of his first UT squad, including two freshmen, went on to accumulate no less than 79 years in the National Football League: Tim Irwin, Brian Ingram, Roland James, Craig Colquitt, Jeff Moore,

Craig Puki, Pat Ryan, Robert Shaw, Danny Spradlin, Jesse Turnbow, Brad White and Greg Gaines.

Irwin was one of the elder statesmen of the NFL in 1994, a veteran of more than a dozen years as an offensive tackle with the Minnesota Vikings. His introduction to Tennessee football in 1976 was a memorable one, painful though it was.

In those days, a picnic for the UT squad at the Lambert Farm in Blount County was the unofficial start of another season.

"Players always looked forward to that picnic," he says, "because it kicked off the season and there was always some great food. One of the favorites was a big bowl of boiled shrimp, already peeled and all. Players would just take that stuff by the handfuls. The older players had talked about how great the shrimp were.

"We went over in buses and I was sitting by big Mickey Marvin on the way over and he kept telling me about the shrimp. I was a freshman and he was a senior and he told me to be sure and be near the front of the line because the shrimp wouldn't last long.

"When they opened the bus doors it was like a herd of wild elephants heading for that shrimp. I was in front, not wanting to miss anything. I was wearing sandals and one of them got hooked on a tree root sticking up and down I went. Mickey was right behind me and he just came right dead over the top of me, not even slowing down, to get to that shrimp. So did some other players. By the time I got there, the shrimp was gone and my toe was a bloody mess. It was broken."

Irwin had signed with Tennessee a year before, Bill Battle's last season as head coach. He decided once and for all to become a Vol after watching Vanderbilt whip Tennessee 17-14 in 1975, an unusual twist because Vandy had been one of three schools he had considered.

"That day, watching Tennessee lose to Vandy, I wanted to come to Tennessee so bad I could taste it. I went in and told Coach Battle the next day that it had made me sick to see Tennessee lose to Vandy and that I wanted to come to Tennessee."

So he signed on with the Vols, an ungainly 6-7, 255-pounder who had been a tight end and nose guard at Knoxville's Central High School. If the broken toe at the picnic had been an unpleasant experience, he hadn't seen anything yet.

As a freshman, he got to hold the blocking dummies for the varsity offensive linemen and it was Irwin's lot to have to hold one for Marvin, a 290-pound All-Southeastern Conference performer and his buddy from the shrimp/broken toe episode.

"When Mickey hit that bag, he would just lift me right off the ground and drive me back several yards," Irwin says. "He took all the hide off the back of my knuckles where my hands would go back into my chest trying to hold that bag. One day he drove me and the blocking dummy into the back side of a seven-man blocking sled and put a pretty good gash on my back. I'll never forget holding those dummies for him; it was one of the worst experiences of my life."

It seemed that whenever Irwin wasn't going through the blocking dummy bit with Marvin, he was fighting somebody on the practice field. "The first couple of years at UT, I fought with just about everybody. I had some good fights with Kim Logan and Jesse Turnbow and Jim Woofter, and Woofter was as peaceful a guy as you'd ever meet. And I had some good ones with Craig Puki, the linebacker. His favorite trick would be when he was wearing a red X that meant he was an injured player, he would sneak up behind you and just knock the hell out of you. He was real bad about that."

Puki's last season was 1979, Irwin's 1980. But their confrontations didn't end on the practice field in Knoxville. Their paths would cross again in the NFL — Puki as a linebacker with the San Francisco 49ers and St. Louis Cardinals and Irwin as an offensive tackle with the Vikings.

THE FOURTH QUARTER

The coaches called it The Fourth Quarter. The players called it something less printable.

By whatever name, the punishing winter conditioning program instituted by Johnny Majors was the first step in shaping the Tennessee football squad of 1977.

In a way, the drills conducted in the athletic "bubble" where the football facility now stands were not a great deal different than those implemented by Doug Dickey beneath the old Section X stands at Neyland Stadium when he arrived at Tennessee 13 years earlier. There were cleaner, more pleasant surroundings, to be sure, but the workouts were long and demanding. And most of the players hated every minute of them.

"That was the toughest physical thing I've ever been through, including 13 years in the National Football League," says Tim Irwin. "Coach (Joe) Avezzano and Coach (Bobby) Roper were the two bad boys of those workouts, along with Coach Majors. They seemed to take a real delight in putting us through it.

"I remember how excited this whole city was when Coach Majors came back. They were playing 'When Johnny Comes Marching Home Again' and all that stuff. Then we met Coach Majors and his staff and they darn near killed us that winter. They didn't wait until spring. I believe they tried to run off as many guys as they could. I started dreading going into that bubble with them as soon as I woke up each day.

"Along about an hour before time to go to the bubble, you could go down through that dorm and see everybody just sitting on the edge of their bed, not saying anything, just worrying. Because they knew what they were getting ready to do. Sometimes it would be an hour and a half of wrestling, mat drills, jumping rope and running. Never stopping the whole time you were in there. When you came out you were just about dead."

John Chavis also recalls the toil, the strain, the sweat. "It was the most grueling thing I've ever been a part of," he says. "There is no question that it weeded out some of the people who were not committed to the program. But there weren't more than probably five or six guys who dropped out because, in a way, the players were excited and looking forward to the new coaching regime."

Chavis, who would join Majors' UT coaching staff 12 years later, went into the winter conditioning program at his normal weight of 226 pounds; he came out weighing 198. But he came out in the best physical condition of his life.

The conditioning workouts consisted of a great deal of running, endurance training, rope jumping, wrestling, agility drills, and hurdles. There were also weight lifting sessions. Based on the results of the fourth quarters of the 1977 season, the Fourth Quarter workouts were a success. Only three teams outscored the Vols in the fourth quarter that season—Florida, Mississippi and Kentucky. Florida and Kentucky won with their fourth quarter superiority.

If anything was more gruelling than the winter conditioning program of 1977, it was spring practice 1977, if for no other reason than the length of some of the sessions. The NCAA had no time restrictions on practices in those days, so a workout scheduled for two hours could easily last three hours or more. "These players simply don't know how to practice," said Professor Majors as he began Football 101 on the UT campus.

At one session, the offensive team was having an unusually difficult day. An irritated Majors shouted: "All right, nobody leaves this field until we score." Forty-seven plays later the offense finally made it to the end zone. The story tells us that the defensive players either weren't very smart or were terribly dedicated.

One of the workouts backfired on Avezzano, the offensive line coach.

"Coach Avezzano had been working us like dogs," Irwin says. "And nothing we did was good enough to please him. He was griping that no linemen were getting downfield ahead of the ball carriers. Finally, he told us to be in the bubble at 6 o'clock the next morning in full pads. That's when we were running the Burma Road drills, a course laid out with blocking dummies. We would do the Burma Road until nobody could go any more.

"Now I don't know for sure who alerted one of the local sportswriters, but I would bet it was Charlton Webb. Anyway, somebody notified him and it came out in the paper what we had been doing. And, as it turned out, they had to count it as one of our 20 spring practice sessions. But it eliminated that 6 o'clock bull."

Player fights became commonplace during spring practice, probably the byproduct of the intense competition for playing time. "It was the most fighting I've ever seen in a football program," says Chavis, who built quite a reputation as a scrapper of the first order. "There would be a fight here, a fight there, but the coaches did a good job of keeping it under control. I just believe that it was a healthy type of competition because the minute we walked off the field we were all friends again."

Danny "Pert" Jenkins, a defensive tackle from Elizabethton, was one of the defensive standouts of Majors' first team and a favorite of the head coach. He was listed at 220 pounds but weighed 205 at most and was overmatched physically every time he took the field. A couple of teammates say he once challenged giant tackle Tim Irwin during that first spring. He went charging into an offensive huddle, all 205 pounds of him, to accuse Irwin of holding him on the previous play. He is supposed to have grabbed Irwin's facemask and screamed, "You —— - ——, if you hold me again, I'll kill you!" Irwin, claiming he had more practice field fights than he can remember, says he doesn't recall a confrontation with Jenkins.

The fans turned out nearly 85,000 strong for Majors' coaching debut at Neyland Stadium. It was the Vols vs. California in the '77 season opener and the Bears had a bit of an edge in the person of assistant coach Fred Malone, who had been on Battle's Tennessee staff the year before. While his familiarity with the Vol personnel might have been a plus for Cal, the Bears were certainly a better team to begin with, and they spoiled the homecoming of the All-America tailback of the mid-1950s, 27-17.

A fumbled punt by freshman Junior Reid, one of Majors' first recruits, cost the Vols dearly. The Bears took over at the UT 14 and scored a decisive touchdown four plays later. Majors consoled Reid, probably remembering a fumble of his own in the 1957 Sugar Bowl game that resulted in a 13-7 loss to Baylor.

Tennessee notched its first victory under Majors, a 24-18 win over a weak Boston College team that had bowed to Texas 44-0 the week before. Lyonel Stewart, a one-time walk on linebacker, wrapped himself around an onsides kick after BC's last touchdown, and explained after the game, "I had it and they weren't going to get it!"

The Vols stumped their toe against Auburn. Trailing 14-12, they had the ball at the Tiger 1 to begin the fourth period but lost a fumble. Jimmy Gaylor's 35-yard field goal try failed as time ran out.

Pat Ryan, a fifth-year senior who had seen very little action in an injury-plagued career, started the first three games at quarterback, then gave way to Jimmy Streater, a stringbean, scrambling sophomore billed as Tennessee's quarterback of the future. Ryan had earned the starting job in '75 but suffered a broken collarbone a week before the opener and missed the season. In '76, he watched from the bench as Randy Wallace ran the show; Ryan's stats that year show one pass attempted and three rushes for 12 yards. Now in '77, he wound up playing second fiddle to Streater, seeing only enough action to attempt 65 passes.

Ryan was an outstanding dropback passer; otherwise he wouldn't have played 12 seasons with the NFL's New York Jets. But at Tennessee he never was given the opportunity to strut his stuff as a passer because the Vols were using offenses more suited to a running quarterback, which Ryan was not. They ran the veer in '75, for instance, then switched to the wishbone in '76, again with Wallace.

There were few bright spots in that 1977 season. Craig Colquitt emerged as an outstanding punter, and he was the only Vol to make the Associated Press All-Southeastern Conference team at season's end. That was one of the few times that Tennessee has failed to land a player at one of the 22 regular playing positions. Colquitt's 52-yard average was instrumental in an easy 41-10 triumph over Oregon State. Georgia Tech thumped the error-plagued Vols 24-8 without attempting so much as one single pass. At a squad meeting the following day, when the players and coaches were to review the game film, the coaches threw the film on a table, said "Here, you all watch this, we're leaving," and walked out of the room.

As expected, Alabama made it seven in a row over Tennessee 24-10, but the Big Orange defense did itself proud that day. It is noteworthy that one of the rarest of penalties helped lead to Tennessee's defeat. In the third quarter, Alabama punted, but the officials ruled that a Vol had clipped while the punt was in the air. Instead of giving the Vols the ball and a 15-yard penalty, the rule specified that possession revert to Alabama and the Tide went on to score another touchdown for a 24-3 lead. The rare call has happened only twice in games involving Tennessee, both at Birmingham's Legion Field. The first one came in the Vol-Auburn game in 1972.

One of Tennessee's infrequent trips to Gainesville, Florida, was memorable for three reasons: a frightening brush with a speeding train, an ugly encounter at game's end and a record run by the Vols' Kelsey Finch.

The near-tragedy occurred as the team and official party made their way to the stadium on game day. They were making the 40-mile trip from their Silver Springs motel to Gainesville aboard three chartered buses. About halfway to Gainesville, as they traveled along State Route 315, they came to an unguarded Seaboard Coast Line railroad track.

Only a few people on the buses noticed that a fast-moving train was approaching, but not the Florida State trooper escorting the convoy nor the driver of the front bus. They made it across the tracks without incident. The driver of the second bus, which carried defensive players, managed to bring his coach to a sudden stop just a few feet short of the tracks as the train came roaring by. Bus No. 3, with members of the official party and a few players aboard, also stopped.

Associate athletic director Gus Manning, who was riding with the state trooper, as has always been his custom at out-of-town games, said he and the trooper never saw the train approaching. They didn't realize there had been a near-tragedy until they arrived at the stadium.

But Majors sure did. He was riding in the right front seat of the lead bus and looked up to see the train fast approaching. "I was reading at the time and I glanced up and saw this train coming lickety-split. It was right on us. We probably didn't miss getting hit by more than two seconds. I remember thinking that the No. 2 bus had been destroyed; there was no doubt in my mind."

Needless to say, Majors was a bit perturbed that the trooper chose to drive through the crossing. "It was dumb, absolutely ridiculous. It was stupid on the part of the trooper. I was absolutely astounded that he would do such a thing and I let him know it when we got to the stadium."

As for the game itself, Tennessee took favored Florida down to the wire before the Gators staged a long drive that set up a go-ahead field goal with two minutes to play. The Vols, unable to move, ran out of downs at their own 42. The Gators, leading 20-17 with 46 seconds left, struck for a touchdown, quarterback Terry LeCount going 36 yards and halfback Tony Green 6.

After the kickoff, Tennessee ran one more play and fumbled, Florida recovering at the UT 33, 13 seconds to go. Green got 15 yards. Three seconds remaining. Timeout, Florida. Then LeCount hit Wes Chandler in the end zone, but he was ruled beyond the end line.

Florida's strategy was more than backup Vol quarterback Joe Hough could take over on the sideline. Hough, a battler of some distinction, became more incensed with each pass and announced before the final play: "If that so-and-so throws the ball again I'm going after him." It has always been assumed that he was referring to QB LeCount and not coach Doug Dickey on the opposite sideline.

In any event, on the final play LeCount went for the end zone — and Hough went for LeCount. The Vols lost their cool, players from both teams poured onto the field and an ugly brawl raged for several minutes, at times threatening to spread into the stands.

After the game, LeCount said the controversial last play was supposed to be a pass-run option. "I guess they meant for me to run it," he said, "but I saw Wes Chandler open. We've been together so much we sometimes do things naturally."

When Hough went onto the field, he had words with Florida offensive line coach Kim Helton, who had appeared to call for the timeout with three seconds remaining. LeCount conferred with Dickey on the sidelines before firing the ball to Chandler.

Helton was decked during the fracas. Several Vols claim they saw Helton gesturing "throw it, throw it" before LeCount's last pass. Dickey later said he told LeCount to run out the clock but two Fort Lauderdale photographers near the Gator bench said Florida coaches called the pass play.

"Hough went clear across the field right toward Helton and that seemed to start the fight," said Alan Williams, Florida's punter that day and later a Knoxville television personality. "It was some fight, too. There must have been four or five piles of players beating the heck out of each other. There were a lot of bloody noses. I remember Majors and Dickey were in the middle of the field trying to separate the players."

Williams supports Dickey's contention that he didn't call either the timeout or the pass play. "It wasn't Dickey," he said. "He didn't know anything about it. He was as surprised as anybody. I think Helton was behind the whole thing. He was standing beside me on the sideline and I noticed him giving signals. It looked like he was trying to get some word to LeCount. Then, when the pass was ruled incomplete, he seemed extremely disappointed."

Although he declined to elaborate on the final play, Majors was visibly annoyed. "I don't know who had the idea of that last pass, but if they need it that badly, God speed. Our day will come."

Senior tackle Pert Jenkins, who played very little because of a leg injury, let his feelings be known. "Coach Majors told us not to pop off but I have one comment," he said. "I used to have a lot of respect for Coach Dickey. He recruited me five years ago. Now I know how Alabama wins the championship even when Florida has better players."

Jenkins had some battle scars from the fight, but claimed innocence. "I was just walking away. Some guy passed me going in the other direction, turned around and smashed my nose and split my lip."

"I told everybody that Tennessee would be a fighting team," Dickey said. "They proved that right up until five minutes after the game."

On the same day that Vols and Gators were trading punches in Florida, Knoxville heavyweight boxer Big John Tate was throwing some of his own in Las Vegas. Big John, who would go on to win the world heavyweight title, K.O.'d Lou Esa—a Floridian—for the sixth victory of his brief career.

Almost overshadowed by the postgame melee was a 99-yard touchdown run by Finch, the longest run in Tennessee history. The Vols, backed up to their own goal in the third period, gave the ball to Finch on a simple off-tackle play, hoping to gain enough yardage to give punter Colquitt room to kick from the end zone.

Once through the line, though, Finch found himself all but alone; only defensive back Chuck Hatch had a shot at him but he missed at about the Florida 30. He cut back twice as his motor began to slow. He very nearly ran out of gas along the way but managed to traverse the 99 yards without falling on his face. As he began his run, Florida fans were shouting, "Hold that line!"

After he finished, they were shouting, "Block that kick!" Unless they decide someday to lengthen the playing field, Finch's record will never be broken because it is statistically impossible to have a run from scrimmage longer than 99 yards.

After a homecoming victory over Memphis State came a 43-14 loss to Ole Miss that Tennessee fans would just as soon not remember. For one thing, it assured a losing season for the first time since 1964. For another, it was the most points scored on Tennessee since 1947. All in all, it was a miserable day.

Tennessee fumbled the opening kickoff, the Rebels converted the bobble into a touchdown and things got progressively worse for the Vols. Over on the sideline, Majors turned to administrative assistant Henry Lee Parker and asked, "Henry Lee, what the hell can we do?" Parker replied: "John, you see that big old clock at the end of the field? Just hope that son of a gun hurries. That's our only hope."

The Vols went on to lose 21-17 at Lexington to one of Kentucky's greatest teams ever. So it remained for Vanderbilt to serve up Tennessee's first Southeastern Conference victory under Majors.

It is worth noting that as the Vols dismantled Vandy that day, 42-7, they were outfitted in all-orange uniforms for the first time ever, courtesy of Johnny Majors. When the Vols took to the field for pregame warmups wearing the all-orange outfits, the crowd of 83,146 was all abuzz.

Chavis remembers how stunned the players were when they got off their buses and went to the locker room. "There were those orange pants laid out at each locker," he says. "It really created some excitement for us. I remember that after we dressed, Craig Puki and I went through a helmet-butting like you see on television nowadays. We just stood there with our hands on each other's shoulders, butting heads and screaming. We were pretty fired up; the intensity level was really something."

Chavis says he didn't like the idea of losing to Vanderbilt, not then, not now. "When we lost to them in '75 it left a bad taste in my mouth. I was from out of state (South Carolina) but I learned very early here at Tennessee that you want to whip Vanderbilt every time you get the opportunity. It was my misfortune to be on a team that lost to Vanderbilt ('75). That was certainly something I didn't forget about right away; in fact I've never forgotten about it."

Chavis, who came to Tennessee in 1975 from Dillon, S.C., without a scholarship, became the first walk on to earn a scholarship under Majors, being awarded one after the Florida game of '77. Although he weighed a relatively light 226, he was the heaviest of the Vols' down linemen that season. Brad White, the other tackle, was 6-3 and 224 and middle guard Jim Noonan 5-9 and 206.

The week after the Vols beat Vanderbilt, Majors received a letter from Bobby Harrison, a World War II fighter pilot and close friend from Lynchburg. "In the letter, he said that '77 team reminded him of a passage from a sermon he had heard from Tom Majors, my great-uncle and a Methodist preacher. Uncle Tom had said, 'It's better to be one foot from hell heading away from it than to be a hundred miles away heading toward it.' "

From the shambles of a 4-7 season, two games worse than Battle's farewell campaign, came unmistakable evidence that Tennessee football under Majors would receive unbridled support from its legion of fans. Although the season was not very good when judged by wins and losses, it was most certainly an artistic success at the box office. The fans came in record numbers, an average of 83,283 per game, putting Tennessee third in the nation in attendance behind Michigan and Ohio State and causing UT officials to take a look at expanding Neyland Stadium.

Despite the disappointments of his maiden season, Majors was upbeat. "I've never been more encouraged about Tennessee football," he declared. "The most positive memory of this past season to my family and me was the support element. The fans stayed with us all the way. Their support will be a big factor in putting Tennessee back on top."

Truer words were never spoken. All through Majors' tenure, and into that of Phillip Fulmer, Tennessee has been among the nation's attendance leaders, year in and year out.

Seventeen years later, Majors looks back at the job facing him when he arrived in Knoxville thusly: "It was like having a runaway truck and trying to stop it with your hands. Like an 18-wheeler going down a mountain and having to get it slowed down and then stopped and finally getting it turned around and headed back uphill."

CHAPTER 17

THE CLASS
OF '78

Tennessee's 1977 season hardly set off dancing in the streets of Knoxville. But nobody felt the sting of a 4-7 record more than Johnny Majors. As a competitor, he knows few equals. So it was not surprising that he launched an immense recruiting campaign that fall and winter.

Vol recruiters fanned out in all directions, but concentrated their efforts in talent-rich Georgia, which had already been a happy hunting ground. Nine of the 29 players signed hailed from the Peach State, more than twice as many as were signed from Tennessee. Signees came from 10 other states: Florida, Ohio, Kentucky, North Carolina, Michigan, Virginia, California, New Jersey, Alabama and Illinois.

The result was the most ballyhooed recruiting class ever assembled in Knoxville, the Class of 1978. Its star attraction was Lee Otis Burton, a strapping 6-6, 230-pound defensive tackle from Americus, Georgia, a *Parade* magazine All-American. He had all the tools—unusual strength, great quickness, exciting speed, a passion for football, and a fierce desire to excel.

If ever a Tennessee lineman wore a "can't-miss" label, it was Lee Otis Burton. His would become a household name in Big Orange Country, but he was struck down by a mysterious malady after that first year and his career ended almost before it began.

There were five other *Parade* All-Americans: running back Glenn Ford from Greensboro, North Carolina; lineman John Gorence from Detroit; lineman Kenny Jones of Nashville; running back Dennis Mahan from Martinsville, Virginia, that state's all-time scoring champion; and lineman Lee North from Tucker, Georgia, son of former Georgia Tech player Bobby North.

Never before had Tennessee rounded up such a collection of freshman talent. Once the celebrated recruits were signed on the dotted line, and Tennessee fans were subsequently beside themselves, Majors threw some cold water on their rosy expectations. He pointed out that the 1978 team would be shaped in the spring, at least four months before any of the freshmen would put on an orange uniform.

Unfortunately, as is the case in most recruiting classes, many of the signees never panned out, were never really heard from again once news of their signings appeared in headlines; players like Al Wollschlaeger of Chicago, receiver Buck Walker of Atlanta, lineman Jim McCarthy of Verona, New Jersey, and back Paul Lee of Simi Valley, California. Lineman Tim Daniels, a giant tackle from Massillon, Ohio, lettered one year and became a medical casualty, a victim of cancer, and had to give up football. All told, 11 of the 29 signees never lettered. Five of them lettered only one year.

Six of them made solid contributions, lettering all four years: Jones, North, running back James Berry, wide receiver Anthony Hancock, linebacker Lemont Holt Jeffers, and kicker John Warren. Tight end Mike "Go" Cofer, running back Terry Daniels, wide receiver Mike Miller and defensive back Mike Terry were three-year lettermen.

Cofer picked up the nickname "Go" a year later when a second Mike Cofer, a linebacker from Knoxville Rule High, signed with the Vols; he was nicknamed "Stop." Go was for offense, Stop for defense.

One of the questions on a Sports Information Department freshman questionnaire that year asked: "What person, living or dead, do you most admire?" One of the Fabulous Frosh, who shall remain anonymous here, answered, "Living." He went on to list his hobbies as "Hurting and fishing."

Another player, answering a question that asked what kind of defense his high school team used, wrote "6-3-2-2." Is it any wonder that his high school team had won a state championship the year before?

Hancock was recruited as a running back, but switched to wide receiver because his arrival in Big Orange Country happened to coincide with that of a number of acclaimed running backs. His resume did not include All-American designation, not even all-state; all-city was the best he could do. He was the last of the 29 players Tennessee signed that year. As it turned out, however, moving to wideout was probably a blessing, because he became the No. 1 NFL draft choice of the Kansas City Chiefs in the 1982 NFL draft.

He had been heavily recruited by Ohio, Michigan, Penn State and Tennessee. Being from Cleveland, he had grown up an Ohio State fan. And being a running back, he had been impressed that Buckeye tailback Archie Griffin had won the Heisman Trophy not once, but twice, 1974-75.

Very few things in Hancock's life had an impact like what happened to him on February 15, 1978, national signing day. Even though he had committed to Tennessee, he was visited that day by not only Majors, but also Ohio State coach Woody Hayes, who battled Majors down to the wire. In the end, Tennessee's highly successful track program might have been the difference. Hancock was an outstanding hurdler and Stan Huntsman's Vol program appealed to him.

"I had grown up a Buckeye fan," Hancock says, "and I had wanted to be a Buckeye. But I thought about what Coach Majors had done, about Tony Dorsett winning the Heisman Trophy and Pitt winning the national championship. I thought Tennessee would be a great opportunity to play sooner. So I had already told Coach Hayes that I was going to Tennessee."

As classes were changing at John Hay High School, Hancock saw Hayes and assistant John Hicks coming toward him in the hallway. He says it was like the parting of the Red Sea, students quickly moving out of the way as Hayes and Hicks approached. He glanced the other way. There came Majors and assistant coach Bob Harrison.

"There I was, a 17-year-old high school kid, and there were two coaching legends coming at me from different sides. I've never been so nervous."

Hicks, an All-America tackle for the Buckeyes in 1973, and Hayes made one last pitch for Anthony to stay in Ohio. But he signed that night with Majors and Harrison.

Hancock arrived in Knoxville with impressive credentials; he had averaged 7 yards per carry as a senior. But he found that the other freshman running backs weren't exactly chopped liver. Mahan had scored an astounding 96 touchdowns. Daniels had averaged 9.4 yards and Berry 8.4. Ford could do it all as a running back, pass receiver and kick returner. Mike Miller, who like Hancock would wind up a receiver, had 9.5 speed in the 100-yard dash.

Hancock got lost in the shuffle, stuck on the scout team for Tennessee's first few games. Disillusioned, he told Harrison, who had recruited him, that he wanted to go home. Harrison, noting that an already-thin receiving corps had lost Robert Malone and Jeff Moore to injury, offered Hancock a chance to play wideout. He took it.

His first varsity play was right out of a storybook, against Alabama at Neyland Stadium.

"I was on the sideline, my first time to dress out," he remembers. "It was all new to me. With eight or nine minutes to go in the game we were behind 30-3. One of the coaches said, 'Hancock, get ready to go in.' And I thought, 'What? Go in against Alabama and against coach Bear Bryant?'

The first thing Hancock did was pull a Thurman Thomas—he couldn't find his headgear. So he borrowed roommates Kenny Jones' helmet and raced onto the field. The only problem was that Jones was a defensive lineman and his helmet was outfitted with all sorts of vertical and horizontal bars on the face mask, so that Hancock could hardly see out.

"Here I was in my first collegiate game, against Alabama and Bear Bryant, wearing a defensive lineman's helmet. I'm in the huddle trying to get the chin strap fastened but the helmet is so big it's turning on my head. Jimmy Streater called the play, a pass to me. I'm supposed to catch a pass against Alabama and coach Bear Bryant.

"I lined up out wide and then I couldn't remember: is it two steps up and one step back, or is it one step up and two steps back? Whatever I did worked because I gained 19 yards on my first collegiate pass."

Streater suffered a hip injury shortly afterward and was relieved by one-time walk on David Rudder, who directed two fourth-quarter scoring marches and completed 11 of 12 passes, two for touchdowns. He hit a school record 11 in a row at one stretch.

The 1978 season had started on the same note as 1977—the Vols losing to a West Coast team. This time it was UCLA, and the Bruins pinned a 13-0 shutout on the Vols while the celebrated Tennessee freshmen watched from the bench. Then it was another dish of West Coast football, Oregon State. The Beavers had a 13-0 lead and the game in the bag with five minutes to go, but hold on! Tennessee wasn't dead.

Following an interference call against Oregon State, Streater ran in from the 2 to make it 13-7. After the Vols recovered a fumble seconds later, Streater hooked up with Jeff Moore on a 44-yard touchdown pass. Moore was in the clear because the Beavers had only 10 men on the field; the free safety who should have covered him failed to reenter the game. The Vols had scored 13 points in a 20-second span to tie at 13-all but Alan Duncan's extra point try that would have won the game was wide to the right.

Auburn ran wild in the first half and swept on to a 29-10 victory at Birmingham, where Tennessee hadn't won since 1969. In making it three losses in a row for the Vols, the Tigers outgained UT 224 yards to 32 in the first half behind future NFL stars James Brooks and Joe Cribbs. Army was no match for the Vols, as usual, bowing 31-13 and giving Majors an opportunity to see some of his freshman players under fire for the first time.

Following the loss to Alabama, Rudder drew the starting QB assignment against Mississippi State, a reward for his sparkling relief performance against the Tide. Quarterback David Marler and receiver Mardye McDole were more than the UT defense could handle in a 34-21 State victory. It was over by halftime, at which juncture the Bulldogs led 28-3.

So six games into Majors' second season, Tennessee was 1-4-1, even worse than the 2-4 record at the same point of the '77 campaign. But there were signs of improvement, most notably in the strong finishes in the losses to Alabama and Mississippi State.

The improvement showed dramatically the next week when Tennessee scored on its first play of the game against Duke. Streater faked a handoff and passed 66 yards to Jeff Moore and the Vols, getting solid performances from all hands, waltzed to a 34-0 triumph.

Then Tennesseee headed for South Bend, Indiana, and the long-awaited first match with Notre Dame, quarterbacked by none other than Joe Montana. The Vols led 7-6 at the half and their supporters, ever-hopeful but realistic, kept fearing the roof was going to fall in. And sure enough, it did. The kicking game, that part of football in which Majors takes immeasurable pride, got them in trouble and they went on to lose 31-14. The Irish blocked a punt, recovered a fumble and kept Tennessee bottled up. The result was two touchdowns and a field goal for 18 points in the third period and a commanding 24-7 lead.

The highlight of the day for Tennessee was an extraordinary play by Burton, the heralded defensive freshman tackle who had by this time earned a starting berth. Irish star Vagas Ferguson hit at left end and appeared headed for a touchdown. Burton overtook him 41 yards downfield. The Tennessee people, Majors included, knew at that moment that here was a player of uncommon ability.

If Tennesseans worried that the Vols might have a hangover the following week against Ole Miss, their fears seemed well founded by halftime, with the Rebels leading 17-7. The second half was a horse of another color, Tennessee outscoring the Rebs 34-0 to post a 41-17 win. Roland James had a 90-yard interception return for a TD, fourth longest in UT history.

Alan Duncan, whose missed PAT had cost the Vols a victory over Oregon State, kicked five field goals to provide the 15-point margin in a 29-14 victory that ended a two-game losing streak to Kentucky. The Vols routed Vandy for the second year in a row, this time by 41-15, as Streater established a new UT record for total offense in a season, 2,011 yards.

With the closing streak of three impressive victories, observers were beginning to look at Tennessee as a pretty good team. Even Majors sounded optimistic: "I think we have turned the corner," he told reporters after the game. "We are a good football team."

The whirlwind finish made it a 5-5-1 season, quite good considering the horrible 1-4-1 start. But most important, the Vols appeared to have momentum on their side. And fans were smiling again in Big Orange Country.

The postscript to the 1978 season is that the Lee Otis Burton story, which had such a marvelous beginning, had a sad ending, at least as far as football was concerned. His development had been slowed by a wrist injury and ankle sprain early that fall and he didn't see action until the third game, against Auburn. Still he was in on 57 tackles in nine games. By the time spring practice 1979 rolled around, he was struck with a mysterious ailment, which caused him to lose strength and to lose some of his coordination. It was initially described as "a chemical imbalance" and "a problem of the central nervous system." UT trainer Mike Rollo says the biggest problem Burton had was with coordination. "Even his walking was unsteady. He just couldn't carry out coordinated activities."

Guillain-Barre syndrome, a rare but serious neurological disorder, was the first preliminary diagnosis. For a time multiple sclerosis was suspected. Burton gave it the old college try as the 1979 season got underway. He got in for only five plays against Utah in the second game of the season. Then it was all over. Two months later, he was sent to Duke University Medical Center for tests. Of all the many doctors who examined him, no one could come up with either a reason for the illness or a definitive diagnosis. There were conflicting diagnoses, in fact.

By the spring of 1980, a resumption of Burton's football career was all but out of the question. But he was determined to try. In the summer of 1981, before what would have been Lee Otis' senior season and more than two years after he first became ill, UT trainer Tim Kerin and a group of doctors put him through some agility workouts. Actually, the doctors were all but certain that he could not return to football; in truth, the session was held out of sympathy for a player who wanted dearly to return to football, but couldn't.

A senior season for Burton never came. Nor did a sophomore season or a junior season.

"He was treated with medication and got back to the point where he could do pretty well in a non-athletic setting," Rollo said. "I saw him a couple of years ago in Atlanta, where he lives, and he was getting along fine. He appeared to be well-toned. Just looking at him, you would never know he had had a problem."

Lee Otis Burton, who but for the illness might have become a Tennessee legend, never played another down.

CHAPTER 18

WHAT ARE RUTGERS?

Ben Byrd's "Free Thought Association" prediction column in *The Knoxville Journal* was strictly tongue-in-cheek stuff, a whimsical takeoff on people who take themselves too seriously at picking football winners. And yet a lot of people claim that one of his columns played a role in one of the most surprising defeats in Tennessee football history, the 13-7 loss to Rutgers in 1979.

This was the setting: the Vols were 4-2 and had a number of things going their way. They were ranked No. 17 in the nation and favored by a whopping 23 points to bounce back from a 27-17 loss to Alabama. They were coming off an open date and were in near top physical condition. But coach Johnny Majors sounded a warning: they could scarcely afford to be looking ahead just one week before Notre Dame came to Neyland Stadium. UT fans took his words as just so much coaching gibberish, as usual. To heck with Rutgers—bring on Notre Dame.

Rutgers, which won the first college football game ever played, was 5-2, having sprouted some football muscles over the past few seasons, even though its schedule had been minor league, for the most part. The Scarlet Knights had been dismantled by Penn State 45-10 and by Temple 41-20. Bucknell could have beaten them with one more field goal. The Scarlet

Knights from New Brunswick, New Jersey, had much football prestige to gain, little to lose other than a football game. But few people took them seriously.

In contrast to the pregame frenzy of the game before (Alabama), there was a low-key atmosphere surrounding this seventh game of the season, even if it was homecoming. Rutgers was not a traditional Tennessee rival; in fact, the two teams had never met before. Conference records were not at stake and Rutgers came into the game without the glamor that attaches itself to a team of more preeminence. Still, a crowd of 84,265 turned out on a perfect football afternoon to watch the Big Orange go after victory No. 5.

Tennessee hadn't lost to an Eastern team since Boston College upset the Vols in the 1941 Sugar Bowl game. Not many people outside the Rutgers football family expected anything other than a Big Orange victory.

Include Byrd in that number, for here is how the sports editor of *The Knoxville Journal* predicted the outcome in his now famous Free Thought Association column of November 3, 1979:

> "RUTGERS AT TENNESSEE—People around here just don't know a lot about New Jersey and the East, and I guess I have been asked a hundred times this week, 'What are Rutgers?' Some people seem to think that they are something like mathematics or physics. Others say that they always come in groups, and that it is impossible to find just one Rutger by itself. One housewife told me that she bought a pound of them at the supermarket last week for 59 cents, but they must have been on sale because another lady said that she usually pays 89 cents a pound for them. This one man who has been up East told me that he doesn't know exactly what Rutgers are, but he's pretty sure that they are quite a bit like yonkers. Now, if I just knew what yonkers were. TENNESSEE."

Rutgers, the breather inserted on the schedule between Alabama and Notre Dame, pulled off the shocker of shockers. The crowd stayed to the bitter end, hoping for a miracle. But the miracle had already happened—for Rutgers. A host of bowl scouts were tight-lipped. The Vols couldn't match muscles with the visitors from the East.

Rutgers offensive tackle Kevin Kurdyla, whooping it up after the game, was to the point: "Well, I guess they now know what a Rutgers is. They know we come higher than 59 cents a pound."

Majors called it "the worst licking I've ever been involved in as a coach." An exaggeration perhaps, but not altogether a falsehood. His team had a paltry 95 yards rushing. Jimmy Streater was intercepted three times. Rutgers had 26 first downs, Tennessee 15.

The Vol coach suggested, in jest it was assumed, that perhaps the loss could be laid at Byrd's feet, but he emphasized that most of the blame belonged to coach Frank Burns and his Rutgers team. Some Rutgers people promised to send Byrd a Rutgers letter jacket, but he never received it. But he did receive a number of letters from both Rutgers and Tennessee fans. "The letters from the Rutgers people were a lot nicer than the ones from the Tennessee people," Byrd says.

The loss infuriated a lot of Tennessee fans, one of whom left Neyland Stadium that day holding two Notre Dame-Tennessee tickets aloft. He announced that he would sell them for 50 cents apiece, $1 for the pair. He got no takers.

If the Vols overlooked Rutgers for Notre Dame, as many people suggested, they didn't go about it half-heartedly. They did it on a grand scale. The preparation for Rutgers was carried out at closed practices. If the Vols were to perform as they did against Rutgers, one wag pointed out, maybe it would have been better to open the practices and close the games.

Just seven weeks earlier, a season of great promise had gotten under way just after an announcement that UT would expand Neyland Stadium. The rousing finish to the 1978 season—three impressive victories and Majors' comments about the program having "turned the corner"—prompted UT officials to boost stadium capacity. They decided to add more than 10,000 seats to raise the seating capacity above 91,000. The old wooden north stands, last temporary seats in the vast arena, would be replaced by a concrete and steel structure, making the stadium into a bowl.

In 1979, despite the so-so records of the previous two years, the demand for Tennessee football tickets became insatiable, partly because of the faith the fans had in Majors. The athletic department had already sold 52,000 season tickets. The fans wanted tickets so badly that they plunked down more than $800,000 for seats that didn't even exist at the time. To get front end money for the expansion, athletic director Bob Woodruff launched a campaign in late 1978, urging fans to join the "Lifetime Seat Option Club."

A lifetime option to buy a season ticket in the new stadium cost $500 and it wasn't unusual to see a hardcore UT fan shell out $2,000 for the right to buy four tickets. And the option didn't even include the cost of the ticket, which at the time was $10.

The lifetime option campaign got half the $1.5 million in front end money and $750,000 was donated by Nashvillian Paul Mountcastle, who had played before 3,000 or so in his days as a Vol in 1911-13.

Yes, Vol fans were convinced that Tennessee's time was coming. The Vols weren't going to continue to wallow in mediocrity.

The team lived up to its billing in the early going, beating Boston College by 12 and ripping Utah by 33. Freshman speedster Willie Gault gave fans a taste of what was to come, his first college reception going 69 yards for a touchdown. Other than that, "Sweet Willie," who would burst on the scene a year later as one of the most dangerous players in the college game, had a relatively quiet season: three kickoff returns for 37 yards, three pass receptions for 95 yards, and six punt returns for 30 yards.

Next up was undefeated Auburn, which had beaten UT three in a row. On the morning of the game the UT Board of Trustees extended Majors' contract three years, through the 1985 season.

That afternoon, there was a game within a game, both teams remaining in their tunnel and trying to outwait the other before taking the field for the opening kickoff. The crowd of 85,936, largest in Southeastern Conference history, grew impatient. Majors laughed it off. "I didn't think Auburn would come out first but I wanted to see," he said. "I knew when the kickoff was scheduled and we were going to show."

Majors had complained that the Vols had been slow starters. Gary Moore took all of 14 seconds to remedy that situation, hauling the opening kickoff back 98 yards for a touchdown and the Vols went on to whip the Tigers soundly 35-17. Ironically, the only other time Moore had a return for a touchdown had been called back the year before—against Auburn.

Jimmy Streater was the talk of the town with his third straight 200-yard-plus performance. He carried 15 times for 106 yards and two touchdowns and completed 12 of 20 passes for 158 yards and another score.

People in Big Orange Country went cuckoo. Majors called the romp his biggest win at Tennessee. The Vols' third victory of the season and sixth in a row over two seasons didn't go unnoticed. Both wire service polls ranked the Vols No. 19 in the nation. CBS-TV was more impressed, putting Tennessee in a tie with Houston for the No. 5 spot. Heady stuff. It was UT's first national ranking in four years.

It didn't last long; Mississippi State made sure that Tennessee's place in the football sun was short-lived. The Vols had climbed into the top 20 on the basis of an 18-point victory over Auburn. They dropped out the same way—with a 19-point loss to State, 28-9. Again it was too much Mardye McDole, hero of State's victory the year before, who caught two TD passes this time. The Bulldogs were a wishbone team and made only token use of the forward pass. But they completed 5 of 6 for 108 yards to go with 320 rushing yards. Majors was blunt in his assessment of the outcome: "It was an old-fashioned butt-kicking, from beginning to end."

Just as *The Journal's* Ben Byrd would unwittingly become an ally of Rutgers four weeks down the line, so Florida coach Charlie Pell was for this game. "Tennessee will beat the daylights out of Mississippi State," he had declared after State had beaten his team 24-10 the previous week. The comment became a headline in one newspaper. One of State's players had a copy made for every player and even tucked his copy inside his uniform for the game. Did it help? "Of course it did," he said. "It made us mad. It gave us the extra incentive we needed."

After three brilliant games, Streater didn't perform particularly well against State and he became the target of fan abuse, most of it racial in nature. He was disturbed but remained silent for the most part. "You're not human if it doesn't affect you," said Streater, a psychology major. "But that's part of the game. I've just got to be able to take it and keep playing as well as I know how. I know I'm not going to be able to please each and every fan that comes into this stadium. And I'll just have to live with that."

At his weekly press conference, Majors acknowledged that the racism existed. He said he didn't often hear comments from people who didn't particularly like a black quarterback. And didn't want to. "There are some sick people in this world," he said.

The yo-yo Vols were at the other end of the string the next week and Georgia Tech fell with a thud, 31-0. Exactly one week after his bad game had precipitated the ugly fan response, Streater threw for two touchdowns, ran for one that was a thing of beauty and had 199 yards for the day before being pulled with five minutes left in the third period. And how's this for a twist? He received a thunderous standing ovation when it was announced that he had broken Condredge Holloway's UT record for career total offense.

Tennessee wasn't just another game to Alabama and coach Bear Bryant. On Monday before the game, Tide defensive tackle Byron Braggs was wearing an orange jersey in the cafeteria at Bryant Hall. Managers put tape over Alabama's crimson-colored helmets and painted orange T's on them for the scout squad to wear. Bryant entered his weekly press conference wearing a smile but said, "I don't know why I'm smiling. I usually get nauseated during Tennessee week."

Maybe the reason for the smile was that his team was undefeated, ranked No. 1 and driving hell-bent toward a second straight national championship, which would come several weeks later with a victory over Arkansas in the Sugar Bowl. Maybe it was because the Tide defense had been spectacular: three shutouts, nine points allowed in five games.

Alabama was favored by 20 points and, prior to the game, the popular question around town was "How much?" Twenty-one minutes into the game, when Tennessee had jumped out to a 17-0 lead, the question became "How?" After the Tide closed to 17-7, Anthony Hancock slipped behind the Tide secondary and Streater fired a perfect strike. Hancock had the ball in his hands and was touchdown-bound, but dropped it.

John Ward, the Voice of the Vols, remembers the play well. "It should have been 24-7 at halftime. Hancock was going to score; it was going to be six points. I have always believed that Tennessee would have won the game if it had been 24-7 at halftime. It probably would have been impossible for Alabama to come back."

Alabama got its wishbone act together in the second half and won 27-17. It was closer than that; Tennessee had a late Streater-to-Hancock TD called back. This loss wasn't as hard to stomach as some of the others in the Tide's eight straight wins over the Vols. They succumbed to superior talent and numbers, but fought the good fight. Majors called it the best effort he had ever gotten as a coach, that his team had a real shot at winning.

Hancock remembers the dropped ball, and also catching the one that didn't count, a 32-yarder from Streater with four minutes to play. "I remember they called a penalty on Phil Sutton and dropped the flag as I was crossing the goal line."

One of Hancock's most vivid memories of his UT career is the day he flattened Majors as the Vols practiced a fake punt reverse at Hudson Field. Majors had been very unhappy with the way the play had been executed the first few times. He finally threw his cap to the ground and screamed for still another rerun.

Hancock, lined up wide, was to circle back and take a handoff from punter John Warren, as he had already done several times. This time, out of Anthony's line of sight, Majors was behind Warren, still pointing out how the handoff should be made as the play started.

"I'm really hauling ass this time," Hancock says. The collision was inevitable. He slammed into the coach and sent him sprawling. But Anthony kept running. "I kept on going because

they teach you that when you get hit you keep on running."
Majors went down in a heap, blood streaming down his face. He
needed six stitches above his right eye.

Despite the loss to Alabama, spirits were high. Then
Rutgers came to town and spoiled homecoming. And the topsy-
turvy season continued: what better way to atone for the loss
than to overwhelm Notre Dame?

The Irish represented the last opportunity for the Vols of
1979 to do something big. Ole Miss, Kentucky and Vanderbilt lay
ahead but they were small fry at the time; the three of them
together had won only six of 24 games. Big Orange Country had
been agog for months over Notre Dame's first visit to the
Volunteer State. That's why nobody had been the least bit excited
the previous Saturday when Rutgers did a number on the proud
Vols; everyone's mind had been on Notre Dame, except perhaps
for Johnny Majors'.

A record crowd of 86,489 showed up, and so did the "other"
Tennessee team. Going from awful to awesome in the space of
seven days, it ripped Notre Dame from stem to stern, 40-18.
Hubert Simpson, who probably spent more time in Majors'
doghouse than anybody ever to wear the orange, rushed for 117
yards and tied a school record with four touchdowns.

It was Simpson who, on the day he signed with Tennessee
in 1976, uttered these famous words, "I've heard that Tennessee
doesn't have a fullback. Well, Tennessee has a fullback now."

He carried a school record 35 times against Kentucky in
1979. Asked if he preferred fewer carries, he said, "I love it. The
coaches call the plays, not us. If they don't give it to me, that's
fine. But I'd like to carry the ball 35, 40 or 45 times every game.
I thrive on contact. I like running inside and slamming into
tacklers. They get knees, shoulder pads and helmet from me."

Simpson's on-field brilliance was matched only by his
string of off-field encounters with police, Majors and academics.
His publicized classroom difficulties had become a topic of
conversation wherever Vol fans gathered. He had been dropped
from school for one year for disciplinary reasons. And Simpson
had earned a reputation, probably well-deserved, as being not
much of a practice player. But he could be hell on wheels on
Saturday.

In a lot of games during his career, Simpson didn't do
much, because he spent a lot of time on the bench; Majors' way
of showing him who was boss. But by the time of the Notre Dame
game he had rounded into a first-class running back—a big,
strong, slashing runner who loved a challenge, be it an opposing
linebacker, a defensive tackle . . . or a coach. Hubert had a knack

for getting under Majors' craw, which he finally did once too often. He missed a practice without permission during two-a-day drills before the 1980 season and was dismissed from the squad. Ironically, he had apparently just cleared the last of his many academic hurdles to become eligible for his senior season.

For as long as Tennessee plays the game, its football fans will remember the magnificent '79 victory over Notre Dame. Not so much that it ranks alongside some of the monumental games in terms of national importance, but because it was over Notre Dame, America's team.

It was for that reason that UT fans decided to tear down the goal posts, a ritual that hadn't been performed at Neyland Stadium since jubilant University of Chattanooga fans had pulled them down 21 years before.

This was, after all, the first time in nearly five years that Tennessee had beaten a Top 20 team, the last time being a 7-3 decision over Maryland in the 1974 Liberty Bowl. Furthermore, it was UT's first upset victory in 52 games, since that win over Maryland. In all of the Vols' 26 victories over that span, they had been favored.

Tennessee's offensive line got plenty of plaudits against Notre Dame. Tim Irwin recalls that it was the first time he received any "ink."

"That was the first time I ever got any recognition at all," he says. "One of the Notre Dame guys said in an interview after the game that Tennessee was a good team, and that that No. 78 (Irwin) was as good as any offensive lineman you'd find anywhere. That year I was honorable mention All-SEC. The next thing you know you find yourself on somebody's All-South team. Then I was first-team All-SEC as a senior."

Along about this time, offensive coordinator Lynn Amedee told Irwin that if he worked hard and stayed healthy he could make a lot of money playing professional football. Amedee must have known whereof he spoke: as the 1994 season approaches, Irwin is preparing to begin his 14th season with the Minnesota Vikings.

Irwin has gone nose-to-nose with some of his old Tennessee teammates over the years, Reggie White, Mike Cofer, Greg Gaines and Craig Puki among them. He has also gone against ex-Vols of more recent vintage like Keith DeLong, Tracy Hayworth and Todd Kelly. He says that White, the Vols' "Minister of Defense" (1980-83), is at the head of the class among NFL defensive stars. "It seems like I've been blocking Reggie White all my life. He is the best. When he wants to bring it, no one else can do it quite like he can."

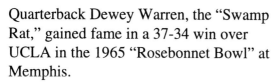

TENNESSEE'S GOAL LINE STAND STOPS L.S.U.

FINAL SCORE: TENN. 3–L.S.U. 3
Baton Rouge, La., October 24, 1964

This goal line stand against LSU in 1964, which preserved a 3-3 tie, was one of the most famous plays in Tennessee history.

Linebacker Steve Kiner was a key figure in the "Jackson Massacre," the 38-0 loss to Ole Miss in 1969.

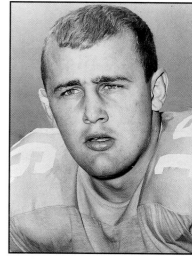

Quarterback Dewey Warren, the "Swamp Rat," gained fame in a 37-34 win over UCLA in the 1965 "Rosebonnet Bowl" at Memphis.

Bobby Majors, last of the five football-playing Majors brothers, was an
All-American defensive back in 1971.

All-SEC Fullback
Curt Watson turned in
one of the great
rushing performances
in Tennessee history,
gaining 197 yards
against Georgia in the
Vols' 17-3 victory in
1969. He later traded
his football togs for a
pilot's uniform as a
member of the Navy's
famous Blue Angels.

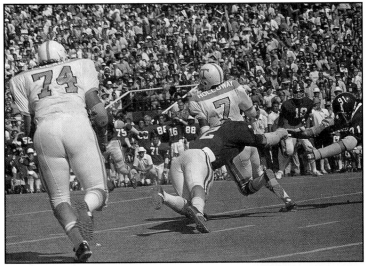

Quarterback Condredge Holloway usually showed his heels to the opposition.

Coach Bill Battle poses with the co-captains of his last Tennessee team (1976), Larry Seivers and the late Andy Spiva (50).

Tony Robinson is set to unload his rifle arm against Alabama in a 1984 victory at Knoxville. A knee injury suffered against Alabama exactly one year later ended his Vol career.

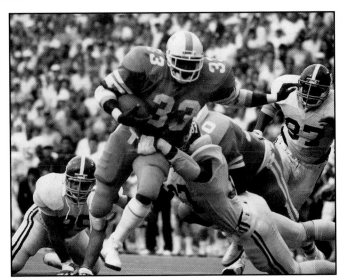

ohnnie Jones
became Tennessee's
first 1000-yard
rusher and is the
Vols' career rushing
champion.

More than 40 years of NFL experience
is represented by these four members of
the 1982 squad: Reggie White (92) of
the Philadelphia Eagles and Green Bay
Packers, Mike Cofer (93) of the Detroit
Lions, Bill Bates (40) of the Dallas
Cowboys, and Willie Gault (26) of the
Chicago Bears and Los Angeles Raiders.

Linebacker Dale Jones was not
only a big-play specialist but also
one of the most popular players
ever to play for Tennessee.

Tailback Chuck Webb, who holds the UT record for rushing yardage in a game (294) was popular with fans, then left for the NFL after two seasons.

All-America center Bob Johnson and coach Doug Dickey are pictured in 1967 and 21 years later after Johnson was elected to the National Football Foundation College College Hall of Fame.

Offensive tackles Charles McRae (left) and Antone Davis, tipping the scales at a combined 610 pounds, were first-round picks in the 1991 NFL draft, McRae by the Tampa Bay Bucs and Davis by the Philadelphia Eagles.

Coach Johnny Majors and grandson Brandon share a playful moment during 1991 Sugar Bowl preparations in New Orleans.

This is one of the most revered photographs in existence, at least as far as UT fans are concerned. The scoreboard at Notre Dame Stadium tells the story of Tennessee's greatest comeback victory ever: the Vols winning 35-34 in 1991, after trailing 31-7 at one point.

Quarterback Heath Shuler could take a licking and keep on ticking.

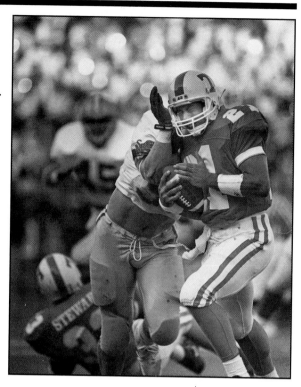

Phil Fulmer as a Vol, 1968-71, and as head coach, 1993.

Play-by-play announcer John Ward (right) and color analyst Bill Anderson, a part of the Tennessee football scene since 1968, bring the action to Vol fans on a 90-station network.

UNIVERSITY OF TENNESSEE
NEYLAND STADIUM

After the rousing win over Notre Dame, the Vols stuck to the up-and-down script the rest of the way. First, they lost big-time to Ole Miss in that most inhospitable of places, Jackson, Mississippi. The Rebels broke away from a 14-14 halftime tie to romp 44-20, the most points scored against a Tennessee team since 1923.

The Vols beat Kentucky 20-17 on Alan Duncan's 25-yard field goal with five seconds left. They trailed Vanderbilt 10-0 at halftime, then roared back behind Streater for a 31-10 triumph. Streater's 85-yard TD pass to Hancock, the longest pass play in Tennessee history at the time, wasn't broken until Andy Kelly to Carl Pickens clicked for 87 yards against Auburn a dozen years later. A psychological ploy by Vandy didn't work. All the Commodore players wore T-shirts under their game jerseys with the words "I HATE UT" emblazoned across the chest.

Tennessee made its first bowl trip in five years, facing Purdue in the Bluebonnet Bowl at Houston, and the Vols kept right in character down to the bitter end of the '79 season. Just as they had done against Vandy, the Vols were hapless, helpless and hopeless in the first half and the opening minutes of the second as they fell 21 points behind. Then, after all seemed lost, they stormed back to make a game of it, going ahead 22-21 but losing 27-22 with a minute and a half to play.

So Majors' third Tennessee team retained its strange hot and cold wave down to the final gun of a tumultuous 7-5 season that was sometimes gratifying but too often disappointing.

CHAPTER 19

HERSCHEL TO THE RESCUE

With the arrival of the 1980s came sweeping changes on the Tennessee staff.

Four assistant coaches departed for one reason or another. Offensive coordinator Joe Avezzano became head coach at Oregon State and took linebacker coach Bobby Roper with him. Assistant head coach Joe Madden wound up with the Detroit Lions and defensive line coach Jim Dyar went into the insurance business. They were the last of the seven aides who had followed Johnny Majors from Pitt to Knoxvillle.

Bill Pace was hired away from Georgia to become offensive coordinator and assistant head coach. He was to coach the quarterbacks but what Pace probably didn't know was that he wouldn't have much in the way of quarterbacks to coach, particularly in 1980. Other new additions to the staff were Dom Capers as secondary coach and John Julies as coach of defensive ends.

In one of life's little ironies, the fourth and last replacement was 29-year-old Phillip Fulmer, hired away from Vanderbilt on Feb. 1, 1980, to coach the offensive line. What extraordinary repercussions that hiring would have a dozen years later!

As Majors and his revamped staff mapped plans for the 1980 season, they saw that the Bluebonnet Bowl game had proved that Tennessee was only a few football players away from being a competitive team—say five or six away. That was a mark of real progress. Three years before, five or six players wouldn't have helped the Vols win even one game. In 1979, that many could have helped win nearly all of them.

Rebuilding a football team that had become as low in talent as Tennessee was a very difficult thing in those days; a limit of 30 freshman players per year was cutting things razor-thin. But the Vols had flat run out of outstanding talent at quarterback; there was no one of the Condredge Holloway-Jimmy Streater stripe, a breed whose lightning-quick feet turned many a loss into a sizable gain. The coaches wondered if they had anyone capable of turning the team into a winner. The answer was no.

The QB roster included junior Jeff Olszewski, who had understudied Streater in '79, junior college transfer Steve Alatorre, Bobby King and freshman Randall Morris, a mid-year high school graduate who had arrived with Alatorre on campus in time for spring practice. With that rather unimpressive list, Tennessee had loaded all the heavy recruiting artillery in search of quarterbacks. Some fans took that as a hint that Olszewski didn't figure too prominently in the Vols' long-range plans. One prospect highly coveted by Vol recruiters was a junior in Joplin, Missouri, Alan Cockrell.

UT had signed six QBs, but two of them, Joe Cozart and Dirk Gentry, were recruited as defensive backs. The others were Jeff Joslin, Alvin Jones, lefty Dwight Singleton and Daryl Dickey, son of the former Vol coach. Singleton, Joslin and Jones never advanced beyond junior varsity status. Morris was converted to running back.

Dickey, suffering a broken leg early in fall practice, dropped off the squad before enrolling in school and returned as a freshman the following fall. As things turned out five years later, that was a blessing in disguise, as Dickey led the Vols to the SEC and Sugar Bowl championships after Tony Robinson was injured.

So Tennessee struggled through 1980 with Alatorre and Olszewski one week, and Olszewski and Alatorre the next. It didn't help matters that quarterback coach Lynn Amedee resigned in June to become head coach at UT-Martin.

Before the 1980 season got underway, a report said Majors was headed for Notre Dame as head coach. He brushed it off thusly: "I can't comment on everything like that that comes along," he said. "Tomorrow somebody in Stone Gap, Virginia, may write that Majors is going to coach a basketball team in Alaska. Somebody else may write that I'm going to be the first astronaut on Mars. I just don't plan to comment on all those stories. I have a football team to coach."

While Majors fretted about job rumors, the schedule, the quarterback predicament, injuries and various other things, it was life as usual for the players. Like putt-putt golf games in Gibbs Hall, the athletes' dormitory.

"We had putt-putt courses laid out through the dormitory," Tim Irwin says. "We would even play down the stairs, much like the Larry Bird-Michael Jordan commercials you see on TV today. For instance, we would play down the steps, around the corner, down the hall and into Kyle Aguillard's room and beneath his bed. That would be one hole. And we would do this for hours. At times there would be several of us walking around like it was an 18-hole golf course. Sometimes we would play all night long."

Aguillard, a lanky tight end from Texas, was one of the putt-putters. He was not only a colorful character, but an extremely talented musician. "He could play guitar and sing like you wouldn't believe," says Irwin, himself a guitarist. "We'd get out in that dormitory stairwell and play guitars and sing. We had a baseball player in the dorm who was taking banjo lessons. He came in with the banjo one day and Kyle strummed it a little. Now he had never had a banjo in his hands but he messed around with it for about an hour and by then he was playing Foggy Mountain Breakdown. It was amazing the things he could do with a guitar.

"But Aguillard was also the biggest sponge I've ever met in my life. He would bum everything you had. He never had a dip of tobacco, never had a guitar pick, never had a guitar string, never had a clean shirt. I caught him using Phil Sutton's toothbrush one night. One time he borrowed Sutton's car and wrecked it."

While the Vol quarterbacking didn't appear to be anything to burst into song about, the wide receivers were little short of spectacular, particularly when it came to speed. Included in their number were three wideouts who would go on to fame and riches in the NFL: junior Anthony Hancock and sophomores Willie Gault and Mike Miller. All three could run like the night wind. The problem was finding somebody to get the ball to them.

A few days before Georgia came to Knoxville for the 1980 season opener, the Southeastern Conference Skywriters were quizzing Bulldog coach Vince Dooley. The discussion naturally got around to his prize recruit, Herschel Walker. Dooley wasn't about to go overboard on an untried freshman, super prospect though he was.

"Herschel does have speed and size (215), and he's making a good adjustment to college football. I don't think he's ready yet, but he's a team man, not a prima donna, and I think he'll learn fast. He has had a lot of publicity and I hope no one expects to see another Dorsett or Simpson out there. Herschel doesn't have those moves. I'm hoping he'll develop them, but they're not there yet."

Dooley was right—Walker would learn fast. He entered the game in the second quarter, with his team trailing 15-2. Starting from the Tennessee 16, he headed for the end zone. Defensive back Bill Bates rushed up to challenge him, going low, drawing a bead on Herschel's pile-driving knees. Walker simply trampled him and flattened two other Vols and kept going. He later scored on a 9-yard run.

Walker later explained his philosophy in simplistic terms. "The shortest distance between two points is a straight line," he said. "I like to run straight ahead."

Tennessee built a 15-0 in the third quarter, then more or less dug its own grave. The Vols' downfall seemed to swing on one weird play, the fluke fumble of a Georgia punt by Bates. The punt called for a fair catch, and Bates said he started to call for one but, seeing a wall of blockers forming on his left, decided to run with it. Sophomore center Joe Happe blind-sided him and knocked the ball loose. It was bobbled by several players from both teams and stayed alive for more than 30 yards. Finally it scooted out of the Tennessee end zone and Georgia had a safety.

The Bulldogs got not only a safety, but the momentum as well. After Georgia had closed to 15-9, Olszewski, who had won a four-quarterback derby for the starting job, lost the ball and the Bulldogs converted the miscue into the clinching touchdown. Except for the fumble, Olszewski performed well, completing 15 of 20 passes for 186 yards and a 36-yard TD to Mike Miller.

Despite the bobbles, the Vols were in a position to win. They were on the move, with a first-and-goal at the Georgia 5, four minutes to go. Glenn Ford fumbled at the Georgia 3 and the Bulldogs ran out the clock. This was the same Glenn Ford who fumbled his way out of the lineup the year before.

Asked what he remembers about the game, Tim Irwin says, "The same thing that everybody else remembers—Herschel Walker running over Bill Bates. But I also remember Glenn Ford fumbling near the Georgia goal. We had that game won. Of course, we had no way of knowing what kind of season Georgia was going to have; we didn't know they would go undefeated and win the national championship."

Anthony Hancock, a junior split end on that Tennessee team, slumped on a bench and leaned against a wall. He was almost in a daze. "I just don't see how we lost," he said. "I just can't see where the game was lost."

Today, he calls that defeat and a similarly disappointing loss to Southern Cal the following week the most frustrating of his career. "The Rutgers game in '79 was bad, but when I think of disappointing defeats I think of Georgia and Southern Cal. Those two games we had in our grasp."

At Majors' Tuesday press conference following the loss to Georgia, one question struck a raw nerve with the coach. One newsman, saying there had been outcries from some Vol fans after star running back Hubert Simpson had been kicked off the squad two weeks earlier, asked Majors if he saw an end to his "honeymoon" with UT fans after three years of rebuilding.

Majors proceeded to inform the media in no uncertain terms that he was (a) sick and tired of discussing the Simpson case, (b) not worried about the criticism that followed Simpson's dismissal, and (c) not concerned about a suggestion that his "honeymoon" might be coming to an end.

"I don't give a damn what some people think," Majors said when asked to respond to the critical tone of some questions on his call-in radio show the previous Wednesday concerning Simpson's departure. "You can't please all the people all the time because it's impossible. You make decisions that are best for the program and that's what I did. And I don't want to keep talking about the damn thing, OK?

"Frankly, I get sick and tired of hearing about the honeymoon crap anyway. I'm a big boy, so don't send me any flowers. All right? . . . I may cry at times, when I feel like it. I don't want any self-pity. I can handle the job I've got. I've been beaten a lot worse than I've been beaten here. I've had worse football teams, worse talent, better talent."

Southern Cal had come into Neyland Stadium riding a 20-game undefeated streak and ranked No. 5 in the nation. Included on the Trojan roster were a number of future NFL stars, names like running back Marcus Allen, tight end Hoby Brenner, defensive back Ronnie Lott, offensive linemen Keith Van Horne, Roy Foster and Don Mosebar.

Just as the Georgia game the week before turned on one play from among dozens, so did this one. Tennessee had been knocked around for two quarters and part of the third, but now the score was tied at 17 with three minutes left, thanks to a spectacular comeback detonated by quarterback Steve Alatorre. He had relieved starter Jeff Olszewski with the Vols trailing 10-0.

The Vols got possession for one last shot at victory. Even if it failed, they had the best tie since Georgia in 1968. As they pushed for what could have been the winning score, and a monumental upset, Alatorre launched a pass into the left flat. Jeff Fisher stepped up to intercept, and that was that.

From the UT 44, USC had time for a couple of passes to move into field goal range. Eric Hipp kicked a 47-yarder and time ran out as the ball sailed through the uprights. Tennessee fans, who had been ready for a jubilant victory party just moments before, let out one loud collective groan. The outcome didn't do much to help the spirits of the Tennessee faithful, but the game graded out as an A+ for entertainment. It's not often that the turning point of a football game comes on the final play.

USC coach John Robinson saluted the Vols and their fans. "The game, the fans, the Tennessee people, everything was great. This represents the best in college football."

He proved to be a better coach than prognosticator. "I don't think we need to feel sorry for Tennessee," he said. "They're going to win their share. I think they'll wind up with an outstanding season before it's over." (The Vols would go on to finish 5-6.)

With Tennessee 0-2 for the first time since 1962, Majors and his staff went back to work. They looked at films over and over, trying to figure what went wrong. The head coach wasn't dismayed. "From four years ago to this stage, just to be competitive with folks like Southern Cal is a definite plus," he said.

It was supposed to be just a warm-up for Auburn, but Washington State and its wonderfully named quarterback, Somoa Somoa, refused to follow the script. Tennessee jumped out to a 28-3 lead, but the Cougars closed to within 28-23 and suddenly they weren't laughing and telling jokes on the Tennessee sideline. But a Steve Alatorre-to-Anthony Hancock pass of 45 yards set up a clinching touchdown and the Vols won 35-23.

And then it was on to the Loveliest Village of the Plains, otherwise known as Auburn. Ten autumns had been peeled off the calendar since Tennessee last won a football game in the state of Alabama. In those years since the 1969 Vols ripped Alabama at Birmingham, Big Orange teams had lost five times each to Auburn and Alabama within the confines of the state of Alabama.

As they raced onto the playing field, the Vols were met by a barrage of oranges, a stunt that served to whip the Tennessee players into an emotional frenzy. They didn't open the game with a kickoff return for a touchdown as Gary Moore had done the year before, but this was about as perfect a game as any Tennessee football team ever played, before or since.

The final was 42-0 and the old line about the Star-Spangled Banner being the turning point of the game was certainly true in this one. The Vols could do no wrong, the Tigers no right. Auburn fans found little to cheer about. One of their biggest ovations of the afternoon was for a five-yard penalty against Tennessee on a kickoff. Olszewski played like Johnny Unitas and Bart Starr rolled into one, completing 11 passes in a row in one stretch.

After the game, the Tennessee players agreed almost to a man that the bombardment of oranges had played a key role in the outcome. "We talked about it on the way down here," Olszewski said. "Some of the guys were saying 'I hope I get hit by an orange.' It got everybody fired up. The Auburn people may think it's fun and a good time, but I think it helped us."

Assistant coach George Cafego sat nearby, munching on an orange. He was asked if it was one of the oranges Auburn students had thrown. "Yeah," he answered. "These people down here don't know you can eat these things. They think the only thing you can do with 'em is throw 'em."

With the emphatic victory, UT fans were asking if Tennessee football had moved into that bright new tomorrow that they had waited for through a lot of disappointing yesterdays. Alabama would answer the question three weeks later, after the Vols had enjoyed an open date and a 23-10 win at Georgia Tech.

UT boosters had chanted "We want Bama!" as their team had dismantled Auburn. So now they had Bama, defending national champion, the nation's top-ranked team. Bear Bryant with his 301 victories. The nation's longest winning streak, 26. The outfit Tennessee hadn't been able to beat since 1970.

The battle lines were drawn. On one hung Johnny Majors' crying towel; on the other, Bear Bryant's. Poor-mouthing at its best.

Majors: "I've never gone into a big game with as many people hurt as this one . . . I don't know who's going to play yet."

Bryant: "Our injuries are the worst we've ever had, by far. We'll just try to get as well as we can. We'll play the game on the field and let the chips fall where they may. If Tennessee embarrasses us, we'll just tuck our heads and come on home and not make any alibis."

Their whining prompted a whimsical column from Randy Moore of *The Knoxville Journal* about coach Paul "Bear" Brantly and coach Johnny Minor. It read in part:

> The Bear said, "Why, we ain't got 'nuff manpower to field a girls softball team, let alone a football team." And Minor grumbled, "I'll tell you how bad we are. We had us an intrasquad game yistiddy and both sides lost."
>
> "You know, son," Bear said. "You pore-mouth almost good as me."

"I poor-mouth better'n you," Minor answered. "In fact, since neither of us got any healthy players why don't we skip the game? We'll have a whine-off, just you and me."

The oddsmakers, who had made the Tide a 15- to 20-point favorite the past three years, were down to a single touchdown on this one. The final was 27-0, Alabama. But those numbers weren't the true measure of the game, which wasn't much of a game at all. It was 37 1/2 minutes old before Tennessee got its first first down. The first half ended with the Vols two yards in the red on offense, 238 yards down on defense. Tennessee finished the game with 59 yards total offense, Alabama with 383.

Tennessee's fourth play of the game was a harbinger of things to come. A pass from Alatorre slithered off Hancock's fingertips in the end zone. What if he had been able to hang on to the pass?

"I'm not stupid enough to say we would have beaten them if we had scored there," Majors says. "That's the kind of thing you can't predict, although one play can make a difference."

Vol tackle Irwin tells how frustrating it was to lose to Alabama year after year. "During my five years at Tennessee, we just never could beat Alabama. That was the biggest regret of my college career, not being able to beat them. If there is one thing I could change about my college days, it would be to beat them."

The long-awaited confrontation between Majors and the team he left behind, Pittsburgh, was more misery for Tennessee. For the second week in a row, the Vols were woefully inept on offense. They scored only six points in the two games, courtesy of a 100-yard kickoff return by Gault against Pitt.

Virginia's 16-13 win made it three straight losses for Tennessee and the fifth of the season on home turf, setting a UT record for that form of futility. Things went from bad to worse. The Vols lost 20-9 to Ole Miss the following week and also lost their captain and great middle guard, Jim Noonan, who suffered a career-ending knee injury.

After trainer Tim Kerin examined Noonan's knee on the sideline, he asked why he had refused to be assisted off the field. Noonan said, "I've never had to be taken off the field in my entire career and I've got a strong feeling this is my last game, so I wasn't going to be taken off in this one."

The team that went 11 quarters with one touchdown from scrimmage in a three-game span at midseason, closed with a bang, getting 12 TDs in the final two games, a 45-14 victory over Kentucky and a 51-13 win over Vanderbilt.

Tennessee's longest football season in years wound up 5-6. Included were losses to four of the nation's top 11 teams: Georgia (1), Pittsburgh (2), Alabama (6) and Southern Cal (11). There was no bowl game. The Big Orange flag was flying at half mast.

CHAPTER 20

MAJORS 1, JOHNSON 0

Alan Cockrell remembers as though it happened yester-day—signing with Oklahoma State coach Jimmy Johnson, he of later Dallas Cowboys fame, and then deciding a few days later he'd rather play at Tennessee.

And he disputes the story that made the rounds at the time: that Johnny Majors stashed him in a motel the night before national signing date so Johnson couldn't get to him. "No truth to that at all," Cockrell says. "I was never in a motel hidden away. There were so many stories going around about a lot of stuff but none of it was true."

Cockrell came out of Parkwood High School in Joplin, Missouri, one of the nation's most recruited players. He was some prospect: at 6-2 and 218 he was big for a quarterback. He could throw *and* run. During his career, he had passed for 3,500 yards and 44 touchdowns and rushed for 1,727 yards and 38 TDs. He led Parkwood to a 14-0 record and the Missouri 4-A championship. He was an outstanding punter and placekicker and a three-year starter in basketball and baseball. To top it off, he was a member of the National Honor Society.

Tennessee, badly in need of a quarterback of Cockrell's talents, apparently had lost him to Oklahoma State when he signed a Big Eight letter of intent on Wednesday. A picture of Cockrell wearing cowboy boots and a big white hat in the *Stillwater (Oklahoma) News-Press* convinced Vol recruiters of as much.

Along about Saturday, Cockrell began to have second thoughts. He imagined playing before 95,000 in Neyland Stadium. He had always played on a winner (Parkwood was 31-3 in his three seasons) and he believed Tennessee offered a better opportunity to win conference or national championships than Oklahoma State. He called assistant coach Doug Mathews, who had been recruiting him for Tennessee.

"Look, Coach Matthews, I've changed my mind," he said. "I don't want to go to Oklahoma State; I want to come to Tennessee. I'm going to sign the national letter with you guys."

Majors and Mathews went to Joplin on Tuesday, the day before the national letter day. That night, they went to Parkwood High's gym where Cockrell was playing in a basketball game.

Cockrell's parents were up in the stands, flanked on one side by the elegantly coiffured Johnson and Dave Wannstedt (later his defensive coordinator with the Cowboys) and by Majors and Mathews on the other. Johnson and Majors had crossed paths before: Johnson had been an assistant on Majors' staff at both Iowa State and Pittsburgh. When the game ended, Alan slipped out a back door. The four coaches waited in the lobby, jaws locked in a tense silence.

"After the basketball game, I went out the back door and left," Cockrell says. "I spent the night with my junior high coach in Riverton, Kansas, about eight miles from Joplin. I had told my dad that I didn't want to be around the coaches, that I had made up my mind and I was going to Tennessee. I didn't want to have to talk to Coach Johnson because I had told them of my decision."

Cockrell didn't tell anyone, not even his parents, where he was going after leaving the basketball game. That night at his junior high coach's home, Alan received a telephone call from Lou Holtz, then the head coach at Arkansas. At first Cockrell couldn't understand how Holtz had learned where he was. And then he could.

"There's no doubt my mother told him," Cockrell says. "Coach Holtz had really charmed my mother. When he came to our house on his second recruiting visit my mom had baked an apple pie. Coach Holtz followed her into the kitchen and helped her do the dishes. He was the epitome of the good recruiter."

The next morning, Cockrell had his parents take the Tennessee coaches to Riverton, where he signed the national letter with the Vols.

"I wouldn't knife Jimmy Johnson in the back, and I don't think he would knife me," Majors said. "But I'd beat him any way I could when it comes to football, and I know the feeling is mutual."

The freshman class of 1981 also included a number of other players who would make solid contributions to the Tennessee program. Players like Johnnie Jones, Chris White, John Cook, Carl Zander, Bill Mayo, David Moon, Jeff Smith, Alvin Toles, Ricky Holt and the McKenzie twins, Raleigh and Reggie. Daryl Dickey, who had signed the year before but fell victim to a broken ankle in preseason practice before he enrolled in school, returned as a born-again freshman.

Mayo was one of Tennessee's juiciest recruiting plums that year. And also a young man of very unusual interests. Majors accompanied assistant coach Bobby Jackson on a visit to Mayo's home in Dalton, Georgia. As they were in the living room talking, Mayo went to his room. When he returned, he was carrying something. He asked Majors, "Do you like snakes, Coach?" and held out a python snake.

"Pythons get real big but this one was pretty small, about six feet long," Mayo says. "Coach Majors acted interested but he didn't seem to want a whole lot to do with the snake. I had a spider also, a tarantula. Coach didn't seem too fond of it either. I'm still interested in those things; in fact, our eight-year-old son got his first tarantula just the other day."

Tennessee was in desperate need of offensive linemen at the time, and Mayo was the No. 1 line prospect in the South. Majors later said he would have handled a rattlesnake that day if he thought it would help him sign the young giant.

UT offensive line coach Phil Fulmer also dropped in on Mayo in the visiting period in January 1981, just before the signing date. Mayo was also into spelunking and he and some of his weekend spelunking mates took Fulmer with them on one of their excursions inside a cave.

"We were in there for an hour or two, I guess," Mayo says. "Everything was fine until Coach Fulmer put his hand on a bat. He let out a pretty big yell. He tells me he had never been spelunking until that day, hasn't been since, and doesn't intend to ever go again."

On a visit to Georgia, Mayo was taken to coach Vince Dooley's home where the coach himself showed him around. They ended up in the den, where the walls were adorned with pictures of past Georgia greats, including Herschel Walker. A bottom row had two empty picture frames. Dooley pointed at one and said, "Bill, one of these frames is for you." Mayo said that alone just about turned him off to signing with Georgia.

If that didn't, then what happened next did. Dooley and an assistant coach showed Mayo a Georgia depth chart, on which Mayo was typed in as a starting guard. "That was corny," Mayo says. "That didn't do much for me either."

The freshman class also included a pair of free-spirited Canadians, Pat Langdon of Burlington, Ontario, and Dale Sanderson of Hamilton, Ontario. They developed a pastime in the dorm that has to rank as one of the strangest ever.

"On Saturday afternoons in the offseason, those guys would stand at opposite ends of the dormitory hall. They both took their clothes off; why they did it naked I'll never know. They were probably 80 feet from each other, both of them stark-naked.

"One would put a pair of binoculars to his eyes and the other would be holding a baseball bat. The guy with the bat would run at the guy with the binoculars until the guy with the binoculars stopped — scared that the guy was right on top of him. I guess you can say it was a form of chicken. But the rest of us would sit there for hours watching those guys do that."

Sanderson saw only limited action at Tennessee, probably no more than 50 snaps all told, and took a medical redshirt with a back injury; Langdon played hardly at all. But Sanderson went on to play 10 years with the Hamilton Tiger-Cats of the Canadian Football League.

Cockrell became one of Majors' all-time favorite players. Majors remembers him as one of the finest athletes he ever recruited. "He threw well enough to be a good passer and he ran the option very well. He had all the ingredients to be an outstanding college quarterback. He certainly helped us break some ice at Tennessee, like beating Alabama in '82."

Cockrell reported to Big Orange Country in late July, two weeks earlier than the other freshmen, to study films and work out with some of the older players. He had shed 10 pounds to reach the 205 prescribed by Majors. In one of his first media interviews, he emphasized that he didn't consider himself the saviour of Tennessee football.

Thirty-eight days later, he might have wished he had gone on to Oklahoma State, where he would be playing against Tulsa instead of Georgia and Herschel Walker in Athens, Georgia. Everywhere one looked in football-mad Athens one saw "We're No. 1" posters and bumper stickers. Or "Give Herschel The Ball" or "Honk If You Love Herschel."

The game was billed as a duel between sophomore stars Walker, the irresistible force, and Tennessee defensive tackle

Reggie White, the immovable object. One newspaper asked "Can Reggie the Great halter Herschel the Magnificent?"

The Dawgs answered the question rather emphatically, opening defense of their national championship with a 44-0 wipeout. It was Tennessee's most decisive loss since 1910 and still stands as UT's worst defeat in the modern era, which began in 1926.

Walker pounded out 161 yards, but quarterback Buck Belue and wideout Lindsay Scott stood out as much as their more celebrated teammate with a pair of touchdown strikes. A crowd of 79,600 was amazed at how easily Georgia did the Vols in, and thousands left early, including virtually all of the Tennessee boosters. The Vols never threatened. Their running game netted 30 yards on 30 carries; the passing game got 122 yards, most of it short tosses into the flat. There is no question that the Vols missed quarterback Steve Alatorre and wideout Anthony Hancock, both out with injuries.

Georgia coach Vince Dooley was shocked by the score. After all, the Bulldogs were supposed to be rebuilding after their national championship year, Herschel Walker notwithstanding. Johnny Majors was caught off guard, to say the least. "We got beat by a much better Georgia team than the one we saw last year," he said.

By Monday, at least one angry Vol fan had put his opinion into print. On a wall along Neyland Drive was a message scrawled in 3-foot high letters: "DOUG DICKEY 1982."

Cockrell's first college action was under less than ideal circumstances. He was thrown into the Georgia game late in the third period with his team trailing 24-0. Most observers figured that the Vol staff had nothing to lose by the move, but Majors said he had planned to play him all along. Cockrell, incidentally, turned in Tennessee's longest run of the day, a seven-yarder just after he went into the game.

In the gloom of the following week, it was the old "Cheer up, Coach, things could get worse" kind of situation. Majors cheered up and, sure enough, things got worse.

If the Vols thought Georgia with Herschel Walker was something, they hadn't seen anything yet. Five days after the Athens Slaughter, they enplaned for Los Angeles and a date with Southern Cal and its great running back, Marcus Allen. So, on successive Saturdays, Tennessee was called on to face the two finest runners in the nation. Allen would go on to win the 1981 Heisman Trophy; Walker would win it the following year. The Trojans had the largest offensive line in college football, larger in fact than their Los Angeles neighbors, the NFL's Rams.

The Vols were as futile against USC as they had been against Georgia. Allen was unstoppable. He scored three times in the first half, carried on three of the first five plays of the third quarter and retired for the night with 210 yards and four touchdowns on 22 carries. Five Trojan quarterbacks played, with very little difference in effectiveness. But there was a silver lining for Tennessee. Cockrell entered the game in the third quarter with the Vols down 36-0 and led an impressive 87-yard touchdown march. Tennessee's first points of the year came on a Cockrell pass to freshman tailback Randall Morris.

Each time Southern Cal scores a touchdown, its mascot Trojan horse gallops around the field. He got a workout as the Trojans romped 43-7, causing Vol freshman guard Bill Mayo to worry that the horse might suffer a heart attack before the night ended.

It was also a frustrating night for another freshman lineman, David Moon. He was on Tennessee's kickoff return team that, like the Trojan horse, also had a busy night, and Moon was continually getting beat by USC's Chip Banks, who went on to stardom with the NFL's New York Giants. Finally, on a fourth quarter return, Moon just blatantly clipped Banks in full view of everyone, but the officials did not call it.

Getting his ears pinned back was a new experience for Cockrell. "I'm coming from a high school that went 14-0 and we were beating teams like Georgia and Southern Cal beat us. So that was kind of a rude introduction to college ball for me."

Tennessee emerged from the first two games of 1981 with the exact record as the year before, 0-2, against the same teams, Georgia and USC. But there the similarity ended. The margin was a mere four points the first time. The second time the aggregate score was 87-7.

This was the low-water mark of the Majors Era. Realistically, there appeared to be no way out. The '81 Vols were young, inexperienced and lacking in depth. They appeared doomed to an absolutely miserable season.

For the first time in his 14-year career as a head coach, Majors was hearing the cry of the wolf. Tennessee fans were disappointed that he had not been able to put that old thunder and lightning back into Tennessee football in his four-plus seasons and they were especially agitated by the lopsided losses to Georgia and USC. Some were quite vocal about it. The popular joke around town was "Johnny Majors is in the fifth year of his four-year rebuilding program." At the same time, some of Majors' most loyal backers took out a full-page ad in both Knoxville newspapers pledging their continuing support.

Fighter that he was, Majors was not about to abandon ship. He went on to turn in one of the very best coaching jobs of his career, for the Vols would lose only twice more in their next 10 games that season.

His first order of business was to install Cockrell as his No. 1 quarterback as preparations began for Colorado State. He had been impressed by the freshman's performance under intense pressure, a feeling shared by USC coach John Robinson, who said, "I really liked Cockrell's looks. He seemed to have a definite plan in mind. He has the sort of bearing about him that you like to see in a quarterback."

Cockrell's move to the first team on Monday's depth chart was greeted by hurrahs from disgruntled boosters. He became the new darling of UT fans in that he represented the "new hope" for a season that had gotten off to a catastrophic start. As the team started preparing for the home opener against Colorado State, Cockrell was joined on the first team by five freshmen: fullback Alvin Toles, offensive guard Bill Mayo, defensive end Ricky Holt and two kickers, punter Jimmy Colquitt and placekicker Fuad Reveiz.

Colorado State fell 42-0 and Cockrell, in his first college start, was everything he was cracked up to be, and then some. He guided the Vols to a 21-0 halftime lead and played only enough of the second half to make it 28-0.

One week later, just as he was beginning to get the "feel" of being a starting quarterback, Cockrell suffered a season-ending knee injury against Auburn. It was the fifth play of the game and he was scrambling when Auburn tackle Donnie Humphrey hit him. "I just started to cut upfield and Humphrey hit me up top, nowhere near my knee," Cockrell says. "But my shoe gripped the artificial turf and turned me around and the knee gave way.

"My dad always told me that if you get hurt, don't lie there on the ground; get up. I knew at the time that my knee was hurt and I was trying to get up. The doctor took one look at it on the sidelines and and said it didn't look good. Next thing I knew I'm in the hospital getting cut on."

With Alatorre back at the controls and Cockrell watching from the sidelines in street clothes and on crutches, the Vols held on to win 10-7 in a most unusual finish. Auburn's bid to win or at least tie died with the clock. The Tigers had reached the Vol 4 with 15 seconds remaining but quarterback Ken Hobby fumbled the snap. The Tigers, out of timeouts, watched helplessly as time expired.

During his hospital stay, Cockrell was swamped by flowers, fruit and more than 50 get-well cards a day, compliments of

Tennessee fans. He was having no visitors, not even Coach Majors for a time. A young nurse, who obviously didn't know Johnny Majors from John Wayne, steadfastly refused to let the Vol coach into Cockrell's room when he dropped by after the surgery. Higher-ups intervened and Majors was allowed to visit.

Three days after his surgery, Cockrell held forth in a press conference at the hospital and brought a few chuckles when he revealed that he had to discontinue pain shots because his sore rump had begun to hurt more than his injured knee.

A week later, Georgia Tech fell by the same 10-7 score, the big play being a 42-yard touchdown pass, Alatorre to Hancock, in the fourth quarter. Hancock was back in action after missing half the season with an ankle injury. The winning margin came on a 25-yard field goal by freshman Fuad Reveiz, who ended up at Tennessee almost as an afterthought.

Reveiz, born in Bogota, Colombia, wasn't exactly unknown to the Vol coaches. They had known about him the year before but thought they had capable kickers on hand. Coming out of spring practice, however, they weren't so sure. About a week before the start of fall practice, they decided they needed to stabilize their kicking.

That Reveiz was available was something of an accident. He had committed early to Florida State, notifying other schools that he was not interested. Two days before national signing date, FSU assistant coach George Henshaw called to tell Reveiz that they were going to give his scholarship to someone else. Reveiz was left with a kicking tee, and no place to use it.

Reveiz was en route to Bakersfield (California) Junior College when Majors caught up with him and his parents by telephone in Las Vegas. "I asked them if they would be interested in coming back to Knoxville, told them I couldn't guarantee them anything, but that we were interested in improving our placekicking.

"They flew back in without knowing whether he would get a scholarship or not. Now, I wouldn't have had him come all the way in here if we didn't have some serious considerations about wanting to find something out there that we didn't have on campus. I wanted to see him face to face, eyeball to eyeball."

Reveiz, 5-10 and 220, had been a high school linebacker in Miami, and hadn't done a lot of kicking. But he was said to have a powerful leg. After he and his parents arrived in Knoxville, they sat talking with Majors at Neyland Stadium while the other Vol kickers were practicing.

One of them was John Warren, Tennessee's only scholarship kicker, who was trying to replace the departed Alan Duncan.

"I watched John that day and he was a straight-on kicker and I knew I could beat him as far as distance and hang time were concerned. I have just never felt that straight-on kickers are as effective as sidewinders."

After watching the Vol hopefuls for a few minutes, Reveiz told Majors, "Coach, I can kick better than those guys."

"I'd say the same thing if I wanted a scholarship," Majors answered.

The mother joined in. "You don't know Fuad," she said. "He means what he says and he can do it."

"I liked his parents and I was impressed by Fuad when I took him in my office for a talk," Majors says. "I just liked the way he looked. I wanted to give him a tryout in the worst way, but of course we couldn't do that. So I finally said, 'Do you think you can handle this?' and he looked me in the eye and said, 'Coach, I can do it.' So I told him he had a scholarship and we shook hands."

Majors acted on a hunch that day, giving Reveiz a scholarship after studying the situation for about six hours. "I didn't know if he could kick a lick," he says, "but sometimes it pays to play hunches."

Reveiz went on to become Tennessee's all-time scoring leader with 314 points. He set a Southeastern Conference record with 18 consecutive field goals in 1984 and holds the SEC record for the longest field goal, 60 yards against Georgia Tech in 1982. Majors' hunch play paid extra dividends for Fuad's younger brother Carlos followed in his footsteps as a Tennessee kicker in 1985-86.

George Cafego, the Vols' venerable kicking coach, called Reveiz "Frank" almost from the first day of practice. Asked why, he said, "I can't pronounce his other name."

The three straight victories over Colorado State, Auburn and Georgia Tech were all but forgotten as Alabama made it 11 in a row over Tennessee in a 38-19 romp. And to top it off, the unlikely hero was a redshirt senior quarterback, Alan Gray. Two weeks before, he had been a fourth-string quarterback whose primary contribution to Crimson Tide football had been as a holder for placekicks.

Reveiz kicked a 28-yard field goal with nine seconds left to give Tennessee a 24-21 decision over Wichita State, but it took one of the wackiest plays ever to unfold on Shields-Watkins Field to make it happen. Midway through the fourth quarter, Shockers tight end Anthony Jones took a pass from quarterback Prince McJunkins and was headed toward the goal with no defender even within shouting distance. He lost his sense of balance and direction simultaneously, inexplicably stepping out of bounds at the UT 25 after a 67-yard gain. McJunkins was intercepted three plays later and Reveiz went on to kick his game-winner.

Ole Miss coach Steve Sloan, whose Rebels were to face Tennessee the following week, offered an explanation for Jones' bizarre run: "I'd say one of those ghosts you've got in that stadium up there just got him. A ghost just jumped up and pushed that boy out of bounds!"

But UT's Willie Gault, he of the flying feet, wasn't about to do any running out of bounds against the Rebels. He ran back kicks for 201 yards and into the record books in a 28-20 win. Aside from improving Tennessee's record to 6-3, the win was noteworthy for another reason: it marked the first time since Johnny Majors came marching home five years before that his UT record had been above the .500 mark, 27-26-1.

On a snowy, bitterly cold day in Lexington, Kentucky, it was man-bites-dog — the winner fired its coach and the loser accepted a bowl invitation. Kentucky took advantage of seven Tennessee turnovers to record a 21-10 victory as Fran Curci coached his last game for UK. He was fired four days later. The Vols accepted a bid to the Garden State Bowl.

The Vols weathered Whit Taylor's 464-yard passing performance—second-highest total in SEC history—to beat Vanderbilt 38-34. Taylor's heroics overshadowed a 319-yard passing performance by Alatorre and Gault's four catches for 217 yards and a touchdown. For aficionados of offensive football, it was some afternoon: the two teams ran and passed for a whopping 1,120 yards. But a defensive back was the man of the hour for Tennessee. Carlton Peoples managed to tip a pass out of the hands of Allama Matthews in the end zone on the final play of the game.

On the same afternoon that Tennessee was beating Vandy at Knoxville, history was being made 250 miles to the south. Alabama beat Auburn 28-17 at Birmingham but it wasn't just another game; it was victory No. 315, with Paul "Bear" Bryant taking that last step onto the pages of football history. The victory moved him past Amos Alonzo Stagg, the game's original grand old man, as college football's winningest coach of all time.

The Tennessee team that UT fans had been looking for through all of 1981 finally reared its head in the Garden State Bowl. The day belonged to Alatorre and Hancock as the Vols beat Wisconsin 28-21. Alatorre completed 24 of 42 passes for 315 yards. Hancock, enjoying the best day of his career, caught 11 of them for 196 yards, including a 43-yard scoring pass. And Willie Gault got in a big lick. The Badgers apparently decided to live dangerously after getting their only lead of the day and sent a kickoff in Gault's direction. Eleven seconds later, Willie the Jet was standing 87 yards away in the other end zone.

The sloppy defensive performance against Vanderbilt had resulted in unusually tough practices in the first two or three days of preparations for the bowl game. It wasn't long before Gault and Reggie White showed up in Majors' office as unofficial spokesmen for the squad. White said, "Coach, we thought that a bowl game was supposed to be a reward for the players. We're working so hard that it's like spring practice and the players aren't happy."

"People who play like we did against Vanderbilt don't deserve a reward," Majors answered. "But if you beat Wisconsin in the bowl, we might take you over to New York City for a big meal in a nice restaurant."

The key word was "might." The victorious Vols ate on their own that night, going their individual ways. Many of them went across the river into the Big Apple. Others did their dining on the New Jersey side.

And so with the impressive upset victory, Tennessee climaxed the long road back from the smoldering ruins of early September. The one-sided losses to Georgia and Southern Cal were all but forgotten.

The success of later teams failed to dull Majors' appreciation of what the '81 team did. "The entire season was a testimonial to a gutsy bunch of players who didn't know they were supposed to be a mediocre team," he said. "Since then, whenever things get tough, I always think back to that team and that season."

CHAPTER 21

A SEASON
OF PROMISE

It took on all the appearances of an old-fashioned political rally: fried chicken, cherry pie, banners, babes in arms, politicians at virtually every turn, introductions, speeches, much applause.

But if this was a political rally, there was only one candidate. And he was Johnny Majors, head football coach, University of Tennessee.

This was the annual meeting of the Davidson County UT Alumni Chapter and the Nashville Big Orange Club, and they turned out more than 1,000 strong. Tennessee's 1982 season might have been still a month away, but you couldn't tell it from the proceedings at the Nashville Fairgrounds. This was more like the south end zone at Neyland Stadium following a Big Orange score.

As it was every year, this Big Orange celebration was staged almost in the shadows of Vanderbilt's football stadium. If you weren't wearing orange, you were in the wrong place. If you weren't thinking orange, you should have gone somewhere else. If it wasn't orange to begin with, someone had slapped some orange crepe paper on it before you got there. About the only things missing were the giant "T" and Jay Julian and his Pride of the Southland band.

The UT Sports Information people were doing a brisk business with their new Vol football brochures. More than 300 were gobbled up at $4 a throw. All three Nashville television stations did live remote interviews with Majors. No fewer than four radio stations managed to get the Vol skipper on the air.

One enterprising outfit was hawking Tennessee-LSU packages. For $442 (from Knoxville) you got four days and three nights in New Orleans. Put up another $40 and they would throw in a three-hour dinner cruise on the Mississippi.

It being election time, more than just a few political candidates had developed a sudden interest in the University of Tennessee. Political lapel buttons probably outnumbered those with Big Orange messages.

In his speech, Majors didn't tell the crowd what it wanted to hear: that the Vols would win them all. He told them he hoped the Vols could come up with a meaner defense.

"I want them to be very mean on Saturday—and then go to church on Sunday and respect their fellow man."

Concerning defensive tackle and future NFL star Reggie White, who became an ordained minister, Majors said he had told him: "Reggie, you can hurt some people on the field and still be a good preacher."

As the 1982 season drew ever nearer, the questions began to mount.

Will Alan Cockrell's rebuilt knee hold up? Can the linebackers back the line? Is the offensive line offensive enough? Will the defense be mean and nasty like the coach wants? Will the coach kick about the kicking game?

Those questions didn't come from the fans; they came from Majors. Associates noticed that he was in the best frame of mind since he had arrived at Tennessee. He was upbeat; privately he felt the Vols were at last able to play with the big boys of college football. He mentioned the "positive finish" of 1981. He liked the attitude and off-season conditioning work of his players. He was impressed by their work habits. There had been substantial progress in academics.

Cockrell was one of the best quarterbacks he had ever had, even though he was returning from a terrible knee injury. The Vols had speed at the wideout positions like nobody this side of the NFL.

To top it off, Georgia and Southern Cal no longer occupied the first two spots on the Tennessee schedule. Mention that and you got the smile that bared that trademark space between Majors' two upper front teeth.

Listening to Majors the Optimist, one wondered how the Vols could possibly fail to make it to the Super Bowl. Then Majors the Pessimist got in his two cents' worth. He was forever telling anyone who would listen that that his team was woefully weak at certain positions. He feared that the Vol defense might surrender too much yardage on the so-called "big plays."

Majors' fears that his team would be "good-hit, no-field" became reality. Underdog Duke struck twice for long-distance touchdowns in handing the Vols a 25-24 setback in the season opener. A 100-yard kickoff return by Greg Boone and an 88-yard pass play revealed soft spots in the UT defense and helped send the Vols to their sixth opening defeat in their last seven openers.

All Tennessee eyes were on Cockrell that day. With his knee heavily braced, he was little short of sensational: 20 of 25 for 239 yards. But Duke's Ben Bennett went him 49 yards better: 288 yards on 19-of-24 passing.

Cockrell's rehabilitation of his injured knee had been a long and painful ordeal. He was in a cast for 12 weeks and on crutches for another four. It wasn't until about mid-July 1982 that he believed he would be able to resume his football career. And he credits Tim Kerin, the Vols' late trainer, with making it all possible. "Without Tim's help there is no way, no way whatsoever, that I could have come back."

The injury cost him some speed and he had to wear a heavy knee brace, which affected his maneuverability. "When I came to Tennessee I had the ability to scramble around," he said. "Maybe not like a Condredge Holloway, but I could move. I ran a 4.6 forty coming out of high school and the injury slowed me down. I was pretty much a passer first and runner second."

The knee continued to give him problems after his football career ended and his professional baseball career began. In the intervening years he has had two more operations on the knee.

Majors, rarely at a loss for words but sometimes searching for just the right one, had that problem at his weekly press conference the week after the opener.

He was asked if the upcoming game with Iowa State would be special to him, inasmuch as he had once coached the Cyclones. He answered, "No, that won't change my attitude at all. I'd like to beat them badly."

Realizing that what he had meant to say was "wanting *badly* to beat them" instead of "wanting to beat them *badly*," he quickly explained. "I'm not talking about beating them badly on the scoreboard; I'd just like to beat them, period. I'd just like to beat them anyway we can beat them. So, please don't misquote me and say I want to beat them badly."

In any event, Tennessee beat Iowa State, and not badly. It was 24-21, the winning margin coming on Fuad Reveiz's 52-yard field goal with four minutes to play.

The following week, it was a double dose of trouble. The Vols were called on to face not only their old nemesis, the wishbone, but freshman sensation Bo Jackson as well. And they weren't equal to either task. The wishbone chewed up 357 yards, with Jackson getting 110 and backfield mate Lionel James 128. Auburn, driven by revenge, stopped its three-game losing streak to Tennessee with a 24-14 triumph. The mercurial Willie Gault twice breezed past the Auburn secondary to haul in TD passes of 38 and 78 yards from Cockrell.

Just three games into the season, Tennessee was at a crossroads. Realistically there had been no expectations that it would be a season of 10 or 11 wins for the Vols, but there were high hopes for 7-4 or 8-3. With a 1-2 record, the players down in the dumps, and Vol fans crying in their beer, those hopes weren't dead, but they were flickering low. Especially with LSU and mighty Alabama looming just ahead.

Washington State was up first, and the Cougars just about put another dent in Tennessee's helmet. The Vols' 10-3 victory left a crowd of nearly 92,000 limp with boredom and also some doubts about their clout on offense. Tennessee gained but 55 yards on the ground and 213 passing.

Late that same night, after LSU had beaten Florida 24-13, more than 2,000 fans, including Gov. David C. Treen, turned out in a heavy rainstorm at the Baton Rouge airport to welcome the Tigers home. "How 'bout them Tigers?" asked the headline in the Baton Rouge Sunday Advocate. Here's what about them Tigers: Three games. Three victories. The nation's highest scoring team. A spot in the national rankings. Talk of a national championship. And Tennessee coming to town.

Now whoever called Tiger Stadium "the world's largest outdoor insane asylum" wasn't just trying to be funny. It is as tough a place to play as there is in college football. Guys who haven't played before 75,000 rollicking Cajun fans on a Saturday night just haven't played. And here came Tennessee, for which playing in a plain, old, everyday stadium would be challenge enough. The Vols were 2-2 and in need of an aspirin or something.

The whole state of Louisiana was caught up in a frenzy. LSU had won 499 games since beginning football in 1893, and entrepreneurs weren't about to let the occasion slip by unnoticed. They were hawking T-shirts printed with "I Was There, LSU vs. Tennessee, Tiger Stadium, LSU's 500th win, Saturday, October 9, 1982."

The idea was flawless but, unfortunately for the T-shirt vendor, it was based on a false premise: that LSU, favored by 14 points, would win the game. The Tigers didn't lose, but neither did Tennessee. The loser was the vendor, stuck with thousands of shirts rendered more or less worthless by a 24-24 tie. It wasn't a total financial catastrophe; many of the 5,000 Tennessee fans walked out of Tiger Stadium with nice souvenirs. The Vols, who had come from 10 points back in the fourth quarter, walked out with a moral victory, their heads held high.

Reveiz got Tennessee the tie with a 52-yard field goal with 1:40 left. He missed another 52-yarder by inches as time ran out. When someone offered that back-to-back 52-yarders are rare, Reveiz said, "I'm coached to make ten out of ten, not nine out of ten." Punter Jimmy Colquitt, the other half of Tennessee's terrific kicking tandem, established a school record that night that still stands, averaging a whopping 53 yards on five punts.

That human rocket, Willie Gault, was at his best, hauling a kickoff back 96 yards for his fourth career kickoff touchdown and returning a punt return 43 yards to put the Vols in scoring position. LSU coach Jerry Stovall, who would be named national coach of the year that season, marveled at Gault's kickoff return. "We tried kicking it away from him but he got over there and caught it anyway. I knew when he drew even with our last man that he was gone. He's a world-class sprinter and I'll welcome any suggestions you guys have on how to keep it out of his hands." Nobody came up with any ideas.

So much for the second Saturday in October. It was time for the Third Saturday in October, the main event. When Tennessee and Alabama square off, nothing else matters. Not anything from the past, not anything in the future.

Bear Bryant always had a special fondness for Tennessee and, as he approached the midway point of his final season of coaching, he was asked his thoughts as he prepared for his last visit to Knoxville.

"I think of all the times I've walked out of that place with a broken heart, broken everything, after being beaten by Tennessee. Yeah, I have some thoughts about Tennessee. I love 'em. But I like to beat 'em."

Which is what the Bear had done for 11 straight years. Not since 1970, when Bill Battle's first Vol team trounced the Tide 24-0, had Bear Bryant walked away from a Tennessee game with a broken heart. Or a broken anything. So when he addressed the question about his thoughts, he was not recalling the Tide's 11-year mastery of the Vols, but how he was dominated by Tennessee and Bob Neyland when Bryant was still several years away from becoming one of the most famous coaches of all time. The Bear never managed to beat a Neyland-coached team, winding up 0-5-2 in seven tries when he coached at Kentucky.

"Tennessee Week has always been and I reckon always will be something special for Alabama," the Bear said. "It was when I was playing, and it is now while I'm coaching. There's a lot going on in Knoxville, with the World's Fair and all, and we're looking forward to coming up there. You've got a wonderful crowd up there. You get eighty or ninety thousand folks in there trying to help your team win. I like that. But it's not very good for our quarterbacks."

Little did he know how special it would be for Tennessee and its legion of hungry fans.

THE STREAK ENDS

Not being a Tennessean, sophomore quarterback Alan Cockrell didn't really comprehend the significance of the Alabama-Tennessee rivalry. That is, not until the morning of October 16, 1982, the third Saturday in October. The day would, in fact, become the most memorable experience of his three-year UT career.

He got up that morning in a West Knoxville motel, where the Tennessee team was quartered, and went downstairs for breakfast and team meetings. He noticed a newspaper headline that asked "Will This Be No. 12 For The Tide?" a reference to Alabama's 11 consecutive victories over Tennessee. The story also told of an Alabama player's plans to handle young Mr. Cockrell.

Alabama was ranked No. 2 in the nation and favored by 13 points. The Tide had just ripped Penn State 42-21; it would be the only loss for the Nittany Lions, who would go on to win the national championship.

"Even though I wasn't from Tennessee, I could still feel something about the rivalry," Cockrell says. "But I don't think I really understood the magnitude of that rivalry until that morning.

"That whole day was unbelievable. The team buses going to the stadium with police escort, traveling along Neyland Drive and seeing all those people alongside the road. Even on the interstate people were rooting for us, waving, blowing their horns. I believe they were lined up the whole 10 miles of that trip. And this was pretty early in the morning. This whole thing is starting to hit me by then. This is a pretty big game, I'm thinking.

"Going out on the field for warmups you could just feel the tension. The quarterbacks went out early and I'm enjoying the scene, the day, the atmosphere. And I noticed over by the tunnel where the visiting team comes out, there was a circle of reporters and photographers moving around and I could see Bear Bryant's hat right in the middle of it. He just walked up to the south goal post, leaned against it and crossed his legs like he always did and looked out on the field. I just wanted to stand there and watch the man for a couple of minutes. That's all I wanted to do."

Less than four hours later, Tennessee had won 35-28 and pandemonium reigned. The goal posts, each of which weighed several hundred pounds, had toppled under the weight of frenzied UT boosters. The one at the north end of the field came down. Fans carrying a section of it took a victory lap around the field. Others were doing a snake dance. They laughed. They kissed. They cried. They screamed. Knoxville had never seen anything like it.

One Alabama fan, caught with his girlfriend in the mass of humanity and all the hoopla, said, "Oh, what the hell. Have a good party."

The gigantic victory party carried over well into the night and even the next day.

Long after the game, most of the goal post at the south end of the field was still standing, even though what remained of it was twisted and tilted at a crazy angle. Late that night, Vol linemen Bill Mayo and David Moon visited Shields-Watkins Field and used a hacksaw to bring down the rest of the goal. They cut it into as many pieces as they had time to and pieces of it can be found in various Knoxville business establishments today. "We were dirt-poor back then and you could barter those pieces for different things," Moon says.

It was an emotional time for all. Mrs. Elizabeth Majors, 68, said she didn't know whether to laugh or cry. So she did a little of both. Her oldest son John, 47, did some of both, too, and so did a lot of his players and so did some Tennessee fans. The Alabama rivalry just does that sort of thing to the Tennessee football family and there was no doubt that the 12-year wait made this one especially sweet.

Beating Alabama was something special for Moon, a native of Meridianville, Alabama. When he was a high school senior, he committed to Tennessee, but scheduled a visit to Tuscaloosa the week of the Auburn-Alabama game. He ended up having dinner at Bear Bryant's house.

"I felt like I had to be able to tell Coach Bryant face-to-face that I was going to Tennessee," Moon says. "I felt that if I couldn't do that, then I was making the wrong decision. And I was able to do it."

The small gathering at Bryant's house that night included Ken Donahue, the Tide's defensive coordinator. He told Moon that if he went to Tennessee he would never be able to beat Alabama. The Vols won three out of four against the Tide during Moon's days at UT, a fact that he never let Donahue forget after he became the Vols' defensive coordinator in 1985.

Most of Tennessee's juiciest triumphs down through the years had been against Alabama, beginning with that historic 15-13 win at Tuscaloosa in 1928. This one ranked right up there with the best of them — 1928, 1938, 1946, 1967. Each of those victories ended periods of Alabama domination and spun the wheel back toward Tennessee. The Vols would, in fact, win the next three games against Alabama to build their own little streak.

For a while, it appeared that Alabama would routinely make it 12 wins in a row over UT, building a 14-3 lead in the early going. A number of Vol fans made a quick exit from the stadium. They should have hung around. When Willie Gault and Alan Cockrell hooked up on a 52-yard touchdown pass midway through the second quarter, the Vols began to gain some confidence. Tennessee finally mounted a two-touchdown lead in the fourth quarter and had to beat back a furious comeback by the Tide.

In the final minute, from the UT 17, Alabama quarterback Walter Lewis threw three times into the end zone. Tennessee fans, having grown accustomed to seeing Alabama find a way to beat Tennessee, kept expecting the worst. The first down pass was incomplete. On second down, cornerback Lee Jenkins raced madly to the corner of the end zone to slap a pass away. On third down, here came another pass, this one to the middle of the end zone, aimed for Tide wideout Joey Jones. Jenkins leaped and batted the ball back toward the goal line where Vol end Mike Terry tucked it away. The clock said 17 seconds to play. Tennessee 35, Alabama 28.

"It's a dream come true," Terry said in the bedlam of the dressing room. "I saw that ball pop loose. It was just hanging there for somebody to catch. Why not me? Glory to God. It was a precious apple."

Senior defensive back Bill Bates had waited a long time to beat Alabama. "I've wanted to beat them since I was so young," he said, "ever since the streak started. Before the game, Coach Majors told us the clock eventually strikes 12 on everybody. Today it definitely struck 12 on Alabama."

Cockrell threw three interceptions in the first half, but emerged as one of the heroes. He completed 8 of 11 in the second half, without an interception. Chuck Coleman rambled for 139 yards and got what turned out to be the winning TD on a 34-yard scamper in the fourth period.

Long after the goal posts had come down, long-suffering Tennessee fans refused to leave the field. When Cockrell finally made his way to the locker room, he found it all but deserted. Most of the players were still on the field, celebrating with their fans. One of the few inside said, "Let's go back out there!" and back they went for an encore, right into the midst of all that madness.

Cockrell had given away his chin strap and his wrist bands. He still clutched the game ball — with both hands. Some fans tried to wrest it away. He even had what he called "serious money" offers to part with it but he declined. He presented it to Majors.

Amid the tumult and the shouting, practically all the UT faithful assumed that this victory heralded the dawn of a bright new era for Tennessee football. Majors, excited though he was, was not among their number. "I've never been one to jump up and down and say, 'Oh, man, we're on the way now,' " he said. "This win will stand out in my memory the rest of my life, but we can't live on it next week."

How right he was. John Ward, the Voice of the Vols, made a speech in Chattanooga two days later and predicted that the Vols would lose to Georgia Tech in Atlanta the following Saturday. They did.

Ward and his broadcast sidekick, Bill Anderson, felt that Tennessee had beaten a team that was not up to Alabama standards, particularly defensively. "I can reflect back on what Bill said in the booth that afternoon. He is a genius when it comes to knowing what is going on on the field. He has a great feel for the game. I remember he was disappointed with the way Alabama looked that day. He couldn't understand why a Bear Bryant team had lost control of the game defensively.

"Tennessee won that day, but I never thought that was the real Alabama team. Alabama just did not look like Alabama. I was reading Bill Anderson all the way through it. His face told me something was wrong out there."

Indeed, it was not one of Alabama's great teams. After bowing to Tennessee, the Tide lost three in a row at season's end, to LSU, Southern Mississippi and Auburn, and finished 7-4. Bama beat Illinois in the Liberty Bowl in Bryant's final game as coach, but for only the fourth time in his 25 years at Alabama, the Tide failed to land a spot in the final top 20.

On Sunday after the stirring triumph, some Vol fans went to Majors' home and wrapped his car in wide strands of orange crepe paper and secured the paper to lampposts and nearby trees. A large color photograph of the car appeared on the front page of Monday's *Knoxville Journal*. It showed Mrs. Majors admiring the handiwork but trying to figure out where to begin the unwrapping job.

The football world was shocked and saddened three months later. On January 26, 1983, less than a month into his retirement, Bear Bryant, the man who had won four national championships and a record 323 games, was dead.

While Georgia Tech coach Bill Curry fretted about his team's lack of offense in a 24-0 loss to Auburn, Majors was warning of a possible letdown by his team in Saturday's game in Atlanta. He pointed out that recent Tennessee teams had played poorly the week following the Alabama game. Except for the previous season, when they beat Memphis State, the Vols had lost six straight after bowing to the Tide.

So Majors came up with a novel scheme to head off a letdown. When the players went to the practice field on Monday, they found a platform covered with blankets and a sheet.

"This is Cloud Nine," Majors told them. "I want each one of you to jump off it and then we'll be down off Cloud Nine and we'll start getting ready to play Georgia Tech."

The ploy failed. Tech caught Tennessee looking the other way and it was no contest. The Jackets asserted their mastery at the start, rolled up 24 first downs and 451 yards and cruised to a 31-21 victory. About the only thing Tennessee fans had to shout about was an SEC-record 60-yard field goal by Fuad Reveiz.

The day before Tennessee was to host Memphis State, a star of the future was showing off his wondrous passing talents for the Vol junior varsity. Tony Robinson completed 11 of 17 passes for 278 yards and five touchdowns and rushed for 70 more in a 41-19 win over Kentucky at Lexington. For the JV season, Robinson completed 15 of 29 passes and seven of them went for touchdowns.

Interestingly, a quarterback from North Carolina named Shuler completed 1 of 2 for 3 yards for Tennessee that day. He was Lamar Shuler of Robbinsville, N.C., a cousin of the Vol QB of a decade later, Heath Shuler.

Reveiz continued his amazing kicking against Memphis State, knocking home five field goals in a 29-3 homecoming victory that stood as the first comfortable victory on home soil for the Vols since the 42-0 conquest of Colorado early in the 1981 season.

Tennessee then faced the Jackson Curse and had to weather a brilliant performance by Rebel quarterback Kent Austin before laying that ghost to rest, 30-17. Austin hit 15 straight passes en route to a 37-for-50 performance afternoon. Reveiz became the SEC's all-time field goal leader with three field goals to push his total to 22.

The Vols nailed down a Peach Bowl bid with a 28-7 victory over Kentucky, and it was Reveiz hogging the spotlight again. The sophomore from Colombia, South America, via Miami was 5-for-5 on field goals and a 55-yard shot at the end of the half was his eighth of the season from beyond 50 yards, an NCAA record.

Reveiz, the name that sportswriters could not spell and fans could neither spell nor pronounce a year before, was suddenly a household word. Youngsters in Big Orange Country no longer wanted to be quarterbacks; they wanted to be kickers. After all, one does not hit 27 of 30 field goal attempts in 10 games and go unnoticed.

When Reveiz had signed on with the Vols just in time for 1981 fall practice, he was introduced to George Cafego, UT's venerable kicking coach and resident homespun character.

Cafego looked Reveiz in the eye. "Son, I'm not going to take Latin to learn to pronounce your name, so your name is going to be Frank from now on. Let's get up there and kick." So Fuad Reveiz was Frank to Cafego for almost four years.

But during a game late in Reveiz's senior season, Cafego approached him on the sideline and said, "Fuad, let's get our mind ready."

Reveiz was dumfounded. "That just blew my mind when he called me Fuad," he says. "I felt right then that I had finally earned his respect and right then that was worth more to me than anything in the world."

Meanwhile, inflation hit the Vanderbilt ticket office, of all places. Vol-Vandy tickets, which once went for a song, were in heavy demand as fans in Nashville grew more and more excited about the game. The face value of a ticket was $15 but in alleyways and dimly lit hallways around Music City the suggested retail price had soared to as much as $100.

This was quite a switch. In years past, Vandy was usually nothing more than the last notch of the season on bowl-bound Tennessee's gun. Rarely had the approach of the game set the football world on its ear. But now the Commodores were 7-3, had won four in a row and were already in the Hall of Fame bowl. The most astonishing thing, however, was that Vandy was favored by 3 points over Tennessee, something that hadn't happened in quite some time.

Whit Taylor, who had stung Tennessee for 464 passing yards the year before, was at it again. Ignoring the sloppy playing conditions, the senior quarterback completed 24 of 42 aerials for 391 yards and three touchdowns as the Commodores slipped and slid to an exciting 28-21 victory over the hated Vols. Some quarterbacks require most of a season to put up numbers like Taylor did in just two games against Tennessee: 34 of 62 passes for 855 yards and five touchdowns.

Vandy's futility against Tennessee had nearly matched the Vols' frustration against Alabama. Thus, 1982 gave Tennessee a look at life from both sides. In 91 years of football, only two other Tennessee teams had beaten Alabama and lost to Vanderbilt in the same season, 1926 and 1948. And the Vols wound up the season the same way they had started it—losing on a big play— to Duke in the opener and to Vandy in the 11th game.

Taylor was all smiles as he talked of beating Tennessee. "All year we've been looking for this day," he said. "Don't get me wrong. We didn't look past any opponent but we never lost sight of this date. I'm not calling it revenge for last year but it was a lot better watching Tennessee try to hit that last pass than it was throwing it last year."

All that remained of a disappointing 1982 season was a Peach Bowl engagement with Iowa. The game appeared to be history at halftime, at which point the proverbial snowball's chances looked good by comparison to Tennessee's plight. Iowa quarterback Chuck Long had dissected the Vol secondary with an incredible first half passing exhibition in which he completed 14 of 17 passes for 289 yards. Tennessee had a measly 87. Most importantly, perhaps, Iowa held a 21-7 lead.

But when Cockrell cranked up the UT offense in the third period, it was a new ballgame. The Vols ran off an incredible 55 offensive plays in the second half. The Hawkeyes managed to win it 28-22 but only after a monumental Tennessee rally that brought the Vols storming up to the Iowa gates in the facing minutes with what would have been the winning touchdown.

It was the final game for Gault, who made All-American in 1982 and is remembered for his extraordinary speed more than any player who ever wore the orange and white. Willie left vapor trails on football fields across the Southeastern Conference and still goes through life as though something is after him. At

Tennessee, he wore No. 26, but players on opposing coverage teams could only guess his number to the nearest digit. UT fans learned very quickly that if it wasn't moving, it wasn't Willie Gault. Whatever he's running from isn't gaining on him. Willie the Jet takes a back seat to very few people in the world when it comes to moving from point A to point B in a hurry. He didn't make the 1980 U.S. Olympic team for being slow.

Gault ran back three kickoffs for touchdowns in 1980 and only one other player in all of Tennessee history, Gene McEver (1928-29-31), ever ran back two. And it took him a whole career to do it. The Chicago Bears picked Gault in the first round of the NFL draft in 1983, only because he slowed down long enough to answer the phone. He went on to a long and productive career with the Bears and Los Angeles Raiders.

Gault gave offensive lineman David Moon a jolt in a game that season. "There I was, just an old country boy from Alabama," he said. "Willie Gault was across from me in the huddle and I looked down at his feet. He was wearing his own signature shoes! There was a velcro strip across the top of the laces and it said something like 'Willie Gault Edition Flyers.' "

Three all-time Tennessee greats were named to the All-Time SEC Team for the first 50 years (1932-82): offensive lineman Bob Suffridge (1938-40), defensive lineman Doug Atkins (1950-52) and linebacker Jack Reynolds (1967-69).

Six UT players made the second team: center Bob Johnson (1965-67), place kicker Fuad Reveiz (1981-84), defensive lineman Steve DeLong (1962-64), linebacker Paul Naumoff (1964-66), defensive back Roland James (1977-79) and kicker Herman Weaver (1967-69). Tennessee's Robert R. Neyland was coach of the second team, behind Alabama's Paul "Bear" Bryant.

CHAPTER 22

"THE RUN"

They called it "The Run."

When tailback Johnnie Jones took a pitch from Alan Cockrell and set sail on a dazzling 66-yard touchdown scamper against Alabama, he wrapped up a 35-28 Tennessee victory and earned himself a special niche in Vol football lore. On Oct. 15, 1983, at Legion Field in Birmingham, another legend entered the football ages at Tennessee, alongside the deeds of McEver, Butler and Lauricella.

The country boy from Munford, Tennessee, with quiet ways and a quick smile, had done nothing in his UT career to indicate that he would go on to establish eight school records on his way to becoming Tennessee's all-time rushing leader and the Vols' first 1,000-yard rusher. In his freshman season of 1981, he had carried only four times for 25 yards. As a sophomore, he gained 421 yards as understudy to Chuck Coleman and Randall Morris.

Three weeks before The Run, in fact, Jones had thought about quitting. He had been upset since he injured an ankle before the opener against Pittsburgh and was sidelined. He didn't see much action in the next game against New Mexico, after missing practice to attend his grandmother's funeral. When he finally got to play, he carried only one time against Auburn and fumbled. He rode the bench for the rest of that game.

"My pride wouldn't let me quit," he said. "It was discouraging but I just had to keep working and things would fall into place for me. Anybody who starts feeling like quitting, they should talk to me first. I can tell them how it is. I can tell them about a day in Birmingham."

So he stayed around. And became a hero in waiting.

There were great expectations as Tennessee lined up against Pittsburgh in the season opener. Johnny Majors had said privately that his 1983 club could be his best at UT, as it ultimately turned out to be. Pitt put a damper on those thoughts, carving out a 13-3 victory on a night when a sensational performance by the Tennessee defense was wasted. Coach Larry Marmie's defenders, who would become known as "Marmie's Army" with their marvelous play that season, didn't even allow Pitt a first down in the first half. The Vols had a number of chances to put Pitt away early, but they broke down on offense on each occasion.

When the Panthers finally got moving, they pulled off one big play, a 56-yard scoring pass, John Cummings to Dwight Collins, and Tennessee was never quite the same.

The Vols polished off outmanned New Mexico 31-6 and two weeks later Majors found himself an embattled coach. Auburn whipped his team 37-14; actually not as bad as the score indicates, but too bad for the paying customers. Many Neyland Stadium fans left early. Many of those who stayed to the bitter end booed during the fourth quarter.

"I know a lot of people are talking doomsday," Majors said. "Baloney! For the first time in six years I see daylight. I know I may sound like a crazy man, but I feel confident we are now building a good program and I'm not going to change my mind one iota."

So, after three games, with a 1-2 record, the Vols had to deal with a certain loss of public faith as well as with such little matters as LSU, Alabama, Kentucky, Vanderbilt and others. A breather, The Citadel, was next up and nobody in Big Orange Country was heard to veto that matchup.

The Citadel fell at Memphis, as expected, 45-6, and defensive tackle Reggie White was almost a one-man gang. White, improving every week, registered four sacks to add to his school career record. Trouble was, there was hardly anyone there to watch the Vols' Minister of Defense do his thing. Liberty Bowl Stadium, capacity 50,180, had 29,829 empty seats that day.

Back home, Alan Cockrell and company disposed of LSU 20-6 and it was the kind of win that made Johnny Majors laugh and tell jokes. There hadn't been too many of those games in the

Majors era — Notre Dame of 1979, Alabama of 1982 and perhaps a couple of others. Cockrell, often criticized in the past for his lack of running, caught the Tigers in a blitz and broke away for a 43-yard TD. "I only wanted to get a first down," he said.

And now we come back to Alabama vs. Tennessee, Legion Field, Birmingham.

It was a most atypical Alabama-Tennessee game; this classic rivalry was steeped in the tradition of kicking duels and trench warfare, not 41-34 shootouts.

The 13-point underdog Vols scored on an 80-yard pass and run, Alan Cockrell to Lenny Taylor, on their first play of the game, but had to rally time after time to stay in the game and, finally, to win. They trailed 27-17 midway through the third period, then 34-24. They finally pulled into a 34-all tie.

As the clock got down to 3:00, Tennessee was faced with third-and-3 from its 34. Timeout. Cockrell met with Majors on the sideline. Majors was on the headphones with offensive coordinator Walt Harris in the press box. They discussed the situation. This might be the Vols' last chance.

Tennessee had enjoyed unusual success that day with the short passing game, the "80 Series." Majors wanted to run a short pass. Harris said he thought Alabama was leaving itself vulnerable to an option play. They argued back and forth. Finally, Majors gave in and said, "OK, Walt, that's what I pay you for; just run the damn thing!"

The call was "48 option." Cockrell was to decide at the line whether to go left or right. He noticed a blitz forming to his right so he audibled the other way. In the din of Legion Field, some offensive linemen were unable to hear the checkoff. One guard pulled the wrong way and didn't block anybody. Cockrell made a fake, started down the line and pitched to Jones, who slashed through the right side of the Alabama defense. He eluded one tackler at the line of scrimmage, made one cut and streaked 66 yards to the end zone. And instant glory. Johnnie Jones had run his way into the Big Orange book of memories, making the final big play in a game that was up to here in big plays.

Following the touchdown and extra point, the first words on the offensive phones in several minutes was Majors to Harris: "Walt, that was a hell of a call I made there, wasn't it?"

Four years earlier, Ed Murphy, a Memphis businessman and former Vol track standout, was helping UT to recruit Jones. His selling point was "Some day you're going to score the winning touchdown against Alabama."

Like another storied run against Alabama, Johnny Butler's 56-yarder in 1939, the touchdown-maker went untouched. Not one Tide player laid a hand on Jones as he sped down the field. "I got the pitch and saw that I had some running room," he said. "Then I saw Tim McGee make a good block, so I cut back over to the right and everything just opened up. I was tired, but I wasn't so tired that it was going to keep me out of the end zone."

Although it was an offensive show like had never been seen in an Alabama-Tennessee game, the Vol defense played a key role. Reggie White and his defensive mates dominated the second half, holding the Tide scoreless for the final 21 1/2 minutes.

Majors' postgame press conference began outside the dressing room but had to be moved to the inside of a nearby bus when officials realized that the crowd prevented any chance of order. "Where do you start?" Majors asked. "There were so many key plays. I don't think I've ever been involved in a game with so many big plays."

Across the way, longtime Alabama defensive coordinator Ken Donahue took the loss hard but saluted Cockrell. "You want it bluntly?" he asked. "We played terrible defense and Alan Cockrell audiblized one great game. We had man coverage on Jones' run; we were blitzing from the left side. Cockrell picked it up perfectly. He did everything he had to do to win. His audibles had a great deal to do with their winning. Make no mistake about it; he did a great job. And I didn't."

Cockrell, playing his finest game, finished with 292 yards passing and three touchdowns. He ran six yards for another score. He can boast of something that very few starting Tennessee quarterbacks can: he never lost to Alabama during his UT career (he was injured and did not play as a freshman).

How profound was Tennessee's second straight victory over Alabama and first win in Birmingham since 1969?

On Monday following the rousing victory, the UT Athletic Department was offering video tapes of the game for $49.95 per cassette. And audio tapes of John Ward's description of the game were going for $9.95 each.

Three of their top four running backs were out with injuries the following week against Georgia Tech, but Cockrell's passing carried the Vols to a 37-3 victory. He threw touchdown passes of 50 yards to Taylor and 55 to Clyde Duncan. Jones, about the only healthy running back, gained 128 yards. And Marmie's Army was at its best. In six games, it had yielded no touchdowns in three outings and one TD in two others.

Giants Stadium in East Rutherford, N.J., seemed like a nice place to be going to play football, but the Vols found out otherwise. A swirling, chilling wind that gusted to 25 miles per hour played havoc with passing and the kicking game. Put the ball in the air and it might wind up in Hoboken. It was that kind of day.

With the wind so strong, the strategy was to simply give the ball to the running backs, point them toward the enemy goal and forget about the forward pass. But with three of their four running backs injured, the Vols were unable to keep fresh men battering at the Rutgers defense. The one back who was available, Jones, kept getting up and having another go at it with the heroic results of 234 yards in 41 carries, both school records. It ended up 7-0, Tennessee.

Majors had alerted his star junior back to that eventuality. "During the week I told Johnnie that Tony Dorsett once carried the ball about 40 times in one game at Pitt and had run 65 yards on his last try," Majors says. "I asked Johnnie if he thought he could carry it 30 or 35 times and he said he could. But at the time I didn't think it would be necessary."

During the game, as the Vols huddled in their own end zone, John Madden, the former Oakland Raiders coach and CBS-TV analyst, walked out of the tunnel at the end of the field. He was spotted by one of the Vols in the huddle. "Hey, that's John Madden!" he exclaimed, and his teammates paused to watch him pass by. What makes it interesting is that Tennessee was nursing a 7-0 lead and was out of timeouts. They got away with it.

Things were looking up. The Vols went home with their first shutout in 29 games, a 6-2 record and its first five-game winning streak since 1973. There was talk of national rankings and multiple bowl invitations.

After an open date, Tennessee bowed to Mississippi 13-10. "It was a football game that the Vols richly deserved to lose," Knoxville Journal columnist Ben Byrd wrote. "If one had to pick Tennessee's toughest opponent of the season it would be a toss up between Auburn and Tennessee. The Vols have been their own worst enemy in at least two of their three losses, Pittsburgh and Ole Miss."

He referred to a series of Tennessee errors that included a fumble one yard away from a potential game-winning touchdown, a pair of costly interceptions, three procedural penalties and a pair of illegal blocking penalties that wiped out long returns that had moved the team into scoring range.

"We tied it up in a bright red package with mistletoe and everything, and handed Ole Miss an early Christmas present," Majors said.

Cockrell was struggling following his lights-out games against Alabama and Georgia Tech. One fan took it upon himself to let Cockrell know in no uncertain terms that he didn't appreciate Alan's performances one bit.

As he headed for the exit toward the Neyland Stadium locker room, a heavy rubber and metal stadium chair came sailing out of the stands. It was supposedly aimed at Cockrell, but hit offensive tackle Curt Singer. Cockrell was hit by a cup of ice.

"The only thing I had any regrets about was that I didn't pick the chair up and keep it," Cockrell said. "It was a brand-new stadium chair. I should have just walked off the field with it. They got the guy who threw it and I later got a copy of an apology he had sent to the university. I never gave it a second thought really.

"The Ole Miss game was one of the low points of my career at Tennessee," Cockrell said. "Before the game we were still in the running for the Sugar Bowl. If we had beaten Ole Miss, Alabama had to beat Auburn for us to go, which didn't happen anyway. But with the loss to Ole Miss we lost all possibility of going.

"We got booed. Those people who boo are die-hard Tennessee people. They wanted us to win, probably worse than we wanted to win ourselves. That may seem silly to say but that's how hard they pull for you. There were times I probably deserved to get booed. But despite the boos and the bad times, my days at UT were great for the most part."

Despite the loss to Ole Miss and regardless of what they did against Kentucky, the Vols were headed for the Citrus Bowl to play Maryland and Boomer Esiason. They got past the Wildcats at Lexington 10-0 with a performance that was a throwback to single-wing days. After a scoreless first half, Citrus Bowl officials celebrated in front of the UT fans as the clock ran down. One bowl member ran back and forth with a bag of tangerines held high.

The Vols had scored just 27 points in their past three games, but won two of them. The defense had surrendered just one touchdown in the past four games and had held six opponents to six points or less.

Majors had said that his team would have to score a lot more against Vanderbilt to win, and he was right. Tennessee won it 34-24 to give Majors his 100th coaching win, but the game was more noteworthy for the performance of Jones, the Vols' great junior running back. He broke his own single-game record with 248 yards on 40 carries, with touchdown runs of 70 and 41 yards thrown in. The entire offense was in high gear with 548 yards and there were big-play touchdown passes by Cockrell; 78 yards to McGee and 85 yards to Duncan.

The 248 yards enabled Jones to become the most prolific single-season rusher in UT history. He shot past the elusive

1,000-yard mark with room to spare with his 1,116 yards.

The awesome Reggie White closed out his home field career with a virtuoso performance. Fighting through double- and triple-team blocks, as he had had to do for much of the season, he had nine tackles, three sacks, and the first interception of his career. As he trotted off Shields-Watkins Field for the last time and headed toward a brilliant professional career, Tennessee fans knew they would probably not see his likes again.

With White leading the way, the 1983 defense went from worst to first. Reggie and friends led the SEC in 1983, a 180-degree turn from 1982 when they ranked last.

The Citrus Bowl game was a corker for those fans who hate to see the offense interrupted by the defense. The Vols won it 30-23 by outscoring the Terps 14-3 in the fourth quarter. Maryland's Esiason, one of the nation's top quarterbacks, suffered a shoulder injury after being sacked by White on the second play of the second quarter and never returned to action. Both Esiason and his backup that day, Frank Reich, went on to NFL careers. And the Vols would meet up with Reich one year later in another bowl game.

Cockrell clutched the game ball as he walked off the field at Orlando Stadium that day. Approaching the exit to the dressing room, he turned and hurled the ball into the stands. "That's the last pass I'll ever throw," he said to teammate Mike Furnas. Cockrell wasn't certain that his football career was over, but he must have had an inkling that it was. Professional baseball beckoned.

"I just felt that if I was a high draft pick I would probably give up football and sign a baseball contract," he says. "Had I been a 15th round draft pick, or a fifth round draft pick, I would have stayed at Tennessee."

He was a first-round selection, the No. 9 pick overall. He signed with the San Francisco Giants and played only two games with the Giants' rookie team in Everett, Washington, before being shipped to Class A Fresno of the California League. As the 1994 season began, he was with Colorado Springs, the Colorado Rockies' AAA farm club, playing the outfield, first base and filling in some at catcher.

The Toronto Blue Jays drafted him out of Parkwood High in Joplin, Missouri, but Cockrell dreamed of playing Southeastern Conference football before 95,000 at Neyland Stadium. Following his knee injury in 1981, he came back to pass for 2021 yards in 1982 and 1683 in 1983, but the injury had affected his mobility. For that reason, he wondered if he should have gone ahead and signed a baseball contract coming out of high school.

Looking back, he thinks he did the right thing. "I would still go to Tennessee and play football," he says. "I just felt back then that if I were given an opportunity to play baseball and I was a high pick that it would be a smart decision. Heath Shuler got that opportunity after his junior year.

"The only difference between the No. 9 pick then and the No. 9 pick now is that today's No. 9 pick is an instant millionaire; the No. 9 pick then got six digits. Times have changed. I guess I was born too soon."

Though he ended his UT football career a year early, Cockrell has continued to follow Tennessee football. That first season in baseball, on a road trip to Reno with the Fresno club, he had a bat boy call a casino to get the score of the Tennessee-Washington State game. And he has managed to attend a few UT games.

The 9-3 finish was the best combined regular season-bowl record for Tennessee since 1972. It was quite a comeback for a team that lost two of its first three games, then won eight of its last nine.

CHAPTER 23

ANOTHER TONY

Two of the greatest talents Johnny Majors ever coached were named Tony—Dorsett of Pittsburgh and Robinson of Tennessee. Dorsett won the Heisman Trophy in 1976. Whatever Heisman chances Robinson had were wiped out by a devastating knee injury in 1985.

Majors called Robinson the greatest quarterback he ever had the pleasure of coaching. Robinson's first practice at Tennessee, which gave a hint of things to come, is indelibly etched in the coach's mind.

"It was the fall of 1982," Majors recalls. "I had seen Tony Robinson on film from high school and it was exciting, just exhilarating, to see all the things he could do throwing a football.

"That first day on the practice field, we lined Willie Gault, a senior, out wide and Tony hit him on the dead run 60 yards downfield, with Willie in full stride. He had the greatest natural touch on the ball I've ever seen. He had the purest arm. He had stuff that Joe Namath and Dan Marino had. He could throw the short pass, the intermediate, or the long. His touch on long passes that first day was something like I had never seen before.

"And Tony could run. When he got out in the open field with those old long legs of his he could do a lot of things."

Robinson had a cannon for an arm but, unfortunately for Majors and the program, Robinson wasn't ready to play his first two years, '82 and '83. "He hadn't really worked hard enough at the detail part of his position—the signal calling, and reading and checking," Majors says. It didn't matter; Alan Cockrell was doing quite well at quarterback. And Robinson was picking up splinters you know where.

Robinson, sure he would be the starter when he arrived in Knoxville, declined to redshirt and considered leaving the program. He went home once, nearly left another time, and almost took his old job back at a hardware store in Tallahassee, Florida.

But with Cockrell having passed up his final year of football to sign a pro baseball contract, Tony Robinson's time had come. Offensive coordinator Walt Harris, who had tutored a number of outstanding college quarterbacks in his career, gave Robinson a course in quarterback play.

Robinson's debut in the '84 season opener was solid: 13 completions in 16 attempts, no interceptions, as the Vols turned back Washington State 34-27 for the first opening day win under Majors. Mark Rypien, later of Washington Redskins fame, completed 17 of 32 for 220 yards for the Cougars. Johnnie Jones picked up where he left off the season before, rushing for 203 yards and two TDs.

Other than the final score, the most significant development of that night was the birth of the Big Orange Wave, a spirited maneuver in which the crowd rises to its feet and whoops it up section by section as the wave rolls around Neyland Stadium. Some observers felt that the wave played a role in the Vols' tumultuous 17-point third quarter. While the stadium was rocking to and fro, the Vols were wheeling and dealing down on the field en route to what was thought to be a commanding 31-16 lead.

After two games, following the Vols' 27-21 victory over Utah, Jones was leading the nation in rushing and was a leading Heisman Trophy candidate. But, for the second straight week, Tennessee built up a healthy lead and then took a nap in the fourth quarter. "Nobody was much in the mood to turn flips and shout after this game," Majors said, "but it is a victory."

A victory it was, the 10th in the last 11 outings for the Vols since their last defeat to Auburn a year earlier. Things looked peachy; Tennessee had pulled into 19th place in the UPI poll. And then Army came to town to botch things. The Cadets outfought, outmuscled, outhustled and outhit a Tennessee team favored by 18 1/2 points and headed back to West Point, with a 24-24 tie.

Jones rushed for 118 yards, his sixth straight performance of more than 100 yards.

The Vols hadn't won a Southeastern Conference opener in five years and Auburn made sure they didn't do it at the Loveliest Village of the Plains the next week. With Jones nursing a sore shoulder and performing far below his normal effectiveness, the Vols had to turn to the pass and it didn't work. Auburn was without its great star, Bo Jackson, but won emphatically anyway, 29-10.

The pounding the Vols took left them facing an uphill climb in the conference race. They were battered and bruised when they went into Auburn, and things were worse when they came out. Linebacker Alvin Toles was lost for the season with a broken leg, fullback William Howard was injured, defensive back/kick returner Charles Benton was out of commission with a neck injury, and defensive backfield mates Charles Davis and Tommy Sims were also among the invalids.

Robinson, back from the injured list, hit some key passes. But he had two throws picked off and gave up a safety in the second quarter when he was blindsided and fumbled the ball out of his end zone. The offense was all but nonexistent, even though the defense came up with five turnovers. Jones gained 67 of Tennessee's 74 rushing yards before trotting off with a shoulder injury in the third period.

An example of Tennessee's futility came on the final play of the first half. Auburn led 16-3 and the ball was one foot from the goal, five seconds to go. Prudence called for a dive play with Jones carrying. Robinson took the snap and Jones went diving into the end zone. The only trouble was, he didn't have the ball. Robinson did, and he was on the ground three or four yards back upfield.

Florida was up next. The last time Tennessee and the Gators met on a football field, in 1977, the Gators threw a pass into the end zone with a 10-point lead and three seconds left in the game. That piece of strategy precipitated a postgame fight and prompted an angry Johnny Majors to vow "Our time will come."

But now, seven years later, Majors said the grudge had been forgotten, although the Gators' attempt to run up the score hadn't been, at least as far as he was concerned.

"I don't have to look back at the film to remember what happened," he said. "I remember it vividly. But I don't think that would have much bearing on this team because we don't have any of the same players or any of the same coaches, except me. It's a different Florida coaching staff, too."

Dickey, the coach of the '77 Florida team, had been forced out a year later and replaced by Charley Pell, himself almost at the end of his rope as he brought his team to Knoxville.

The offense that was missing at Auburn resurfaced against Florida. But the defense was nowhere to be seen as the talented Gators romped to a 43-30 victory. Not since the infamous 35-31 loss to Georgia in 1973 had a Tennessee team scored as much as 30 points and lost.

The offense had seldom been better than it was against the Gators. With Robinson turning in a brilliant performance, the Vols struck early and often and actually outgained Florida 551 yards to 509. Robinson set school records for pass completions (29), individual total offense (389 yards) and first downs passing (18). But the defense, which looked good at times, was especially vulnerable to misdirection plays and screen passes. Florida quarterback Kerwin Bell completed only nine passes, but they went for 201 yards.

A year earlier, defensive coordinator Larry Marmie had been the toast of the town. His Tennessee defense ranked No. 1 in the SEC, a key factor in a 9-3 record and a turnaround from 1982 when it was dead last. He was named the conference's assistant coach of the year, and other schools tried to hire him away from Tennessee. But now his defense had done another turnaround; it was in shreds and tatters and ranked last in the SEC again. The defensive unit, which had lost the great Reggie White, had few takeaways and ranked far down the list in SEC statistics.

Marmie was undaunted. "We all know that football is a game of highs and lows," he said. "If you have peaks, you've got to have the valleys too. I guess we're in a pretty big valley right now."

The battle with Alabama went down as one of the greatest comebacks in Tennessee history. For a change, the two old rivals weren't fighting for the SEC lead. Alabama was 2-4, had even lost to Vanderbilt. Tennessee was 2-2-1, so it was more a matter of trying to steer clear of the conference cellar.

No matter. A crowd of 95,422 turned out at Neyland Stadium. After all, this was Alabama vs. Tennessee.

The Tide could have more or less written an end to Tennessee's season. The Vols trailed 27-13 with five minutes to play. Many Tennessee fans had already conceded Alabama a victory, streaming for the stadium exits. They may have escaped the inevitable traffic jam, but, boy, did they ever miss a comeback.

Majors was on the headphones to his man upstairs in the press box, offensive coordinator Harris. "There's still enough time," Majors told him. "You can do it. It's going to be close, but you can do it."

Late in the game, the Vols faced fourth-and-3 at midfield. Fullback William Howard was sent crashing into the line. Assistants in the press told Majors that it was first down. Bama coach Ray Perkins was sure Howard had been stopped short. Vol network announcer Bill Anderson, also high above the action, had to side with the Tide: "I can tell from up here it's short," he told his audience.

Referee Jimmy Harper signaled first down. Perkins nearly went beserk, striding onto the field as far as the wire to his headphones would allow. He was angry and asked for a measurement. Harper declined. The Tennessee drive continued, and Robinson fired a 17-yard TD strike to Tim McGee to cut it to 27-20. And still the fans left.

The defense stopped Alabama on the next series and Andre Creamer returned a punt 45 yards to the Bama 11. On the third play, Jones smashed in from the 1, making it 27-26 and setting up a two-point try with 2:09 to go.

That was the clincher, the two-point play. Robinson faked a pitch to Jones and cut inside to the end zone. Ironically, it was the same play the Vols had used to spring Jones on his memorable 66-yard TD run against Alabama a year earlier. It wasn't the prettiest or best-executed play of the season, but it was by far the biggest.

Creamer went from goat to hero that day. With his father and sisters somewhere up there in the huge crowd, he was beaten on a 68-yard touchdown pass 35 seconds before halftime. But he came back to set up the winning touchdown with that punt return.

Majors was ecstatic after UT's third straight win over Alabama. "I've been in this game a long time and I don't remember being involved in a comeback like that, ever. Usually I get myself pulled together pretty quickly after a game, but it took me 45 minutes to get my heartbeat back to normal after this one."

Later that night, a popular night spot on the Cumberland Avenue "Strip" erupted in a chorus of "Go, Johnnie, Go" when Jones wandered in. But the shy tailback became embarrassed and left. Fuad Reveiz's on-field celebration was rudely and painfully interrupted when a fan, looking for a souvenir, yanked the placekicker's helmet off his head. The helmet was recovered; Reveiz's twisted neck recovered, too.

Jones and Reveiz rushed and kicked their way into the UT record book as the Vols hung up their second straight eleventh-hour victory, this one 24-21 over Georgia Tech. A 19-yard scamper in the first half made Jones the school's all-time rushing leader with 2,429 yards, 65 more than Curt Watson had in 1969-71. And Jones didn't realize it until a reporter asked him about it after the game. Reveiz made a first-half field goal that erased Gene McEver's career scoring record that had stood for more than 50 years.

But a more significant Reveiz field goal that day was the one that won the game, a 22-yarder with 38 seconds remaining. That made the record 4-2-1 heading into the November stretch run.

Memphis State was no match for Tennessee, falling 41-9 as Robinson passed for 186 yards and two touchdowns and ran for 69 yards, including a 25-yard TD jaunt on an audiblized quarterback draw.

The Vols converted more followers a week later with a 41-17 romp over Ole Miss at Jackson, burying the Jackson Jinx for the second straight time. "Our offense was fun to watch today," Majors said as he knocked on wood. The defense wasn't far behind; the Rebels got 14 of their 17 points against Tennessee reserves in the fourth quarter. Jones went past 1,000 yards rushing for the second straight year. Reveiz hit two field goals, his 15th and 16th in a row, breaking his own SEC record of 14 straight set two years earlier.

Bowl talk swept Big Orange Country. One newspaper said the Vols were headed for San Diego to play undefeated and third-ranked Brigham Young in the Holiday Bowl. Another said Tennessee would go to the Sun Bowl at El Paso to face Maryland in a rematch of their 1983 Florida Citrus Bowl battle.

Newspaper No. 2 was on the mark; the Vols accepted the Sun Bowl invitation a week later. BYU went on to beat a 6-5 Michigan team in the Holiday Bowl and was crowned national champion. The Cougars went 13-0, but their schedule was hardly frightening: Pittsburgh, Baylor, Tulsa, Hawaii, Colorado State, Wyoming, Air Force, New Mexico, Texas-El Paso, San Diego State, Utah, and Utah State.

Tennessee football was beginning to look a lot more like Tennessee football. With Kentucky coming to Knoxville, the Vols had a 6-2-1 record and an excellent shot at 8-2-1, which would be their best since the '72 team went 9-2.

It remained for Kentucky to mess things up. The Wildcats grabbed two fumbles and two interceptions in claiming a 17-12 victory. A key play came late in the game when UT linebacker

Reggie McKenzie was called for roughing UK punter Paul Calhoun. McKenzie said he was sure he made no contact.

"The judgment is that if there's enough contact to crack a raw egg, then you have a five-yard penalty," said veteran SEC official Bert Ackermann of Knoxville. "On the other side of the coin, you have to ask yourself if the kicker contributed to the action. Sometimes he causes it."

In any case, referee Robert Aillet called it roughing, and Kentucky benefited greatly, getting the five penalty yards and a first down. More importantly, it kept the ball away from Tennessee in a game that ended with the Vols at the Wildcat 13. It ended with Robinson trying to stop the clock with a high throw out of bounds. The trouble was that Tony took a couple of steps back before heaving the ball. Had he fired it low and immediately, he might have been able to save just enough time for one more play.

The season finale, a 29-13 victory over Vanderbilt, was the Tim and Tony Show; Tim McGee was catching what Tony Robinson was throwing. Robinson completed 20 of 31 for 273 yards; McGee made an early bid for 1985 preseason All-America honors with 10 catches for 190 yards and two touchdowns.

Robinson shattered Jimmy Streater's UT record for total offense, finishing with 2,089 yards, 78 more than Streater's 1978 total. Tony also wiped out a 28-year-old UT record for season passing accuracy, his 61.7 percent bettering the mark held by none other than Johnny Majors. Jones smashed his own single-season rushing record of 1,116 yards by running for 1,290 and winning the SEC rushing title for the second straight year.

The Vols put on a marvelous first-half performance. The lead was 21-0 and the game, from all appearances, was Tennessee's. Once the second half began, however, Maryland took control; Tennessee took a siesta.

Less than three minutes into the third period, Maryland had ruined Tennessee's hopes of a shutout, and the Terps went on to score 22 unanswered points to take a 22-21 lead. Pete Panuska, a little-used running back, earned his scholarship in 12 seconds as he returned a kickoff 100 yards to put UT on top 27-22 and lift the Vols' sagging spirits.

With less than two minutes remaining, Tennessee's hopes of victory were swelling with the loping strides of Robinson as he neared the end of a neatly executed 22-yard quarterback draw. The Vols were moving into position for Reveiz to trot onto the field, kick a routine field goal and win the game.

But Maryland's Al Covington delivered a vicious lick to Robinson. Something popped out. A football. The Terps recovered. It was all over but the shouting.

After Tennessee had dominated the first half, Maryland posted incredible statistical advantages in the second: first downs (16-2), rushing yards (186-30), passing yards (177-52), total yards (363-82), time of possession (23:57-6:03) and points (28-6).

The Maryland quarterback that day, Frank Reich, ranks as one of the all-time masters of the comeback. Check his credentials: Six weeks earlier, he had been at the controls when Maryland roared back from a 31-0 deficit to beat Miami 42-40—the biggest comeback in college history. He gained everlasting fame nine years later as the quarterback who led the greatest comeback in NFL history, the Buffalo Bills' 41-38 win over the Houston Oilers after being down 35-3 in the third quarter of a 1993 playoff game.

Reveiz found it a difficult way to end his career, standing powerless on the sideline as the Vols drove downfield. He was hoping for one last chance at a field goal. "The worst feeling was when Coach Majors came up to me after Tony's fumble with about 15 seconds to go and said, 'It's over.' "

Though he went out on a losing note, Reveiz had quite a college career. He broke the legendary Gene McEver's UT scoring record with 314 points, set an SEC record of 18 consecutive field goals as a senior and kicked nine field goals of at least 50 yards, including a 60-yarder against Georgia Tech in 1982.

CHAPTER 24

A CHAMPIONSHIP SEASON

All Tony Robinson wanted was a little shut-eye.

It was the eve of Tennessee's season opener against UCLA, and the Vols were watching film. Quarterback Tony Robinson was sitting in the front row, alongside freshman quarterback Jeff Francis.

"The projector was in the back of the room," Francis recalls. "After a couple of minutes I looked over at Tony and he was sound asleep. I nudged him and said, 'Wake up, Tony.' He says, 'Don't worry; just let me know when they turn the projector off. I gotta' get some sleep.' "

The nap must have been more beneficial than anything he might have learned from the film. The next afternoon, before a nationwide television audience, Robinson established school records for passing (387 yards) and total offense (417).

By the time the 1985 season arrived, which was to be Johnny Majors' ninth year as head coach, the Big Orange faithful felt their favorite school had about settled in as a middle or barely upper division Southeastern Conference entry. By and large, the Vols played competitively against nearly everybody, and Alabama was no longer a problem: Three straight victories had corrected that situation, at least for the time being. An SEC athletic director had publicly labeled the conference as divided between the "haves" (Alabama, Auburn, Florida, Georgia, LSU, and Tennessee) and the "have-nots" (Kentucky, Mississippi State, Ole Miss, and Vanderbilt). Vol partisans were happy to be included among the former. Their school had appeared in four consecutive bowl games, none of them the giants of the holiday extravaganzas, but still it was apparent the football program, if not spectacular, at least was on solid footing.

But all that changed in 1985 when a breakthrough occurred that would change the face of Vol football drastically for at least the next decade. At last, Johnny Majors would achieve the first step toward reestablishment of Tennessee among the elite of college football: The Big Orange would win the Southeastern Conference championship, the first for Tennessee in 16 years but also the first of three that would come Tennessee's way over a six-year period extending through 1990.

A new athletic director had come on board, one Doug Dickey, the head coach of that last Tennessee team to win an SEC championship in 1969. He succeeded Bob Woodruff, the man who had hired him as the Vols' head coach in 1964.

Facts regarding the season opener with UCLA would seem to have added up to a Vol victory: quarterback Robinson, 25 of 35 passes for 387 yards, 417 yards total offense, named SEC, AP and UPI offensive player of the week; defensive back Chris White, three interceptions, SEC defensive player of the week.

Alas, those were impressive individual feats, but, sad to say, they didn't add up to a Tennessee victory. A resourceful UCLA team, trailing by 16 points with five minutes left, tallied two touchdowns and a pair of two-point conversions, to gain a 26-all tie before 94,370 fans at Knoxville. The decisive play for the Bruins on the final touchdown was a 44-yard pass from substitute quarterback David Norrie to Mike Sherrard. Why was it so decisive? Because it came with the ball on the UCLA 3, third and 10. It was a terrible way to let a victory get away.

The Vols were downcast after losing their big lead. Receiver Joey Clinkscales probably spoke for the whole squad when he said, "I'll tell you why it feels so bad. You hate to come out of a game the same way you went in, without a winner." Nobody polled the Bruins, but it is safe to say they were absolutely thrilled to leave Knoxville with a tie.

Very likely the thought of a Southeastern Conference championship began to germinate in a few minds two weeks later when the Vols again entertained a nationwide audience on ABC with an astonishing 38-20 creaming of Auburn. It wasn't your garden variety Auburn team, either. This was an outfit that came to Knoxville ranked No. 1 in the nation and featuring the great Bo Jackson. Majors unabashedly acknowledged the outcome as "one of the sweetest" victories of his career.

With Robinson hitting his favorite target, Tim McGee, the Vols jumped to a 24-0 lead. When it appeared Auburn might rally, Tennessee tacked on two fourth-quarter touchdowns to win going away. Robinson, who was a deceptively elusive runner, kept the defense loose with his combination of skills. He riddled the highly regarded Auburn defense for 259 yards and four touchdowns on 17 completions.

Perhaps more significantly, the Vol defense turned Jackson every way but loose. The soon-to-be Heisman Trophy winner, whose vast athletic skills later allowed him to play major league baseball as well as pro football, was held to 80 yards, a paltry sum considering he had already put together back-to-back 200-plus yard games in 1985. Majors called attention to the job the defense did on Jackson: "Jackson is a marvelous athlete with great ability. You are scared every time he has the ball. Our defense swarmed him constantly, and everything he got came the hard way."

Sports Illustrated sent a crew to Knoxville to cover the game. The emphasis, of course, was to be on Jackson. Writer Rick Reilly wound up writing not about Bo, but about Robinson, "the biggest thing in Tennessee since Dolly Parton left Pigeon Forge." Reilly described Robinson, who graced the *SI* cover of October 7, 1985, as "a quarterback built along the lines of a tent pole."

"Man, just think about it," said McGee, who caught six passes for 163 yards and a touchdown. "We had nothing to lose. This is Auburn, the No. 1 team with the No. 1 Heisman guy. We could've lost 50 to nothing and everybody would have said, 'Typical Tennessee team.' Now, we've got Tennessee back on the map."

Much of the credit for the surprisingly easy victory went to Ken Donahue, Bear Bryant's defensive assistant at Alabama for 19 years, who had just returned to his alma mater as defensive coordinator. Jackson had averaged 163 yards against Donahue at Alabama, but Donahue managed to lasso him this time. Jackson gained only 80 yards on 17 carries before leaving in the third period with a bruised knee.

"I was glad to see Bo go to the sideline," Donahue said, " and I'll be even gladder to see him graduate."

After dealing with giants UCLA and Auburn in impressive fashion, the Vols nearly spilled the milk the next week against little Wake Forest. "A natural letdown," decreed the media, "following two highly emotional games." "Nonsense," responded

Majors, who gave credit to the undermanned but game Demon Deacons for holding Tennessee to a 31-29 triumph. "We may not have looked as crisp as we did in earlier games," Majors told reporters, "but Wake Forest had an awful lot to do with it."

Everything appeared to be going well two minutes into the final period with the Vols ahead, 31-14, and the coaches getting ready to rest the regulars. But hold on! Here came those Demon Deacons, White in command, to post two touchdowns. And then came, with one minute left, an onside kick intended to set up a field goal that would have earned Wake Forest a one-point victory.

Carlos Reveiz, who had succeeded his brother Fuad as the Vols' placekicker, had to fight winds that gusted up to 17 miles per hour as he rifled through a 52-yard field goal in the third period. Reveiz's shot and a goal-line stand the Vols mounted moments before halftime were credited in postgame analysis with playing pivotal roles in the victory.

But for the second time in three weeks, some fans left Neyland Stadium feeling as though Tennessee had lost. The more philosophical souls in attendance, noting that the Vols had struggled, figured that it is better to look bad and win than to look good and lose. On their first possession, the Vols needed 12 plays to go just 38 yards to score. That's struggling.

"We had 'em all the way," Majors said, tongue planted firmly in cheek. "Seriously, though, I was tickled to death to walk out of Neyland Stadium with a 31-29 victory."

Happy to escape the feisty Demon Deacons' booby trap, Tennessee next prepared for a mammoth outing against Florida at Gainesville where two superb quarterbacks would be matching skills. But the contest wasn't decided on the basis of Tennessee's Tony Robinson vs. Florida's Kerwin Bell. Believe it or not, it hinged on the kicking game, an area in which Florida enjoyed a decisive edge that steamy, sultry October afternoon.

Consider just one sequence in which the time it took to run only two plays turned the game completely upside down: Florida is pinned at its own 7, third-and-25. A short run is followed by a 63-yard punt, but on the return Tennessee is penalized for a clip. So now Tennessee has possession, all right, but the ball is on the Vol 8. And so it went throughout the afternoon, as the Gators' outstanding punter, Ray Criswell, kept UT at bay. Uncharacteristically, Tennessee's punting suffered through a lackluster performance.

Majors' analysis of the 17-10 defeat was right on target: "Summarizing, I thought our defense played well enough to win. But field position and punting were what killed us. We had our backs to the wall because of Criswell's great punting." In retrospect, maybe the Vols' showing wasn't all that bad. Tony Robinson, who completed 26 of 36 passes for 300 yards, was still firing for a game-saving touchdown in the final minute of the fourth quarter.

Although the Vols lost to Florida, the two teams would go on to tie for the conference championship with 5-1 records. And Tennessee would get the Sugar Bowl invitation because the Gators were declared ineligible for the SEC title because of recruiting violations.

Vol fans thought they saw their SEC title hopes sprawled out hopelessly on the artificial turf of Legion Field one week later. Robinson lay crumpled on the ground with a severe knee injury that would end his college career. It came in the opening minutes of the fourth quarter of a classic battle with Alabama in which Tennessee held a 16-7 lead.

Trainer Tim Kerin went to Majors. "It's bad, Coach," he said. "I'm afraid Tony's out for the year."

Majors called Donahue in the press box, informing him that Robinson was lost so he could adjust defensive plans. He asked Donahue not to say anything to offensive coordinator Walt Harris; he didn't want Harris concerned at the moment. "We were in four-down territory at the time," Majors said, "and we wanted to put something on the board."

After Reveiz kicked a field goal, Majors called Harris. "Keep your chin up," he said. "Tony won't be back in the game and is probably lost for the season. But we're going to have to put that out of our minds now and concentrate on winning the game."

When the Crimson Tide drove to a touchdown that cut the margin to 16-14 and the Vols couldn't get a drive going without Robinson, even the most gung-ho Tennessee supporter was afraid the jig was up.

But the fans failed to take Dale Jones into account. For sure, they weren't figuring on Jones making a defensive play that will forever rank as one of the greatest in Tennessee history. This one was certainly the most crucial one since Bill Majors, Wayne Grubb and Charles Severance ganged up on Billy Cannon in the 1959 LSU game. How the junior defensive end from Cleveland did it still ranks as one of the great mysteries of sport, but some way or other Mike Shula's pass was first batted into the air by Jones from a distance of no more than eight or 10 feet, then snatched by Jones, all in the same motion. He hugged the ball to his chest and fell to the ground. The most unlikely interception in UT history turned the momentum back Tennessee's way, and the Vols held on for their fourth consecutive victory over the Tide. The

South's greatest football rivalry had produced another classic: Tennessee 16, Alabama 14.

Many of the fans there that day still remember the play that might have been. After Robinson was injured, it was a less-gifted but also less error-prone Daryl Dickey who entered into the game. His first pass was right into the hands of an Alabama linebacker, who dropped it. Had he held on to the ball he probably could have run it back for a touchdown.

Before Robinson left the game, the skinny senior had guided his team to a touchdown and two field goals, and he had the Vols in position for another field goal when the injury occurred. Robinson was a superb quarterback, gifted in both passing and running. His loss could have been a mortal blow from which the 1985 Vols would never recover. From that point, it would be up to Dickey, a fifth-year senior, to handle field general responsibilities if the Vols' slim SEC title hopes were to remain alive.

How well Dickey did his job would be the central theme around which the rest of the season would revolve. It was a big plus that Dickey, son of the Tennessee athletic director, had a solid football mind, a keen sense of responsibility and a confidence in his ability.

Frankly, the outlook didn't appear too promising a week later when the Vols were unable to sustain an offense for 59 minutes and needed a heroic 51-yard field goal by Reveiz with four seconds left to salvage a tie with Georgia Tech, 6-6. Dickey, unspectacular with his passing most of the way, drove the Vols to within Reveiz's kicking range to set up the tying field goal. This, take note, was against a Georgia Tech team not likely to be confused with the one five years later that brought a national championship to the Flats. Few customers among the 94,575 left Neyland Stadium that afternoon making plans for a holiday trip to New Orleans.

Dickey was undefeated as a starter. He was also winless, with his only other start resulting in a 24-24 tie with Army the year before. With Robinson at the controls, Tennessee had averaged 400 yards of offense in five games. With Dickey handling the team, the Vol offense managed just 258 yards against Tech. "I take responsibility for that," he said. "We lacked execution, and it's up to the quarterback to help our team execute."

Robinson, just out of the hospital, made a surprise visit to the Vol dressing room before the game. "I didn't even know he had been released," Reveiz said. "We're all in there putting on our pads and you hear that familiar voice saying, 'Come on, boys!

Let's get it up!' " Teammates agreed that the visit gave them a lift and broke a lot of the tension.

By early November, the Vol defense had risen from the shambles of an almost disastrous start to a level of proficiency that not even the most rabid Vol fan could have foreseen in mid-September. So *The Knoxville Journal* launched a "Name The Vol Defense" contest. It began as an informal little undertaking with a grand prize of an orange and white football autographed by the Vol defensive starters. Its retail value: about $24. The promotion sired a monster of sorts; the *Journal* received thousands of entries, with 533 suggested nicknames ranging from "Angry Orange" to "Ziegler's Zombies." The contest deadline had to be extended for a week.

The winning nickname turned out to be "Orange Crunch." It beat out "Rocky Stops" and "Crunch Bunch."

Two other non-conference foes would be met before Tennessee returned to SEC combat. Rutgers didn't offer much opposition in suffering a 40-0 pounding at Knoxville, and the Vols managed to stave off Memphis State, 17-7, at Liberty Bowl Memorial Stadium. The win over Memphis State came with great difficulty and wasn't nailed down until the Tigers ran out of downs at the Vol 10 on a fourth-quarter touchdown bid.

As the three non-league tests passed by, Majors saw signs in Dickey of remarkable progress in decision-making and in physical skills. Most Tennessee fans had dismissed the idea of an SEC championship in 1985, but Majors wasn't joining the skeptics in a death watch.

When the offense is adjusting to a new quarterback, as Tennessee's was after Robinson's injury, there is one time-tested recipe to stay in contention with your opponent: Take the charge to him with solid defense. In the 34-14 win over Ole Miss at Knoxville on November 18, Chris White, a Vol safety, dominated the game as few defenders ever do. Maybe a Reggie White occasionally, as happened two years earlier, but a defensive back? And yet, it happened. The ever-alert White, who had been touted earlier as a future quarterback, snared two interceptions and blocked a punt, essential plays in the victory over the Rebels.

Majors lauded the play of White and his old Bradley County teammate, Dale Jones, who harrassed Ole Miss quarterback Chris Osgood unmercifully. The freshman Osgood completed only four of his 20 passes. "White and Jones were excellent," Majors said. "Chris seems to be around the ball on virtually every play and comes up with key interceptions. Of course, Dale Jones is one of the premier defensive ends in the nation."

With a 3-1 SEC record and heading into traditional season-ending clashes with Kentucky and Vanderbilt, Tennessee was on the brink of nailing down its first league title since 1969. And yet, the idea still hadn't sunk in with fans. The reason? Daryl Dickey still had not been tested enough under fire to convince the Orange faithful he was an adequate replacement for the sidelined Robinson. Young Mr. Dickey was about to make believers out of the doubters.

Halftime at Lexington on November 23 found the Vols clinging nervously to a 6-0 lead on the strength of two Reveiz field goals. Dickey and mates had been unable to establish a consistent offense in the first two quarters, but coordinator Ken Donahue's defensive troops had repulsed all Kentucky forays into Vol territory. In the third quarter, Dickey's hand turned hot. He found the ubiquitous Tim McGee for touchdown passes of 37 and 12 yards, turning the game into a rout by the time the final period started. With Dickey hitting 13 of 19 pass attempts, Tennessee crushed the Wildcats, 42-0.

Majors credited the victory to a third-quarter scoring sequence by the Vols. "Our ability to take the second-half kickoff and march downfield for a touchdown was pivotal. And for that we can thank a memorable play in which Daryl Dickey broke out of a trap and hit Tim McGee deep in Kentucky territory. Tim then used his exceptional athletic ability to squirm across the goal line."

On November 25, Tennessee cracked the Top 10 in the Associated Press poll for the first time since 1972. The news drew a long, low whistle from Majors and loud whoops from several of his players.

All of a sudden, with oft-beaten Vanderbilt the lone remaining hurdle to a conference championship, Vol fans awakened. They began to smell the roses. Their team needed to beat Vanderbilt the next Saturday at Neyland Stadium to earn a trip to the Sugar Bowl. UT students, most of whom had gone home for Thanksgiving, returned to campus early in order to be among the 97,372 who set an attendance record.

The suspense was short-lived. With five minutes left in the opening period, the Vols, en route to a 30-0 shutout, had taken command on a Dickey-to-McGee pass and a Reveiz field goal. The Neyland Stadium goal posts came down. For the second week in a row, Daryl was named SEC player of the week. Not only had he provided the quarterbacking artistry needed for a championship, but he had achieved the amazing distinction of throwing 106 passes without an interception. He had his most productive day against Vandy: 22 of 32 passes for 299 yards and three TDs.

Majors in his postgame comments summed up the season neatly: "This is the most distinct and responsive group of champions I have ever been around. The championship teams I have been involved with in the past may have had more experience, strength and speed at certain positions, but as a group, this is the most remarkable one in terms of improvement since spring practice and since a period of reconstruction at midseason."

Bob Woodruff, who retired as UT athletic director that fall, talked to the Vol squad concerning Tennessee tradition two days before the Vandy game.

"Coach Woodruff claims he's the world's worst speaker," Majors said, "but he held the team's total attention for eight minutes. After it was over they gave him a continuous ovation as he left the room."

On to the Sugar Bowl, where the Vols faced a "hopeless" task, sidetracking the Miami Hurricanes, who to a man thought they, rather than Penn State, deserved to be ranked first in the polls. The Hurricanes, under the flamboyant Jimmy Johnson (a Johnny Majors protege), were prohibitive favorites. Few teams have ever gone into a major bowl more firmly entrenched as underdogs as the Tennessee team that took the field at the Louisiana Superdome. That Miami would beat the Vols was a foregone conclusion. How decisively they would prevail was the only question. But a funny thing happened to Miami on the way to its championship coronation . . .

A sea of orange (Tennessee's shade, not Miami's) gave a Neyland Stadium appearance to the Superdome as the teams trotted out for their pregame workouts. Everybody from Tennessee who could buy, beg, borrow or steal a ticket was on hand in New Orleans, even if not in a very optimistic frame of mind. The Superdome seats about 78,000 and estimates of the number of Tennessee fans on hand were in the 50,000 range. Vol faithful, overjoyed at being invited to the party, were prepared to take their licks. After spotting Miami a touchdown lead, the Vols roared back to post a 14-7 halftime lead en route to a 35-7 thrashing of the cocky Hurricanes.

The interaction between the Tennessee players and their fans that night was somethng to behold. The better the Vols played, the louder the UT fans cheered. And the louder cheers provoked still better play.

A fiendish pass rush by the Orange Crunch defense, combined with the big play performance of the Vol secondary, made Miami All-American Vinny Testaverde look like just another quarterback. He spent much of the night running for his life and was sacked seven times for minus-84 yards. A year later, he would win the Heisman Trophy. The Vols intercepted four passes and forced three fumble turnovers.

On its front page of January 2, 1986, *The Knoxville Journal's* main headline, set in massive size type, said simply, "CRUNCH!"

Dickey, forever shedding his second-string label, had a productive game and deservedly won MVP honors on the basis of providing excellent direction. But it was the defense that really stole the show. Besides holding Miami's heralded running game to 32 net yards, the Vol D registered four interceptions, seven sacks and four tackles for lost yardage. In fact, one press box minion voted for defensive coordinator Donahue as MVP, and game stories, with Majors leading the cheers, credited the upset victory largely to the planning and attention to detail of the single-minded Donahue.

Over the last seven games, the Orange Crunch defense posted three shutouts (Rutgers, Kentucky, Vandy), and gave up just 34 points: Georgia Tech (6), Memphis State (7), Miami (7) and Ole Miss (14).

(Incidentally, if Miami had won, the Hurricanes would have had their national championship because Penn State bowed in the Orange Bowl to Oklahoma, a team Miami had defeated in regular season play. As it turned out, Oklahoma was named No 1, Penn State No. 3, Tennessee No. 4 and Miami dropped to No. 9.)

Coming away from New Orleans, Vol fans felt good about their football team and where it was headed. But even the most optimistic among them probably didn't realize that Tennessee had entered a Golden Era that would continue at least until the mid-1990s.

Several days later, Pittsburgh, which had lost Majors to Tennessee nine years earlier, tried to rehire him. Majors was offered a lucrative contract, one he called "tempting," but he turned it down. UT offered him a six-year contract, through the 1991 season, and boosted his salary package by $20,000. His new contract was worth more than $250,000 a year.

The 1985 Vols will live in memory as the team that restored the Tennessee tradition. They were the first Tennessee team to win an SEC championship since 1969, the first to go to a major bowl since 1970, and the first in 15 years to wind up in the final top 10 rankings. The 9-1-2 record landed the Big Orange at No. 4 in both the AP and UPI final polls. Once again, Tennessee walked tall across the college landscape.

CHAPTER 25

ORANGE SHOES

Somewhere in Russia there are 100 pairs of orange Nike football shoes, compliments of the University of Tennessee Athletic Department.

The shoes were virtually new when shipped to Russia in 1990. They had been worn only once, on October 18, 1986, when Tennessee played Alabama—and lost 56-28. No wonder people in Big Orange Country were glad to see them shipped halfway around the world. For most Vol fans, the moon would have been the destination of choice.

Following the Alabama debacle, UT equipment manager Roger Frazier dutifully packed them away in a downstairs storage room at Stokely Athletics Center. Four years later, athletic director Doug Dickey received a letter, and therein found a perfect excuse to dispose of 100 reminders of a painful day in Tennessee history once and for all.

"Coach Dickey got this letter from someone in Russia saying they were starting American football there," Frazier says. "They asked if we could donate any football equipment, so we sent them the orange shoes. We didn't keep a single pair."

Frazier says the only pair he knows of today is owned by Hugh Ray Wilson, an avid UT fan who operates Hoorays Sports Bar and Grill in Knoxville's Old City.

Most of the players who wore them and most of the fans who saw them are in agreement: good riddance. In a word, they were gaudy to the point of being tacky. If truth be known, the decision to outfit his team in orange shoes probably ranks high on coach Johnny Majors' list of things he would like to change.

Long before Football 1986 ever reared its head, it was obvious that enthusiasm over Tennessee football was reaching an all-time high. The aura that surrounded the Southeastern Conference and Sugar Bowl championship season would continue; the 1986 Orange and White spring game left no doubt of that.

The 1985 SEC champs put away their football togs the night of January 1, after dismembering Miami in the 1986 Sugar Bowl. It became an unusually short offseason. Just 114 days later, on April 26, diehard Tennessee fans turned out 73,801 strong for the Orange and White game at Neyland Stadium. The crowd exceeded by more than 30,000 the previous largest turnout anywhere on the planet for an intrasquad scrimmage.

It afforded Vol fans their first opportunity to salute their champions following their conference and bowl championships. The Orange and White game itself featured a quarterbacking confrontation between sophomores Randy Sanders and Jeff Francis, who were to battle in the fall for the job vacated by Daryl Dickey.

It was probably the first football game ever played where the size of the crowd was a bigger story than the game itself. And this particular spring game was a good one, with Francis and Sanders slugging it out for the quarterbacking job. Sanders' Orange team won 24-14, with Randy completing 12 of 16 passes for 149 yards and two touchdowns. Francis wasn't far behind, with 10 of 15 for 110 yards.

Enthusiasm might have been at fever pitch, but the spring game was played beneath a dark cloud of sorts. Back on January 8, with the '85 championship season and Sugar Bowl victory still fresh in their minds, Tennessee fans got a jolt. Tony Robinson, the pet and pride of Big Orange Country, the people's choice, and former Vol teammate Kenneth "B.B." Cooper (1981-84) were arrested by Knoxville police on felony cocaine charges, accused of selling cocaine to an undercover officer.

The news was made even harder to take because the way in which Robinson had handled the adversity of a career-ending injury endeared him even more to the hundreds of thousands of people who followed Tennessee football across the state and beyond its borders.

Robinson pleaded no contest to three counts of delivering cocaine and was ordered to serve 90 days at the Knox County Penal Farm. The sentence was extended after he violated terms of his work-release program.

During the 1987 NFL players strike, Robinson was granted a release to play with the Washington Redskins. In 1989, while playing with the Virginia Storm, a minor league team based in Fairfax, Virginia, he was arrested for failing to appear for a scheduled probation hearing in Knoxville. He was returned to jail.

In the days that followed the Robinson-Cooper drug bust, Knoxville and Nashville newspapers investigated the UT sports program, and there were allegations of booster involvement with football and basketball players, claims of free hotel rooms and use of boosters' cars. UT president Edward Boling ordered an in-house probe of the athletic department. Robinson was found to have been using a Vol booster's car, and a credit card belonging to the booster was found in Robinson's possession. There were widespread reports of players selling their tickets for cash, allegedly done with the knowledge of the UT coaching staff.

On August 20, six months after the start of the investigation, the in-house committee released its final report. A limited number of violations of NCAA rules were confirmed. Tennessee was placed on a year's NCAA probation, with no sanctions. Majors received a reprimand. The booster linked to Robinson was told to disassociate himself from the program.

Robinson's was a sad story—a once-promising career wrecked by drug convictions, jail time and run-ins with the courts.

UT was destined for another black eye. On Friday before the 1986 season opener against New Mexico, *The Knoxville Journal* reported that 28 Tennessee players had violated NCAA rules during the 1985 season by arranging free admission to games for non-relatives and non-student friends. That gave UT officials less than 24 hours to review the 1985 complimentary-pass lists, during which infractions by additional players were discovered, and to consult with the NCAA to determine which players would be suspended.

It was agreed that UT would suspend 10 players for the New Mexico game, including starting linebacker Kelly Ziegler and placekicker Carlos Reveiz, whose suspensions had been announced during the summer. Ten was the minimum number the Vols could suspend under the agreement with the NCAA. The cases of other players went under appeal.

"If all 60 of their players were ineligible, I don't know if it would be good enough to help us," said New Mexico coach Joe Lee Dunn, whose team was a 23-point underdog. But Dunn sided with Tennessee. "It's a little far-fetched," he said. "When it's come to where a guy can't let his fiancee get into a ballgame, something's wrong."

After all the legal maneuverings, the Vols went on to turn back the Lobos 35-21 and everybody on the Tennessee side was glad to have that game out of the way. A sidelight: after years of strolling the sidelines in coaching togs, Majors was wearing coat and tie, which he does to this day.

The Tennessee players decided on a one-game boycott of the media in retaliation for the reporting that led to the suspensions, so there were no postgame player quotes to be heard or seen.

Francis, impressive in his starting debut, completed 19 of 32 passes for 230 yards without an interception. Walk-on kicker Phil Reich, subbing for the suspended Carlos Reveiz, was 2-for-2 on field goals of 33 and 30 yards.

As things turned out, the NCAA discovered that there had been widespread violations of the "pass-list" rule. But the season went on.

Francis' debut as the starting quarterback had been sparkling for the most part, but not faultless. Quarterbacks coach Walt Harris decided that Francis should work, not on his passing, but on his voice, because his teammates had been unable to hear his snap count as they were in scoring position early in the game. After having first-and-goal at the 4, the Vols suffered two procedural penalties in a span of three plays and had to settle for a field goal.

Consequently, Francis had to spend several sessions with a speech therapist in an attempt to strengthen his voice. "This guy had me work on using my diaphragm more in speaking," he says. "It was the most embarrassing thing I've ever had to do, sitting there in the office and having to call out signals. I don't know that it helped; when you have 95,000 people screaming I don't care how loud you are, it's going to be difficult to hear. After that, whenever those offensive linemen would miss an audible at the line, they had a built-in excuse: 'I couldn't hear Francis.' "

Francis says the players weren't really mad at the media over the pass-list incident. "First of all, I don't think the suspensions had any effect on the game. I think we were sort of let down because it was a kind of unwritten thing; it was a way that you could make a little money, by selling your complimentary tickets. We were disappointed that we weren't going to be able to do it again."

While Tennessee was slipping past the outmanned Lobos, developments at Syracuse, New York, caused Johnny Majors and his staff more than a little concern. Mississippi State and its great quarterback, Don Smith, upset Syracuse 24-17.

Even so, the Vols were favored by 23 points the following Saturday. Smith handled everything Tennessee could throw at him. The folks who claim that one man can't beat 11 hadn't seen State's gifted senior field general at work. He applied the coup de grace on a 62-yard touchdown run in the fourth quarter to bring his team back from a 23-20 deficit to a 27-23 triumph. He also threw TD passes of 43, 12 and 5 yards.

It didn't help matters that Francis suffered a shoulder injury on Tennessee's third offensive play. Sanders played well in relief and was in charge as the Vols, down by four points, made their last bid with 4:30 to play.

Just in case any of his teammates were feeling the pressure, Sanders made a brief speech in the huddle: "If there's anybody here who doesn't believe we're going to score a touchdown, just go to the sidelines." Nobody departed. On third-and-15 from the Bulldogs' 16, freshman Terence Cleveland broke clear in the end zone, but Sanders' pass was about a foot too high for the 5-8 Cleveland.

Just after the 1986 season, his freshman year, Sanders had a scary fall in the shower that left him with amnesia. It happened when several players began throwing cold water on each other in the shower. He was continually asking questions, prompting teammates to write on a notepad: "You fell in the shower and hit your head and you can't remember anything." The night of the mishap he had a date with his girlfriend. He couldn't remember her phone number. Later, when it came time to take her home, they got in Randy's truck and he began to drive.

After a few minutes, he said, "This may sound stupid, but where do you live?" She gave him directions to her house, but to this day he doesn't remember driving back to the dormitory. He recovered his memory after three or four days.

Tennessee was no match for Auburn. The Tigers, still smarting from a 38-20 loss at Knoxville the year before, pummeled the Vols 34-8. The final indignity was a touchdown by quarterback Jeff Burger with three seconds to play. Actually, the Tigers didn't want to score. Coach Pat Dye sent in instructions to Burger to down the ball and run out the clock.

Burger called "kneel down" in the huddle and tackle Tracy Searls grabbed him and said, "You better not kneel down. Stick it in there."

Burger took the snap, backed up and waited for a Tennessee player to challenge him. None did. Finally, he simply stepped into the end zone, completing a quarterback sneak to end all quarterback sneaks. It could have been called a quarterback crawl, because it was accomplished on hand and knee while no one was watching. Certainly not game officials and Tennessee players.

"What was I supposed to do?" Burger asked after the game. "I guess I was wrong to do that but Tennessee let me do it. They sort of quit on the play. They just stood there and watched me."

"An appropriate ending to an imperfect day," said a disappointed Majors.

Francis remembers the day quite well. "That was my first road game as a starter," he says. "I can remember not knowing what was going on in games because I was a sophomore. It was terribly hot that day and it was just a bad day all around. I remember looking over at their players during a TV timeout, seeing the size of their arms and then looking at ours. I knew we were physically outmatched.

"Then we played down there my senior season. It was so different from my sophomore year. I looked at our guys in the huddle who were freshmen and sophomores and I knew what they were going through. In the three years I played, Auburn was by far the strongest team we played. They had the best defense in the country."

Just when Tennessee fans thought it couldn't get worse, it did; insanely worse. Texas El-Paso had just been bushwhacked 69-7 by Iowa the week before, was coming off a 1-10 season and had won but 25 games in the preceding 16 years. The Vols were prohibitive favorites in spite of their 1-2 record.

The Miners slugged it out with Tennessee before losing 26-16 in a real snoozer. The air was filled with boos because Tennessee chose not to fill it with footballs, sticking with a conservative game plan of old-fashioned power football with William Howard carrying more often than not.

Things went from bad to worse a week later. In a tune up for Alabama, the Vols lost 25-21 to an Army team that beat Tennessee at its own game—kicking. At one point the Vols had a 21-7 lead, then allowed the Cadets to score 18 points in the fourth quarter. The killer came when Army blocked a punt at the UT 10. Cadet Reggie Fullwood picked up the loose ball at the 2 and stepped into the end zone for the winning TD with 35 seconds to play. Tennessee football had long prided itself on its kicking and protecting the kicker but the way in which Army won was almost as painful as the loss itself.

Nobody was more unhappy than Majors. "I don't know of a week when I've ever been more anxious to put a game behind me

. . . We did about as many different things as we could do to lose this game."

The Vols didn't have to do much to lose the next one, orange shoes or not; Alabama saw to that. The Tide rolled up 457 yards rushing and most of it came on one play, Toss Sweep 28, a quick pitch to sophomore tailback Bobby Humphrey on a sweep to the left side of the Tennessee defense. Twenty-seven times quarterback Mike Shula pitched to Humphrey, and 27 times the Vols failed to stop it. Humphrey finished with 217 yards and three touchdowns. Alabama scored a touchdown on eight of its first 10 possessions and converted eight of 11 third-down situations. The scoring drives were 74, 43, 12, 74, 62, 48, 80 and 56 yards.

Oh, yes, the final score was Alabama 56, Tennessee 28. It was the most points ever scored by either team in the storied series. And one must go back to 1893, when North Carolina scored 60, to find a worse defensive performance by a Tennessee team.

Almost overlooked in the wreckage was a fine performance by the Vol offense, which managed to register 408 yards and four touchdowns. Francis was a hero in defeat, completing 23 of 30 attempts for 309 yards. In back-to-back games, against Army and Alabama, the sophomore completed 50 of 66 passes for 643 yards.

Francis remembered the crushing defeat on an April afternoon eight years later.

"Alabama got us down 21-0 very early but we came back to cut it to 21-14 and Neyland Stadium really erupted; our fans really got into the game. Then Alabama just rammed the ball down our throats. They lined up and played smash-mouth football."

Humphrey said he detected something in Tennessee's once-feared Orange Crunch defense. "Tennessee is usually a good, fired-up defensive team. The hitting was the same, for the most part, but I could tell by looking into their eyes that something was different out there."

Majors was more to the point: "The Tennessee defense never showed up." Amen.

Ray Perkins, with his first win over Tennessee after three losses, was surprised to learn that the Tide had run Toss Sweep 28 twenty-seven times. "That has to be a record for a team of mine," he said. "But we ran it early with success. Why stop? Tennessee never solved it."

The record after six games was 2-4, and the two victories were over teams that could hardly be called heavyweights, New

Mexico and Texas-El Paso. Playing for pride was about all that was left for the Vols.

Georgia Tech pinned a 14-13 defeat on the Vols a week later, dodging a bullet in the process. With 1:49 to play, Carlos Reveiz, who had been the nation's most efficient kicker the season before, slipped on his approach to the ball and banged what would have been the winning field goal against the right upright.

The football gods had not been smiling on Tennessee. Two of the six losses could have gone the other way; they could be traced to an overthrown pass against Mississippi State and a blocked punt in the dying seconds of the Army game. That was the difference between 4 and 2, which the Vols could have been, and 2 and 4, which they were.

The Vols beat Memphis State 33-3 and, while the Vols didn't look like world-beaters, they sure didn't resemble the Tennessee team of the past several Saturdays.

The long-dormant Orange Crunch defense was at it again in an emphatic 22-10 victory over 20th-ranked Ole Miss that ruined the Rebels' Sugar Bowl dreams. Fullback Howard was a workhorse, carrying the ball on 16 consecutive plays as the Vols battled to retain possession in the fourth quarter. Howard set an individual game NCAA record with his 16 straight carries.

The Vols got an invitation to the Liberty Bowl following a 28-9 conquest of Kentucky, a bid based largely on economic considerations. The Memphis bowl folks made no secret of the fact that they wanted a host team whose fans would come early, stay late and spend money in the interim. Tennessee fans certainly met that requirement, as they still do today.

The SEC's hottest team took a 5-5 record to Vanderbilt a week later and came away a 35-20 victor. It was not one of the more spectacular victories in UT history, but it was an awfully big win for the program. Much had been expected of this team. It had come into 1986 riding a five-year wave of winning teams and bowl appearances, topped off by the SEC championship and Sugar Bowl victory.

The Vols took another giant step in the Liberty Bowl, getting past a good Minnesota team 21-14. Francis, playing perhaps his finest game, engineered the winning touchdown drive and won Most Valuable Player honors. Jeff completed 22 of 31 passes for 243 yards and hooked up with Joey Clinkscales on the winning TD pass of 15 yards. Francis finished the '86 season as the NCAA's seventh-ranked passer.

CHAPTER 26

THE COMEBACK KIDS

After all the trials and tribulations of Tennessee's 1986 season—investigations, drug raids, inquiries, interrogations, newspaper charges—it was probably too much to expect that the 1987 campaign could get off to an untainted start.

It didn't.

In the very first game of the season, Tennessee vs. Iowa in the Kickoff Classic at East Rutherford, New Jersey, controversy reared its head, trivial though it was. Hawkeye kicker Rob Houghtlin accused Vol placekicker Phil Reich of using an illegal tee. Houghtlin said he was not questioning the tee Reich used to kick a 20-yard field goal, but the Hawk squawked that the tee Reich used for kickoffs was taller than two inches, the maximum the rulebook permits.

"It was at least 2 1/2 inches," Houghtlin said. "I saw it in pregame warmups." He claimed such a tee would allow a kicker to get more height and distance on the ball.

Nonsense, Reich countered. He said he shaved the bottom of the tee so the legs actually looked higher. "But it's two inches," he declared.

All tees aside, Tennessee won the game, and a new star was born, running back Reggie Cobb. The redshirt freshman from

Knoxville's Central High gained 138 yards on 25 carries in the Vols' 23-22 victory over the highly regarded Hawkeyes and he would blossom into one of Tennessee's finest running backs ever. But the story of the game was a 96-yard fumble return by outside linebacker Darrin Miller.

The senior from Flemington, New Jersey, shocked the Hawkeyes and a national television audience when he intercepted an errant pitchout at the UT 4 and rambled to the far end zone. His teammates kidded him about nearly running out of gas on the return. Paul Naumoff, Vol linebacking star of the mid-1960s, joked on a television show that Miller's run was one of the greatest in Tennessee history, "but also one of the longest in elapsed time." Knoxville sportscaster Bob Kesling, co-host with Naumoff on the Friday night show, said Miller's run took long enough for one pursuing Hawkeye to be knocked off his feet three times by the same Vol blocker.

There was an interesting note to the game. When Tennessee lined up to attempt the winning field goal with three seconds remaining, former walk-on center Nick Zecchino snapped the ball to walk-on holder Lee England, who placed it down for walk-on kicker Reich, who hit the game-winning 20-yarder. Reich received a scholarship almost immediately after the game.

The Vols butchered Colorado State's Rams 49-3, but it wasn't a case of Tennessee being sharp as much as it was the Rams having a tendency to self-destruct. They fumbled the opening kickoff at their own 14 and the Vols turned that into a 7-0 lead. Two more turnovers led to UT touchdowns before halftime. It wasn't the best of nights for Colorado State punter Brian Glazer. He had one punt blocked and popped up another one that went for minus-three yards before Glazer himself was able to down it.

The record went to 3-0, only the second 3-0 start in 11 seasons under Johnny Majors, in an impressive 38-10 romp over Mississippi State in the Vols' first visit to Starkville since 1950.

The big play came early. With State's Hank Phillips apparently headed for a 76-yard touchdown run in the first period, Vol defensive back Terry McDaniel overtook him and stripped the ball at the UT 15, where it was recovered by Darrin Miller, who had made the big grandstand play against Iowa two weeks earlier. Thus inspired, the Vols drove back 85 yards to a TD, and the rout was on.

After an open date, Tennessee was staring defeat in the eye against No. 3 Auburn, trailing by 10 points with seven minutes to go. But Jeff Francis drove the Vols 55 yards to a field goal and 56 yards to a touchdown to forge a 20-20 tie with 1:20 to play.

The tie offended a large number of Tennessee fans, who were upset that Majors decided to take the sure one point and a tie, rather than go for two and a possible victory.

Following the game, Auburn coaches let it be known that they had wanted Tennessee to go for two, their awesome defense probably giving them the courage to make such a wish. "It wasn't just the best decision Majors could make," one of them said. "It was the *only* one."

Looking in the rear-view mirror, the Vols had everything to gain and very little to lose. Auburn finished 5-0-1 and won the Southeastern Conference championship. LSU (5-1-0) was second and Tennessee (4-1-1) third. Had the Vols made a two-point conversion and won, they would have tied LSU and Auburn for the championship. UT's lone defeat was to Alabama three weeks later.

If the Vols had tried for two and failed, they would have finished tied for third place. As it was, they played it safe and still finished third. The consequence of Majors' decision wasn't so easy to see at the time, but as it turned out, the tie was as damaging to Tennessee's title hopes as a loss would have been.

A few days later, Majors received a call supporting his decision to go for one. The caller was Florida State coach Bobby Bowden, whose team lost to Miami 26-25 that season after going for two and failing. The call was of considerable significance: The Seminoles wound up 11-1 and No. 2 in the final poll behind 12-0 Miami.

Francis feels that he turned in perhaps the sharpest performance of his career that day against Auburn. His statistics were not overwhelming (13 of 20 for 166 yards) but his timing and execution were. He "bought some time" on a key play on the tying TD drive. Facing third-and-14, he could find nobody open but eluded the Auburn pass rush long enough to dump the ball to Charles Wilson, who broke a tackle and gained 13 1/2 yards. Cobb slammed in from the seven on the next play.

No Tennessee team in recent years had enjoyed a game in which everything fell into place quite like it did on October 10, 1987.

California, the team that had spoiled Majors' first game as UT coach 10 years earlier, ran into a UT team that could do little wrong. The Vols scored on their first five possessions, had a 31-0 halftime lead and cruised to a 38-12 victory. Francis was at his best, completing 21 of 26 passes for 220 yards and two TDs. The Orange Crunch defense was so overpowering that after 15 minutes of play, Cal's total offense was minus-12 yards. Coaches are always preaching balanced offense. Tennessee's was that day: 220 yards rushing and 220 yards passing.

As the game drew to a merciful conclusion, UT students in the southeastern corner of Neyland Stadium reminded everyone that it would soon be another Saturday of a different kind. "We want Bama, we want Bama," they chanted. And Bama they were going to get. The two old foes of many a stirring October battle were to meet in Birmingham a week later.

While Tennessee was feasting on Cal that day, Alabama was stumping its toe against lightly regarded Memphis State, 13-10, a development that probably hurt Tennessee more than it did the Tide. It might have been dynamite news for UT fans, but not for the Vol coaches, who certainly didn't welcome anything that would help make the Tide any tougher mentally.

Whatever the reason—Alabama taking out its frustrations on UT, the Vols having a bad night, or a combination of both—it was a 41-22 disaster for the Big Orange. The last time Murphy's Law was so hard at work against Tennessee was in 1969, when Ole Miss drubbed the undefeated and third-ranked Vols 38-0 at Jackson, Mississippi.

It wasn't much different on this night in Birmingham. Tennessee, again undefeated and ranked in the top 10, was a study in futility. The Tide, meanwhile, could do no wrong, scoring a couple of inexpensive touchdowns (on a 90-yard bomb and Gene Jelks' 63-yard punt return) and getting another big break when Keith Davis' fumble on first-and-goal at the Bama 8 sailed into the hands of cornerback Jelks.

The game started slipping away from Tennessee just after the last strains of the National Anthem. With third-string quarterback Jeff Dunn making his first collegiate start and all but unknown to the Tennessee people, leading the way, Alabama had a 21-0 lead 14 minutes into the game.

It was obvious at the outset that Alabama was sky-high and Tennessee wasn't. "I thought we were excited about playing the game," a dejected Majors said. "We helped Alabama some, but they did a lot to help themselves too. You've got to give them credit."

Going into the game, all signs had pointed to a smashing Tennessee victory. The coaches felt confident to the point of cockiness. One of them was asked his prediction hours before kickoff. He answered "Pick a score," implying that the Vols could win by any margin they chose. As things turned out, however, it was Alabama that picked a score. For the Vols, it was the first loss in almost exactly a year. They had gone 9-0-1 since losing to Georgia Tech on October 25, 1986.

For Bill Curry, in his first year as Alabama head coach, it was a giant victory. His team had already lost to Florida and Memphis State and had barely beaten Vanderbilt, so he was hardly the most popular guy in Tuscaloosa, Alabama, where folks think that if you didn't play for Bear Bryant you can't coach football, at least at Alabama. A brick hurled through Curry's office window more or less underscored that notion.

For Francis, it was a shock, even though he had a fine day statistically: 26 of 44 for 358 yards. "I don't think I've ever been more disappointed than I was in the '87 Alabama game," he says. "We got to Birmingham and I was never more prepared for a game than I was for that one. We got down early and I ended up throwing four interceptions. It's a situation where you want to win the game so bad that you try to do too much; you try to win it yourself. That was a big mistake. I wanted to make it happen and I forced a couple of passes that I shouldn't have thrown. I made some decisions that I normally wouldn't make, but it was because I wanted so much to win that game.

"I remember Jelks' punt return. And then there was a real questionable call that went against us. Dunn bounced a pass to a receiver and the officials called it a completion and they went in to score. That just broke our back."

Another thing broken was Tennessee's almost incredible streak of 11 games "covering" the spread. The last time the Vols had failed to beat the spread had been against Washington State in 1986.

The spread said Tennessee by 14 over Georgia Tech a week later, and the bookies hit it right on the button, UT winning 29-15. And, just to make the bookies look good, the Vols squandered a 29-0 lead in the second half.

The Tennessee team that had been held to 51 yards rushing by Alabama gained 321 yards against Tech, and there were two reasons for that: (1) offensive line coach Phillip Fulmer challenged his troops after they were manhandled by Alabama and (2) Francis suffered a severe ankle injury in the early going that would keep him out of the lineup for three games.

With Francis on the shelf, freshman Sterling Henton and junior Randy Sanders stepped forward. Sanders, who became a placekick holder after losing the starting job to Francis the year before, spearheaded three scoring drives against Tech.

Boston seemed like a nice place to be going, but it turned out not to be for Tennessee's football team. The fans who had been clamoring for the flashy Henton got their wish and those who had been wondering why Francis was the starting quarterback got their answer.

Sanders got the starting call, and proceeded to throw interceptions on his first and third passes of the day. In between, he one-hopped a screen pass to Anthony Miller that had touchdown written all over it.

Henton came on in relief and played well, though he made some freshman mistakes that turned out to be costly. Gaining confidence as the game wore on, Henton directed two long scoring drives as the Vols sought to come back from a 20-3 deficit. They finally bowed 20-18.

Tennessee, which had stumbled around in two of its previous three games, went into the November stretch with a 5-2-1 record, and needing to win to finish 9-2-1 and land an invitation to one of the better bowls.

Henton got his first start against Louisville and he passed with flying colors in a 41-10 romp. Fans who saw it will probably always remember his dazzling 16-yard tippy-toe, tightrope-act scamper down the west sideline for a touchdown. Cobb continued his heroics, rushing for 127 yards on 20 carries.

All the old grads went home in a festive mood following a 55-10 homecoming victory over Ole Miss. The 55 points were the most scored by a Tennessee team since the 1960 outfit got 62 against Tampa.

It was a banner day for the offense, which piled up 578 yards, the highest total since they began keeping track of total yards in 1944. The Vols rushed for 368 yards. The last time a UT team got more yardage on the ground, 1971, Reggie Cobb was three years old, Johnny Majors was two years away from a job at Pittsburgh, and Bill Battle was the toast of Big Orange Country. They got 390 that day against California-Santa Barbara. One year later, the Gauchos gave up football.

The day before Tennessee all but destroyed his Rebels, coach Billy Brewer gave Majors his opinion of the sensational Cobb, who had been making some big tracks on the football field: "I think Reggie Cobb is the best pure tailback in our league." The next afternoon, Cobb carried only 13 times for 81 yards and three touchdowns and moved to within 87 yards of a 1,000-yard season.

Kentucky, Tennessee's most enduring rival, battled the Vols to the bitter end in one of the best of all Vol-UK games.

Michael Whitehead, an almost forgotten Vol of 1987, was credited with one of the biggest defensive plays of the season, a spectacular fourth-down stop on Kentucky star Mark Higgs that preserved a 24-22 Tennessee victory at Lexington. The Wildcats, trailing 24-20, were driving for the game-winning score with under two minutes to go.

Whitehead, who had dropped from starting middle guard to second team to third, went from scrub to hero by slamming into Higgs on fourth-and-goal from the Tennessee 2-foot line. Whitehead lost his helmet in the collision.

The game was still on the line at the end when Vol punter Bob Garmon danced away the final seven seconds in the back of the end zone before stepping out to give the Wildcats an intentional safety that left them two points short. It might have been the biggest three-yard loss in many a year for Tennessee.

Francis played exceptionally well in his first game after a three-week layoff with an ankle injury. He was the starter and directed the Vols 59 yards to a field goal and 68 yards to a TD in the final period as Tennessee rallied from a 20-14 deficit.

Francis was more or less left on his own in a crucial situation on the winning TD drive. He and quarterbacks coach Walt Harris had developed an unusually close relationship that year, almost to the point of being able to read each other's mind.

"It was third-and-9 and we were down three points (20-17)," Francis says. "Having worked with Coach Harris, I sort of knew that what he was saying was 'I don't know what to call; just go up there and find a good play.'

"I ended up checking to an audible and I threw to Terence Cleveland for a touchdown. That was a good example of reaping the benefits of studying film and putting in all that hard work."

The Vols spotted Vanderbilt a 28-3 lead in the second quarter before rallying to win 38-36 in a wild shootout. Coach Watson Brown's imaginative offensive scheme produced four touchdowns in Vandy's first four possessions and left Majors scratching his head.

"How in the world they do it, I don't know," he said. "Reverses, keepers, whoopee passes, the Statue of Liberty play; they come at you with a little bit of everything."

It was all Tennessee could do to get back in it. Credit Francis, the consummate field general, for that. He was booed by the home crowd early in the game but played intelligent football in bringing his team back from a 25-point deficit. He got the last laugh.

Cobb, the new hero of Vol fans, gained 140 yards on 27 carries to boost his season total to 1197 yards, second highest single season total in UT history behind Johnnie Jones' 1290 in 1984.

Francis credits the experience of the Alabama game six weeks earlier with getting the Vols in position to win over Vandy.

"Obviously, Vanderbilt wasn't the quality team that Alabama was, but I think that having gone through that Alabama game caused us to not panic against Vandy. The coaching staff should get credit for that. We just slowly pecked away at Vandy's lead and ended up winning. And I think a lot of that had to do with what happened at Alabama, where we didn't handle the situation very well."

The '87 Vols had one last comeback up their sleeve in the Peach Bowl. Indiana led 22-21 with a little more than four minutes to play, so in the end there had to be another of those fourth-quarter rallies by Tennessee.

Just before the Vols returned to the field, offensive guard John Bruhin turned to Francis on the sideline and said matter-of-factly. "Don't worry, Jeff. We're going to drive it down there and score. We're going to win." The Vols came thundering toward the finish line behind Francis and Cobb to win 27-22 and post yet another comeback victory.

It was the fifth time that the '87 team had picked itself up off the floor in the final period — Iowa (23-22), Auburn (20-20), Kentucky (24-22), Vanderbilt (38-36) and Indiana (27-22). Those scores add up to 132 points for Tennessee, 122 for the opposition. It is easy to see that the final record, 10-2-1, could have been 6-6-1, 7-6 or 6-7 had the ball taken a different bounce here or there in five games.

In any event, Tennessee had its first 10-win season since 1972, with bookend victories over the Big Ten, over Iowa in the opener and Indiana in the finale. And it rounded out the best three-season record in Majors' 11-year tenure as head coach: 26-8-3.

The good times that Tennessee's numerous and faithful fans had long awaited seemed to be at hand. No one had any inkling that a catastrophic season lay just ahead.

CHAPTER 27

NO JOY IN VOLVILLE

Ken Donahue came up with perhaps the best line from the miserable 1988 season, a campaign during which there weren't many good lines, period. Midway through the six consecutive defeats, someone asked if the play of his defense was giving him nightmares.

"No," he answered, "when you don't get any sleep you don't have nightmares."

We can think of Tennessee's 1988 season as one long U-turn. After dropping their first six games, the Vols came back to win their last five and lay the groundwork for a stunning championship 1989 season.

UT's '88 media guide may have unintentionally sounded a warning:

"The prospect of playing four Southeastern Conference games by mid-October has underscored the need for coach Johnny Majors to have the Tennessee Vols in fine fettle when they burst out of the starting blocks for the 1988 season.

"By the time the leaves have turned deep orange in the nearby Smoky Mountains, UT will either have some impressive scalps on its belt or will have been bloodied by some of the biggest ogres in college football."

As things turned out, UT was bloodied by some of the biggest ogres in college football, and by a couple of not-so-big ones. The first month and a half of the 1988 campaign became a nightmare, one misery after another. Nothing Tennessee tried worked; nothing the other side tried failed to work, or so it seemed. There was no joy in Volville.

There is no denying that the first half of the schedule was a meat-grinder. Majors pointed that out before the season began, and he got no argument from Gil Brandt, personnel director for the Dallas Cowboys. Brandt said on a visit to Knoxville that he couldn't recall a college team taking on a more demanding schedule in its first six outings.

Things went from bad to worse in Big Orange Country, not only in its heart, Knoxville, but in other areas as well. As the defeats began to mount, Nashville disc jockey Duncan Stewart was perched atop a billboard, vowing not to come down until Tennessee won a game. Another deejay, Joe Grant, followed Stewart's lead and set up shop on the roof of Wartburg's Village Mart shopping center. In mid-October, after the losing streak had reached six, fans began to warn both of them to bundle up, that it looked like it might be a cold winter. One wag pointed out that it was only 337 days until the 1989 season opener against Colorado State.

After two weeks, a strong gust of wind accomplished what the Tennessee team couldn't, bringing Stewart down from his "Go Big Orange" billboard. He avoided serious injury when he slipped from a steel girder near the top of the billboard catwalk. He was able to grab the top rung of the ladder, which prevented him from falling some 30 feet to the ground. He suffered a leg injury and was treated at a hospital then, undaunted, resumed his Vol Vigil on crutches, but on the ground.

Georgia started all the agony between the hedges at Athens. The Bulldogs, knowing full well that defense would be the chink in Tennessee's armor, simply lined up, ran straight ahead and dared the Vols to stop them. Which Tennessee couldn't do.

But Georgia could. The Vols trailed 21-17 in the third period and were poised to take the lead when Bryan Kimbro recovered a fumble at the Georgia 16. They moved to a first-and-goal at the 1. After two unsuccessful running plays, quarterback Jeff Francis was blindsided and lost the ball at the 13. The Dogs then marched back downfield for an insurance touchdown and it wound up 28-17.

Francis, entering the game needing 194 yards to oust Alan Cockrell as Tennessee's all-time passing yardage leader, responded with 354 yards on 25-of-38 passing. Francis picked up a new member for his fan club. "He's the best quarterback I've seen in a long, long time," said Georgia coach Vince Dooley.

Duke, Tennessee's old nemesis from 1976 and 1982, led by a quarterback whose name made him sound more like a secretary of state than a passer, put another dent in UT's helmet with a 31-26 upset. The Blue Devils, 13-point underdogs, were better than advertised (they went 7-3-1 that season) and, with quarterback Anthony Dilweg and batterymate Clarkston Hines wowing the Neyland Stadium crowd, were quick to point that out. They built up a 24-7 halftime lead, with Tennessee's only points coming on a Preston Warren interception return of 30 yards. It was the only mark against Dilweg, who completed 21 of 32 for 311 yards.

Tailback Reggie Cobb rushed for a career-high 182 yards, but Francis had an off-day, at least until the fourth quarter when the Vols scored 19 points and threatened to make a game of it. Tennessee got 19 points and almost 500 yards from the offense, but looked sorry doing it.

Neyland Stadium's boo-birds were vocal through the long night, disagreeing with calls like sending fullback Roland Poles up the middle with Tennessee trailing by 18 points with five minutes to play. Or Francis running the option on a crucial fourth-down play earlier in the fourth period. Or not throwing more to Cobb. It was very obvious that the Vols had a long way to go, and a short time to get there.

A week later, LSU was at Neyland Stadium, seeking its first victory in 11 trips to Knoxville. The Tigers got it with room to spare, turning the Vols every which way but loose in a 34-9 romp. The afternoon was rainy and windy. There were about 25,000 no-shows and no one was quite sure if that was a result of the weather or the Vols' dreadful showings in the first three games. Lucky for them.

Randy Moore of *The Knoxville Journal* caught the tone of the game this way:

"There was a time Saturday when Tennessee looked terrific.

"Every formation was precise, every move was crisp and every call was executed flawlessly.

"Then halftime ended, the band returned to the stands and the Vol football team returned to the field.

"After that, things quickly returned to normal—normal at Tennessee this season, meaning the offense stops itself and the defense stops nobody."

Although Tennessee wouldn't actually hit bottom for a couple more weeks, you would have had trouble convincing Vol fans that that point hadn't already been reached.

The statistics were brutal. Total offense: LSU 503 yards, Tennessee 199. First downs: LSU 25, Tennessee 9. Time of possession: LSU 38 minutes, Tennessee 22. Tennessee's 12 possessions ended like this: Punt. Punt, Fumble. Punt, Punt. Halftime. Punt. Touchdown. Field Goal. Punt. Punt. End of game. No wonder UT fans started streaming for the exits in the third quarter.

Francis, looking like a man trying to paddle an aircraft carrier in the North Atlantic, suffered through a horrible day: 4-of-12 for 71 yards. The game marked the debut of freshman quarterback Andy Kelly, who would go on to break all of Tennessee's passing records in the three years ahead.

Tennessee trailed Auburn by only 10-6 at halftime. Francis got a word of encouragement from backup Randy Sanders. "If we don't turn the ball over, I don't think we can lose," he said.

Perhaps he forgot to knock on wood. Tennessee proceeded to lose three turnovers in the third period, and Auburn converted them into 21 points and a commanding 31-6 lead. The final, 38-6, was UT's worst defeat since a 43-7 loss at Southern Cal in 1981.

Senior tailback Keith Davis, Tennessee's leading rusher with 21 yards, was almost numb. "This is like a dream," he said. "Sometimes I think, 'Am I awake? Is this all happening?' It's hard to believe but we've got to keep coming back."

Tennessee has played few games like this one, good in the first half, hideous in the second. Auburn won the first half, 10 points to 6 and 256 yards to 173. The Tigers won the second half as well, but by 28-0 in points and 204-2 in total yards.

Cobb suffered through probably the worst game of his career, gaining a mere 12 yards on nine carries and fumbling twice inside the Vol 30. Afterward, he dejectedly told reporters that he had lost the game single-handedly. Later on, he revised that evaluation slightly: "I had a lot to do with it" is the way he put it.

September turned out to be one of the ugliest months in Tennessee football history. In those 30 days, the Vols had lost their first four games by a combined score of 131-58.

If there were any lingering doubts that the 1988 team was among the worst since Tennessee went big-time 60 years before, they were swept away by the flood of Washington State touchdowns in a 52-24 disaster. Quarterback Timm Rosenbach put on a show with 21 completions in 32 attempts for 352 yards and five touchdowns.

As if the score itself weren't bad enough, the Cougars rolled up 618 yards of total offense—the most ever against a Tennessee team—and averaged 9 yards per play in a spectacular offensive display. A more alarming statistic was this: Tennessee had allowed more points (183) in five games than the 1985 SEC championship team did in 12 games (140). In the last three games, the Vols had been outscored 122-39.

After Washington State had ripped his defense for 52 points, Majors came up with one of the more memorable under-statements of the season: "It was quite a mismatch between their offense and our defense." He could have underscored that by pointing out that 24 other Tennessee teams had gone AN ENTIRE SEASON without giving up as much as 52 points.

Washington State was by no means the cream puff on the schedule that many fans had expected. The Cougars scored at least 24 points in every game, finished 9-3 and wound up No. 16 in the nation.

Alvin Harper put himself in the record book with 12 pass receptions against the Cougars, bettering the record of 11 shared by Johnny Mills (1966), Gary Kreis (1969) and Larry Seivers (1976). But nobody noticed. And very few cared.

All anyone in Big Orange Country cared about was what had happened to Tennessee football. Majors promised that the open date before Alabama would produce some changes in the way the defense went about its business. "We're not going to just stay with the same things," he said. "But the changes will be in deployment and, we hope, in execution."

There were cries for Majors' scalp. Rumors were rampant; the most popular one was that Majors would be fired. Another was that he would resign. Still another said Majors would dismiss at least half his staff. When the university called a press conference for Wednesday following the Washington State game, it was generally accepted that somebody's head was about to roll. It was whose head that was so surprising.

Majors had to make a very difficult decision. At the press conference, he announced that Donahue, his friend and one time mentor, had resigned and that assistant coach Doug Mathews would succeed him as defensive coordinator.

Big Orange fans were taken aback. How could Tennessee fire the man who had been recognized as one of the greatest defensive minds in the game? The coach who had devised the defensive scheme in the 35-7 demolition of Miami and quarterback Vinny Testaverde in the 1986 Sugar Bowl. The man responsible for the great Alabama defenses under Bear Bryant.

Ken Donahue, 63, had been called the hardest-working coach in football. There were stories of his years at Alabama, where Bear Bryant prided himself on working longer hours than any coach in the business. Even the Bear finally had to concede to Donahue.

"No matter what time I get there, Donahue's already there," the Bear said.

Many knowledgeable observers felt that the game had passed Donahue by, that he had lost his grip on the game. Offensive coaches began to outsmart him in the game of X's and O's. In 1986, Alabama had used the same play over and over to overwhelm his defense to the tune of 56 points. Washington State had driven the final nail four days earlier with that 52-point, 618-yard explosion.

Tennessee's defense had obvious personnel weaknesses, but more and more the Vols appeared to be caught in bad defensive alignments. The players said they hadn't felt comfortable with the defensive game plans, that they were out of the past.

Donahue denied that his departure was a sign that Majors had made him a scapegoat. "That's not true. Our personal relationship is unchanged. Somehow or other I just didn't seem to be able to get the job done like I felt it should be done, and maybe somebody else can. I hope so, because the players deserve it. They've worked these past few weeks and at times seemed to be showing some improvement, but just couldn't get there."

There was no joy in Volville. Most of the '88 season was already down the drain, but the Vols showed they hadn't thrown in the towel, slugging it out with Alabama before falling 28-20. For the first time in 1988, Keith DeLong and his defensive mates held the opposition below 400 yards, held the Tide to 299 yards in fact. DeLong, a senior, made 19 unassisted tackles against Bama, intercepted a pass and sacked quarterback Vince Sutton. He was well on his way to All-America recognition, racking up honors at the same pace as his famous father, 1964 Tennessee All-American Steve DeLong.

For a change, Vol fans couldn't blame defeat on the defense. DeLong and pals played well enough for Tennessee to win, but out of perhaps a dozen excellent opportunities, the offense managed only two scoring drives, and one of them came too late to do anything except reduce the final margin to eight points. The rushing statistics bore out the offense's ineptness: 33 carries for just 97 yards. Cobb was handed the ball 23 times, but could manage only 47 yards.

It was mid-October and the record was 0-6. Not since 1909 had a Tennessee team lost six straight games in a season. Never had one lost seven in a row. Majors needed another defeat like a drowning man needed a bucket of water. Already the fans were out shopping for tar and feathers and a rail on which to ride him out of town.

Memphis State, which in 11 meetings with Tennessee had drawn back 11 nubs, was favored by two points to extend Tennessee's losing streak to seven. As the Vols' team buses drove into the Liberty Bowl Memorial Stadium parking area that morning, Memphis State fans hurled oranges and insults at the Vols. "Oh-and-six, oh-and-six, oh-and-six," they shouted, referring to Tennessee's season record. During warmups, Memphis State students and cheerleaders began to chant "We're going to kick some Vol ass." UT players were infuriated. "We went to the dressing room before kickoff and a lot of our guys were really ticked off that that had happened," Francis says.

The Vols broke a 10-10 tie with an impressive second half show by the offense and carried on to a 38-25 victory. The streak had ended. As the Memphis State players trudged off the field with MSU's 12th straight loss to Tennessee, delirious UT fans got the last laugh with their own chant: "Oh-and-12, oh-and-12, oh-and-12."

Sophomore Tony Thompson came off the bench after Cobb suffered an ankle injury in the second quarter and was an instant star. He got 124 yards on 28 carries, scored two touchdowns and had a two-point conversion run.

Already there was talk about Tennessee winning its remaining four games and finishing 5-6. Which is exactly what happened.

Two teams from the wrong side of the tracks met on homecoming Saturday and fortune smiled on the home team. Tennessee beat Boston College 10-7 on Chip McCallum's 43-yard field goal. The Vol offense struggled mightily, so it was left to Preston Warren to make his second interception return for a touchdown of the season, a 31-yarder in the second quarter. It was one of four Tennessee interceptions during the afternoon, the first time the Vols had turned that trick since the '86 Sugar Bowl.

The Eagles got a massive stroke of bad luck at the end. When they came out of the huddle on third-and-19 at their own 20 with just over a minute to play, a wide receiver lined up on the line of scrimmage outside the tight end. That made the tight end an ineligible receiver, and as soon as he cleared the restraining zone to run his pass route, the line judge let fly with his flag.

The wideout, Marcus Cherry, raced downfield to grab Mike Power's desperation heave away from two defenders and then romped into the end zone for the score that would have put BC on top. But the infraction nullified the play and the Vols held on to win. The call was made by an East Coast Conference member of the split officiating crew, so the Eagles couldn't base their case on home cooking.

BC coach Jack Bicknell was livid just the same. During the ensuing rhubarb with the officials, BC was assessed three consecutive 15-yard stepoffs for unsportsmanlike conduct. That made it 17 penalties for 165 yards against the Eagles. Francis proceeded to down the ball three times as Tennessee ran out the clock.

"I don't know what the officials saw or didn't see," Bicknell said. "I just know that they're not very nice people, and I'm sure they would say the same thing about me."

Majors acknowledged the stroke of luck. "But who deserves some good luck more than Tennessee?" he asked. "We've had our share of the other kind."

Tennessee visited Oxford, Mississippi, for the first tme since 1951 and came away a 20-12 upset winner over Ole Miss. The defense turned in its top performance of the year and the much-maligned offense, which had laid an egg against Boston College the week before and had been in a deep slumber for most of the season, silenced the critics, at least for the time being.

Tennessee's sudden turnaround impressed the oddsmakers so much that the Vols were made three-point favorites over Kentucky. A 28-24 victory over an honored old opponent put the goal posts in jeopardy for the first time in a long while.

There are few things that arouse the emotions of Tennessee football fans more than the way their quarterback plays. And in his farewell appearance before the home folks, Francis gave them something to remember him by, an absolutely flawless performance. It was unquestionably the finest day of his career, made even more impressive by the 100 percent miserable weather conditions. His numbers were 27 of 37 for 282 yards, four touchdowns, and no interceptions.

"Francis was the difference," said Kentucky coach Jerry Claiborne. "We tried to confuse him, but he's a smart passer. He did a heck of a job of making us take our people off the ball. We thought we might intercept one of those sideline passes, but he'd spot it every time and just throw the ball away."

Rain and gale force winds that sometimes made an airborne football look like a free-floating balloon greeted Tennessee and Vanderbilt in the season finale. Thus shorn of their passing attack, the Vols resorted to old-fashioned football—slamming between the tackles—and it paid off in a 14-7 triumph. Senior tailback Keith Davis had a career-high 162 yards and made some crucial runs in the late going when Tennessee needed to control the ball.

Kent Elmore, who won the SEC punting title with a 44.3-yard average, unloaded an 81-yard quick kick in the first quarter. "Don't you know Bowden would have loved that one?" Majors asked after the game. The quick kick was one of the late Bowden Wyatt's favorite weapons when he was Tennessee's head coach in the 1950s and Majors was his star tailback and quick-kicker.

Tennessee's five-game winning streak might not mean much by some standards, but for a team that had lost its first six games of 1988 it was quite an accomplishment to win five after having to circle the wagons at midseason.

The Vols of 1988 had made a trip through football hell, and lived to tell the tale.

The turnaround of '88 probably represented some of the best coaching of Majors' long career. He shuffled personnel. He shuffled coaches. And even as losses mounted, he kept morale high.

"One thing I really respect about Coach Majors is that he was so positive, even though we were losing," said San Francisco 49ers linebacker Keith DeLong, an All-American at Tennessee on that 1988 squad. "That's when I gained all the respect in the world for him.

"Coach is a position I'd never want. Football is so big at Tennessee. If they lose, he gets the blame. If they win, everyone takes the credit."

CHAPTER 28

SAD SACKS
NO MORE

The talk on the football field is not always about football, especially during television timeouts.

The game: Tennessee is playing UCLA at Neyland Stadium on an unusually hot September afternoon. In the second period, the Bruins punt.

Television timeout.

The Tennessee offensive unit trots onto the field. Vol quarterback Andy Kelly calls the first down play, taking 10 seconds at most. Do the Vols then discuss the play? The magnitude of this early intersectional game? The national rankings?

Vol guard Patrick Lenoir looks down as he stomps his feet. Kelly says, "Patrick, what are you doing?"

Lenoir: "Check this out, man. This is cool. Watch this."

He walks to the middle of the huddle and begins stomping his feet harder. As he does, sweat oozes, then squirts through the mesh top of his shoes. It isn't long before all the Vols are stomping their feet. And a good time is had by all.

Tennessee and Alabama are locked in a tense struggle of unbeatens at Birmingham. The Southeastern Conference lead and a high national ranking are at stake. The Tide, holding a 16-14 lead, punts.

Television timeout.

The Vol offense takes the field; Kelly calls the play.

Tackle Charles McRae, his back to the huddle, is staring at the large sign across the front of the east side upper deck that says: "Welcome To Birmingham, Football Capital of the South."

Kelly, thinking that McRae is probably searching the stands for his family or friends, asks, "What are you doing?"

McRae, pointing to the sign: "Come here and look at this. Is capital spelled right? I think maybe it should be spelled with an 'O.' " By the time the game resumed, most of the players got into the discussion. (The "A" spelling is correct.)

The 1989 season had a very humble beginning, a boring 17-14 victory over a weak Colorado State team. It was no thing of beauty, and Tennessee fans may have been disappointed at the final point spread, but they could think back only one year to realize that an unimpressive three-point victory beats the devil out of a loss by whatever score. On the corresponding Saturday of 1988, the Vols lost to Georgia to begin their infamous 0-6 start.

Two fumbles, one on the center-quarterback exchange that denied the Vols a touchdown late in the first half, and one by Andy Kelly that set up the Rams' only TD later in the final quarter turned what should have been a comfortable win into a close one. Footballs still take funny bounces, and the Vols were pretty fortunate that the one they were playing with didn't take any more than it did.

What made the narrow win of even more concern was the fact that perhaps the most demanding six-game gauntlet in UT history lay just ahead. UCLA, Duke, Auburn, Georgia, Alabama and LSU read more like a death march than a schedule.

The Vols were 15-point underdogs when they teed it up against UCLA in the Rose Bowl, their first visit to the mammoth stadium since the 1945 Rose Bowl game. UCLA was expected to contend for the Pac-10 championship, despite having lost quarterback Troy Aikman, the top pick in the previous spring's NFL draft.

Few Tennessee teams have ever played such a near-perfect game; the Vols had not one turnover or penalty as they thrashed the Bruins 24-6.

UCLA coach Terry Donahue sounded like 1988's Johnny Majors in his postgame remarks. "It was an absolutely flawless performance by Tennessee. They were a faster, quicker, more physical team and gave us a real beating. I was surprised at the way we were manhandled physically."

There was a reason the Bruins were manhandled. Following the disastrous 1988 season, Majors ordered an overhaul of the winter weight training program. The Vols had admittedly been the SEC's weakest team; only two players could bench press more than 400 pounds in 1988. By the fall of '89, every starting offensive lineman could bench 400 or more.

As the final horn sounded on the Vols' seventh straight victory spanning two seasons, they headed not for their dressing room, but for the northwest corner of the playing field, just in front of sections 13 and 14. There, on a starry night in California, they exchanged high-fives with many of the 5,000 or so ecstatic Big Orange fans.

The Vols unveiled a new tailback sensation, redshirt freshman Chuck Webb, to go with junior Reggie Cobb. Webb gained 134 yards on 22 carries and Cobb 78 on 14. It didn't take the media long to seize on the rather obvious nickname for Tennessee's new 1-2 tailback punch: the Cobb-Webb offense.

That either of them was playing surprised some people. Cobb had been suspended by Majors the previous February, reportedly for failing three drug tests. Webb was arrested a couple of months later and charged with stealing a check from a teammate and attempting to cash it. He pleaded guilty and performed community service. Both were reinstated in the fall.

"People make mistakes," Majors said. "They work it out or they have to leave."

Observers hailed the impressive win over UCLA as one of the milestone victories in UT history. But it later lost some of its glitter when the Bruins proved they weren't as good as advertised, stumbling through 1989 with a 3-7-1 record.

A workmanlike 28-6 victory over Steve Spurrier's offensive-minded Duke team avenged the 31-26 loss of a year before, boosted UT's record to 3-0, and cleared the decks for an early season showdown, Tennessee vs. Auburn. To heighten the suspense, both teams had open dates. CBS was sending its national coverage crew to Knoxville. *Sports Illustrated* would staff the game.

Down in Auburn, Alabama, coach Pat Dye noticed a difference in the way his team was going about preparing for Tennessee. "Ain't no doubt they were in a different frame of mind today than they've been," he said. "We worked them last week. Today they worked themselves."

Up in Knoxville, Tennessee, the Vols weren't about to forget the 38-6 pounding they took at Auburn the year before. Cobb, in particular, remembered the two costly fumbles he made in that game. He talked of healing some of the scars, even though he would be going against the nation's No. 1 defense against the rush.

"This is an opportunity to find out what you're made of," he said. "When you play against the SEC's No. 1 defense, that tells you what kind of running back you are."

The kind he was was worth 225 yards to Tennessee in a dramatic 21-14 win over the nation's No. 4 team in a steady downpour. His tailback sidekick, Webb, added 93 yards, giving the Cobb-Webb offense 323 yards on 41 carries for the day.

Cobb's 225 yards wasn't far behind the best rushing day anyone ever had against an Auburn defense, a 233-yard effort by Alabama's Bobby Marlowe in 1951. The highlight of Cobb's performance was a nifty 79-yard touchdown scamper early in the second quarter.

Meanwhile, the Tennessee rushing defense was at its best, holding the Tigers to 31 yards on 29 rushes. Reggie Slack hit 18 of 40 passes for 285 yards, including an 83-yard TD strike to Alexander Wright in the fourth quarter. The Vols took advantage of two center snaps over the Auburn punter's head for safeties.

"We're not the same team they beat 38-6 a year ago," Cobb said. "They made some remarks this week, saying I wasn't going to be a factor in the game."

Offensive coordinator Phil Fulmer, for one, liked what he saw of the Cobb-Webb offense.

"Those two guys are fabulous players," he said. "At least we're smart enough to give them the ball enough times that they can make something happen with it."

Vol linebacker Shazzon Bradley's postgame comments made it easy to understand why he would dabble in professional boxing following his football career: "We're weird characters. We've all got a little intelligence but not a whole bunch. We just like to go out there and fight it out — best man wins."

Many of the Tennessee players who celebrated that day were the same athletes who, at the same time a year before, were being figuratively stoned in public for being the worst Tennessee football team of modern times. Now they were 4-0, winners of nine in a row and ranked No. 6 in the nation. Only three teams had longer winning streaks: Notre Dame (16), Miami (12) and Fresno State (11).

Many people feared a letdown following the emotional victory over Auburn and it almost came to pass. The Vols slipped past Georgia 17-14, but Majors wasn't about to throw it back. "This is the Southeastern Conference," he said, "and in this league you take a win whenever you can get it."

Georgia more or less ignored Tennessee's feeble passing game, massing as many as eight players up front in an effort to disable the Cobb-Webb offense. It slowed UT's running game a bit, but Cobb gained 106 yards on 20 carries, Webb 83 on 11. The running game had to carry the day because the aerial game was nowhere to be seen. Sterling Henton completed 3 of 8 for 34 yards and Kelly 1 of 3 for 12 yards.

So Tennessee and Alabama, who had waged many a memorable 100-yard war over the years, headed for the Third Saturday in October with pristine records, the first time that had happened since 1973.

But while Tennessee was struggling to edge Georgia, Alabama was sending an ominous message with a 62-27 drubbing of Ole Miss. And the Tide did it without its No. 1 quarterback, Jeff Dunn. In his absence, backup Gary Hollingsworth passed for 363 yards and five touchdowns.

Before they got together in Birmingham, Tennessee football took a blow to the solar plexus. Nine days before the game, while the Vols were enjoying an open date, the Cobb-Webb backfield that had carried the Vols to a 5-0 record and the No. 6 national ranking suddenly was no more. At a team meeting before practice that day, Majors informed the squad that Cobb had been dismissed from the team for a violation of team rules. The action was reportedly for failing a drug test. He had been indefinitely suspended eight months earlier for violating an unspecified team rule. Sources at that time said he had failed three drug tests.

Cobb was reinstated in July, about a month before pre-season practice began, and proceeded to average 123 yards a game as half of one of college football's most dynamic 1-2 punches in years.

His dismissal was the talk of Big Orange Country. Most everyone was supportive, including his ex-teammates, but there were some who weren't. One sign spotted by a television camera said, "Lynch Reggie."

Cobb was chosen early in the second round of the 1990 NFL draft by Tampa Bay, where he became a standout running back. The Green Bay Packers signed him as an unrestricted free agent in the spring of 1994.

The Vols, shaken by Cobb's dismissal, went grimly about their business of preparing for Alabama. "It's a jolt," said tailback Tony Thompson, who moved up a notch on the depth chart with Cobb's departure. "But this team has been through a lot of adversity before and we've come through a lot. I guess we'll see how we come through on this one. This team is a close-knit group, not like teams of the past. We don't have much to say right now. Everybody will probably pull together a lot harder."

That was also the opinion of Auburn coach Pat Dye, who had seen Cobb rip his team for 225 yards two weeks earlier. "That shocks me," he said, "but it probably will make Tennessee a better football team, because they'll all pull together and play harder than they've been playing. And they're already playing as hard as I've seen a Tennessee team play."

In a game in which two imposing defenses were expected to dominate, Hollingsworth, a 6-4 stringbean, picked up right where he had left off against Ole Miss, passing the Vol secondary silly as the Tide rolled to a 47-30 victory. He set an Alabama record with 32 pass completions (in 46 attempts) for 379 yards. For Bama coach Bill Curry it was a fitting 47th birthday present: one point for each of his years.

Hollingsworth completed 32 of 46 for 379 yards and three TDs. He didn't beat the Vols deep; he didn't have to. He kept flipping little nickel and dime passes to various receivers as they meandered almost at will through the Tennessee secondary, which laid an egg on Legion Field before the national television cameras.

Henton, yielding the first-team job to Kelly during this game, got off to a nightmarish start: 0-for-3 passing, two sacks for minus 19 yards, two badly thrown balls. He was in for only 11 offensive plays, then gave way to Kelly, who went 15-for-28 for 226 yards and directed Tennessee to 30 points.

The defeat was disappointing but not fatal to Tennessee's championship hopes. "This was just a loss," Majors said. "It wasn't a disaster."

What was disastrous was the last couple of minutes of the first half and the first five minutes of the second. Over that span, the Tide scored a pair of touchdowns and a field goal, 17 points, without Tennessee putting one play in motion. The only time the Vols touched the ball during this stretch was a fumble on a kickoff return that set up the second Alabama TD in the third period.

Some Tennessee fans insisted that the loss of Cobb doomed the Vols, but in truth he wouldn't have made a difference, simply because Cobb did not play defense, which is where the game was lost.

Vol linebacker Darryl Hardy probably said it best: "Everything Alabama did worked. We'd play run; they'd pass. We'd play pass; they'd run."

As despondent Tennessee fans headed back home, they saw a homemade sign on the northbound side of Interstate 59 near Gadsden, Alabama, that told the story: "CALL AIRPORT — DEFENSE MISSED THE PLANE."

The defeat knocked Tennessee from No. 6 to No. 11 in the Associated Press poll. The Tide, which had been No. 10, replaced the Vols in the No.6 spot.

If the fans thought Hollingsworth was something, they hadn't seen anything yet. LSU's Tommy Hodson completed 31 of 49 passes for a whopping 438 yards and four TDs. He passed LSU to an early 14-0 lead but the Vols gained the upper hand and went on to a wild 45-39 triumph.

In two games, the Vols had surrendered 63 completions in 95 attempts for 817 yards and seven touchdowns. The joke at the corner pub went something like this: "When the Lord handed out pass defense, Johnny Majors thought he said 'plastic fence' and said he didn't need any."

Only a surprising show of poise by sophomore Kelly and his offensive mates averted an LSU blowout. "I thought we did a good job of staying calm, not panicking and not trying to get those 14 points back all at once," Kelly said.

The Tennessee staff, at wit's end over the pathetic play of the secondary, went for a quick-fix, making redshirt freshman wide receiver Carl Pickens a two-way player by using him at safety in addition to wideout. And what a stroke of genius that looked to be —Pickens batted down two passes and returned an interception for a touchdown as the Vols battered Akron 52-9. On offense, he caught a TD pass that was nullified by a penalty.

Pickens did it again the next week against Ole Miss, intercepting a pass that led to Tennessee's go-ahead touchdown in a 33-21 win. But the afternoon belonged to Webb. Tennessee's resident Mr. Excitement put on a show that Tennessee fans will never forget.

Webb piled up an amazing 294 yards against the Rebels, breaking the school record of 248 yards set by Johnnie Jones in 1983 against Vanderbilt. Believe it or not, one of his best runs of the day was a two-yard gain when he was hemmed in by two defenders for what should have been a five-yard loss.

In one game, in the space of three hours, Webb gained almost three-fourths as much rushing yardage (294 to 416) as coach Johny Majors had gained in his entire first season with the Vols. And in so doing, he pushed his season rushing total to 1,091 yards to become only the third Vol in history to surpass 1,000.

Kelly, the quarterback who handed off to and then admired the dazzling Webb, remembers him as a private person. "Chuck didn't say much. Off the field he was awfully quiet. The thing that sticks out in my mind today is that when he first came here I knew he was good but I wasn't sure about his attitude. I wondered what he would be like in a game. You know, when the chips were down, was he going to be one of those guys who will step forward or would he be one of those guys who wouldn't give his all?

"But once he got out on the field, he gave it everything; running, blocking, anything he was asked to do. I thought he did pretty well in practice, but he would take it to a different level on game day. On game day he was just a different player. Get him in the huddle and he wanted the ball. He wanted to be the guy everybody looked up to.

"That day against Ole Miss, when he got 294 yards to set the record, Chuck was in a zone. He wanted the ball EVERY play. If the play wasn't going to him he acted like he was mad. But even when he didn't get the ball he was carrying out his assignment to a T. It was amazing how he would go from a quiet guy to a guy who wanted to carry the team. And he could do it."

Tennessee kept possession of the Beer Barrel for the fifth straight year, overcoming a shaky start to whip Kentucky 31-10 on a cold and windy day in Lexington. UK led 10-9 at the half but the Vols took control in the third period and went out to outscore the Wildcats 22-0 and chalk up a 213-19 advantage in yards in the second half. Webb picked up 145 yards on 27 carries, moving to within 54 yards of Johnnie Jones' school single season rushing record. He was a cinch to get that against Vanderbilt in the season finale.

The second half was Tennessee's best half of the season defensively. The key play came when UK, leading 10-9, faced fourth-and-1 at the Vol 34 early in the third quarter. Mark Moore and Darryl Hardy broke through to throw Alfred Rawls for a six-yard loss. And that was that. A Cotton Bowl invitation was just around the corner. All the Vols, 25 1/2-point favorites, had to do was show up against Vanderbilt. Or at least most everybody thought.

By late Saturday afternoon, Majors could say "I told you so." He had warned that beating Vandy would not be easy. He had pointed out that the Commodores had played Tennessee tough for three straight years.

After the Vols huffed and puffed their way to a 17-10 victory, Majors looked pretty smart. Despite what the fans might have thought at times, he carried a lot of grey matter beneath that coaching cap, and didn't have to have someone remind him to put up his umbrella when it rained.

The victory, the tenth in 11 games, gave the Vols a share of the SEC championship with Auburn and Alabama and nailed down an invitation to the Cotton Bowl to face Southwest Conference champ Arkansas.

One discouraging note: Webb, sidelined by an ankle injury, missed out on a chance at Jones' single-season UT rushing record. In fact, he wasn't even at the game, electing to go home to Toledo, Ohio, for the weekend. Tony Thompson filled in admirably, gaining 128 yards on 33 carries.

A crowd of 10,000 or so gathered at Thompson-Boling Arena to cheer the Vols and witness the official bowl invitation and acceptance. Majors told them they were the greatest football fans in America. "We're the champs and you're the champs," he said.

A 31-27 Cotton Bowl victory over Arkansas gave Tennessee its best overall record since 1970, 11-1. And it was another virtuoso performance by Webb that helped Tennessee register its 600th victory.

Webb rushed for 250 yards and his 78-yard touchdown run in the third period gave the Vols a seemingly comfortable 31-13 lead. But the Razorbacks scored twice in the fourth period to narrow the gap.

As the '89 season got underway, there was sad news for Tennessee football. Gary Roach, a quarterback on the teams of the mid-1970s, died in Knoxville in mid-August after a long battle with leukemia. He was 35.

Athletic director Doug Dickey received a $30,000 raise in early December, his second increase in three months, boosting his salary to $130,000. He had received a $6,000 raise on October 1. The $30,000 compensation was intended to dissuade Dickey from possibly taking the job of SEC commissioner. After the salary package was approved by the UT athletics board, Dickey withdrew his name from consideration as commissioner.

For Majors and his squad, the crowning point of the season was not the Cotton Bowl bid and victory but the share of the conference title brought about by Auburn's 30-20 victory over previously undefeated Alabama on the final day of the regular season.

The sad sacks of 1988 had become the SEC co-champions of 1989.

CHAPTER 29

THAT SICK FEELING

Years after his college days, Andy Kelly still dreams about Alabama-Tennessee games. They are all nightmares, even those dreams in which Tennessee wins. Because Tennessee never managed to beat Alabama while Kelly was a Vol, 1988-91.

"I'll dream that we've lost to them," he says, "and I'll wake up in the middle of the night with that same sick feeling I had walking off the field in Birmingham my senior year. Sometimes I even dream that we've won, and it feels even worse when I wake up and realize it was just a dream."

He wakes up ill. But he has nothing on the thousands of Tennessee fans who got that sick feeling on the Third Saturday in October in both 1990 and 1991. They thought the Vols should have won both those games from Alabama.

The 9-6 loss in 1990 was especially bitter because, as in 1989, it knocked the Vols from the undefeated ranks. They were 4-0-2 heading into their mid-October showdown with the Tide.

Defensive tackle Tom Fuhler, just arrived at Tennessee from a junior college, got the 1990 season off to a refreshing start with his candor during a preseason interview:

"We're ready to make a run for the national championship," he declared. "We'll beat Alabama because they have no coaches.

We'll beat Bill Curry at Kentucky because he has no players. Auburn . . . well, that was a mistake for Auburn to be ranked No. 1 in preseason. We're just going to have to stomp 'em for that.

"Notre Dame? Forget about it. They have no coaches *or* players."

Now, that kind of commentary might be great in World Championship Wrestling, but not in college football, where coaches hire people whose only purpose in life is to be on the lookout for "bulletin-board" material from opposing teams. Like Fuhler's, for instance.

Needless to say, Fuhler's utterances did not go unnoticed by coach Johnny Majors.

Fuhler's remarks notwithstanding, Tennessee went on to reach midseason without a loss in its 100th year of intercollegiate football. That was a story in itself, a half season of feast or famine.

It began in Anaheim, California, where the famous Disneyland complex took on a definite orange hue the week of August 19-26. There were about 7,000 Tennessee fans on hand to see the game, enjoy the festive atmosphere and take in the sights of Southern California. Half a world away, it was a different climate. Iraqi troops had invaded Kuwait three weeks earlier.

Tennessee and Colorado, both coming off 11-1 seasons, met in the first Disneyland Pigskin Classic, the first game of the college season. The game was billed as a duel between two Heisman Trophy hopefuls, Colorado quarterback Darien Hagan and Tennessee tailback Chuck Webb. But as NBC beamed the game across the country, Vol quarterback Andy Kelly stole the show, completing 33 of 55 passes for 368 yards and three touchdowns. Webb got his yards, all right, and most everybody else's as well, accounting for all but four of Tennessee's 135 on the ground. Kelly got off to a horrible start but looked like the second coming of Johnny Unitas in the fourth period. He led Tennessee to 21 points in the final 10 minutes and his fourth-quarter statistics were downright amazing: 17 of 26 for 234 yards and touchdown tosses to Carl Pickens and Alvin Harper. Incredibly, UT ran 33 offensive plays and gained 282 yards in the fourth quarter alone.

It ended in a thrilling 31-31 tie, but the Vols came awfully close to winning. On the game's final play, Webb got into the secondary and appeared to be touchdown-bound. But a Colorado player had an angle on him and Webb, after a 25-yard gain, tried to get out of bounds to stop the clock and set up a winning field goal try by Greg Burke. Had the field been a couple of yards narrower, it would have worked.

Six days later who should appear at Neyland Stadium with his University of the Pacific team but Walt Harris, Tennessee's offensive coordinator of 1983-87. Whereas Tennessee's 31-31 tie with Colorado the week before had been college football at its best, Tennessee vs. Pacific wasn't. The Vols had a 31-0 lead after one quarter and went on to a 55-7 victory over the woefully outmanned Tigers.

If Harris had held even the slightest hopes of an upset, they were dispelled pretty quickly. By late in the first period, Pacific had completed four of seven passes—one to split end Jason Edwards and three to Tennessee defensive backs.

The game will long be remembered not for the one-sided victory, but as the game in which Tennessee lost Chuck Webb to a serious knee injury. The gifted sophomore tailback, who many experts thought was on the way to becoming a legendary college running back, was tackled at the end of a broken pattern run that netted only a couple of yards. His legs were cut out from under him, and Tennessee's national championship hopes, real or imagined, were cut out from under Webb's legs.

Although his knee was severely damaged, he limped to the sidelines under his own power. Asked later why he did so without help, he said, "If my leg was broke, I would have walked off the field. It was a pride thing with me. I wouldn't get carried off the field."

After he learned of the severity of Webb's injury, Majors uttered one of the more quotable quotes of his 16 years at Tennessee: "Disgruntled alumni aren't the coach's worst enemy; injuries are."

Majors gave an indication of the kind of breathtaking talent he had lost when he said, "I've always said that Tony Dorsett was a once-in-a-lifetime runner for any coach to have. Now it looks like Chuck Webb is a twice-in-a-lifetime runner."

Majors had been down the injury road before. He lost his first two quarterbacks at Pittsburgh in 1976, and the Panthers still managed to win the national championship. He lost the great Tony Robinson to a knee injury at midseason in 1985, and the Vols went on to claim the SEC title and beat Miami in the Sugar Bowl. He lost several key members of the offensive line for the dismal first half of the 1988 season, and the team rallied to win its last five games.

Webb was gone, but the cupboard was anything but bare. Tony Thompson, who had sparkled in games against Memphis State in 1988 and Vanderbilt in 1989, stepped into Webb's tailback spot and would perform more than admirably. So admirably, in fact, that he would come within 29 yards of Tennessee's single season rushing record of 1,290 yards, set by Johnnie Jones in 1984.

"We lost a great player when Chuck Webb went down," Kelly says. "When you lose a player like that you're bound to feel it. But I don't think the guys lost their confidence in our ability to win games. Losing Chuck definitely hurt our offense; he could make plays when a play really shouldn't have been made.

"A guy could miss a blocking assignment and nobody would notice because Chuck could make a quick move and make the tackler miss him."

Webb never played again at Tennessee, opting for a professional career instead. He signed with the Green Bay Packers but encountered knee problems again.

Ironically, Webb's father had bought a $1 million insurance policy on his son's legs just a few weeks before. The Lloyds of London policy would protect the Vol star against an injury that would cost him a professional career.

Thompson got off to a shaky start against Mississippi State a week later, fumbling the ball away at the State 3 early in the game. His teammates gave him plenty of vocal support. "Don't worry about the fumble," Kelly told him. Teammates slapped him on the rump.

"The guys on this team stick together," Thompson said. "They just told me to hold on to the dad-blamed ball."

Thompson did as he was told. He held on throughout a 69-yard touchdown run. He held on just as tightly on his next carry, an 80-yard TD scamper that opened Tennessee's lead to 17-7.

Before his day was done, Thompson had a lot of fans asking "Chuck Who?" He wound up with 248 yards and the two touchdown runs as the Vols crushed the Bulldogs 40-7. The Vol defense stepped forward to take a bow after holding State without a touchdown (the Bulldogs' TD came on a punt return). The defense, in fact, had allowed but one touchdown in the previous eight quarters.

The 5-7 Thompson may have felt 10 feet tall after his spectacular 248-yard performance, but he had to share the spotlight with offensive guard Bernard Daffney. The 6-7, 300-pound Daffney earned a niche in Tennessee football history when he lumbered 32 yards on a "fumblerooskie" play for the Vols' third touchdown. On the play, Kelly took the snap, then laid the ball on the ground behind the right ankle of center John Fisher. Kelly faked a handoff and rolled toward right end. After the pursuit followed, Daffney scooped up the ball and rambled around the other end.

After the game, Daffney at first tried to convince the media that it hadn't been a preconceived play, that he had merely picked up a fumble and run with it.

Finally, though, he couldn't let the charade continue. He broke into a huge grin and asked, "How'd it look on TV?"

Daffney was not the first Vol ever to score on a hidden ball play, but he most likely was the last. The NCAA outlawed fumblerooskie-type plays the next year.

The Vols were favored by 39 over 1990 Breather No. 2, otherwise known as Texas El-Paso, and they had almost covered the spread by halftime, when they led 35-0. The final was 56-0, and Tennessee had outscored its last three opponents by 151-14, a fact not lost on the voters in the Associated Press poll, who put Tennessee at No. 6.

Auburn and Tennessee staged what looked like a replay of the Disneyland Pigskin Classic of four weeks earlier, only this time it was Auburn playing catch-up instead of Tennessee. The Vols let a 26-9 lead slip away in the fourth quarter as Tiger quarterback Stan White came out firing from the hip and it ended 26-26. White completed 30 of 58 passes for 338 yards and three TDs.

The Vol staff was roundly criticized for having gone too conservative after building a big lead. Four times the Vols took over in Auburn territory; yet the offense could convert only one of the possessions into a score. It inspired a joke that made the rounds in Knoxville for a week or so after the game:

"Did you hear that the Vols' offensive players couldn't get in the dorm the other day? It seems somebody put an end zone in it."

When old friends Majors and Auburn coach Pat Dye met at midfield for the traditional handshake, Dye said he wished the two teams could meet again and decide a winner.

"That just suits the you-know-what out of me," said Majors.

There was a postscript. Tennessee had one last shot at victory, moving downfield in range of kicker Greg Burke, but his 34-yarder drifted left. After Burke trotted off the field, a sideline camera showed a cup of ice, thrown by Vol center John Fisher, hitting Burke's headgear. The ESPN announcers mistakenly said that Fisher was throwing the ice at Burke because of his missed field goal, when, in fact, Fisher had aimed at the cameraman.

"Nobody in the stadium felt worse than Greg," Kelly remembers, "and as he was walking off the field John went to meet him, to console him, pat him on the butt and tell him to keep his chin up.

"John saw the cameraman getting in Greg's face with the camera and that ticked him off. He threw at the cameraman and he beaned Greg right in the head. On TV it looks like he was throwing it right at Greg but he wasn't."

Burke ended up in trainer Tim Kerin's doghouse that season. The Vol kicker was on curfew, meaning he had to be in his room by 11 p.m. However, he needed to be out past curfew one night and, like something out of a movie, put a mannequin in his bed. He was caught red-handed.

At practice the next day at Neyland Stadium, equipment manager Roger Frazier and assistant Max Parrott outfitted the same mannequin in full game uniform, complete with headgear and Burke's No. 27 jersey. The coaches called for the PAT/field goal team, of which Burke was a member. By the time he got on the field, there was the mannequin, standing over the ball, in a kicking pose. Burke received additional curfew restrictions from Kerin, but not before everyone had a good laugh.

Tennessee led Florida 7-3 at the half of a defensive struggle but it wasn't that way for long. Junior college transfer Dale Carter hauled the second half kickoff back 91 yards to score and the rout was on. The dazzling run ignited a 28-point third quarter and brought this observation from Carter: "On a kickoff or punt return, I think 'Can't nobody stop me.' If there's a hole, I'll find it."

Carter's return seemed to rejuvenate the UT offense; the Vols didn't go into their customary shell after mounting a sizable lead. And once the bloodthirsty crowd got into the game, things got out of hand for the Gators. It marked the first time in four years that Tennessee had held an SEC opponent without a touchdown. And it was probably the finest defensive performance by a Tennessee team since the '86 Sugar Bowl.

The victory shoved Tennessee to No. 3 in the AP poll behind Miami and Virginia and caused ESPN announcer Tim Brando to make a reappraisal of the Vols. After the 26-26 tie with Auburn, he had said, "Well, this second tie knocks Tennessee out of the national championship picture." After the smashing victory over Florida, he said, "Well, this victory keeps Tennessee in the national championship picture."

One thing for sure: the win kept the bowls interested. There were scouts on hand from nine of them—Sugar, Cotton, Orange, Fiesta, Gator, Florida Citrus, Hall of Fame, Peach and Sunshine.

Majors instituted a new wrinkle for Tennessee football the following week—the Vol Walk. He invited Tennessee fans to form a human corridor for the Vols on their seven- to 10-minute walk from the Neyland-Thompson Football Complex dorm to Neyland Stadium.

Majors, ever the comic, had a ready answer when asked why it was decided to stage the walk. "Well, it probably beats swimming up the river."

Then it was the Third Saturday in October. And, lo and behold, Tennessee was favored by 11 points. The oddsmakers weren't impressed by the 2-3 Tide in Gene Stallings' first season as head coach. Neither were the voters; Alabama was unranked in the polls. It was shades of 1987, when Tennessee also was favored over the Tide, albeit by a mere 2 1/2 points. And, as in 1987, all signs pointed to a Tennessee victory.

Senior tackle Antone Davis felt uneasy that day, just as he had three years earlier.

"I remember that we were in a real good mood in the meeting room before the '87 game, and I didn't feel good about that," he said. "I kept thinking, 'You all better get ready for this thing.' "

In their press packets, writers covering the game found a press release boosting Alabama kicker Phillip Doyle for All-America honors, along with a prophetic quote from Stallings: "He is deadly accurate and pressure doesn't bother him."

Three hours later, Doyle calmly kicked a 47-yard field goal to give the Tide a dramatic 9-6 victory.

No one could explain the low-scoring game; after all, the average score in the series had been 43-25 over the previous four years.

One answer was that Tennessee's offense, which had averaged 42 points in six games, was all but non-existent against Bama. The Vols made just eight first downs. Quarterbacks Kelly and Henton combined to complete only 9 of 25 passes for a measly 51 yards and had two intercepted. The running game was good for only 125 yards, with Thompson the leading ball carrier with 48 yards. Alabama's offense wasn't much better: 11 first downs, 118 yards passing, 104 rushing.

The loss was Kelly's first as the starting quarterback. He had a 10-0-2 record entering the game.

Doyle's winning field goal came just after Burke had attempted a 50-yarder that would have won it for Tennessee with 1:35 to play. But Stacy Harrison broke through to block it and set the stage for Doyle.

The game was a throwback to those old Alabama-Tennessee games of another time, when defense and field position were the rage and 9-6 games were the rule rather than the exception.

On the sidelines two minutes before the game ended, Ben Byrd of *The Knoxville Journal* was talking with Scott Hunter, quarterback of Alabama's great teams of the late '60s. "The only people enjoying this game are Gen. Neyland and Coach Bryant," Hunter said.

Burke's field goal try was then blocked, prompting Byrd to suggest that the number had just been trimmed in half. "I'm pretty sure the general left after that," he said.

The Vols may have been No. 3 in the national polls going into the game, but they were No. 1 in the hearts of Vol fans. ESPN cameras panning the crowd routinely zeroed in on Big Orange boosters with their index fingers aloft in the popular "We're No. 1" pose.

After the defeat, at least one Tennessee fan was still holding his finger on high as he stalked past the Alabama rooting section following the game. However, it wasn't the index finger this time.

A victory over Alabama could have done wonders for third-ranked Tennessee. No. 2 Miami's loss to Notre Dame would have elevated the Vols into the No. 2 spot behind Virginia and lent championship overtones to the UT-Notre Dame game three weeks later.

After an open date, Tennessee got back on track with a 41-20 win over 32-point underdog Temple, the Vols using the kicking game to score 14 first-quarter points. Kelly, the target of much verbal and written abuse for not having played well against Alabama, enjoyed his best all-round day in many weeks. But the highlight of the afternoon was the introduction of Vol players of 50 years before.

By early November, Chuck Webb, lost for the season after a Game 2 knee injury required surgery, was working, prompting one reporter to ask Majors if there was a chance that the gifted tailback might get back in action in 1990. The answer was an emphatic no.

"Chuck's a tough kid," Majors said, "but he's not the Bionic Man."

The remark brought to mind one that Majors' wife Mary Lynn often used during the years at Pittsburgh, when Lee Majors, television's "Six-Million-Dollar Man," was a close friend of the Majors family and sometimes a guest in their home. In those days, Mary Lynn loved to joke about having the "Six-Million-Dollar Man" and the "Six-Dollar Coach" under the same roof at the same time.

Majors the actor was not related to Majors the coach. His real name was Robert Lee Yearby and he played high school football at Middlesboro, Kentucky, not far from Knoxville. He regularly attended Tennessee games and Johnny Majors was his hero. Johnny once gave him a chin strap after a game. Although he went on to fame and fortune, Robert Lee Yearby never realized one of his greatest ambitions—playing football at Tennessee. But because he so admired Johnny Majors, he called himself Lee Majors when he became an actor.

The sweat from the Temple game hadn't even dried when Tennessee people began looking ahead to Notre Dame. The meeting with the Irish at Neyland Stadium produced the biggest ticket crunch in UT history. Newspaper ads ran for weeks before the game, some of them asking as much as $190 per ticket. One ad asked $600 for a pair in Section UU, but that wasn't all; the seller would throw in a free Bahamas trip for two with the tickets.

A crowd of 97,123, second largest in Tennessee history, crammed its way into Neyland Stadium and every one of them left thinking they had seen college football played at the highest level—a free-swinging duel between two very talented, well-coached teams. The game turned into a slugfest with a combined offense of 925 yards, 516 by Tennessee and 408 by Notre Dame.

The Irish stuck mostly to the ground, rushing for 316 yards and scoring three rushing touchdowns against a Vol defense that hadn't surrendered one since the fourth quarter of the Colorado game. The Vols threw more passes that day than any Tennessee team had ever thrown (60), completed more (35) and gained the most yardage (399).

Notre Dame's celebrated Rocket Ismail, swift as the wind, scored the game-winner on a 44-yard dash with a little more than three minutes left. But Tennessee came ever so close to pulling it out.

Down 34-23 with three minutes left, Kelly capped a 10-play, 68-yard drive with a 23-yard strike to Alvin Harper. Carl Pickens, who set a school record with 13 receptions that day, recovered an onsides kick with just under two minutes left.

"When we got the onsides kick, I just knew we were going to win," Kelly says. "I told them in the huddle, 'Guys, we have time. We're going to go down there and score and we're going to win this game.' "

With less than a minute to play, the Vols had the ball at the Notre Dame 21. Harper streaked toward the end zone and had a step on the safety. But cornerback Rod Smith moved in front of Harper and shook down the echoes with a leaping interception of Kelly's pass at the goal line.

Of the 846 passes Kelly threw in a four-year UT career, that is the one he would most like to have back.

"We had beaten Smith a little earlier with the same play," Kelly says. "This was the same play, same end zone, same corner. On the play, we tried to isolate him on the corner. We ran Pickens on a short route and Harper a post corner in behind him. Smith baited me, and he made a good play. He stayed up on Pickens and invited me to throw the ball. Just as I released it, he either read it or made a guess; I don't know which. When I threw the ball, I didn't see him breaking away from Pickens.

"If I had kept my eyes on him for maybe another second, I could have dumped it to Pickens and at least got another down or Pickens could have gotten a first down or out of bounds."

It wasn't the end of the world, but you couldn't have convinced Andy Kelly. He was consoling teammates after the game and when he got to Fisher, one of his closest friends, he broke into sobs.

Despite the defeat, it was a day to remember for Kelly. He set school records for pass attempts (60), completions (35) and passing yardage (399).

The defeat ended Tennessee's 21-game November winning streak. It was, in fact, the only November loss for Tennessee in a 36-game stretch over nine seasons.

A week later, the Vols laid all their hopes of a triumphant season on the line against an Ole Miss team that had come to be far better than it was supposed to be. After two unexpected losses by Auburn, the winner would emerge as a clear-cut leader in the race for the Sugar Bowl. Majors called the game the biggest challenge any of his Tennessee teams had ever faced.

Tennessee played just well enough to win, 22-13, and the Vols won it because they built up a 20-7 lead and were able to milk the clock with a couple of long possessions that left little time for the Rebels to play catchup. Kelly turned in his third straight stickout performance by completing 19 of 23 passes for 174 yards. Thompson got 106 yards on the ground and 6-2, 232-pound Greg Amsler got 63 more on 13 carries from the tailback position.

Kentucky was a 27 1/2-point underdog but played the Vols off their feet before losing 42-28. The Wildcats led by 14 points twice in the first half; then the Andy Kelly Aerial Show started. The junior quarterback threw a school-record five TD passes, three of them to Pickens, who tied a school record. In four outings since his bad game against Alabama, Kelly had completed 88 of 163 passes for 1,137 yards and eight TDs.

Thompson, whose career had been marked by injuries, brief stints on defense and long stints on the bench, got 79 yards to become the fourth Vol to pass the 1,000-yard rushing barrier. And, to top it all off, he was elected captain.

He saved his best for Vanderbilt, zigging, zagging and juking his way for 236 yards and tying a school record with four touchdowns. Tennessee won easily 49-20 to wind up 8-2-2, claiming its second straight SEC championship and a berth opposite Virginia in the Sugar Bowl.

The Vols, down 16-0 at halftime, managed to claw their way back from a lethargic first half to subdue Virginia 23-22. And Tennessee's 100th year of football ended in much the same way it began more than four months before — with Kelly rallying his team to escape almost certain defeat.

A stern halftime lecture may have had something to do with it. An angry Majors told the Vols, "You are Southeastern Conference champions and you'd better start acting like it!"

Kelly hit 14 of 17 passes for 141 yards and a TD in the fourth quarter alone. Ironically, his fourth quarter passing statistics against Colorado 127 days before had been precisely the same, 14 of 17.

Dan Dierdorf of ABC's Monday Night Football crew, which covered the game, summed up the battle of New Orleans and Tennessee's gutty comeback thusly: "This was a perfect example of a team not losing its cool."

CHAPTER 30

TIME TO RELOAD

In the off-season, Tennessee had served as the National Football League's No. 1 farm team. Nine offensive players off the 1990 Southeastern Conference championship squad were taken in the 1991 NFL draft, stripping the Vols of much of the firepower that had established school records for points and total offense.

As the Vols of 1991 gathered for fall practice, the search was on. Graduation had wiped out the running back corps and had cut deeply into the wide receiver ranks, traditionally Tennessee's stock in trade. A major restructuring was in order but, to make things a bit easier, UT returned two of the finest players in the nation in quarterback Andy Kelly and wideout Carl Pickens.

But fall practice 1991 will be remembered for the arrival of Heath Shuler, the prodigiously talented quarterback from Bryson City, North Carolina, just across the Smoky Mountains from Knoxville.

Observers could see right off that Shuler was an arsenal unto himself. He made a tremendous impression on his very first day of practice, displaying a quick release and uncommon zip on his passes. His throws, in fact, had so much velocity that few of the rookie receivers were able to handle them.

A young walk-on receiver, Chip Robertson, felt the full effect of a Shuler pass. He was running a hitch route as Shuler took a three-step drop and fired the ball. It hit off the screw of Robertson's helmet, and put a gash in and deflated the ball.

From the standpoint of sheer quarterback talent, Shuler was probably as good as Johnny Majors had ever signed—tall (6-3), rangy, athletic, intelligent and with a fine arm. Draw up the ideal college quarterback, and he would look like Heath Shuler. If calamity were to befall Kelly, the gifted Shuler would step into the breach.

The schedule was a coach's nightmare. The Vols had to open against a Louisville team that had demolished Alabama (34-7) in the Fiesta Bowl, although the Cardinals had suffered heavy graduation losses and were not ranked in the Top 25.

But five Tennessee opponents were: Florida (5), Notre Dame (6), Auburn (17), Alabama (22) and UCLA (24). And the other bad news was that the Vols would get three of the toughies in a row: Auburn, Florida and Alabama. Worse news was that the Vols had to play at Florida and at Alabama. The worst news was that there wasn't a taffy pull anywhere on the schedule.

Back-to-back SEC championships made Tennessee a juicy target, and brought out one of Majors' favorite expressions: "The higher you are on the flag pole, the harder the wind blows."

Louisville, the opening opponent, found out early that Messrs. Kelly and Pickens could play the game. They hooked up on a 75-yard touchdown pass on Tennessee's third snap of the season and Pickens added a 67-yard punt return for another TD in the fourth quarter as the Vols won 28-11 in a game billed as the biggest in Louisville's history.

Some Vol fans thought they saw the second coming of Reggie Cobb and Chuck Webb when freshmen Aaron Hayden and James "Little Man" Stewart became the first Tennessee backs in 18 years to each run for more than 100 yards in a game. Hayden gained 109 yards and Stewart 101 as the gifted tandem fell just one yard short of accounting for exactly half of Tennessee's total offense.

There was little doubt that the coaches had suddenly solved what had been their most pressing problem—bolstering a position that had been woefully weak in spring practice.

And what did Majors have to say about the spectacular debut of his freshman tailbacks? Nothing too profound: "I was very pleased with the freshman tailbacks."

Majors spent the night before the UCLA game the way he usually spends the night before a big game—sleeping soundly. But he spent the first part of it helping the University of the South at Sewanee celebrate its 100 years of football at a reception and banquet. He spoke, but he was there mainly because of his sentimental ties to the school where his father, the late coach Shirley Majors, gave the Tigers their only undefeated teams of this century, 1957 and 1963.

The Vols beat UCLA 30-16 in the sun-baked oven they call Neyland Stadium, where concession people were charging—and getting—$1.50 for a cup of water.

It was defense that did UCLA in. With Tennessee, it no longer was "Speed Kills." Now it was "Defense Decapitates." Cut the head off and the body dies. UCLA's Tommy Maddox, one of the nation's top quarterbacks, could vouch for that. He spent most of the afternoon running for his life. The UT defense sacked him, socked him, harried him, hurried, him, swatted his passes and generally made life miserable for him. Just like the Vol defense had treated Louisville's Jeff Brohm nine days earlier.

Meanwhile, Kelly, the quarterback a lot of people refused to appreciate, and Pickens were at it again, collaborating on a 34-yard touchdown to give the Vols an early lead and they were in command all the way.

Moving from the football field to the courtroom, the UT football program escaped the full wrath of the NCAA on September 18 when the Committee on Infractions let UT off with relatively minor penalties following an investigation of several months.

The committee imposed a two-year probation but decided not to levy any sanctions and accepted the university's mild self-imposed restrictions on scholarships and the size of the coaching staff. It was regarded as a best-case scenario for Tennessee, which could have been banned from postseason play and television appearances.

The football program had been charged with five violations described as major, with the focus on alleged recruiting violations by assistant coach Jack Sells, who had since been fired, and a controversial summer football camp that the NCAA claimed was an invitation-only camp for outstanding prospects.

The NCAA report said it was "a unique case in which the institution should receive less than the full set of minimum penalties otherwise required by NCAA legislation."

The investigation had begun in January 1990 after the NCAA received an anonymous letter alleging the UT senior camp was illegal. The NCAA investigated the summer camp in early 1990, then expanded its investigation to Sells.

And then it was back to the football field.

The clock read 5:45. The Vols trailed Mississippi State 24-20, with the ball at their own 12-yard line. Neyland Stadium's south end zone must have looked 10 miles away. The Vols had to run the table, with no misses. Bear Bryant used to have a favorite saying about that sort of situation: "That's when they come up with something their mamas and papas gave them."

Kelly's game-winning touchdown pass to tight end Mark Adams, when everyone in the stadium was expecting the throw to go to Pickens, brought smiles to a lot of faces, not the least of which was the one belonging to offensive coordinator Phil Fulmer, sitting in the coaches' booth high atop the stadium. He must have known what he was talking about earlier in the season when he described Kelly as "the glue that holds our offense together."

The addition of Arkansas and South Carolina to the SEC in 1991 necessitated a two-division setup, under which a number of traditional games played on a year-in and year-out basis all but came to a close beginning in 1992. One of the victims was Auburn vs. Tennessee, a rivalry that had stood for college football at its best for nearly four decades. They met in 1991, but since they were placed in opposite divisions, they would not meet again in regular season play until 1998 at Auburn and 1999 in Knoxville. Under the SEC's 5-2-1 schedule format, they would play every eighth and ninth year.

Perhaps it was the seeming end to the rivalry that attracted a crowd of 97,731 to Neyland Stadium, the largest crowd ever to see a game at the Home of the Vols. And they saw Tennessee at its best in a 30-21 victory engineered by Kelly.

It was a dazzling offensive display. Kelly threw three touchdown passes, completing 23 of 35 for 355 yards, and Stewart ran for 141 yards as the Vols piled up 557 yards. The highlight was a Kelly-to-Pickens TD pass of 87 yards, longest in Tennessee history.

The Vols had arrived at the one-third mark of the season with a 4-0 record, a No. 4 national ranking, an open date and a great many maniacal fans. They were riding in the fast lane of college football. This rather happy turn of events was happening just three years after Tennessee football had been 0-6 and up to its neck in embalming fluid.

The outlook was bright because the '91 Vols had a couple of things going for them that recent Tennessee teams had lacked: a dandy quarterback who could be dynamite when the occasion demanded and a beastly defense that could all but choke the life out of an offense, particularly one that liked to throw the ball. The pass rush had been raising unmitigated hell with opposing quarterbacks. Defensive coordinator Larry Lacewell had come up with a nifty little scheme in which he sent four defensive ends, and no tackles, after the other team's quarterback. The leader of the pack was a newcomer, end Chris Mims. At 6-6 and 261, he was a frightening sight to quarterbacks and a joyful sight to NFL scouts.

In his senior season, Kelly had become a master at getting the ball into the end zone. He had done it often enough, and by whatever means necessary, to have a 19-2-2 record as a starting quarterback. Even in those two defeats (Alabama and Notre Dame in 1990), he had put his team in a position to win. In the two ties, the Vols had scored 57 points, so it was hardly a case of offensive breakdowns.

Strange as it seemed, Tennessee was in the chase for a national championship. But as good as Tennessee looked, observers said the Vols couldn't cut it because the murderous schedule still included road games at Florida, Alabama and Notre Dame. And the observers were right.

As the Vols headed for Gainesville, Florida, there was bad blood between Tennessee and Florida. Anti-Tennessee sentiment in Florida had reached a crescendo a month earlier when the NCAA more or less acquitted Tennessee of charges that assistant coach Sells broke recruiting rules and that UT had run an illegal summer football camp.

Florida supporters were furious. To them, Tennessee had been the villain in the Gators' being stripped of the 1984 SEC championship. UT had always been pictured as the culprit in that episode, although the defrocking was done by a vote of the SEC membership.

That the Gators remembered having their tails kicked almost into Ft. Loudoun Lake when they visited Knoxville the year before probably had a lot to do with their 35-18 victory this time. Tennessee presented Florida five turnovers and a blocked punt, all gift-wrapped. The Gators scored off four of the six miscues, and on an interception return for a touchdown, and that was that.

The Vols didn't beat themselves; on this day, the better team won. Although Kelly threw for 392 yards, he was intercepted three times. Tennessee's rushing game netted a measly 49 yards. Stewart, who had gone past 100 yards rushing in three of Tennessee's first four games, carried eight times. He got zero yards.

The name of Jack Sells, the fired assistant coach, surfaced again. It was revealed that he had faxed diagrams of Tennessee plays to Florida defensive coordinator Ron Zook, a former Tennessee coach and a close friend of Sells', three days before the game.

Zook at first denied the story but Florida later admitted to the charges. He also fired verbal potshots at Majors and UT athletic director Doug Dickey, his one-time bosses: "If we got something that could have really helped us, then Johnny Majors should be more concerned with where the leak is on his staff.

"I think it's Tennessee trying to hurt Jack (Sells) some more and they've already run the guy out of coaching. Either that, or it's that Doug Dickey has a vendetta against Florida, which I've heard."

Twelve days after the game, according to a complaint filed with Chattanooga police, Sells claimed that he had been assaulted in a Chattanooga restaurant. The complaint said that a man approached Sells in the restaurant and inquired if his name was Jack Sells. Sells said yes. The man then struck him in the eye and fled the restaurant. Sells reportedly was the victim of a similar attack earlier but declined to file a complaint that time.

The SEC investigated and released this statement regarding the fax matter: "The commissioner has determined that no violations of conference regulations occurred. It was further determined that the incident did not involve findings of ethical misconduct by any institutional personnel. The conference considers the matter closed."

On to Birmingham and 5-1 Alabama vs. 4-1 Tennessee. Into the third period of this duel at high noon before the ABC cameras they went, a battle of evenly matched teams, Tennessee leading 6-3. For almost three quarters, Alabama-Tennessee was everything Tennessee fans were always hoping it would be, but rarely was.

The Tennessee staff elected to play it cozy in the second half, more or less forcing the offense to keep its gun holstered, and hoping the defense could hold on. If the Vol D had managed to hold on, it would have been a great bit of strategy. But the defense didn't hold on. After 30 minutes, with the score still 6-3, the world blew up in UT's face. Bama marched 70 yards to a touchdown early in the fourth quarter and struck for two more in a span of a minute and a half. It was 24-6 Alabama, six minutes to go. The Vols' road had suddenly become long and the hill steep. Their dream turned into the same old nightmare. They did come back to score twice, but Alabama won 24-19.

The loss set off a storm of protest among Tennessee supporters. Many fans, and even some Vol players, complained that the decision not to pass had cost Tennessee the game.

Their complaints were not without grounds. Going back to the previous year's 9-6 loss to the Tide and carrying into the fourth period of this game, Tennessee had gone seven quarters and two-thirds of another without scoring a touchdown. And this was with an offense that had set school records for yards and points in 1990 and was even ahead of that pace in 1991.

As if to underscore the fact, in the five games following the loss to Alabama, the Vols averaged just under 500 yards per game. And twice in that five-game stretch they set school records for total offense in a game, 603 yards against Memphis State and 606 against Vanderbilt.

Back home in Knoxville, the switchboard at WIVK Radio lit up even while the game was still in progress. Irate Tennessee fans began calling in their gripes to the station long before the postgame call-in show was to go on the air.

Sports talk show host Mike Keith said he had never seen anything like it.

"We were sitting there in the studio and Alabama had just scored to go up 24-6 with six minutes to go," he said. "And we started getting calls right then. Some people just wanted to cuss somebody out. Understand, this was still during the game. Some people wanted to be put on hold for an hour and a half to be on the Final Scoreboard show so they could gripe. They were ready to do that because they were so furious."

Kelly looked back nearly three years later. "We watched on film what Alabama had done the year before and I really felt confident. After the game, some of our guys said in the paper that they thought we didn't get a chance to show what we could do. I think there was a stretch in the third quarter when we ran the ball a ton and didn't get a chance to throw it."

He remembers his teammates being confused by the strategy. "Coming off the field, a receiver would ask me, 'What are we doing? Why don't we start throwing?' And I'd try to keep everybody calm. I'd say, 'Let's do what we're told and execute it and do the best we can.'

"All of a sudden, bam! Alabama gets a long punt return and we're down 24-6. What made everybody question the play calling in that game was because when we got down 24-6 we opened up and threw everything at them and all of a sudden we are on the board with 19 points and we have the ball and a chance to win.

"Everyone looked back and asked why we didn't come out in the third quarter or even the second quarter and just air it out and let whatever happens happen. Everybody thinks if we had done that we would have scored and probably won the game. We would have scored more and probably Alabama wouldn't have had that burst and scored the points that they did.

"We felt we were a better team than Alabama, both in '90 and '91. They had a solid defensive team both years but, to be honest, their offense wasn't very good. And both those years our defense, for the most part, played well enough for us to win. The offense just didn't get it done.

"You can't imagine how much we wanted to beat Alabama. In the preseason you could ask which game we would most want to win and everybody on the team would pick the Alabama game. Maybe that had something to do with it; maybe we wanted it too much. We had poise and confidence and a lot of smart guys. I don't think that we choked."

Fulmer defended the decision to put the wraps on the offense, saying the call was made by the entire staff at halftime.

"I don't think it was sitting on the lead," he said. "I think it was being smart. We go in at halftime and Alabama has a grand total of 73 yards total offense. And it was relatively obvious at the time that they couldn't move the football against our defense. We had been very nice to people in the past in giving them things that got them back in the game. And we were determined as a staff — we talked about this very thing at the half — that we couldn't turn the ball over."

Tennessee took out its frustrations on Memphis State, one of its favorite whipping boys, romping to a 52-24 triumph for its 13th win in as many games against the Tigers. The Vols, on a mission and playing at home for the first time in more than a month, got a 169-yard rushing effort from Hayden. Kelly was on target, hitting 28 of 37 for 319 yards and a touchdown. Dandy Andy carried three times from scrimmage and gained just three yards. But on those three carries he scored two TDs and earned a first down.

The Vols were back on the winning track, but there were people who suggested that the frustrating defeat at Birmingham, coupled with the loss at Florida a week earlier, had robbed the players of that intangible called desire. After all, their hopes of SEC and national honors had been shot.

As November 9, 1991, dawned, the season that had shown so much promise a month before had come down to one game: Notre Dame.

THE MIRACLE AT SOUTH BEND

Lindsey Nelson, the golden-throated Hall of Fame sportscaster who calls Knoxville home, knew the predicament Tennessee's Vols faced as they prepared to face Notre Dame at

South Bend, Indiana, in 1991. That predicament is called the Notre Dame mystique.

Lindsey, a Tennessean through and through, had closer ties to Notre Dame than anyone in Big Orange Country. He was the long-time television commentator for Irish games and still felt a close relationship with the Notre Dame family.

But he had even closer ties to the Tennessee family that went back more than half a century, back to the late 1930s when he tutored Vol athletes and performed other tasks in the UT Athletic Department.

"I was there 13 years and I saw a good many football teams come into South Bend on Friday and go out to the stadium for the first time," he said. "They would loosen up and just leave their game right there in the mystique of Notre Dame.

"They get out there and they realize that this is one of a kind. There is no other school or institution in this country like Notre Dame. It surprises people when they see that stadium for the first time. They expect the stadium to be something grandiose, and it isn't. It seats 59,075, and they have never added a seat since the day they built it in 1930.

"When Bill Dooley was coaching at North Carolina, he took his team up to South Bend and on Friday afternoon the team was dressing and he and I were standing out there on the turf. Bill looked around and said, 'My gosh, do you realize that Knute Rockne coached here? And the Four Horsemen played here?'

"Bill was awed. As it turned out, Notre Dame had an easy time the next day because I think Bill conveyed to his team what the mystique had done to him on Friday. And it will do that to a lot of people."

The first time Tennessee played at Notre Dame, in 1978, coach Johnny Majors asked Nelson, then the voice of the Irish and one of the world's foremost announcers, to speak to the Vols at their Friday afternoon workout.

"The funny thing about that," Nelson recalls, "is that Dan Devine, the Notre Dame coach at the time, had asked me to speak to his squad too. I said, 'Dan, I've got to beg out of this because my alma mater's here for this game.' "

Majors asked Nelson to tell some Casey Stengel stories, and there was no better teller of Casey Stengel stories in the world than Lindsey Nelson. He had also been the play-by-play announcer for the New York Mets when Stengel was the Mets manager.

"John wanted to loosen them up a little, let them laugh some," he said, "because that's the best thing to do. I didn't get into the mystique thing at all."

Neither did Majors. Either time. This time he pointed out that the ghosts of Notre Dame wouldn't play a single down.

"A lot of our players don't know who Joe Theismann is, let alone George Gipp and the Four Horsemen," he said. "We're not going to make a big deal of it."

The week of the game, there was a mad scramble to pair the following week's Miami-Florida State winner and Notre Dame in a national championship game. The scramble was based on the assumption that a Notre Dame victory over Tennessee was a foregone conclusion.

When the Vols and Irish teed it up that day, it marked the 300th game in the ancient stadium, and the 100th consecutive sellout.

Twelve minutes into the game, the Irish could almost cry "Bring on the Miami-Florida State winner!" They led 21-0, the highlight being Tom Carter's 79-yard interception return of a Kelly pass. Just before halftime, Notre Dame's lead was 31-7 and the Irish were threatening to add more humiliation to an already humiliating situation. They had the ball at the Tennessee 9, first-and-goal.

And then it happened, an inconceivable run of events that, had any one of them not taken place, Irish eyes would have been smiling. Every one of them was indispensable in what would become the most astonishing Tennessee victory of all time.

Here, in chronological order, are those little bits of good fortune that fell into place for Tennessee, or the bad fortune that befell Notre Dame:

(1) It is second-and-goal at the 5, but harried Irish quarterback Rick Mirer fails to throw the ball away and instead takes a 10-yard sack, courtesy of defensive end Chuck Smith.

(2) On the next play, an incomplete pass, Majors elects to decline a holding penalty, making it fourth-and-goal from the 15 and setting up a Craig Hentrich field goal try from 26 yards away.

(3) UT linebacker Darryl Hardy breaks through to block the field goal attempt. Cornerback Floyd Miley emerges from the pile of humanity with the ball and sets sail on an 85-yard touchdown run.

If Miley is overtaken on his trip to the end zone, there will be precious little time left for the Vols to try to score. Miley's TD comes with 14 seconds left in the half. So, instead of trailing 34-7, the Vols are down by 31-14. But still given up for dead.

(4) Kicker Hentrich is injured on the play, a development that would prove devastating to the Irish later in the game.

(5) The Tennessee defense, ripped from stem to stern in the first half, is faced with the prospect of having to pitch a virtual

shutout after halftime. (Which it would almost do after adjustments to slow the Irish running game.)

(6) Quarterback Kelly, under heavy pressure, throws a pair of incompletions from the Notre Dame 30. But on fourth-and-4, he connects with J.J. McClesky for 14 yards and a first down at the 16. The Vols score three plays later to make it 31-21.

(7) Notre Dame manages only a field goal in the second half, a 20-yarder by Hentrich on fourth-and-goal from the 3 late in the third period. Almost ominously, Hentrich is injured again on the ensuing kickoff and will not return to action.

(8) Following a 2-yard Carl Pickens reverse and two incomplete passes, it is fourth-and-8 at the Notre Dame 28. Kelly hits Cory Fleming down the sidelines for 20 yards. The Irish are penalized to the 4 for a personal foul, from where Aaron Hayden scores to make it 34-28, 9:03 to go.

(9) Mirer, who has thrown four straight incompletions, is intercepted by Dale Carter at the Notre Dame 45. The clock reads 5:09.

(10) After Kelly moves his team to the 26, the call comes down from the press box; screen pass left to Hayden. The play almost doesn't get off the ground when Hayden, trying to move into position to take the pass, is hooked at the line of scrimmage by a defender. But the play works to perfection because the Irish are caught in a full blitz. Hayden was so wide open he could have run to Kalamazoo.

(11) Vol freshman kicker John Becksvoort adds Tennessee's 35th and winning point. To this day, Vol fans shudder to think of the consequences had he missed.

(12) In a beautiful display of hurry-up offense, Mirer moves his team downfield and, on a great call, runs a quarterback draw to the Tennessee 9.

(13) Sophomore walk-on kicker Rob Leonard, who has never attempted a field goal in college, faces a 26-yarder. If he makes it, the Irish walk off the field a winner.

Holder Joe Sexton has trouble handling a low center snap. And charging hard from the outside comes Jeremy Lincoln, who is about to earn his four-year scholarship with one giant leap. He almost overruns the kicker but manages to at least partially block the ball with his rump. (In his postgame interview, Lincoln remembered to thank his mother for giving him a large rear end.)

Pandemonium erupts on Tennessee's side of the field.

There it is—the bizarre chain of events that could have happened, had to happen, and did happen. Take away any one of them, and it is very unlikely that Tennessee would have pulled off its miracle victory. In 299 games played in the stadium they call "The House That Rockne Built," no team had ever recovered from a 24-point deficit to defeat the Irish.

Where did this stirring victory fit in the overall blueprint of Tennessee football?

Was it the Vols' biggest triumph ever? Possibly. The most thrilling? Hardly. The most satisfying? Absolutely not. The most illogical? Definitely.

As big victories go, Tennessee's 1928 win over Alabama has to remain up there above all the others. It was without question the win that got Tennessee off and running in the world of college football. Call that one Big Victory 1-A on the list. The win over Notre Dame was Big Victory 1-B.

As far as football purists are concerned, the Miracle at South Bend can in no way rank above UT's 6-0 decision over Georgia Tech in the epic battle in Atlanta in 1956, Majors' All-American year at Tennessee. That one was later voted the second greatest college game ever played. Call it Big Victory 1-C.

There have been other memorable Big Orange triumphs: 14-13 over LSU's defending national champions in 1959; the 21-0 victory over Alabama in 1939; the 17-0 thrashing of Oklahoma in the 1939 Orange Bowl, the game that put Tennessee into the bowl business.

As for most thrilling, the win over the Irish is probably a notch below some other ones of the modern era. The 37-34 conquest of UCLA in the 1965 "Rosebonnet Bowl" game at Memphis is probably first on the list. And beating Alabama 35-28 in 1982, the victory that ended the Tide's 11-game winning streak over Tennessee, was another thriller.

As for satisfying wins, beating Notre Dame at South Bend is hardly run-of-the-mill, but most Tennessee fans will agree that beating Miami in the 1986 Sugar Bowl is No. 1 in that category. And always will be.

As for amazing victories, this one was No. 1—by a mile.

They just can't happen like this one did.

Majors was asked if he regarded it as the biggest win in Tennessee history.

"I certainly wouldn't disagree with that assessment," he answered. "There's never been a bigger one, in my opinion. The Sugar Bowl win over Miami was awfully big. But for the time and place, there's never been a bigger one than the one at South Bend. There was great exposure and media coverage. I understand that 20 million people in Europe saw it."

Remarkably, Kelly says, the Tennessee players never quit believing they could win, even when the score was 31-7.

"The thing that sticks out in my mind today is that, even

when we were getting pounded in the first half, nobody got really down. No one panicked. No one threw in the towel. We just kept prodding each other on the sidelines, saying things like 'Let's stay in it; let's stick with the game plan.' "

Kelly says Majors did an extraordinary job at halftime of making the players believe they could still win.

"Coach Majors got to the locker room before we did and he had written on the board the number of turnovers and mistakes we had had, and the number of points Notre Dame had scored as a result. It seems like it added up to Tennessee 14, Notre Dame 10; in other words, they had earned 10 points and we had given them the rest.

"Coach said, 'Guys, we are being very good to Notre Dame. We are giving them points. We cannot give them points and win this game.' That was pretty obvious and everybody realized that. But seeing it on the blackboard, and knowing that we had played well except for the few mistakes, made us realize that if we played well we could still win.

"Coach told us that if we stopped making mistakes, stopped turning the ball over, that we could get back in the game. Nobody laughed. I think everybody looked at that blackboard and it rang a bell. I believe what Coach Majors did that day had the biggest impact of any halftime or pregame speech that I ever heard him give. When he wrote it on the board, it clicked in everybody's mind.

"As we started back on the field, we said, 'Let's do what we came to do. Let's stick to the game plan and do what we were told all week. And things will work out. If we don't win, at least we will give Notre Dame a fight and give ourselves a chance to win.' "

Tennessee and Notre Dame have played four games and the series couldn't be much closer: Each has won two games and Tennessee leads in points scored 118 to 117.

Before the Vols had even departed South Bend, bowl talk swirled through Big Orange Country. But Majors was having no part of any rap sessions regarding bowls.

"I am concerned only about the Mississippi bowl," he said, a reference to the fact that Tennessee was to meet Ole Miss at Neyland Stadium. The last thing he wanted was for his players to let Saturday's heroics make them fat and lazy.

By Monday, it was all but official that Tennessee would meet Penn State in the Fiesta Bowl in Tempe, Arizona. So the Vols found themselves struggling to concentrate on the task at hand Saturday, Ole Miss. But they managed to sleepwalk their way to a 36-25 win. Stewart broke out of his slump with 215 yards on 38 carries.

Tennessee was an 18 1/2-point favorite over Kentucky at Lexington but the Wildcats said they would have none of that and played the Vols off their feet before bowing 16-7. The Vols used three field goals by Becksvoort, a 149-yard rushing day by Stewart and a defense that allowed Kentucky to cross midfield only once.

Gerry DiNardo, in his maiden season at Vanderbilt, said he figured Tennessee considered the game with the Commodores a joke and even questioned whether the annual in-state showdown could even be considered a rivalry.

"If it is a rivalry," he said, "it needs to be played like a rivalry. When you go 2-19 or whatever it has been in recent years, I'm not sure that's a rivalry. I'm not sure how seriously UT takes it. I think the other side probably looks at it as a joke."

DiNardo had already developed a distaste for orange. He once chased away a practice field visitor because he was wearing an orange rain jacket. During a radio show, he requested that orange tape be removed from his microphone. Later on, he steadfastly refused to use the word "Tennessee," choosing to refer to UT as "That university in the east end of the state."

The Vols gave him a rude welcome in his first visit to Neyland Stadium, rolling to a 45-0 victory and establishing a school record for total offense (606 yards) along the way. And, for the first game in Tennessee history, three runners gained more than 100 yards each: Stewart with 145, Hayden with 115 and Moose Phillips with 107.

In a game teeming with the feelings of a bitter rivalry and spiced by a pregame tussle, Tennessee unloaded both barrels on Vandy, its most enduring but least endearing opponent. The skirmish erupted as the Vols headed for their locker room before the kickoff, but was halted before any damage could be done.

The game was anything but boring. The Vols uncorked a fake field goal and worked it for a touchdown, Kelly firing a strike to Shazzon Bradley in the end zone and giving the senior defensive tackle a play to remember.

Along about the middle of the fourth quarter, with Tennessee leading 38-0 and the Commodores' plodding I-bone offense going nowhere, Larry Woody of The (Nashville) Tennessean yelled to Ben Byrd of The Knoxville Journal a few seats down the line in the press box and asked in mock seriousness: "Hey, Ben. Is butt-kicking two words or hyphenated?"

Tennessee won nine of 11 regular season games and Big Orange fans everywhere were convinced that the Vols were better than Alabama and should have been 10-1. But the Vols had had to play with one hand tied behind their backs on the Third Saturday in October.

The eligibility clock ticked away for Kelly, the King of Comeback, but not before he broke virtually all of Tennessee's passing and total offense records.

The Fiesta Bowl was one Tennessee fans would like to forget. The Vols led 17-7 in the third quarter but Penn State responded with a comeback to rival Tennessee's at South Bend. The Nittany Lions converted Vol turnovers into 35 points, scored four touchdowns in less than five minutes and swept on to a shocking 42-17 victory despite Tennessee's big edge in total yardage, 441 to 226.

CHAPTER 31

THE BUYOUT

The most significant day of the 1992 football season was a Friday. A Friday the 13th. In Memphis, coach Johnny Majors walked into a news conference on November 13 and wrote an end to his Tennessee career with this statement:

"Since I have not been given the opportunity by the UT administration to remain as head football coach past this current season, I am, effective December 31, 1992, relinquishing my duties connected with the University of Tennessee."

As Majors headed into the 1992 season, there was no indication that it was to be his last at Tennessee. Far from it. He was coming off a 9-3 year, one highlighted by the rousing comeback victory over Notre Dame. Tennessee had the best five-year record in the Southeastern Conference and Majors' popularity, which had survived the dismal days of the 1988 season, hadn't been as high since the year he arrived.

Majors, a Tennessee legend if ever there was one, was entering his 16th year as boss of the Vols. His face adorned the cover of the Vol press guide to acknowledge that he was about to embark on his 25th year as a head coach. He and his team and staff seemed poised to make the 1992 campaign a fruitful one. Majors seemed destined to coach at Tennessee for as long as he wanted.

The year, however, was full of surprises. It will be remembered as much for events off the field as for what happened between the white lines on Saturdays. It would be difficult to recall a year with more tumult, more distractions.

With the exception of a 5-6 record in 1988, the UT program had been on the upswing since 1983. There had been bowl trips, a bevy of All-Southestern Conference and All-America selections and a seemingly endless stream of talent to Knoxville.

The 1992 team would be a youthful one, but Vol fans knew, instinctively perhaps, that the ingredients were there for another outstanding season. They eagerly looked forward to the debut of heralded sophomore quarterback Heath Shuler, who came out of Bryson City, North Carolina, with superstar written all over him. He would live up to all the advance billing, and then some.

What happened in 1992, however, almost defies belief, as the Vol program took one blow after another before steadying itself in December.

Despite the loss to Penn State in the Fiesta Bowl, Tennessee had had another successful recruiting season and an uneventful spring practice. Uneventful except for a pitched battle between Shuler and fellow sophomore Jerry Colquitt, from nearby Oak Ridge. One would replace the departed Andy Kelly and it was a competition that would not be resolved, publicly at least, until just before the season opener with Southwestern Louisiana.

In late May came the first episode in a bizarre sequence of events that would rock Tennessee football to its very foundation. Majors, in Milan to attend a banquet for former Vols John Fisher and Earnest Fields, was taken to a Memphis hospital after experiencing chest pains. An angioplasty procedure was performed to clear a coronary artery and he was released a day or so later. Vol fans breathed a sigh of relief and began the long wait through the summer.

Majors wasn't his usual self during the annual Big Orange Caravan's goodwill tour of the state. People said he complained openly about his contract and the fact that several SEC coaches were paid higher salaries. He couldn't understand how basketball coach Wade Houston could receive a $33,000 raise in May 1991 after losing 22 games the previous season.

He could have signed a contract extension in September 1991 that would have provided him a $50,000 to $60,000 raise through the 1996 season. He declined, holding out for a contract that would run through 1998.

The first salvo in the war came at a party in June. Majors got into a quarrel with Bill Johnson, the Sparta banker who had played with Majors at Tennessee and had been a very close friend. They reportedly almost came to blows. The ramifications of that spat would not be realized for several months. Whether anyone knew it at the time, the fierce in-fighting had begun.

A couple of months later, just before the start of fall practice, esteemed head trainer Tim Kerin died suddenly of an aortic aneurysm. Kerin had come with Majors from Pittsburgh and had been closer to the head coach than anyone else on the Vol staff. Kerin was bestowed the highest honor in the athletic training profession on June 11, 1993, when he was inducted into the National Athletic Trainers Association Hall of Fame.

Vol players paid tribute to Kerin during the 1992 season by wearing a shamrock with "TIM" on their helmets in honor of his Irish heritage.

On August 24, Majors and Dickey agreed verbally on a contract to run through the 1998 season, but without an immediate salary increase. It was not the time for a raise for the football coach; there had even been a petition signed by UT and state employees protesting a raise. Majors understood that he would get a raise when other UT employees got theirs, probably sometime within the next six months. Later that day, he experienced some chest discomfort.

The next afternoon he left practice early for what he assumed would be a routine medical examination. Because of his angioplasty procedure in May, and Kerin's death three weeks earlier, Majors was unusually mindful of his health.

As Knoxvillians were getting ready for work the next morning, they learned from a live television report from the entrance to University Hospital that Majors was undergoing quintuple-bypass surgery at that moment. It appeared to be nothing more than a minor and temporary setback.

Dickey turned the reins of the program over to Phillip Fulmer, the assistant head coach and offensive coordinator.

Majors says that while he was in the hospital, he asked his wife to remind Dickey that a contract had been due on Majors' desk the morning of his surgery. Mrs. Majors said that when she mentioned it to Dickey, he only smiled and said nothing.

Fulmer led the team into the new season. With Majors watching on television and Shuler starring on the field, Tennessee dumped Southwestern Louisiana 38-3. The Vols fell behind 3-0, then pulled away with a 24-point second quarter.

Playing Georgia at Athens was a demanding early assignment for Tennessee and Shuler. But the sophomore quarterback did the job with the aplomb of a veteran. He directed a 14-play, 80-yard drive that won the game for the Vols, keeping the drive alive with a 22-yard pass to Ron Davis on fourth-and-14 at midfield. Shuler himself scored the winning touchdown on a 3-yard run.

Shuler looks back on that game as the day he came of age as a college quarterback. "Just the feeling of driving the ball 80 yards to win," he says. "That was something. And hitting that fourth-down pass to Ron Davis was awfully big. Our team really united in that game. We became one. There were young guys on the field that day, me included, who matured more in that one game than you would ever think possible."

There was a seemingly insignificant footnote to the Georgia game. The Vols wore white pants on the road that day for the first time since 1982, an obvious departure from the orange pants that Majors preferred. It would turn out to be not so insignificant.

"I don't know how many interim head coaches there have been in the history of college football," said an elated Fulmer. "But none of them, I'll bet, have been involved in more exciting games than I was in this one."

Majors held an impromptu press conference the next Friday, the day before the Florida game, and said he would be back the next week to observe the Cincinnati game from the press box.

The next day, when the press box was dedicated to longtime trustee and Athletics Board member Tom Elam, the Vols dominated fourth-ranked Florida 31-14 in a game best remembered for a driving rainstorm in the second half that flooded Shields-Watkins Field. Shuler scored two touchdowns and threw a 66-yard TD pass to Moose Phillips. The defense, meanwhile, held the Gators' high-powered offense to 278 total yards.

On Sunday, the day after the Florida game, Majors returned to work unannounced, surprising everyone, including Dickey and university president Joe Johnson. It had been only 26 days since his surgery. Some observers suggested that the early return was due to Majors' concern that Fulmer was getting too much credit for the 3-0 start and the heady victories over Georgia and Florida.

With Fulmer still at the helm, the Vols overpowered Cincinnati 40-0 after leading by only 14-0 at halftime. The highlight was a nifty 77-yard punt return by sophomore Shawn Summers.

When the team departed for Baton Rouge, Majors was back in command. And the Vols were back in their orange pants, by golly. They sputtered a bit on offense but the defense pitched a second straight shutout and held the Tigers to 169 yards.

Tennessee was 5-0 and ranked No. 4 in the nation, a much too generous ranking, Majors would point out later. Arkansas, a

21-point underdog, drove the first nail in Majors' coffin as the Vols blew a 24-16 lead late in the fourth quarter. There were two major breakdowns in the kicking game, that phase of football that is as dear to Majors' heart as any other; he has often said that he devotes more time to the kicking game than any coach in America. First, Orlando Watters hauled a punt back 71 yards to make it 24-22. Then Tennessee's inability to cover an onsides kick cost dearly. The Hogs moved into position for Todd Wright to kick a 41-yard field goal with three seconds left to give his team a stirring 25-24 victory.

In terms of what it did to Tennessee poll-wise and bowl-wise, the loss to Arkansas was one of the most damaging to the program since the Jackson Massacre of 1969. Not to mention what it did to the Vols' coach. Had the Vols won, they almost certainly would have played in the SEC championship game no matter how they fared against Alabama a week later. And Majors might well still be employed at UT.

The largest crowd ever to see a Tennessee-Alabama game turned out the next week and the Tide made it seven in a row over the Big Orange 17-10. Statistically, it was no contest. Bama, on its way to the national championship, piled up 378 yards, 23 first downs and 77 offensive plays to Tennessee's 194 yards, 7 first downs and 49 offensive plays. Even so, Tennessee held Alabama scoreless in the second half and had a chance to win before an interception sealed the verdict. One fan showed his displeasure by hitting Majors with a cup of ice. Nail No. 2.

Here the schedule-maker dealt Majors and Tennessee a lousy hand. The Vols had two open dates in three weeks sandwiched around a game at South Carolina. When a 5-0 team becomes a 5-2 team with a two-week lull in the schedule, criticism is more plentiful. People talk. People complain. Newspapers generate "source" stories.

Majors was criticized on radio call-in shows and in newspaper columns. Some complained that he had ruined the team's chemistry with his early return, that the Vols had performed much better under Fulmer.

It was a tense team that flew to Columbia the next week. It showed on the field, where the Vols had all sorts of trouble with Steve Tanneyhill, USC's pony-tailed freshman quarterback, who kept them off balance all day and exhibited some braggadocio in doing it.

Tennessee, trailing 24-17, made one last stab at victory late in the game. Shuler found fullback Phillips in the right flat and the sophomore from Nashville broke eight tackles on a spectacular 39-yard run to the end zone. The run would have been remembered for a long time to come had the Vols been able to make the ensuing two-point conversion.

They didn't. The conversion failed and Tennessee lost 24-23, the second one-point loss in three games, the third straight defeat and perhaps the final nail in the coffin. The second open date didn't help matters. Some people speculated that a coaching change was in the works. Most people speculated that those people didn't know what they were talking about.

Majors says he and Dickey reached a second agreement a few days before the South Carolina game, an arrangement whereby he would get an extension through 1998, but with no immediate raise. Majors says the offer was "suddenly and mysteriously" withdrawn a week later following the loss to South Carolina. Dickey said that contract talks would not resume until the end of the season.

On Wednesday before the Memphis State game, Dickey and Majors conferred again. Majors claims Dickey told him, "John, you don't have the option to coach here after this year."

The options he did have were to take a job as associate athletic director, or clear out. Majors replied that he had agreed to an extension of his contract and wasn't about to back down.

The buyout on the two remaining years of his contract was to be $600,000, the money to come from athletic department funds. Dickey said there were eight to 15 university people who joined in the decision to buy out the final two years of Majors' contract.

After the second open date following South Carolina, there was another tense road trip, this one to Memphis to meet Memphis State. On that Friday morning, the media reported that Majors was out and Fulmer was in.

That night, Majors made it official, announcing at a press conference that he was through as Tennessee's head coach. He read from a prepared statement. From the tone of his voice, there was no mistaking that he was bitter for having been literally shoved out the door.

The unlikely setting was the Wilson World Hotel in East Memphis. Oddly, it was not too far from old Crump Stadium, where Majors had made his Tennessee debut against Mississippi State as a sophomore tailback in 1954. He made the longest run of his UT career that day, an 81-yard touchdown romp in a 19-7 Tennessee win.

"I will complete this season as head football coach and assistant athletic director," he said. "Having spent 23 years of my life at UT—as a player, student assistant coach and head coach—

I truly appreciate the support I have received from thousands of the most loyal fans during the good years as well as some of the leaner periods.

"During these years, I have had the pleasure of coaching some of the finest young men in the world. This current group of players, though young, are dedicated, talented and have the potential for greatness.

"The University of Tennessee is a wonderful place and I am fortunate to have been associated with so many good people— friends, contributors, supporters, players and coaches.

"I am happy to say that my doctors say my health is excellent and, contrary to some rumors, I was given the OK to return to work when I did.

"Since the days of watching my dad, the late Shirley Majors, coach, I have developed a very competitive spirit concerning football. I played hard; I coached hard; and I demanded a lot of myself and those who surrounded me.

"Sometimes in the heat of the battle, I occasionally said things that, upon reflection, I wish I hadn't. But that's been my style and it has brought me more success than failure.

"I still love the game of football and, if there's an opportunity to coach elsewhere, I would certainly consider it. But, in the meantime, we're all going to focus on the games ahead, beginning with tomorrow's game against Memphis State."

There was little doubt that Fulmer, considered to be a promising head-coaching prospect by the UT administration, would be moved up to head coach.

The football world was shocked. How could this be? Johnny Majors had been born to the orange. What Babe Ruth had been to baseball, Muhammad Ali to boxing, Michael Jordan to basketball, Johnny Majors had been to Tennessee football.

The next day, Tennessee made it 14 wins without a loss against Memphis State, but it didn't come easy. The Vols were down 7-0 just a little more than a minute into the game but went on to win 26-21. The UT defense held the Tigers to minus-1 yard rushing.

Majors and the Vol seniors made their final Neyland Stadium appearance against Kentucky. Majors ran through the giant "T" after the seniors. Even his 78-year-old mother, Elizabeth Majors, and other members of the Majors clan, ran through the T.

After which Tennessee won impressively. The Vols scored on their first two possessions and posted a 34-13 victory. Charlie Garner, Tennessee's new tailback sensation, rushed for 138 yards and scored his first UT touchdown.

Majors got an unexpected victory ride atop some of his big linemen to midfield to meet Kentucky coach Bill Curry.

The Vols rallied for 22 points in the fourth quarter to beat Vanderbilt 29-25 and send Majors out a winner. The three closing victories gave Tennessee an 8-3 record and a bid to the Hall of Fame Bowl at Tampa. On December 4, a week after the Vandy game, Majors told his squad that he would not be coaching them in the bowl game. He accepted the head coaching job at Pittsburgh two weeks later.

As expected, Fulmer was named head coach on Sunday night after the Vandy game. The terms of the five-year contract, through the 1997 season, included $100,000 base pay and $200,000 for radio and television responsibilities.

The Vols were at the top of their game against Boston College at Tampa, rolling to a 31-7 lead before BC scored 16 points against Vol subs in the closing minutes to close the final gap to 38-23. Shuler, the MVP, completed 18 of 23 passes for 245 yards and two touchdowns and ran for two more. Backup quarterback Jerry Colquitt threw his first career TD pass, a 48-yarder to Cory Fleming.

UT president Johnson later said that "unsatisfactory relationships in and around the athletic department" led to Majors' ouster. Majors said he asked Johnson the reason and he replied: "John, you just don't know how to treat people. You must have made a lot of people mad last summer."

Johnson had been quoted in the November 5 issue of the *Washington Post* as saying, "I am a great admirer of Johnny Majors. He represents his alma mater very well." On November 13, eight days later, Majors announced in Memphis that he was out as coach.

Majors never tried to hide his anger, his bitterness. He thought that Fulmer, Bill Johnson, Joe Johnson and Dickey had conspired to force him out. *The Knoxville News-Sentinel* printed a letter on November 28, the day after the Vanderbilt game, in which Majors' sister-in-law, Karen Majors, accused Fulmer of a "closed-door mutiny" against the coach. She also charged that Fulmer and Bill Johnson had conspired to get Majors' job.

The newspaper obtained telephone company records that showed that Fulmer made 26 calls to Johnson during a two-month period that fall. Fulmer and Johnson both insisted they talked about Johnson's bank refinancing Fulmer's house. Both denied a conspiracy.

In the fall of 1993, a national football magazine carried a "Coach's Corner" article, with Majors' byline, which said in part:

". . . Last year was obviously an unusual one for me at the University of Tennessee. I had a quintuple-bypass operation done August 25—on the eve of the 1992 football season. During my four-week absence while I was recuperating, an assistant coach who had been with me for 12 years (Phil Fulmer) walked the sidelines in my place and in view of some of the circumstances that later developed, he apparently grew fond of the limelight. I later found out that Fulmer and one of my best friends and former teammate, Bill Johnson, who's on the board of trustees, spent an inordinate amount of time on the phone, which is highly unusual at such an important and critical time of the year (during football season).

"The team won its first three games with Fulmer serving in my place, and when I came back, we won our next two to make us 5-0. We jumped to an all-too generous No. 4 ranking in the national polls.

"We dropped our next two games — by one point to Arkansas in the final seconds of the game and by seven points to eventual national champion Alabama. At that point a bizarre sequence of events began. First the athletic director, Doug Dickey, offered me a six-year contract extension to remain as Tennessee's head coach—an offer that was endorsed by the school's president, Joe Johnson, and one to which I enthusiastically committed. Then, suddenly and mysteriously, Dickey withdrew the offer a week later following a loss to South Carolina. Dickey told me I could stay in an administrative position with the school instead.

"Needless to say, after 16 years in which we went to 10 bowl games and won SEC championships and built a program that can challenge for the national championship for the next several years, I felt I'd been victimized by betrayal and deception on the part of some of the highest-ranking people at the University of Tennessee. I said, 'No thank you; you can fire me instead.'

"None of this might have happened if I hadn't had the heart problems, but I'm not a negative person, and I'm focusing on the future and not the past. I still have great fondness for the players I left behind at Tennessee, and I wish them well in the coming season . . . "

Also in the fall of 1993, at the SEC Media Days in Birmingham, Fulmer told the writers and broadcasters that he was glad to be Tennessee's new head coach, but said he couldn't comment on Majors' departure because, as he put it, "I was not part of that process."

The News-Sentinel sent writer Jimmy Hyams to Pittsburgh just before the 1993 season began to interview Majors. Hyams wrote that Majors was still so bitter about his ouster from UT that he refused to say the name of the school, referring to it as "my alma mater" or "my former employer."

Hyams' article went on to quote Majors:

"I don't have any trouble saying the 'state of Tennessee,' he says. "I've got too many things to look forward to to be bitter. Other than a handful of people, I've got nothing to be angry about."

"He won't quote them by name," Hyams wrote, "but the handful of people are UT president Joe Johnson, athletic director Doug Dickey, Board of Trustees members Bill Johnson and Jim Haslam and Vols coach Phil Fulmer."

"The state deserves better," Majors says.

"Fulmer was asked five weeks ago if his relationship with Majors would survive. 'Probably not,' Fulmer said.

"Told of Fulmer's comment, Majors said: 'I have nothing to say about that or about that person. I've got better things to talk about and think about with my life. I have no reason to elaborate or expand or even discuss such a subject that doesn't interest me.' "

Majors accomplished a great deal for Tennessee during his 16-year tenure. He did a great deal in the area of public relations for the university. He became one of college football's most visible coaches. His program was widely regarded as one of the best. To many people, he *was* Tennessee football.

Majors might have painted himself into a corner. But no matter what he might have done to bring on his ouster, no matter what demands he placed on the administration, he deserved a far nobler farewell.

CHAPTER 32

PURSUING
A DREAM

The interview room at Thompson-Boling Arena underwent a drastic change between 4:30 and 6 p.m. on Sunday, January 9, 1994. Down came the Lady Vols' backdrop for basketball coach Pat Summitt after her team's solid victory over LSU earlier that afternoon. In its place went the men's interview backdrop. The time had arrived for a long-awaited announcement by Heath Shuler concerning his future. Would he take the plunge into the murky waters of the National Football League draft, where his presence would reportedly be worth mega-millions, or would he return for his senior season as quarterback at Tennessee, where his God-given skills would presumably provide the Vols a shot at the 1994 national championship?

All signs pointed to Heath's departure, but then the weather bureau often says all signs point to snow in Knoxville. It rarely happens when they predict it, so maybe this too was a false alarm. Vol fans hoped so, anyway.

At precisely 6 p.m., Shuler entered the Ray Mears Room accompanied by his father and mother, Joe Benny and Marjorie, by brother Benjie and by coach Phillip Fulmer and his wife, Vicky. The sight of Shuler and Fulmer marching together to the platform may have momentarily nourished fans' expectations he was staying at UT but, if so, they were quickly disabused of any such notion.

Reading from a prepared statement, Shuler declared his intention to pursue his "dream," playing quarterback in the NFL. Just like that, the Heath Shuler era in Tennessee football ended. But memories would abound concerning the impact the vastly talented youngster from Bryson City, North Carolina, had on the 1993 Vol football campaign, a season that began on the practice field in the sweltering humidity of early August.

As August headed into September, Fulmer was getting restless, his players antsy. The suffocating heat of two-a-day drills was now behind them and the opening of the season only days away. "We've practiced hard, and I think we've accomplished a great deal," Fulmer told reporters at his Tuesday afternoon press conference before the opening game against Louisiana Tech. "I think we're ready to play somebody other than ourselves." Not just the Vol players and coaches were ready; so were their fans. The crowd of 95,106 that was on hand for the 7 o'clock kickoff began gathering on campus shortly after noon. Early birds lined Yale Avenue for the Vols' ceremonial walk to the stadium, led by Fulmer, who acknowledged fan support with a wave of the arm and an occasional handshake when he recognized a particular friend.

A good omen came in pregame warmups. After 29 years of having the Tennessee bench on the west side of the field, a practice begun by Doug Dickey, it was moved to the east side to conform to new Southeastern Conference rules regarding crowd control. Lo and behold, not one coach or player, not even Smokey the mascot, peeled off to the right after charging out of the dressing room. It was clear the Vols had their minds on their business, much to the regret of a distinctly underdog and undermanned Louisiana Tech team.

If Fulmer was ready for something other than more intrasquad scrimmages, the Vol players shared that sentiment. Tennessee crushed Tech 50-0, scoring a touchdown only eight plays into the game and otherwise stamping the performance with the Heath Shuler brand—13 of 23 pass completions, 200 yards, three touchdowns, no interceptions. The supposedly porous defense not only pitched a shutout; it ravaged the Bulldogs with seven tackles for lost yardage and registered two sacks. By halftime, Tennessee was cruising with a 36-0 lead, allowing Fulmer to give his reserves plenty of opportunity to strut their wares in the latter stages of the game.

Fulmer expressed pleasure in postgame comments about the Vols' fast start. "One of the best things to come out of the game was our chance to use a lot of our young players. That is going to be important as we go through the season. Depth is something we need to develop."

Louisiana Tech is Louisiana Tech, but Georgia is some-thing else. Both may be called Bulldogs, but Georgia's teeth dig a lot deeper. Even if Ray Goff's club was in for a subpar season, the Georgia tradition and the presence of dead-eye quarterback Eric Zeier made for a dangerous encounter. The Bulldogs hung in gamely until less than two minutes remained in the half, at which time Tennessee clung to a 7-6 lead. With 1:46 left, Charlie Garner raced into the end zone from the 2, and only a minute later, Shuler capped a three-play drive by locating Cory Fleming in the end zone for an 8-yard touchdown pass.

From that point, the defense took over, limiting Zeier to 114 yards passing for the entire game and keeping the Bulldogs out of the Tennessee end zone the rest of the way. Statistical highlights in the 38-6 Southeastern Conference win included 107 yards rushing by Garner and seven pass receptions by Fleming, including two for touchdowns. The emergence of Gar-ner, a dipsy-doodle runner of the first stripe, told future oppo-nents that they over-concentrate on Shuler at their own peril.

Fulmer complimented the defense, still trying to establish itself as something other than a potential Achilles heel. "A defensive stand we made early in the game after an interception set a tempo that we were able to maintain the rest of the way. Believe me, it is a real achievement to keep a team like Georgia from scoring a touchdown." The Vol skipper was less ecstatic about the 10 penalties called against Tennessee in the first half, a problem that came back to haunt the team in the Florida Citrus Bowl. "That is something we will be working to correct," Fulmer promised. But other than that, he could find nothing wrong with his team's performance.

Even before the season got under way, the September 18 meeting between Tennessee and Florida at Gainesville was already billed as the game of the year in the SEC. The media so anointed it, disregarding such historically classic rivalries as Alabama-Tennessee, Georgia-Florida and Auburn-Alabama. When Florida miraculously escaped an upset the previous Saturday at Kentucky, the game lost a slight amount of its luster, but it turned out to be the pivotal contest as far as Tennessee's SEC chances were concerned. It doomed the Vols to playing catch-up football the rest of the season—and to no avail.

Before 85,247 fans, some of whom would be excoriated later for coarse behavior toward their Tennessee guests, Florida jumped to a commanding lead. It was downright embarrassing how quarterback Dany Wuerffel riddled the defense and how Errict Rhett sifted through the line as the Gators built a three-touchdown lead. But two bombs from Shuler, 54 yards to Fleming and 41 to Billy Williams, cut the lead to 21-14 at halftime. Tennessee, losing by a final of only 41-34, was almost always trying to trim a lead of more than seven points. Shuler, in a classic passing display, rifled three more TD tosses of 70, 13, and 5 yards as the Vols made it close but never seemed on the brink of going ahead. The five TD throws equaled a school record set three years earlier by Andy Kelly against Kentucky.

There were some bright spots in the statistics, such as Williams' three touchdown catches, equalling a school record, and certainly Shuler's bombs not only provided good stats but they were what kept Tennessee in the game. In the game for sure, but not victorious, as Fulmer lamented after the game. "Let's understand that our offense can't count on Shuler and Williams to do it all," he declared. Pointing to a running game that netted only 76 yards, Fulmer added, "It was very disappointing that we could never get our running game going. With the running backs we have, there should never be a game where we net less than 100 yards."

The loss put the Vols up Shea's creek without benefit of paddle as far as the Eastern Division of the SEC was concerned. With Florida ranked ahead of UT on the basis of head-on competition, the Vols could notch a championship berth only if the Gators were to lose twice along the way. And while Auburn dealt them a 38-35 setback, a second SEC loss never materialized. As it turned out, the Vols and their fans pulled in vain. Outside help never came.

The test of the 1993 squad's toughness came one week later when LSU arrived in Knoxville, smarting from some tough times in Baton Rouge and hoping the Vols might be mentally down after the loss to Florida. Tough luck, Tigers. Tennessee displayed a resiliency that produced a 42-20 victory and gave a pleased Phillip Fulmer the satisfaction of seeing the running game respond to the challenge he presented after the Florida game.

Coaches are forever in pursuit of a balanced offense, their theory being that it is necessary to establish a running game to make the passing attack work, and vice versa. When the Sports Information Department staffers delivered the statistics to the dressing room after the game, they reflected a coach's dream: 251 yards rushing, 234 passing. Tom Hutton continued his quality punting with a 46-yard average.

Was Fulmer surprised that the Vols were able to shrug off the loss to Florida and play well after an emotional letdown? Not really, but he did acknowledge being concerned while getting ready for the LSU game. "We were keeping our eyes open for signs of a bounceback," he said. "About Wednesday we began to feel the team had its mind where it needed to be." Fulmer mentioned a key play by Shuler, one that revealed the quarterback's versatility. "On our first touchdown drive, as we have come to expect, Heath made the great play we needed to keep the drive alive. We faced third-and-10 at our 38. Heath's receivers were covered, but he managed to scramble for 18 yards." A touchdown by James Stewart six plays later gave Tennessee a lead it never surrendered.

The Vols were sailing along smoothly by this juncture, gaining stature in the national rankings, establishing their quarterback as a legitimate Heisman Trophy candidate and getting a rhythm of balanced offense and defense. Opposing coaches must have lain awake nights trying to figure how to control Shuler without giving a green light to the stable of running backs. Next would come a victory over homecoming foe Duke that not only would leave the old grads in a happy frame of mind but would stir talk that maybe even a national championship was not out of the question for the Vols.

Everybody got into the act during the 52-19 pounding of Duke. Or so it seemed, as several unknowns played a role, and others achieved something far removed from their normal line of expertise. Examples: defensive end James Wilson intercepted a pass; walk-on Greg Johnson blocked a punt; seldom-used linebacker John Emery recovered the blocked punt for a touchdown; backup quarterback Jerry Colquitt connected with a touchdown pass.

That isn't to suggest that Mssrs. Shuler and Garner were taking the day off. Far from it. In fact, the appearance of an army of reserves became possible because Shuler had tossed four TD passes and Garner had ripped through the Duke defense for 129 yards on 10 carries. A pretty good day at the office for those two worthies. About the only disconcerting note in the entire late afternoon (4 p.m. kickoff) performance came after Shuler had drilled a 14-yard scoring strike to Fleming midway through the second period, running the score to 28-0. Duke's Leroy Gallman carried the ensuing kickoff through a stunned band of Vols the length of the field to put the Blue Devils on the scoreboard. Even Gallman's masterpiece was blunted, however, when Paul Yatkowski blocked the extra point.

While distributing accolades after the game—and there were plenty to go around—Fulmer paid tribute to a young man whose dependability at his specialized assignment may have been taken for granted. But not by Fulmer. "We don't dare overlook John Becksvoort's landmark achievement," he said. Becksvoort connected on seven extra points to run his streak to 89, breaking Greg Burke's mark of 87. By the time the regular season ended, Becksvoort would run his PAT streak to 122, and he would miss only one of 13 field goal tries.

Elation created by the almost picture-perfect victory over Duke gave way by Monday to trepidation concerning an especially dangerous game at Little Rock the following Saturday. Under first-year coach Danny Ford, a proven hard-line winner, Arkansas was undermanned by Razorback standards, a problem that was reflected in the team's won-lost record (3-2 at the time). But Fulmer and the rest of the Vol staff knew they would be in for a fierce struggle. Their concerns were fully justified on that bleak October afternoon. The Razorbacks trailed by only 21-14 starting the fourth quarter.

It was here, locked in a monumental defensive struggle, that Fulmer experienced one of his prized memories of the 1993 season. Don't think for a minute that the old line coach instincts in him didn't resurface as the Vols launched an 84-yard touchdown drive that clinched the victory. It was time-honored, root-hog football at its best. Garner here, Stewart there, and finally the cherry on top of the sundae: quarterback Shuler disdaining the pass and blasting into the end zone on foot from the 7. More than six minutes went off the clock, and it resolved affirmatively any question about whether the pass-minded Vols could grind it out in the trenches.

Fulmer couldn't disguise his joy with the victory, achieved before a loud and highly partisan crowd and in less than ideal weather conditions. Wind swirled through most of the game at a 20-mile-per-hour clip. "We knew Arkansas would keep fighting back, scratching and clawing all the way," Fulmer said. "We gave up a lot of yardage, but we pretty well lived up to the old adage about defense: Bend but don't break. There were a lot of defensive plays that saved our neck."

As it turned out, the tie with Alabama a week later had no effect on the Vols' hopes for a berth in the SEC playoff game and a chance to go to the Sugar Bowl. Florida destroyed that dream by winning out in the SEC after its loss to Auburn. What the tie did do, however, was deny Tennessee relief from its most frustrating problem of recent years, an inability to beat Alabama even in seasons that found the Vols rated ahead of the Tide in the final polls. Not since 1985 had Tennessee experienced the sweet taste of victory in the South's most storied football rivalry. But on October 16, 1993, at Birmingham's Legion Field, only a miracle comeback could deprive the Vols of their long-awaited triumph. And be dipped if it didn't come! The miracle, that is, not the triumph.

The Crimson Tide's comeback began with 1:44 left and Tennessee leading 17-9. From its 18, Alabama drove goalward behind the passing of quarterback Jay Barker. Barker to David Palmer for 15, to Palmer for 22, and to Kevin Lee for 17 and a first down at the 1. Then Barker went up and over the pile to make it 17-15. For the conversion, Alabama put the multi-talented Palmer under center. Palmer then did what he does best: run. He ran to his right, ran a little more and finally ran right into the end zone. It was a tie game, sayeth the scoreboard, but Alabama celebrated a victory, and Tennessee mourned its loss.

The reason for the Vols' gloom? Tennessee had dominated action in no uncertain terms, stymieing the Alabama offense and putting points on the board with a Shuler-to-Craig Faulkner pass for 30 yards, a 34-yard Becksvoort field goal and a 73-yard burst by the darting, slashing Garner. A deeply disappointed Fulmer summed up Tennessee's feelings succinctly: "When you're leading by eight points at that stage of the game, it's awfully tough to leave with a tie, especially when you're playing in a rivalry like Alabama-Tennessee."

The Tennessee coach then looked on the bright side: "The scenario that produced the tie was disappointing, but our squad has every reason to hold its head high. There are some good things out there if we keep the superb attitude that this team has had since we began practice back in early August." The truth of those words would react to the Vols' favor when they next saw action, two weeks later against South Carolina.

To put it bluntly, but not unfairly, South Carolina was no match for Tennessee, which used the open date after the Alabama game to give Shuler's slightly injured shoulder time to heal. Consider these highlights of the 55-3 massacre: Garner galloped 60 yards for a touchdown on the second play of the game. The Vols amassed 569 yards total offense, 335 yards rushing, 234 passing. By halftime the lead was 38-3. Shuler was 13-for-23 for 171 yards. Garner and Little Man Stewart each accounted for more than 100 yards rushing. UT defenders turned in seven sacks and eight lost yardage tackles. South Carolina gave up five turnovers, Tennessee none. Overall, not a cheery day for the beleaguered Gamecocks, whose coach, Sparky Woods, would be seeking new employment at season's end.

True to the coaches' doctrine, Fulmer found a few clouds in an otherwise sunny sky: "As pleased as I was with this victory, I have never been involved in a game that didn't leave us plenty of areas where we needed improvement." But going into the Louisville game, even the Vols' cautious head coach would admit his team was playing at an extremely high level of competence.

And a high level of competence, Fulmer knew, was exactly what the Vols would need against a Louisville team that had gained national ranking with solid performances over big-name opponents. Howard Schnellenberger's charges had sustained only one loss, to undefeated West Virginia by two points, when they came to Knoxville on November 6. The Cardinals had ridden the passing of Jeff Brohm to victories over Arizona State and Texas and had already accepted a bid to the Liberty Bowl.

But when Tennessee scored touchdowns on its first two possessions, Louisville's bubble burst, even though the Cards made it much tighter than the 45-10 final margin indicated. The visitors cut the lead to 24-10 at the start of the fourth quarter, igniting a rally that was nipped in the bud minutes later when DeRon Jenkins intercepted a Brohm pass at the Vol 29. Tennessee regained its first-period form and tallied three touchdowns in an impressive stretch run. One of the scores came with a little razzmatazz, Fleming handing off to Nilo Silvan on a punt return that covered 69 yards. Shuler had a sparkling game, connecting on 21 of 30 passes for 215 yards.

Finally, the Vols turned their attention to two respected old rivals, Kentucky and Vanderbilt. The Wildcats, a successful season earning them a bid to the Peach Bowl, were chomping at the bit for a chance to take on the highly ranked Vols in their Commonwealth Stadium lair.

Clicking on all cylinders, the Vols didn't seem especially perturbed because of the inhospitable environment. Whether it was Commonwealth Stadium or Neyland Stadium, on that specific afternoon Fulmer fielded a Vol team that scored the first time it had the ball and didn't let up until it had notched the most one-sided victory in series history, 48-0. Shuler, who completed 23 of 34 pass attempts for 221 yards and three touchdowns, fired a pair of six-pointers to Fleming, the Vols' career TD receiver. Garner passed the 1,000-yard threshhold for single-season rushing when he slashed through the Wildcats for 186 yards.

A week later, the artificial turf of Neyland Stadium took a beating in its swan song as the Vols raced to a 62-14 thumping of Vanderbilt, bringing the 1993 regular season record to 9-1-1 and earning the Vols fifth place in the CNN-USA TODAY Coaches poll and sixth in the AP. A 27-point outburst in the second quarter put the game out of reach of the Commodores. While the senior, Garner, was breaking loose for 151 yards, Stewart, a junior, was staking his claim for future participation by registering three TDs. Larry Marmie's defensive troops weren't slouching around, either. They kept Vandy out of the end zone until the final minutes.

Beating Vanderbilt never gets tiresome for a Tennessee man who grew up in the middle part of the state. The UT coach out of Winchester is no exception.

Within hours of the final horn, workmen began removing the ersatz grass, several layers of which had covered the floor of the stadium since 1968. Much to the delight of an overwhelming majority of fans, the real McCoy would be trod upon again in 1994. Or as one grass partisan put it, "The way God meant it to be." Tennessee ended up with a record of 125-38-7 on artificial turf.

On to Orlando and the USAComp Florida Citrus Bowl went the Vols and a good time was had by all until shortly after 1 p.m. on New Year's Day. From that point on, the fun was all Penn State's. Against a backdrop of "Please Stay, Heath" banners, Tennessee jumped out to a 10-0 lead, then went flatter than yesterday's root beer. Penn State, a 10-point underdog, romped to a 31-13 victory. The Vols appeared lifeless against the Nittany Lions, who dominated both lines of scrimmage, offense and defense. One perplexing development was Tennessee's inability to solve Penn State's three-man pass rush, which more or less invited the Vols to run. They managed but 135 yards on 29 rushes. Media representatives advanced any number of theories to explain the loss—injuries and illness, too much Mickey Mouse, a slippery turf.

Fulmer would have none of it. "It's been a long time since we've been physically whipped the way we were by Penn State," he said. "I tip my hat to coach Joe Paterno for the way his team played. We need to learn from this."

They will be hard lessons for a team that had bludgeoned its last four opponents 210-27, had averaged 42.8 points per game for the season, and had an offense so sophisticated that the opposition rarely knew where the next bullet was coming from.

Perhaps the plunge from rocky top to rocky bottom could be traced to Tennessee's easy November schedule. The Vols were never challenged after the Alabama game on October 16. After all, Penn State is not Vanderbilt. The Nittany Lions may wear plain vanilla uniforms, but they play block-and-tackle football with the best of them. "I think we had to shoot all of our guns in the first part of the season," Shuler said. "That has a lot to do with the momentum."

With Shuler gone, there was obviously going to be a need in the fall of 1994 for more hard-nosed football by a team whose snout had been unceremoniously bloodied in its last outing. The fiercely competitive Fulmer could hardly wait for spring practice and the opportunity to mold a championship contender to fly the Big Orange banner in 1994.

CHAPTER 33

HEATH SHULER

    Heath Shuler became not just a football star in Big Orange Country, but a celebrity, a kind of public property. The demands on his time became so ovewhelming that his main fight every day was for privacy and free time.

    He was a Tennessee Vol and, as such, Tennessee fans believed they owned him. They would think nothing of accosting him in public places and usually they had him surrounded. He got all the aggravation that Michael Jordan or Tom Cruise gets without any of the monetary benefits.

    A motherly lecture years ago prepared him for the limelight. Somehow Margie Shuler knew that her older son would become a star. But how was she to know he would become the most popular athlete in any sport in University of Tennessee history?

    "My mom told me a long time ago that it might come to this," Shuler says as he discusses his celebrity status. "When I started playing I could see that the autograph thing might become a hassle, and said so. And she said, 'Look at it like this, Heath: if they're not asking you for your autograph, then obviously you're not playing well. So, which do you want —to play well and have them ask for your autograph, or for them to never ask for your autograph because you didn't play well?' "

When he got to UT, he quickly became the people's choice like no other athlete who ever pulled on an orange jersey. Fans idolized him as much for his wholesomeness as for his enormous football talents. His boy-next-door image set him apart. No Tennessee athlete in any sport has ever had to endure the adulation like Heath Shuler. Not Johnny Majors, not A.W. Davis, not Condredge Holloway, not Johnnie Jones, not Tony Robinson.

He has never had a drop of alcohol or smoked a cigarette. In a fifth grade science class, he observed two rats for a week. One drank water and the other Pepsi. The one that drank Pepsi shook uncontrollably and died several days later.

Since that time, Shuler has had neither caffeine nor carbonated beverages. Only fruit juices, water, milk, etc.

"He started giving up a lot of things early in life for athletics," his mother says. "I really believe he doesn't know what a Pepsi tastes like."

When the apple of temptation visited Knoxville at the end of the 1993 season, Shuler bit. His storied Tennessee career was over. It was catastrophic for many Vol fans. The thought of Shuler not returning for the 1994 season brought tears to their eyes. But it is a safe bet that just about every one of them wished him Godspeed with the Washington Redskins of the National Football League.

They enjoyed him for three years and, to their way of thinking, it is better for him to have skyrocketed three times, amazing the people still standing on the ground, than never to have shot through the sky at all.

After all, he could have taken his marvelous talents and movie-star looks to Tuscaloosa. He almost did. He was recruited by virtually every Division I-A school in America. He narrowed the list down to 64, then to eight. He visited all eight, either officially or unofficially. It came down to North Carolina, Tennessee and Alabama. Then it was Tennessee and Alabama.

Alabama coach Gene Stallings wanted him in the worst way. "I can't guarantee you a whole lot at this university," he told Shuler. "But I can tell you one thing: your sophomore year you will win the national championship."

And who should win the national championship in 1992, Shuler's sophomore season? Alabama, of course.

Head coach Johnny Majors made a big impact on Shuler's decision. "He came to our house and was a real down-to-earth person in talking to my mother and father. He is a great person."

But the clincher, Shuler says, was David Cutcliffe, Tennessee's offensive coordinator and quarterbacks coach. The two of them hit it off in the beginning. They ended up more than coach and pupil; they became close friends.

"Coach Cutcliffe played the biggest role. He had a really great attitude about football. And he's also down to earth, a real inspiration. He is the real reason I came to UT. It came down to who I was going to be coached by. You see more of your position coach than you ever do your head coach. So I knew I would spend most of my time with him, and we had such a great relationship."

When Shuler announced on January 11, 1994, that he would forgo his final season at Tennessee, he did so with no regrets, no looking back, no thoughts of what might have been. Even though he would have been the odds-on favorite for the '94 Heisman Trophy.

"I look at the Heisman Trophy that I didn't win and say, 'Geez, it's a materialistic thing.' I'm happy and I'm satisfied. It meant more to me to see Bubba Miller make a great block or for Jeff Smith to make a great trap block than to win the Heisman. I just love to see other people perform at their peak.

"I would get just as big a kick out of seeing my brother Benjie catch a pass from me, a touchdown pass. That would be more of a highlight for me than any Heisman Trophy you could give me."

Shuler was a favorite not only of the fans, but the media as well. Veteran Knoxville television sportscaster Bob Kesling put it this way: "If you asked Heath Shuler to be somewhere, he would be there 15 minutes early. If you needed him to stick around and do something extra on the Vol Network, for instance, he would do it. And he would never complain. I never heard him ever say no, he didn't want to do something he was asked to do."

Shuler was a leader like few Tennessee football players have ever been. When he practiced, he practiced with a purpose. When he played, he played with enormous confidence, creating a wake in which his teammates wanted to be swept up and carried along. Regarding his leadership qualities, *Sports Illustrated* said, "A quarterback must be a leader. Heath Shuler is a Schwarzkopf with a dynamite arm."

Chuck Culpepper of the Lexington *Herald-Leader* captured much of the Heath Shuler mystique in this column from from November 20, 1993:

> KNOXVILLE — Dear Heath,
> Hi. My name is Erin (last name withheld) and I am 11 years old and in the sixth grade. I love the UT Vols and watch all the games on TV, but the best thing about the Vols is their quarterback. You. I think you are so cute! In or out of your

uniform you look really good. Your passes are cool and always good . . .

I was at the Wynonna concert Friday, November 12, 1993, in Knoxville and I saw you. I can't believe we were in the same building. When she said, "(Number) 21, come out here," I started screaming my lungs out. When you came out I thought my lungs were going to burst . . .

Excuse me, God. One little question.

Is this fair?

Did You have to give Heath Shuler *everything?*

Pleasant enough that No. 21, as the University of Tennessee's junior quarterback has coaxed NFL franchises into a covetous mode. Fine, too, that he is so good-looking you almost have to squint just to stand next to him. But for him to lead the league in unforced charm? To possess wit? To conduct chatterbox press conferences, the breeziest this side of Boomer Esiason?

The least he could do is be a devout bore.

But Shuler, born on New Year's Eve, is the kind of person you'd seek for the next barstool. He can speak in slight drawl about deer hunting in Pulaski and make it sound like the chase scene from The French Connection. He is gregarious without drowning you. "I don't eat greasy foods," he said, "but I do eat 'em because some of 'em are so goooood." How can you beat that?

One thing about barstools, though: Order for yourself. Shulers attends parties, but he doesn't drink, not even soda.

Back home in Bryson City, North Carolina, he made a goal-driven pact with himself to abstain in this life. When he was in the fifth grade. Lord, help us.

Heath, You have some great fans at the Knoxville Post Office. Good luck! We sure enjoy watching you.

Somebody just jotted that one on the back of an envelope addressed to Shuler. That is not to be confused with the elementary classroom in Lebanon, Tennessee, that decided one of the first tasks of cursive writing should be letters to Heath. Or the woman from western Tennessee who writes in weekly, "Hey. It's me. You played well." Or the fathers, Shuler said, "wanting me to meet their daughters." Or the Knoxville waiter who got $15 from his table to venture to Shuler's table for an autograph. Shuler signs pictures, jerseys, caps, about 200 signatures per week, as if by mandate. Ellie Wilson, who handles his mail for the sports information department, is in awe of a 21-year-old so comfortable with all of this.

The 6-foot-3, 220-pound son of a mailman and a yogurt-shop owner hauls around the autumn mood of a state in which, on Sunday night radio, you can hear a Tennessee football show followed by a church service.

Shuler's shoulders seem patently unchallenged by the weight.

Walking around town, he spots those runt Shulers wearing their must-have orange "21" jerseys, and it almost makes the real Shuler break into full giggle. "Sometimes," he said, "it's even like it's a character, as opposed to being really me. It's just like somebody else, somebody famous, like an actor or an actress. But I want to make an impact on young kids."

> Dear Mr. Shuler,
> I am a kindergarten teacher at Cedar Bluff Primary School. My 24 boys and girls are studying community helpers this month. I asked them to choose a famous person to write, and they picked you . . . You are a good role model for children.

The Shuler brothers make sure to have lunch every Friday and to talk by telephone almost every night. They hugged in Neyland Stadium during a 50-0 win over Louisiana Tech after Benjie, a freshman receiver who was a four-sport phenom at Swain County (North Carolina) High, scored a mop-up touchdown on a pass from backup Jerry Colquitt.

Commotion ruled the sideline on behalf of Benjie, everyone offering congratulations, including Heath, who is older by 3 1/2 years. "And then Heath did something I never would have expected," said Dr. Larry Fields, the Vols' chaplain from the Central Baptist Church of Bearden. "He said, 'Go tell Jerry he threw a good pass. Thank him.' How many people would have even thought of that at that time?"

Fields is certain Shuler carries imperfections. The Bible says he must. But in addition to Shuler's arm and mobility, he flourishes in the spiritual-leadership category. Which figures. On the field, he prefers the stone-cool Joe Montana approach; no insult intended, but he wasn't really into Jim McMahon with the '85 Bears. More into Walter Payton. More into quiet. Yet during halftimes, he is all the time walking around to the different units of the team, doling out encouragement.

On the night before Tennessee beat LSU 42-20, the team watched The Program, Hollywood's attempt at depicting college football.

The next day, the Volunteers huddled for the first play.

Per usual, everyone was a tad nervous starting out.

Borrowing from the movie, Shuler suddenly said, "Boys, time to put the women and children to bed and go looking for dinner."

Everyone cracked up.

"I think we went about 80 yards for a touchdown," receiver Craig Faulkner said.

> My 5-year-old son, Tony . . . has made a point to tell his Mom and I that he definitely wants Heath Shuler's autograph. We are all big Vol fans—distance here in North Dakota does not dampen our support . . .

Shuler will belong to more than just Tennessee soon enough, going headlong into the NFL. He has never said anything to the contrary that he will remain at Tennessee for his senior year and head for the NFL in 1995. For now, he hopes just to go to New York as one of the top Heisman Trophy candidates. "That's just opportunities. That's why you play ball, opportunities."

But about that NFL thing . . . Everyone with a larynx asks.

"Just today, probably five or six times so far," he said last Tuesday at shortly past noon.

"What will stop it?"

"January the eleventh."

The NFL's declaration day.

A mischievous reporter asked if maybe Shuler shouldn't say he's leaving, to get a rise out of people.

Without a trace of arrogance, Shuler said aloud, "How many heart attacks do you want to cause in this state?"

* * *

Through his storied career at Tennessee, through all the honors and all the fan worship, Shuler was ever the small town boy. Brad Zimanek of the *Nashville Banner* wrote about it in this article during the 1992 season:

> About mid-afternoon, Heath Shuler walks toward one of the two major intersections in Bryson City, North Carolina, tucked in a plateau of the Smoky Mountains.
>
> Even though it is the height of the leaf season, one of the primary tourism money-makers in the economically strapped region, it is relatively quiet.
>
> That is until people began to recognize Shuler.
>
> The University of Tennessee sophomore quarterback moves toward the middle of the street. Cars stop. People open their

windows and stick out their hands. Horns honk. A mini traffic jam ensues, but no one seems to mind. This is their hero and he is back home, if only for the weekend.

"You never go through town and not wave," Shuler said. "Every car that goes by, except for tourists, you know . . . You know everyone."

Shuler heads down Everett Street and ducks into Champions Locker, the only sporting goods store in town. Owners Ron and Theresa Marley have been waiting for him. Tennessee T-shirts, sweatshirts, jackets, hats and photographs in need of Shuler's signature are piled up on the counter.

Like the picturesque backdrop of the many hillsides in Swain County at this time of year, orange is the predominant color.

"We just can't keep anything (UT) in the store," Theresa Marley says.

It's not hard to figure out why.

"All the kids want to be like him," Theresa Marley says. "Every mother in town wishes that he was their son or that their daughter would end up marrying him some day."

Shuler's itinerary rivals that of any experienced by the gospel group, The Inspirations. Other than Shuler, they are the most noted Bryson City products and sing at the Victory Baptist Church where the Shuler family attends services each Sunday.

Some of his other friends who were away at college and those still living in the vicinity trickle into his home on Toot Hollow Road, making the gravel driveway resemble a used car parking lot.

Two of his closest buddies to show up are Adam Clawson, a renowned athlete in his own right who finished 21st in slalom kayaking at the Summer Olympics, and Tommy Cabe, one of Shuler's primary targets throughout high school.

Before attending that night's Swain County homecoming football game—where Shuler's No. 21 jersey was to be retired at halftime—he has to eat dinner.

Only the traditional pregame meal will do: hamburgers at Nabers Drive-In. It is the same ritual he and his teammates lived by while winning three consecutive state championships for the Maroon Devils from 1988-90.

His dad, Joe Benny Shuler, says only half-jokingly that his son has eaten 1,000 Nabers cheeseburgers—with the trademark cole slaw topping—while growing up.

Bryson City follows Shuler every step of the way.

On the weekends of home games in Knoxville, anywhere between 30 and 50 people make the two-hour drive through the mountains.

Not all of those can afford tickets to the game, but they will sit outside Neyland Stadium to be part of the atmosphere and wait to sneak in when the gates are opened late in the game.

If someone is unable to catch Saturday's game on TV or the radio, they can catch up with how their native son did by listening to WBHN-AM in Bryson City on Thursday afternoons.

It's when they play a 30-minute radio show that Shuler tapes with broadcaster Gary Peterson the previous night from his Gibbs Hall dorm room.

"It's something I can do for this community," Shuler says.

And they keep asking for more. He walks into the gate before Swain County's game and plays to the crowd as if he were Bill Clinton or George Bush: shaking hands, signing autographs and acknowledging graciously anyone who wants to get close to him.

"He'll shake every hand that's stuck out there," Swain County defensive coordinator Rod White says. "He'll talk to every little kid and he'll sign every autograph if he has to be here all night. He's our county role model. The adults look up to him for what he does. The kids look up to him for what they could be and what he has become.

"If he didn't play another down for the University of Tennessee, he's our hometown boy."

His fan following started when Shuler was a sophomore for the Maroon Devils.

After a game at Murphy, a little girl tugged on the shirt of Shuler's mother, Margie, and asked if she could have Heath's autograph.

He consented, but made her go behind the school bus so no one else would see him. Even then, he told her not to tell anyone. Times have sure changed.

In these parts he is a prince.

"Own this county?" White questioned. "He wouldn't even have to ask for it. They would give it to him."

Despite the adulation, his feet appear to be firmly planted on the ground. "Yes sir" and "No Ma'am" preface any response to his elders.

The Board of County Commissioners certified October 23, 1992, as "Heath Shuler Day" throughout Swain County. Not bad recognition for a 20-year-old.

"This is a small town . . . there's only 7000 people in the entire county," Swain County coach Boyce Dietz says. "We are extremely proud of him. He's carrying the torch for all of us."

TENNESSEE'S ALL-TIME TEAM
(As selected in fan balloting, November 1990)
Modern Era (1941-89)

OFFENSE

RECEIVERS
Willie Gault (1979-82)
Stanley Morgan (1973-76)
Larry Seivers (1974-76)

LINEMEN
Tim Irwin (1977-80)
Bruce Wilkerson (1983-86)
Harry Galbreath (1984-87)
Eric Still (1986-89)
Bob Johnson (1965-67)

BACKS
Condredge Holloway (1972-74)
Reggie Cobb (1988-89)
Curt Watson (1969-71)
Hank Lauricella (1949-51)
Johnny Majors (1954-56)

PLACEKICKER
Fuad Reveiz (1981-84)

DEFENSE

ENDS
Doug Atkins (1950-52)
Dale Jones (1983-86)

TACKLES
Reggie White (1980-83)
Marion Hobby (1986-89)

MIDDLE GUARD
Steve DeLong (1962-64)

LINEBACKERS
Keith DeLong (1985-88)
Steve Kiner (1967-69)
Jack Reynolds (1967-69)

DEFENSIVE BACKS
Bill Bates (1979-82)
Eddie Brown (1971-73)
Bobby Majors (1969-71)
Roland James (1976-79)

PUNTER
Craig Colquitt (1975-77)

KICK RETURNER
Willie Gault (1979-82)

PRE-1940 TEAM

ENDS
Bowden Wyatt (1936-38)
Graham Vowell (1914-16, 21)

LINEMEN
Abe Shires (1938-40)
Bob Suffridge (1938-40)
Ed Molinski (1938-40)
Herman Hickman (1929-31)
Nathan Dougherty (1906-09)

BACKS
Gene McEver (1928-29, 31)
Beattie Feathers (1931-33)
George Cafego (1937-39)
Bob Foxx (1938-40)

PLACEKICKER
Buck Hatcher (1915-16, 19-20)

PUNTER
Bobby Dodd (1928-30)

KICK RETURNER
Gene McEver (1928-29, 31)